STUDIES IN CULTURAL HISTORY

Awash in a Sea of Faith

AWASH IN A SEA OF FAITH

Christianizing the American People

JON BUTLER

HARVARD UNIVERSITY PRESS
CAMBRIDGE, MASSACHUSETTS
LONDON, ENGLAND
1990

Printed in the United States of America
10 9 8 7 6 5 4 3 2 1

This book is printed on acid-free paper, and its binding materials have been chosen for strength and durability.

Library of Congress Cataloging-in-Publication Data

Butler, Jon, 1940–
Awash in a sea of faith: Christianizing the American people / Jon Butler.
p. cm. — (Studies in cultural history)
Includes index.
ISBN 0–674–05600–0 (alk. paper)
1. United States — Religion. I. Title. II. Series.
BL2525.B87 1990
200'.973 — dc20

89-35770
CIP

For

Roxanne

Ben

Peter

CONTENTS

ILLUSTRATIONS

ACKNOWLEDGMENTS

Many kind people helped with this book. Ross Beales, Anne Braude, John Brooke, Nancy Cott, William Cronon, David Brion Davis, John Demos, Jay Dolan, David Donald, Ann Fabian, Clarke Garrett, Carolyn De Swarte Gifford, Nathan Hatch, Kathryn Hermes, Christine Heyrman, Diane Kaplan, Allen Kulikoff, Charles Lamb, Ned Landsman, D. Michael Quinn, Carolyn Park, Michael Perman, Elfrida Raley, Robert Remini, David Ruderman, Harold Selesky, Judy Schiff, Jan Shipps, Allen Stokes, Harry Stout, Daniel Uchitelle, and Mame Warren lent documents, answered questions, gave advice, and offered materials I never would have found on my own. Richard J. Link took an extra and unusual step to help a stranger when he descended to the crypt of the First Presbyterian Church in Newburyport, Massachusetts, to obtain the only known photograph of George Whitefield's casket taken before it was covered with a slate slab in 1933.

Librarians at many institutions—including those at the American Baptist Historical Society, the Dedham Historical Society, the Friends Historical Library at Swarthmore College, the Historical Foundation of the Presbyterian and Reformed Churches, the Historical Society of Pennsylvania, the Ipswich Historical Society, the John Carter Brown Library of Brown University, the Maryland State Archives, the Massachusetts Historical Society, the Methodist Archives at Drew University, the Newberry Library, the New Jersey State Archives, the New-York Historical Society, the Presbyterian Historical Society, the Rhode Island Historical Society, the Seventh Day Baptist Historical Society, the South Carolina Historical Society, the South Caroliniana Library at the University of South Carolina, the University of Illinois at Chicago, the University of Minnesota, the University of Notre Dame Archives, and several libraries at Yale, including the Divinity School Library, the Sterling Memorial Library, the Yale Archives and Manuscripts, and the Beinecke Rare Book and Manuscript Library—offered the invaluable assistance that makes books possible.

A Senior Faculty Fellowship at the Institute for the Humanities at the University of Illinois at Chicago enabled me to begin the book, and a John Simon Guggenheim Memorial Foundation Fellowship and a Yale Senior Faculty Fellowship made it possible to finish it.

A long time ago Darrett Rutman and John Howe encouraged my work in ways that make me happy to restate my appreciation here. Eric Monkkonen's friendship and advice have affected every chapter of the book. The enthusiasm and craft of Aida Donald, Elizabeth Suttell, and Elizabeth Gretz demonstrate why working with Harvard University Press is such a pleasure.

Portions of four chapters, now greatly condensed and often drastically revised, previously appeared in other publications: "The Dark Ages of American Occultism, 1760–1848," in *The Occult in America: New Historical Perspectives,* ed. Howard Kerr and Charles J. Crow (Urbana: University of Illinois Press, 1983); "Enlarging the Bonds of Christ: Slavery, Evangelism, and the Christianization of the White South, 1690–1790," in *The Evangelical Tradition in America,* ed. Leonard I. Sweet (Macon, Ga.: Mercer University Press, 1984); "Magic, Astrology, and the Early American Religious Heritage, 1600–1760," *American Historical Review* 84 (1979), 317–346; and "Enthusiasm Described and Decried: The Great Awakening as Interpretative Fiction," *Journal of American History* 69 (1982–83), 305–325.

Finally, a special acknowledgment. For nearly twenty years I have been privileged to work with scholars in American religious history who are drawn together by a concern for their subject rather than by ideology, politics, or religious affiliation. When we have disagreed about things, as is inevitable, our discussions have emphasized a common desire to understand religion in America. I have appreciated their support and example.

Awash in a Sea of Faith

Introduction

RELIGION IN THE AMERICAN PAST

Strange things happened in American religion in the 1980s. A conservative president, firmly backed by fundamentalist and evangelical Christians, allowed his daily schedule to be guided by horoscopes obtained from a San Francisco astrologer. Prominent television evangelists were defrocked after admitting to extramarital affairs. Revivalists declared that God had spoken to them directly and demanded that they salvage their debt-ridden ministries and hospitals. Bitter contests to control powerful church bureaucracies, colleges, and faculties occurred among Catholics and Southern Baptists. In an age of scientific medicine, fundamentalist Protestants and traditional Catholics performed and experienced miraculous healings, and "New Age" religions touted "harmonic convergence," "soul merge," "channeling," and "rebirthing," primarily to affluent, college-educated, white, and Anglo-Saxon Americans. Despite complaints about "secular humanism" and eroding religious values, over 97 percent of Americans polled on religion expressed a belief in God, and 60 percent regularly attended public worship, figures that stood in marked contrast to polls in Western Europe, where 40 percent of respondents said they did not believe in God and less than 10 percent regularly attended church.

If modern American religion is complex and bumptious, so too were its earliest manifestations. We do not always know this through its written history, however, much of which concentrates on the familiar themes of New England Calvinism, evangelicalism, voluntarism, and declining religious adherence. The nation's spiritual eclecticism, demands for ecclesiastical power and authority, persistent belief in miracles and other forms of divine intervention, and rising rather than falling church adherence are sometimes awkwardly appended to accounts that stress the Puritan origins of American religion and culture. Much of that traditional history is appropriate in certain instances, especially in New England. But elsewhere—and even in New England—this perspective slights America's rich religious complexity and is ultimately unable to explain Christianity's extraordinary power and its highly variable expressions in nineteenth- and twentieth-century America—a society where, by the traditional formulation, religion should have been weak, rather homogeneously evangelical, thoroughly uncoercive, and dominated by the direct descendants of Puritanism.

This book is an attempt to open up the discussion of the first three centuries of the American religious experience by reconstructing a more complex religious past, one that reflects processes of growth and development far removed from a traditional "Puritan" interpretation of America's religious origins. Some of the book's suggestions may startle the reader. It proposes that we attach less importance to Puritanism as the major force in shaping religion in America and more importance to the religious eclecticism that has long been prominent. It suggests that the eighteenth century may have left a far more indelible impression on the American religious tradition than did the seventeenth century. It offers an explanation for why so few people went to church on the eve of the American Revolution and why more attended on the eve of the Civil War. It attempts to determine the importance of quasi-Christian or non-Christian religious beliefs about magic and the occult. It stresses the role of authority and coercion in advancing Christianity in America. It explores beliefs in divine intervention as a persistent theme in American religious history. It argues that a rising Christianity directly shaped the colonies' system of slavery and, in combination with slavery, created an African spiritual holocaust in America. It describes a widening range of spiritual alternatives that turned antebellum America into a unique spiritual hothouse, even as organized religious expression of all kinds, including Christianity, appears to have been losing ground in Europe. Finally, it argues that quite contrary to Cotton Mather's well-known (and well-justified) fears, the story of religion in America after 1700 is one of Christian ascension rather than declension—Christianization rather than dechristianization—and of a Christianity so complex and heterogeneous as to baffle observers and adherents alike.

Throughout this book, religion is taken to mean belief in and resort to superhuman powers, sometimes beings, that determine the course of natural and human events. This is what philosophers of religion call a "substantive" rather than a "functional" conceptualization. It describes what religion is rather than what religion does, and it is based on the work of the anthropologist Melford Spiro. With minor modifications in Spiro's formulation, religion here is associated with supernaturalism, with supernatural beliefs, and with the conviction that supernatural beings and powers can and do affect life as humans know it. Those who hold such views are taken to be religious. Those who reject or ignore them are not taken to be religious.[1]

In their avowal of a transcendent God, early modern Judaism and Christianity obviously fit a supernaturalist conceptualization of religion. But so do other beliefs and behavior that Americans knew well and that figured prominently in their mental world. These include the notorious "magical" and "occult" beliefs of astrology, divination, and witchcraft. Magic and the occult arts, with Christianity and Judaism, are here treated as religious phenomena, however different their specific manifestations or their means of imploring and manipulating supernatural power. All of them predicated the existence of superhuman powers, and all of them offered techniques to invoke other-worldly powers to control nature and affect mankind. I seek to determine the interaction of these beliefs, regardless of the extent to which they may have been disapproved of, detested, or feared by men and women of the time. I thus reject Bronislaw Malinowski's well-known judgment that Christianity and Judaism are true religious systems because they are broad, philosophical, and ethereal—existential—and that magic, astrology, and occultism are inferior because they are narrow, practical, and mundane. Malinowski was wrong about the facts, in any case. Magic, astrology, and the occult were subtle, complex, and sophisticated systems of religious practice, as their many sixteenth- and seventeenth-century manuals revealed, and Patrick Collinson has even wondered whether this complexity could allow them any real popularity. Nor was Christianity devoid of magic, at least in practice. Early modern parish clergymen and priests complained that parishioners interpreted church rituals, such as baptism, as magical rites that could ward off disease or bring other desired results.[2]

This inquiry examines not only churches but the laity that was the object of so much attention from theologians, ministers, and religious institutions. We do not know what we should about lay religion in Europe, and despite much cant about lay authority in America, we know surprisingly little about how it has fared in the society where the people were first declared sovereign. For example, only recently have historians acknowledged that American church adherence or membership rose rather than declined between 1650 and 1950, though much American political rhetoric from the 1840s to the present has assumed a contradictory set of "facts."[3]

The scope of this book, therefore, includes "popular religion." The term has become the subject of some controversy, particularly when it has been equated with spiritual and religious radicalism. No such equation is forwarded here. The term popular religion in this context means no less and no more than the religious behavior of laypeople. It is defined by its clientele rather than by its theology, by its actors rather than by their acts. In the period I am discussing, popular religion was not necessarily anticlerical or anti-institutional, nor was it necessarily rooted in occult or quasi-pagan folk customs. Popular religion was what the laity made it. In some historical instances it emerged as anti-institutional, anticlerical, occult, or pagan. In others it became closely linked to religious institutions and leaders — to ministers and churches, rabbis and synagogues, and others. Historians cannot deduce lay or popular religion from sociological conditions and theological principles or read the characteristics common to one time and place directly into others. Popular religion must be analyzed in particular historical settings among real people in real places across real centuries.

Christian adherence is here taken to mean a regular or steady attachment to institutional Christianity. The definition of adherence involves analytical and practical difficulties. On the one hand, the law in most European nations and states assumed the Christian adherence of all subjects except Jews. On the other hand, clergymen of all Christian groups agreed that the law never guaranteed real Christian practice. Measures of that practice are often difficult to obtain. In the state-supported churches, statistics of church attendance, including visitations by bishops, were often only erratically kept and lacked basic information about the population — the souls "at risk" to attend church or take communion.

Attendance and membership statistics among dissenters were no better kept; Richard Vann explains that Quakers, for example, did not even develop a modern concept of membership until the 1690s, forty years after their founding. Sometimes the available figures concerned attendance, sometimes "communication," the term Church of England officials used to describe the taking of communion. Church attendance and communication were hardly the same, yet discrepancies between them can be falsely magnified. Anglican clergymen, for example, typically exaggerated church attendance but for whatever reason gave very precise (and usually very low) figures for communication. The latter cannot be explained away by reference to a lay "scrupulosity" that led laypeople worried about their personal unworthiness to stay away from communion—their absence thus a measure of their piety. Theodore Bozeman has noted that historians have been more taken with scrupulosity than were clergymen of the time; even most New Englanders who stayed away were indifferent, not exceedingly pious.[4]

Finally, American religious development is approached here within the context of the early modern European religious environment. It would not have been necessary to stress this point some years ago, when historians linked early American history to European and especially to English history and elucidated colonial maturation in a transatlantic imperial context. Paradoxically, social and community studies have turned historians inward, or at least away from Europe. Community is equated with residence. It is defined too often by land deeds and town boundaries, too seldom by habits of mind and memorable tradition, even tradition that reaches back across the Atlantic.

Such a narrow view of community is especially unhelpful in understanding American religious history, where a transatlantic focus is a sine qua non. In the seventeenth and eighteenth centuries as much as today, religion was a learned habit of the mind, and for English-speaking settlers, the religion they had learned came from Europe. Much mythology to the contrary, the close connections between early modern Europe and America, the conscious resort to European models by American colonists, and the overwhelmingly derivative nature of early American society make it impossible to understand America's religious origins apart from Europe.

Yet America's most enduring religious patterns were also created, not merely inherited. The developments of the years between 1550 and 1865 make it clear that neither the substance nor the dynamic of America's religious development was inevitable or "given." Americans were neither implicitly nor necessarily religious or Christian. America's religious identity emerged out of choices made among many available religious forms. America's spiritual pluralism, including an often powerful indifference to things religious, was apparent in its European forebears before colonization, and their pluralism became even more complex in the New World social and cultural environment. In sum, the ultimate success of lay Christianization in America, all the more notable in contrast to the apparent decline of popular Christian practice in Europe, came about through complex processes at work in places far beyond the narrow confines of Puritan New England and with powerful consequences, some intended and some not, stretching far beyond pulpit and even pew. In this setting America and American religion were born.

THE EUROPEAN RELIGIOUS HERITAGE

1

In 1606 James I chartered the Virginia Company to propagate Christianity to native Americans, heathens who the English imagined were living "in darkness" and in "miserable ignorance of the true knowledge and worship of God." A quarter century later the Puritans created covenanted Christian communities in New England for themselves. They said they would follow "the counsel of Micah: to do justly, to love mercy, to walk humbly with our God." They would know that they had succeeded when God commended them, as John Winthrop described, with such "praise and glory, that men shall say of succeeding plantations: 'The Lord make it like that of New England.'"[1]

The rhetoric about converting Indians and establishing Christian communities in America masked startlingly lethargic Christian practice and complex religious belief found among prospective colonists and the laity generally in Europe. In actual fact, Christian adherence among the English and other Europeans was quite different from that implied by James I and John Winthrop. In the sixteenth and seventeenth centuries state-supported Christianity found itself beset by reformers from within and by dissenters from without. Laypeople held views on the natural and the supernatural that ranged from church-approved orthodoxies to officially denounced varieties of magic and the occult, with an occasional village atheist thrown in for good measure. If church attendance is any indication, Christianization—meaning a regular if not vigorous attachment to Christian institutions, theologies, and norms—was in a crisis that continued unabated as Europeans poured out of the Old World into the New. And the problems were not recent. Since the time of Constantine and the "conversion" of the Roman Empire, the Christianization of Europe's people had continued to be a major task of the church, not something to be assumed. As might be expected, the consequences of these unwanted religious complexities soon appeared in the English settlements of British North America.

What did religion mean in early modern Europe? Historians usually write in terms of churches and worshipers—Catholics, Lutherans, Anglicans, Puritans, Presbyterians, Congregationalists, Baptists and so forth. The European laity thought in these terms as well. They sustained churches by adhering to theological and ecclesiastical principles, and they destroyed churches by overturning theological and ecclesiastical traditions.

But early modern Europeans also thought about religion in broadly generic terms, often with remarkable sophistication and daring. Henry Fielding's caricature of England's official religion in *Tom Jones* (1749) accurately depicted what the law allowed on the subject. As Fielding's Parson Thwackum put it, "When I mention religion, I mean the Christian religion; and not only the Christian religion but the Protestant religion; and not only the Protestant religion, but the Church of England." Rigidity was Thwackum's means of managing the lay religious eclecticism he neither condoned nor perhaps even understood. For European laypeople, religion involved much more than the church. Religion was concerned with the transcendent, the unearthly—things and forces that seemed both beyond and superior to nature. This focus on the supernatural and supernatural powers—rather than on the church, whether state church or dissenting church—made popular sense of the traditional Catholic Mass. A miracle occurred there—an unnatural, otherwise impossible, transformation of bread and wine into Christ's body and blood. Supernatural belief likewise underwrote Protestantism. English Midlands Baptists expressed this with remarkable untutored eloquence in their creedal statement of 1655: "Wee beleeve that there is one only true God which is one God who is eternall, allmighty, unchaingable and incomprehensible, infinite; who is a spirit haveing his being of himselfe and giveth being to all creatures and doth what he will in heaven and earth moveing all things according to the counsell of his own will." These early Baptists asserted the existence of a supernatural power ("eternall, allmighty, unchaingable and incomprehensible"), identified its gender ("he"), sidestepped the problem of its material existence ("a spirit haveing his being of himselfe"), and acknowledged both its freedom and its power ("moveing all things according to the counsell of his own will").[2]

The breadth of early modern supernaturalism underwrote more than Christianity, however. Magic, astrology, and divination—what detractors then (and moderns now also) called the occult—thrived in it as well. Practitioners of these arts and crafts could be found throughout England and the Continent during the entire early modern period. The laity obtained magical charms and amulets from "wise men" and "wise women" to keep away disease. They patronized astrologers who predicted the future, explained the past, and cured illnesses. They accepted the existence of witches as a way to explain unexplainable things; sometimes they sought the influence of a "cunning person," "wise man," or "wise woman" to help themselves or to help or harm someone else.[3]

People naturally took an interest in what religion did, that is, in how it "functioned," as sociologists and theologians now put it. Above all, religion explained. It explained unprecedented floods, disappearing animals, catastrophic diseases, and the sudden deaths of children and adults. These became, variously, acts of God, events that stemmed from irrepressible forces in the heavens, and the tragic results of diabolical forces unleashed by witchcraft. Specific religious practices also invoked the supernatural to transcend nature in many ways. Thousands of Catholic shrines dotted pre-Reformation Europe, including England, celebrating deliverance from the cruelties of nature and man alike. Protestants castigated Catholic miracles as "magic" and, therefore, as blasphemous, but they themselves prayed for relief from drought and famine. That common people found little difference in these traditions is suggested in the history of England's Essex County, east of London. There, in the birthplace of English Puritanism, some thirty Elizabethan-era wise men and wise women invoked supernatural power each year to relieve local residents from disease, disability, and distress, even as Calvinist clerics inveighed against both Catholicism and magic.[4]

The expansive, eclectic early modern view of religion produced a plethora of responses from those who were the object of so much attention from the churches, their ministers, priests, and other religious practitioners. Although significant portions of the populace believed in the supernatural, not everyone exhibited the exclusive loyalty to Christianity that the churches taught and demanded. Some expressed multiple forms of religious belief. Sometimes they turned to churches and orthodox Christianity, and sometimes they turned to practitioners of magic, divination, and astrology. Anticlericalism fueled lay disaffection and occasionally exposed a straightforward irreligion that denied religious sentiment in any form, including Christianity and magic. In this often chaotic milieu, Europeans chose from a bewildering variety of religious expression and sometimes opted to make no choice at all. These decisions are not easily recognizable centuries later. At times they verge on the irrecoverable. Often they are misconstrued. Still, they existed. Our task is to determine how, during the centuries of American colonization, Europeans made their choices and what their actions implied for the transfer of Europe's religious heritage to New World society.

The Protestant Reformation, which formally began in 1517, a quarter century after Columbus discovered America, unleashed events that thoroughly restructured traditional relationships between institutional Christianity and potential lay worshipers. In many areas new institutions housed religious truth — Lutheran in some German principalities and states, Calvinist in Geneva and England. In Protestant nations, more insistent reformers in turn criticized the new religious establishments as corrupt and illegitimate with a vigor that easily matched the strength of their antagonism toward Catholicism.

Amid this change, one island of stability remained. While theology and liturgy shifted, it was government that continued to establish official faith. The Protestant Reformation reinforced rather than reduced the inclination of Western governments to sanction and shape Christianity. Reformers' complaints aside, well into the eighteenth century most Christian worship occurred in congregations sanctioned, supported, and sustained by the government. In fact, the Reformation probably increased government activity in religion. In England government activity transformed and magnified religious reformation by creating the new Church of England, which for a century became the principal battlefield of religious reform in that nation. In France the Edict of Nantes (1598) established boundaries for Protestant activity, and its revocation (1685) capped a campaign of repression that virtually stripped the country of its Huguenots. In Germany the doctrine "whose Prince, whose Church" established the legal boundaries of religion within principalities; Catholics moved to find protection from Catholic princes, Protestants from Protestant princes. Throughout Europe, legislation established the ecclesiastical order and theological configuration that the state would permit its laity to follow.[5]

Hence, a Reformation paradox: the priesthood of both the state and the state church rivaled the distinctive Protestant doctrine of the priesthood of all believers. More than one scholar has noted that the rise of the early modern state in England and France took nourishment from religious crises. These crises were in part created by the state, and state intervention benefited secular authority at least as fully as it benefited religion. Thus if the modern state was not born of religion, it certainly was not born exclusively of modernizing secularity either.[6]

State churches formed institutional Christianity's common denominator in Europe on the eve of colonization. Historians have often been hostile to these institutions. As did many at the time, they have criticized them as lethargic and corrupt and have contrasted their seeming perfunctoriness with the reputed vigor of dissenting, often sectarian, churches. Yet the problems of state churches really bespeak their importance, especially in shaping popular or lay religion. Put simply, it is impossible to understand preindustrial lay religious practice without understanding state-supported Christianity. This was true in nations with Protestant establishments—England, Scandinavia, the Netherlands, and parts of Germany—as well as in those with Catholic ones—France, Spain, Portugal, and other parts of Germany. Everywhere, the state churches established the principal forms of Christian worship, doctrine, and moral teaching available to the overwhelming majority of Europe's populace, a hegemony created by the state and with a power that accounted for its frequent derision by contemporaries, reformers, and later, historians.[7]

Official Christianity enjoyed the expanding coercive powers of the rising state. Many laws, especially those that proscribed heresies and established the mechanisms for levying and collecting church taxes, antagonized the laity, who resented intrusions into both conscience and wallet. But in the short run these laws performed crucial heuristic functions. Above all, they brought the state's rising prestige to Christianity. Christianity was true not only because the Scriptures said so but because the state said so. Coercion made the point forcefully. Blasphemy statutes, demands for church attendance, and the collection of taxes dramatically reminded men and women of their Christian obligations. Whether the law and coercion could promote piety remained a matter of great controversy. But at the least, the law demanded regularity, and out of regularity came attendance, listeners, and perhaps even piety.[8]

Legal proscriptions established intellectual and social boundaries beyond which respectful men and women should not stray. Laws prohibited heresy, meaning corrupt doctrine. They forbade blasphemy, meaning ridicule of Jesus and the resurrection. By sanctioning the moral norms of the Ten Commandments, they proscribed a long list of illicit behavior ranging from premarital sex to theft and social discord. Transgressions usually produced modest punishments, at least by standards of the time. Offenders were fined and whipped and sometimes carted through the village while their peers pelted them with garbage, mud, and stones. Occasionally they were jailed. The more serious transgressions of heresy, blasphemy, and witchcraft called for death. Indeed the threat was double, because by law, transgressions offended the state as fully as they offended the church. When Henry VIII executed the abbot of Glastonbury and destroyed the ancient Catholic monastery there in 1539, he charged the abbot with treason rather than heresy—a subtle point, perhaps, but one that escaped neither the abbot nor Henry. English, Scottish, and French witchcraft prosecutions occurred as often in civil courts as in ecclesiastical ones; the crimes alleged against neighbors (and hence against the state) were as important as the crimes alleged against Christianity.[9]

The population itself demonstrated the influence of institutional Christianity in society. Vast numbers of men and women labored in the service of state-supported Christianity and made up the largest bloc of nonagricultural workers in early modern Europe.

Several censuses of Rome and Bologna taken between 1570 and 1640 reveal that those serving as priests, monks, or nuns could easily amount to 10 percent of the adult population; evidence from Tuscany suggests that the total there might have approached 15 percent of the adult population. The ratios among Protestants were inevitably lower, since they had abolished monasteries and convents. But the number of Protestant clergymen remained impressive nonetheless, especially considering the suddenness of the Protestant revolution. In 1600 some fifteen to twenty thousand Protestant ministers, most now married, served congregations in Germany, the Netherlands, France, Switzerland, and even Italy, and another eight to nine thousand men ministered in the new Protestant churches in England and Scotland.[10]

The landscape—"the land shaped by mankind," in John Stilgoe's phrase—further bespoke Christianity's demanding presence in early modern society. The constructed environment teemed with church buildings, chapels, shrines and other symbols of Christianity's claim to the religious allegiance of the early modern laity. By 1600 at least a half million such buildings filled up the Continental and English countrysides, and many parishes contained two, three, or more churches or chapels. Perhaps ominously, buildings often outnumbered priests and ministers, and church authorities continuously complained that they could not recruit sufficient clergymen to fill their parishes.[11]

Most early modern churches possessed little elegance. Rural buildings, especially, reflected an eclecticism stemming from the accidents of ancient preservation, unmovable stone foundations, and tight vestry budgets. The more expensive churches of major market towns and the cathedrals of cities reflected both the financial power of urban places and the importance of these buildings in demanding religious adherence from an often indifferent, recalcitrant people. Even destroyed church buildings could be made to proclaim Christianity, at least the kind demanded by the state. Although Henry VIII demolished Glastonbury abbey in 1539, he allowed the old church tower to stand atop Glastonbury Tor to remind the Somerset laity not only of Christianity's claim to their adherence but also of the Crown's power to destroy as well as create religious practice in a society where such things could not be taken for granted (see Figure 1).[12]

Thus the landscape taught as well, not unlike the law. The

Christian buildings that loomed across the countryside proclaimed Christianity's truth and demanded adherence with a ubiquity that made these commands incessant. Residents of thickly settled English counties seldom lived more than three to four miles from a church or chapel of the Church of England. For believers the buildings "sacralized" the landscape. They provided physical locations for the ritual invocation of the supernatural. At a minimum, this involved public worship on Sabbaths, weekdays, and holy days and publicly conducted familial ceremonies such as baptisms, weddings, and funerals. Sacralization involved the dead as well as the living. Burying grounds consecrated by ecclesiastical officials surrounded most rural European church buildings. Their occupants might sometimes proclaim Christianity more vigorously in death than they had in life.[13]

The Protestant Reformation initiated many changes in European society and culture. Among its most immediate and obvious

1. Glastonbury Tor, St. Michael Church tower.

effects was extensive physical destruction, carried out by the laity, both Protestant and Catholic. Henry Barrow, an Elizabethan separatist, claimed that Catholic buildings, "in their old idolatrous shapes," could "never be cleansed of this fretting leprosy, until [they] be desolate, [and] laid on heaps." Their idolatry "so cleaveth to every stone, as it by no means can be severed from them whiles there is a stone left standing upon a stone." Protestants smashed Catholic statues, burned Catholic catechisms, and destroyed Catholic shrines. Catholics, in turn, hanged or burned Protestant supporters, destroyed Protestant buildings, and during the Wars of Religion in the 1580s stuffed pages of the Geneva Bible into disemboweled Protestant soldiers and laypeople to show their contempt for these heretics: "They preached the truth of their God. Let them call him to their aid."[14]

Protestantism also destroyed old cultural patterns and institutions. Protestants abolished the celibate priesthood, shut down convents and monasteries, and encouraged, even forced, thousands of priests to marry. In England they returned perhaps a hundred thousand previously cloistered men and women to the general population. They eliminated old rituals (novenas, masses for the dead, and Corpus Christi parades), reduced others (feasts for Epiphany and Christ's Passion), and thoroughly transformed the old Lenten period by shifting attention from material abstinence to spiritual contemplation.[15]

Destruction and death — cultural, architectural, and personal — thus possessed real popular significance. Throughout Europe, antiheresy campaigns attracted a broad following. The laity often rushed to participate in the destruction and church officials did not always hold them back; at least people were learning to hate those they attacked. Yet at the same time, state ritualization of this destructiveness constrained its dangers. Royal and magisterial authorizations for such enterprises worked to limit antagonism toward other social and governmental institutions, including the state and the state church.[16]

The Reformation also reshaped social behavior. Large numbers of men and women achieved literacy and began to read the Bible, apparently in response to the renewed emphasis on biblical texts. Preaching increased everywhere. In modestly sized English villages, reforming ministers gave weekday and market day lectures. The crowds worried local officials, however, even those who were sympathetic to reform. When listeners began asking questions about doctrine and scriptural interpretation Elizabeth I ordered the lectures suppressed, for fear that they were encouraging religious radicalism. Social rituals of death also changed. Englishmen who before the Reformation had endowed masses in their wills stopped doing so and sometimes even used them to attack Catholicism. An English laborer, Edward Leach, turned his will into a personal theological testament just before his death in 1644 by bequeathing his soul "into the hand of god my creator Redeemer, and sanctifier, fully trusting and assuredly believing to be saved only by the death and resurrection of Jesus Christ, the son of god, and by no other means."[17]

Social characteristics shaped the dynamics and substance of lay interaction with Christianity in early modern Europe. An unusual religious census taken in 1584 in Antwerp showed that poor people made up the bulk of adherents to all three major religious groups—71 percent of Catholics, 60 percent of Calvinists, and 59 percent of Lutherans. But rich and middle-class residents formed a larger proportion of Protestant congregations than Catholic ones. Only 13 percent of Catholics came from the city's richest taxpayers, while Calvinists and Lutherans drew slightly more than 20 percent of their followers from those ranks.[18]

Social standing affected religious practice in England as well. By law, all English subjects were presumed to be Anglicans. But Anglican strength lay in the church's middle- and upper-class parishioners. They attended services with relative consistency, served as its vestrymen and other parish officials, and furnished the bulk of the taxes paid to support church activities. In general, poor people displayed far less involvement with the church. They seldom held parish offices, rarely became clergymen, and by all accounts stayed away from worship in large numbers. The Puritan movement of the seventeenth century refined rather than reversed this pattern. It too drew adherents from all ranks, but contemporaries did not call it a gentry movement for nothing. Middling merchants and substantial landholders made up its steadiest and most common followers. Participation and even leadership among the poor, especially among weavers and laborers, increased during the English Civil War and Commonwealth periods, but after the Restoration of 1660 the Puritan movement for the most part retreated to its rural and gentry origins.[19]

Kinship and seasonality also shaped religious adherence and practice. Although Catholic and Protestant doctrine alike laid responsibility for salvation at the doorstep of individuals, kinship obviously reinforced and stimulated individual adherence to institutionalized religion. Affines moved in and out of Protestant and Catholic congregations and brought spouses, children, grandparents, aunts, uncles, and cousins with them. Elizabethan Catholicism survived by taking root within aristocratic families, a strategy that preserved as well as constrained it. Similarly, when Protestantism came under attack in France in the 1680s, it declined precipitously when whole families abjured, as happened by the thousands, yet found social crevices for survival when whole families persevered. Seasonality — like the landscape, a combination of human shaping and nature — also paced and molded Christian practice. Death had surprisingly regular patterns. Funerals occurred more often in the winter than in the summer. Marriages occurred most often between the months of June and December, least often between January and March and never during Lent. So strong was the latter tradition that not even English Baptists performed Lenten marriages, despite the Protestant repudiation of Catholic ceremonialism. Baptisms expressed yet another seasonal pattern. They were held most frequently between November and May, least frequently between June and November, and they often did not immediately follow births. In the seventeenth century, English parents often allowed an interval of ten to fifty days between birth and baptism, and in some places in the eighteenth century, September alone suddenly accounted for over a third of all baptisms, despite far more even spacing of births, all for unclear reasons.[20]

Localism and regionalism played havoc with loudly touted "national" religious policies. Although the law usually decreed a uniform national religious practice, local patterns proved difficult to dislodge. Local saints whose cults energized village religious practice in sixteenth-century Spain were thoroughly unknown elsewhere, including, often, in Rome. English Puritanism flourished east and immediately west of London but seldom to the south. Farther west and to the north indifference (some said paganism) reigned until, in the 1660s and 1670s, residents suddenly took to Quakerism. Why? A special clergyman or peculiar local conditions? Emergent urbanization? Population changes? As with the vagaries surrounding seasonality, definitive answers remain elusive.[21]

The flux in early modern European religion distressed Protestant and Catholic authorities. Part of their worry derived from the knowledge that Christianization was a problem rather than a fact — something still to be achieved rather than something attained long ago — and that the problem was persistent rather than new. From the fourth to the twelfth centuries Christianity had commanded a steady allegiance from only a minority of Europe's people. As late as the thirteenth century, Humbert of Romans complained that his parishioners still ignored Christian worship. When the Fourth Lateran Council in 1215 imposed an obligatory yearly confession on every Catholic taking communion, its action did not reflect deeply entrenched Christian practice in the laity but the church's continuing inability to lock the population into regularized attendance and adherence.[22]

Incomplete and erratic lay Christianization continued in early modern Europe. The 1584 Antwerp census that revealed the Reformation's class dimensions also revealed that a full third of the city's ten thousand surveyed households did not even claim a religious affiliation, and the indifference transcended class lines. Between 30 and 40 percent of household heads in rich, middling, and poor households expressed no commitment to any religious group. Worse, amid the proliferation of religious groups in post-Reformation Antwerp, household heads expressing no religious commitment now outnumbered the adherents of any single group: 40.0 percent of those surveyed failed to specify any religious commitment, 29.6 percent said they were Catholic, 21.0 percent said they were Calvinist, and 9.4 percent said they were Lutheran.[23]

Germany exhibited similar erratic patterns of church adherence. Some areas witnessed substantial advances in lay Christianization in Lutheran form. Rural clerics near Strassburg, for example, reported much success in teaching the young and won a major battle against Sabbath tardiness, even though sermons, which were often long, had taken on new importance in Lutheran worship. But other places reported abysmal churchgoing and widespread ignorance of elemental Christian beliefs. Only 10 to 15 percent of the adults regularly attended Sabbath worship in some towns. Gerald Strauss offers a gloomy summary of Coburg's visitations by Lutheran bishops between 1577 and 1589: "Nothing seemed to avail against widespread absenteeism from divine service and catechism sermons . . . there was near-universal blaspheming, widespread sorcery, wife-beating and neglect of children, [and] general refusal to fulfill congregational obligations . . . In some villages one could not find even a single person who knew the Ten Commandments."[24]

The situation in France was both different and similar. Visitations by Catholic bishops revealed a strong trend toward "seasonal" conformity. More than 90 percent of adults took communion at Toulouse's Easter masses in the 1590s, but the bishops worried about superficial faith. Only 2 to 5 percent of the adults who took Easter communion attended weekly mass or repeated their communion at the other great Catholic church festivals in the year, and their absence could not be explained by Protestant inroads, which, the bishops all agreed, were minimal. France's Wars of Religion in the 1580s and 1590s strained this tenuous lay Christianization further. Except at Easter, churchgoing sagged, and the catechization of children and youths vanished. As France explored the New World, its remaining priests struggled not only to restore buildings damaged or demolished in the wars but to salvage the mental habits of a populace among whom regular Christian practice was weak even under good conditions.[25]

The English situation was little better. A Hertfordshire reformer, Humphrey Roberts, complained in 1572 that on Sunday "a man may find the churches empty, saving the minister and two or four lame, and old folke: for the rest are gone to folow the Devil's daunce." A 1574 visitation by the Puritan-leaning archbishop of York, Edmund Grindal, complained of slack Sabbath attendance in most parishes despite an intense sermonizing campaign in the archdiocese. The situation had not improved by the time of Elizabeth's death. In 1603 an East Sussex visitation likewise reported poor Sabbath attendance. In some parishes only three or four persons took communion. In other parishes no communicants appeared. A decade later William Harrison, a Lancashire minister, noted that "for one person which we have in the church to hear divine service, sermons and catechism, every piper (there be many in one parish) should at the same instant have many hundreds on the greens."[26]

The ambivalence of the European laity toward Christian practice hints at rejection of supernatural belief and atheism. The great

French historian Lucien Febvre argued in *The Problem of Unbelief in the Sixteenth Century* that unbelief was impossible in early modern society because supernaturalism was implicit in the culture. Witch hunts thus were not merely understandable but were an inescapable consequence of the widespread belief in gods, demons, priests, ministers, and magical healers. More recent scholarship, however, has uncovered intriguing expressions of agnosticism, unbelief, and atheism in early modern society. Keith Thomas found the infamous "village atheist" very much alive in sixteenth- and seventeenth-century England. Individuals of the time denied the existence of the Christian god, of heaven and hell, and rewards for good behavior. Sometimes they even dreamed about such things. Lady Monson, wife of Sir William Monson, consulted an astrologer after many disturbances while sleeping: "She thinks the Devil doth tempt her to do evil to herself and she doubteth whether there is a God." Others did more than dream. One Yorkshire man denounced preaching as "bibble babble" and said he cared "not a fart of my tail for any black coat in Wensleydale . . . I had rather hear a cuckoo sing." Another dismissed sermonizing as "sharp shitting in a frosty morning."[27]

Unfortunately, atheism's breadth and social significance remain difficult to ascertain. Unbelief lacked the institutional manifestations so obvious in its opposite. At best it was documented by scandalized ministers and priests who found such views alarming and, on occasion, profitable to slight or to exaggerate, depending on the circumstances. Those of the early modern period and later historians alike often confuse atheism with anticlericalism, although, as Febvre demonstrated in the case of Rabelais, anticlericalism might also signal reform tendencies. Worse, unbelief was illegal. Atheism, heresy, and blasphemy brought death, and contemporaries knew well to guard against such opinions. It was one thing to ignore Sabbath services, quite another to denounce one god or many. Better, safer, to keep silent.[28]

Erratic lay adherence to institutional Christianity also reflected the breadth of lay religion and the inability of institutional Christianity to corral and discipline it. To satisfy their spiritual needs the laity turned not merely to the churches but to magic, astrology, and other forms of divination. Specifying the relationship among these religious forms is difficult. On the one hand, Robert Muchembled has argued for an immense gulf between Christianity and magic. He says that occultism took root in a distinctive "popular" culture that was not nearly as Christianized as was elite culture. During the age of Louis XIV an elite Christianity successfully warred against many aspects of popular culture to bring about the demise of many of its manifestations, including magic. On the other hand, David Hall stresses the continuity of the "worlds of wonder" across the early modern religious spectrum and among both laypeople and the learned clergy and theologians. From Christian miracles to wondrous events to occult healing, early modern men and women often saw little disjuncture between Christianity and magic, astrology, and divination.[29]

The social spectrum of popular interest in the occult further complicates the question of relationships. All substantial evidence reveals that occultism's appeal transcended class, age, and gender. Wise men and wise women drew clients from the wealthy, the middling, and the poor. Queen Elizabeth commissioned horoscopes from John Dee, the mathematician, whose house was ransacked by fearful neighbors worried about rumors that he had conjured angels on the head of a pin. Merchants, lawyers, and servants consulted occult practitioners. William Lilly, the astrological physician, saw as many as four thousand clients a year in the 1640s and cast horoscopes to plan battle strategy for parliamentary leaders during the English Civil War. Even clergymen came. The bishop of Rochester came to Simon Forman, an acquaintance of Shakespeare's, hoping for a richer preferment, and in the 1640s, a clergyman secured a horoscope from Lilly to determine whether the nation's new Presbyterian system "would stand here in England."[30]

Occult practitioners displayed equally diverse social characteristics. Dee, Forman, and Lilly, among others, claimed university training and membership in England's intellectual elite. But others inhabited a far different world. The wise men and wise women who provided magical cures to the general population were most often illiterates who had learned their secrets from earlier practitioners. Their success lay in their appearance of precision, their intimate knowledge of their clients, and a certain gullibility in the public. Some practitioners simply tricked people. The Lincolnshire antiquarian Abraham de la Pryme, himself a former learned practitioner, arrested a fortune-teller who used "old mouldy almanacks, and several sheets of astrological schemes, all drawn false and wrong." Other practitioners cleverly manipulated their clients' desire for wonder, amazement, and certitude. Richard Gough, a Stuart antiquary, described how one man's wish to learn secret truths ultimately revealed a previously hidden crime.

> Reece [Wenlocke] had a cow, which was stolen away, and it is reported that he went to a women, whom they called the wise woman of Montgomery, to know what was beecome of his cow; and as hee went, hee putt a stone in his pockett, and tould a neighbour of his that was with him that he would know whether she were a wise woman or not, and whether she knew that hee had a stone in his pockett. And it is sayd, that when hee came to her, shee sayd, [thou] hast a stone in thy pockett, but itt is not soe bigge as that stone wherewith thou didst knocke out such a neighbour's harrow tines.[31]

Men and women sought out occult practitioners to "resolve, direct, and helpe," as an Essex Puritan, Thomas Pickering, put it. Astrological physicians such as Forman, Lilly, and William Salmon linked the health of the body to the motions of the stars. They believed that the earth was a microcosm of the heavens and that the stars revealed the course of life. Horoscopes uncovered the individual's relationship to the controlling forces of the universe. Using this or similar knowledge gained through divination, those who were perceptive could design remedies made of astrologically correct herbs and waters that would bring them into a positive, harmonious relationship with the universe and heal their afflictions. Wise men and women found lost or stolen objects, clothing, household items, cattle, and children. They foretold the best day to sail and good days to begin business ventures, marry, and conceive children.[32]

The laity of early modern Europe often saw little difference between the supernaturalism invoked through magic and that pursued by the churches. Before the Reformation, Catholic shrines offered thousands of opportunities to seek divine intervention through prayer in seemingly impossible situations. Protestants eschewed shrines, but they did not thoroughly eschew healing. The "cure of souls" was difficult to separate from a cure of bodies for Protestants and Catholics alike. Richard Baxter, the great English Civil War Presbyterian, found himself beset by parishioners seeking both spiritual and physical cures. "I was crowded with patients, so that almost twenty would be at my door at once." He finally hired a physician and abandoned his physical healing "unless in consultation with him in case of any seeming necessity."[33]

Not all Protestants repudiated divine healing. English Baptists claimed both to have witnessed and to have performed divine healings in the 1650s and the 1690s. Quakers practiced divine healing openly. Thousands of English men and women were drawn to George Fox between the 1650s and 1680s because he performed miraculous cures regularly. Although miraculous cures remained suspect among Anglicans, Presbyterians, and Independents, such cures played a major role in other, more enthusiastic, Protestant groups of the late seventeenth and early eighteenth centuries. Michael MacDonald argues that a "non-conformist thaumaturgy," variously characterized by exorcisms, raising the dead, and curing the mad, spread across seventeenth-century English Protestantism through Dissenting leaders such as John Durrell, George Fox, and Oliver Heywood to inform London's "French Prophets" of the early eighteenth century, then found new expression in the career of the Anglican reformer turned Methodist, John Wesley, who wrote a medical text that went through as many printings in the eighteenth century as did his spiritual writings.[34]

Europe's wise men and wise women linked Christianity and occultism in ways that often offended their more learned counterparts. Keith Thomas describes a seventeenth-century amulet inscribed simply "Jesus Christ for mercy sake, take away this toothache." But the learned also sometimes pursued the relationship. An Anglican minister confronted by an insane woman driven to fornication "finally gave her an Amulet, viz. some verses of John I written in a paper to hang about her neck, as also certayn herbes to drive the Devil out of her." John Butler, another Anglican clergyman, demonstrated that horoscopes cast in biblical times would have predicted Christ's birthdate. Lilly's seven-hundred-page *Christian Astrology* attempted to synthesize the two potentially competing views. Salmon apparently belonged to Dissenting congregations even as he cast horoscopes and practiced an astrologically based medicine in the 1680s and 1690s. Even Baptists proved reluctant to condemn all occult practices. In the 1650s, when a Baptist congregation asked "whether the practice of astrology in physick be lawful," the Midlands Baptist Association merely advised its members to "be very cautious how they meddle with the practice of it" while it "waite[d] on the Lord for further light in it."[35]

Yet other occult practices strayed far from even the loosest constructions of Christian doctrine. Black pottery "Bellarmine jars," buried at building entrances, warded off diseases and evil events. Inscribed with the face of a bearded man (perhaps the French cardinal, Bellarmine, whom English Protestants would have associated with the Devil), they contained metal nails (believed to have "conductive" power), human or animal urine (believed to be a universal animal fluid), small felt hearts, crosses, Bible verses written out on tiny pieces of paper, and chicken feathers (a mysterious item).[36]

University-educated elites drifted toward complex, highly intellectualized forms of occultism. They did not deny Christianity; they sought to perfect it by unlocking its shackled secrets. The Jewish mystical and occult writings contained in the Cabala had earlier attracted Pico della Mirandola and other Italian Renaissance figures and now intrigued the Anglican Richard Hooker and even Quakers. The magical and mystical works of the sixth-century A.D. Egyptian priest, Hermes Trismegistus, mistakenly believed to have written about 200 B.C., attracted readers with revelations that seemed to prefigure Christ. The healing theories and practices of Paracelsus, the German physician, and his disciple, Johann Baptiste van Helmont, synthesized Christianity, Hermeticism, and alchemy.[37]

The career of a conservative Buckinghamshire Anglican minister, Richard Napier, stunningly reconstructed by Michael MacDonald, reveals how Hermetic-Christian occultism could shape life for common men and women in early modern England even when they neither knew nor understood its underlying principles—a situation not unlike the modern practice of medicine. Between 1590 and 1630 Napier synthesized Elizabethan Calvinism, Hermeticism, neo-Platonism, and alchemy while serving the parish of Great Linford as both minister and physician. To a coterie of late Elizabethan and early Stuart intellectuals, Napier was a "magus," a man comparable to the three wise men of the New Testament and who could conjure angels much as John Dee did. To the less sophisticated, Napier was a healer. Ill, maimed, and distraught patients endured journeys of more than fifty miles to see him, and his neighbors, unlike those of the better-known Dee, do not appear to have been scandalized by his methods. Napier cast horoscopes, made amulets, and prescribed astrologically correct herbs. He took away enchantments and resolved doubts. He consoled. He prayed. And he did not kill, something blood-letting physicians could seldom claim.[38]

Still, Napier remained reticent to advertise his beliefs and practices, and his caution speaks directly to the relationship between Christianity and magic in early modern society. Though many found them part of a common world of wonders and acceptable within Christian circles and even to the law, others were not at all so generous. A wide range of critics, led principally by clergymen, believed that magic—epitomized in its evil forms in witchcraft—was explicitly anti-Christian, a view that directly opposed the laity's ecumenism on the matter. These clergy saw magic as a direct competitor for the laity's spiritual allegiance. Thomas Pickering made the point bluntly in 1608: "as the Ministers of God doe give resolution to the conscience, in matters doubtfull and difficult," he wrote, "so the Ministers of Satan, under the name of Wise-men, And Wise-women, are at hand, by his appointment, to resolve, direct and helpe ignorant and unsettled persons in cases of distraction, loss, or other outward calamities." William Perkins believed that only public ignorance encouraged the laity to believe "that a man may seek to wizards and soothsayers without offence, because God hath provided a salve for every sore." John Gaule argued that the laity's resort to magicians, wizards, and occult healers increased in the 1640s and 1650s because neither church nor state was "at leisure to examine and suppress it." And when a Puritan ministerial association in Cambridge warned laypeople in 1655 about spiritual impostors, it complained not about unrepentant Anglicans or even Catholics but about "witches, wizard[s], and fortune tellers."[39]

The rise of Dissenting Protestantism—in England, Puritanism—further complicated Christianization in early modern Europe. In Switzerland, the Netherlands, a few German principalities, and, of course, England, Protestant Dissent challenged state church Christianity's formal monopoly of public religion. It encouraged adherents to propound their own versions of Christian doctrine and, especially, to criticize that propounded by state church theologians. In the latter's eyes, this dissent stimulated endless cycles of religious extremism—social and spiritual radicalism at Munster, anabaptism in Switzerland and the Low Countries, and Familism, Fifth Monarchism, Ranterism, Muggletonianism, and Quakerism in England.[40]

Protestant Dissent had both individual and collective appeal. If it slighted state church emphasis on public ceremonies such as baptism, marriage, funeral rites, and communion, it also sustained intense individual spirituality through congregations of similarly affected individuals—the gathered saints. Whether among Calvinist Baptists, Congregationalists, and Presbyterians, who stressed human depravity and God's grace, or among Quakers, who stressed the possibility of inward spiritual growth in all persons, the Dissenting experience provoked a profound sense of separation from and superiority to society. Congregational discipline confirmed that separation and superiority. As Michael Walzer describes, it was in the congregations that members testified to faith, revealed "dealings" with the Lord, confessed failings, and criticized sermons. These incessant inspections bleached neighborliness, kinship, and traditional social practice in an acidic bath of reformed Christianity. Intriguingly, Dissenting congregations expelled members for disciplinary lethargy rather than for sins. Some members simply could not endure the disciplinary strain. Some were expelled because they refused to accept or to administer discipline. Few were ejected because they stole, lied, or committed adultery. They were Adam's descendants, and their sins were inevitable. It was their commitment to discipline, not to sinlessness, that made them "saints."[41]

Puritan practice therefore opened a serious breach in the public Christian ritual of early modern England. It shattered the old union of liturgy and life cycle that traditionally brought English men and women into at least momentary contact with Christian ritual and doctrine. Commonwealth Puritans indeed increased sermonizing. Baxter, Shaw, and other Commonwealth ministers delivered Sabbath sermons, preached on weekdays, and spoke to groups of young people. They also increased catechizing. Baxter took particular care to teach elemental Christian doctrine to children and families. But he apparently taught only those he admitted to communion, and it is not at all clear that his efforts really outstripped those of his hard-working Anglican predecessors and successors.[42]

The Puritan turn from public ritual to congregational piety removed significant interaction between institutional Christianity and many segments of English society. Most important, the Commonwealth interlude broke one religious pattern that had commonly prevailed: baptism for virtually all English children. Between 1649 and 1660 only those parents who adhered to or were allowed inside state-supported Presbyterian churches usually obtained baptism for their children. As a result fewer than 15 to 20 percent of newborn infants were baptized, an estimate that includes parishes where ministers who were only lukewarmly committed to the Puritan cause violated their instructions and baptized nearly all children anyway.[43]

Yet Dissent itself soon failed as an effective model of successful Christian organization. Stung by the Restoration, Dissenters dropped from no more than 5 percent of England's adult population in the 1670s to less than 2 percent by 1700. Effective government persecution and surprising institutional lethargy among Dissenters caused the decline. Baptists, Presbyterians, and Independents withered in the face of lawsuits, arrests, confiscations, and imprisonments. The Act of Toleration of 1689 did not reverse the process. By 1715, Dissent counted fewer congregations and fewer adherents in England than it had in the 1680s. Quakers sustained their numbers through family growth, kinship connections, and the loyalty of children to the faith of their parents, and they almost entirely abandoned the proselytizing that had created the movement in the 1650s. As a result, after 1680 the Society of Friends hardened into a "tribal" movement, living off descendants of its first converts, not unlike the fate of the New England Puritans.[44]

In its decline, English Dissent intensified its regional and provincial roots. Although Anglicans feared that the Act of Toleration would strengthen Dissenters, they actually retreated into persisting local loyalties. This parochialism quickly led to institutional manifestations that were all the more obvious in a movement once characterized by extraordinary institutional strength. The Presbyterian-Independent union of 1689 lasted only two years and in 1691 shattered into regional gatherings of highly variable strength. A year later the national assembly of Calvinist Baptists, also formed in 1689, divided into two regional bodies and further fractured churches already split into Calvinists ("Particular" Baptists), Arminians ("General" Baptists), and Seventh Day Baptists.

Presbyterians and Independents remained strong in only a few areas (such as Devon in the southwest or Essex in the east), Baptists retained their largest followings west and northeast of London, and Quakers were concentrated in England's north and east. A third of the surviving Dissenting groups remained isolated outside these regional centers and found it even more difficult to support clergymen and sustain a rich denominational life. In short, few offered compelling models for survival, much less expansion, in the New World.[45]

Popular and learned occultism also shifted after 1680. Although historians, usually citing the advance of "Enlightenment" and scientific movements, have argued that magic, astrology, and divination disappeared in the early eighteenth century, they actually underwent a remarkable folklorization. This transformation allowed them to survive in the largely illiterate and poor segments of English society even as they did indeed often disappear from elite and literate segments of society.

Occultism's disappearance among Europe's educated elite did not stem from the rise of modern science. Recent studies, among them MacDonald's work on Napier and Betty Jo Teeter Dobbs's on Isaac Newton, reveal a crabbed and complex relationship between science and magic. The career of Isaac Newton, who spent years trying to perfect alchemy and conjure angels while he revolutionized the laws of physics, suggests just how complex that interrelationship might have been. Like Napier almost a century earlier, Newton kept his alchemy and conjuring secret because it was suspect and even dangerous. As Keith Thomas points out, Reformation leaders attacked Catholicism and magic together and labeled both as pagan. They ridiculed the Mass as magical, and they noted that the veneration of relics closely paralleled the manipulation of physical objects and "sympathetic magic" practiced by wise men and wise women. Parliament thus banned both white and black magic in 1559, and its action was as much part of its attack on Catholicism as it was an attempt to suppress magical healers and practitioners.[46]

Occultism also came under strong intellectual attack. Isaac Casaubon exposed the Hermes Trismegistus texts as frauds. Criticism of astrology focused on its inconsistencies. Identical twins with identical zodiac signs and "nativities" lived unidentical lives. Astrology could not incorporate new astronomical findings about the heavens. Its predictions were vague and usually wrong. Beliefs about witches also faced criticism. Germany's Johann Weyer and England's Reginald Scot denied the existence of real witches and witchcraft. Accused witches, they believed, were deranged and mentally ill individuals whom the Devil had tricked into thinking they could harm people through magic. The effects they produced should either be laid directly at the Devil's doorstep or explained as natural but misinterpreted happenings.[47]

Dedicated adepts refused to surrender. As late as 1677 Richard Saunders wrote of geomancy that "in this Art, . . . our Saviour Jesus Christ is Via Vita & Veritas . . . he that entreth not by him goeth out of the way." Others sustained the claim that Old Testament figures such as Adam, Moses, and Solomon had accepted and sometimes practiced astrology. Almanac makers gleefully reported deaths of critics and claimed that they had predicted them. Still, the accelerating critiques cast occultism in a thoroughly defensive posture, especially among elites. Isaac Newton's continuing but secret quest for alchemy's "greene lyon" in the 1690s looked backward into a disappearing intellectual universe. His *Principia Mathematica* looked forward and performed intellectual transformations any magus might have admired.[48]

Magic's dislodgment from educated culture at least helped remove the terror-ridden witch trials from the European countryside, though this did not happen everywhere. Witch trials even increased in seventeenth-century Scotland, where they served as one of several instruments of government centralization. In some German principalities they rode waves of intense anti-Catholic and anti-Protestant sentiment that did not ebb until the 1690s. But the trials slowed and even disappeared in other German principalities and in France, England, and Spain. French appeals courts overturned convictions and slowed prosecutions. In Spain's Basque provinces a Jesuit priest, Antonio de Salazar, quashed witch hunting with late medieval legalism and almost modern experiments to test witnesses' veracity. Witch prosecutions in England's Puritan-dominated Essex County, long notorious for its trials, fell from a hundred each decade in the 1580s and 1590s to fewer than ten each decade by the 1650s; the Essex courts, moreover, acquitted a greater proportion of the people they tried and executed none of those they convicted after 1645.[49]

Complex causes produced this change. Magistrates did not always abandon their own belief in witches. But they increasingly refused to convict specific people of specific witchcraft crimes. Magistrates viewed accused witches as they had long viewed local wise men and wise women—people to be ridiculed, perhaps pitied, but not punished. True, England's Puritans struck out against the trend. England's only large witch trial of the Tudor-Stuart period occurred in Essex County, where some forty people died during a real witch hunt in 1645. Yet even at the time it was recognized that the Essex affair constituted an aberration and that it only highlighted the decreasing number of trials occurring around it.[50]

Yet if witch trials declined, magical practice in the general population did not always simultaneously decrease. In the 1740s and 1750s there were still men and women who feared alleged witches and continued to patronize a seemingly declining number of occult healers and practitioners. They consulted wise men and wise women for healing; guided by astrological charts or, more likely, by rumor of some special supernatural property, they sought out herbs; they still filled "Bellarmines" with red-felt hearts, metal objects, and human urine and buried them at their doorsteps; they read almanacs that continued to print the "anatomy" and occult healing formulas; and they continued to interpret baptism as a quasi-magical protective rite rather than as a Christian initiatory ceremony.[51]

The patrons of this eighteenth-century magical and occult practice, however, now emerged almost exclusively among those whom Natalie Zemon Davis calls "little people"—farm laborers, the unemployed, day workers, the illiterate, the abject poor, and the great masses of the underemployed and relatively poor. The bishops, titled nobility, and office holders who had once seen astrologers, the well-known mathematicians, theologians, and university professors who had once investigated Hermeticism and alchemy, and the ministers and church members who had once linked Christianity and occultism in daily life all vanished as patrons of magic and occultism. No longer viable among the nation's intellectual elite, stricken from those segments of Christianity where they had once been found, and absent from printed literature except almanacs and some popular medical publications, occultism and magic now lodged almost wholly in a very special segment of the population that had never before been so independent and, as a "folk," so isolated.[52]

* * *

The withering of Dissent and the folklorization of magic further complicated the already vexed relationship of Christianity, magic, and popular or lay religion. Colonists arriving in America in the late seventeenth century could only look back at even more complex configurations of religious practice and indifference at home than had been available to their predecessors. Everywhere in Europe, state church Christianity endured significant change, not all of it positive. In England, Restoration clerics found little improvement in popular piety after the Commonwealth experiment in national Presbyterianism. Weekly church attendance remained low and Easter communication scandalously so. Terling's rector cited 55 percent of village householders for nonattendance in 1679. A decade later Robert Meeke reported "many to hear but few to receive," despite his own intense labor to increase church attendance. Since Dissent was experiencing its own decline, the problem could scarcely be laid to competition. Nor would it improve with a new century. In the 1730s the rector of Bladon droned on with familiar complaints: "Most men are now-a-days become but too indifferent to religion in ev'ry shape . . . there are, in all places, more absentees than dissenters." The crisis of popular and public faith, by all accounts, deepened rather than receded in eighteenth-century England.[53]

The French pattern was no more encouraging. Over 85 percent of French adults still performed "Easter Duties" through the 1730s, but strong geographic variations in this ratio appeared by mid-century. In rural districts surrounding Chalons only 60 to 70 percent of adults took Easter communion. The rate plunged to less than 25 percent in Paris and Rouen. Other signs of ambivalence abounded. Wealthy men decreased their church gifts and dropped Christian phraseology from their wills. Bourgeois families sent fewer sons to the priesthood and fewer daughters into convents. Whether these changes signaled French "dechristianization" before the Revolution depends on our estimation of lay Christianization in the seventeenth century. But at the time observers did not need comparisons to recognize that even before the Revolution, Christianity still did not command lay respect in the ways the church required, the law demanded, and the landscape suggested.[54]

The state churches bore significant responsibility for the continuing lethargy in public Christian practice. In England vast inequalities characterized priestly wealth; a third of Leicestershire's priests reported incomes of less than £30 sterling in the late seventeenth century, and a third of the parishes, usually the poorest ones, had no clergyman at all. Problems invaded the upper clerical ranks as well. Some bishops simply failed to perform the rite of confirmation, whose blessing, conferred after elementary Christian doctrine was learned, qualified parishioners for communion, usually at age sixteen. Bishop Thomas Smith did not hold a single confirmation in his Carlisle bishopric between 1684 and his death in 1702. His successor confirmed over five thousand persons in one year—a vulgar exercise, perhaps, since he often confirmed hundreds at a time without effective teaching or examination, but preferable to Smith's indolence.[55]

In the wake of persistent, even deepening, lay indifference to institutional Christianity, Europe's Catholic and Protestant leaders launched major efforts to expand proselytizing. After 1720 and especially under the leadership of Benedict XIV, a desire to expand evangelizing missions emphasizing explicitly "popular" preaching led to the formation of the Passionists (1720) and Redemptorists (1732), both of whom worked throughout Catholic Europe. Devotionalism paralleled this popular evangelization. It renewed the personalization of faith long evident in the cult of the saints so bitterly criticized by Reformation leaders. Now devotionalists focused on Christ and Mary. Italian and Spanish Franciscans developed the ritual of the stations of the cross to encourage the laity to replicate Christ's journey of sacrifice through Jerusalem prior to his death and resurrection. The culmination of this process was the great age of Mariology, which swept past its origins in the eighteenth century to triumph in the nineteenth and twentieth centuries. Its beginnings were signaled in Bohemia, where the number of shrines to Mary rose from two in 1655 to over forty by 1700; by the middle of the eighteenth century the Gothic basilica at Mariazell was attracting as many as 150,000 pilgrims per year.[56]

While Dissent receded in England, Anglicans launched a major effort at religious and social reform within their denomination. Reforming bishops such as Henry Compton, Edmund Gibson, and White Kennett laid responsibility for the nation's continuing spiritual lethargy directly at the feet of the Church of England. They found the solution in evangelization, not evangelicalism—that is, in spreading the Word rather than in demanding individual conversion experiences — and they found the means in clerical reform and active proselytizing. They instituted clerical conferences to demonstrate model sermons, discuss parish difficulties, and reshape pastoral labor to increase lay adherence. They pressed other bishops to perform confirmation ceremonies, and they advocated increased diocesan visitations to inspect parish facilities and review clerical performance.[57]

Anglicans also promoted reform of a visual sort. The late seventeenth century was the first major period of English church construction in over a century. The great London fire of 1666 accidentally reshaped the city's sacred landscape and brought forth plans to construct some fifty new urban church buildings with funds donated by Queen Anne. The London scheme largely failed, however, and far more new church construction occurred in the countryside. Surviving seventeenth-century English church buildings are rare in part because successful eighteenth-century efforts to rebuild dilapidated structures replaced the relatively few Anglican churches that had gone up in the previous century. If the new structures lacked architectural distinction, they certainly were no more ungainly than their predecessors. Their aesthetic qualities, in any case, were far less important than their attempt to redress population shifts and reassert Christianity's visual demand for lay adherence.[58]

Finally, Anglican reformers reshaped parish activity. Some Anglican clerics formed midweek "religious societies" for Bible reading and moral training, specifically organized to attract young men (but not, apparently, young women) between eighteen and twenty-five, the age when it was believed the nadir of religious interest was experienced. Societies for the "Reformation of Manners" sought suppression of lewdness, drunkenness, and blasphemy with stiff fines and whippings as punishments. The not so secret indulgences of some of their own backers, however, soon brought the movement considerable criticism. Charity Schools for poor children taught obedience, Christianity, literacy, and proto-industrial skills in a curriculum unembarrassed in its attempt at social control. Catechetical training took up the greatest part of their scholars' day, and at year's end the students were paraded before Charity School supporters, most of them members of the aristocracy and gentry, to demonstrate the success of the venture.[59]

Two famous societies capped the Anglican reformers' campaigns. The Society for Promoting Christian Knowledge (SPCK), founded in 1699, provided books for Charity Schools and an enormous range of popular tracts advancing personal morality and Christian faithfulness; it remained Europe's leading publisher of Protestant tracts down to the twentieth century. The Society for the Propagation of the Gospel in Foreign Parts (SPG), formed in 1701, became central to the religious development of Britain's American colonies; it promoted Christianity among English colonists, who sometimes strayed farther from regular Christian practice in the New World than they had in the Old.[60]

Reform and sectarian movements also took on new life and were perhaps even stimulated by renewed state church proselytization. Germany's Pietist movement originated within its state-supported Lutheran churches in the 1690s. Especially in Prussia it gained strength precisely because state officials appreciated Pietism's fusion of personal piety and personal industry. England's Methodist movement, led by John and Charles Wesley, likewise emerged in the 1740s from within the Church of England. Unlike German Pietism, Methodism soon earned Anglican enmity. It remained politically conservative, nonetheless, and in 1776 John Wesley angrily withdrew Methodist preachers from America after colonists supported the Declaration of Independence. Religious radicals both in England and on the Continent renewed the interest in supernatural intervention and curing despite Enlightenment ridicule. Huguenots defeated in the War of the Camisards fled to London in 1706, where they joined with radical German and English "Philadelphians" to fashion a new sectarian alliance whose followers cured disease and raised the dead. In Paris, *convulsionaires* took Catholic devotionalism and emphasis on miracles beyond limits approved by the church. They besieged the city's largest cemetery in the 1740s, believing that they could witness a raising of the dead. Only violent confrontations with civil authorities, backed by the church, ended the episode.[61]

Renewed evangelization and radical enthusiasm probably revitalized adherence more among the already churched than among indifferent and lethargic laypeople. The decline of French adherence to Catholic life and ritual continued unabated and reflected problems elsewhere in European Catholicism. A rare Portuguese survey taken after the disastrous 1755 earthquake revealed no change in religious practice despite the catastrophe. Though 90 percent of town adults took Easter communion, less than 10 percent confessed their sins as canon law required. Yet Lisbon prostitutes reported a brisk business in forged confession certificates, a suggestion that among Lisbon's wealthier men, social propriety required at least the signs of Easter communion.[62]

A 1743 visitation report from Yorkshire provides a remarkably detailed view of vagaries in lay Christianization in mid-eighteenth-century England. A full third of Yorkshire's approximately 680 parishes furnished no visitation statistics because they lacked a minister, probably because they were small and remote. Neighboring clerics preached and offered communion only irregularly, and most vacant parishes held out little hope of improving their circumstances in the near future. Furthermore, Dissent did not fill the void. Although Yorkshire became a major Methodist stronghold after 1780, Baptists, Presbyterians, and Quakers counted only a few congregations there in 1743. All but a few of these Dissenting congregations, moreover, existed in the larger parishes that also contained Anglican clergymen. As a result the rural villages that lacked Anglican priests also lacked Dissenting worship.[63]

Village size and population density strongly colored Yorkshire church attendance and communication. Christianization fared best in middling parishes, worst in the largest ones. Parishes of ten to forty families demonstrated the most consistent record of Anglican worship and communication; 57 percent of their adults took communion at Easter and 48 percent on other occasions throughout the year. Parishes with forty to one hundred families reported a drop in regular communication to about 29 percent and in Easter communication to 44 percent. Parishes of a hundred or more families reported only 20 percent of eligible adults at regular worship and only 31 percent at Easter rites. Communicants in small villages proved less fickle in their worship than did parishioners in larger places. In small parishes only slightly more people took communion on Easter than at other times, but in large parishes Easter brought out more than twice as many communicants as were seen at other communion services, though both regular and Easter communication remained far less common than in Yorkshire's small parishes. In Yorkshire's large parishes, then, worship and communication were both uncommon and shallow.

As urbanization advanced, Yorkshire's largest town and city parishes exhibited particularly bleak spiritual records. Parishes of over 1,500 potential communicants accounted for nearly a third of Yorkshire's population, and 75 to 90 percent of their potential churchgoers lacked a steady affiliation with institutional Christianity. On average, their rate of Easter communication was 8.7 percent, and none claimed Easter communication rates topping 20 percent. In 1743 Halifax, Yorkshire's largest parish, reported only 150 regular communicants among some 6,200 families (15,150 adults) and only 260 communicants (2 percent) on Easter. The Halifax rector blamed this lethargy on neither lay scrupulousness nor Dissent. Nobody suggested that Halifax's laypeople were so pious that they felt unworthy to take communion. Furthermore, Baptist, Presbyterian, and Quaker activity accounted for few additional churchgoers, and Dissenters had in any case almost wholly abandoned vigorous proselytizing since the 1689 Act of Toleration. What would happen to Halifax's Christianity as urbanization increased?

The Yorkshire visitation revealed the fragile adherence to Christianity among the early modern European laity. Despite cathedrals, chapels, legal establishments, and Christian-dominated education systems, all of Europe's Old World societies extended a most perplexing religious heritage to their New World colonies. If Virginia and Massachusetts authorities intended to expand European Christianity into the wilderness, whose Christianity would it be—that of the law, the church, the ambivalent laity? Old World Christianity had long been sheltered and supported by a complex infrastructure of theology, law, and social process. What would happen in the New World where an ecclesiastical order had yet to be established, where the law had yet to be written or enforced, where the land lay without Christian sacralization, and where men and women were strangers to each other except, perhaps, in their longing for material gain and in their undisciplined, expansive, and sometimes ambivalent expressions of spiritual interest?

THE CRISIS OF CHRISTIAN PRACTICE IN AMERICA

2

It is a commonplace to describe American religion as a seventeenth-century invention. The Puritans of New England, the Catholics of Maryland, even the first Virginia settlers, who were described by Perry Miller as more "at home with Calvin and Loyola . . . than with Thomas Jefferson and the Benjamin Franklin of *The Way of Wealth*," intended to Christianize Indians and fashion Christian societies in the New World wilderness. Their enterprises transcended individual will and national intentions. As late as 1682 the quietistic William Penn too voiced millennialist expectations: "God will plan American [*sic*] and it shall have its day . . . The 5th kingdom or Glorious day of [Jesus?] Christ . . . may have the last parte of the world, the setting of the son or western world to shine in."[1]

Colonists planned less well than God. The religious patterns that emerged in the seventeenth-century colonies did not conform to sweet visions of a triumphant Christian future. In the Chesapeake Bay area of Virginia and Maryland, surprisingly resilient early lay Christian enterprise fell away to an awkward localism and then brought forth an expanding secularism that challenged even rudimentary Christian custom. In Massachusetts, Christian commitments as often produced tension and disorder as peace and harmony. By the 1690s Maryland authorities had reason to wonder whether Christianity would even survive the transit to the next century, while New Englanders fretted about real religious decline in societies that had once measured astonishing levels of Christian adherence. Pennsylvania aside, the Restoration colonies of New York, New Jersey, Delaware, and North and South Carolina exhibited extraordinary spiritual discord and sectarianism as well as a remarkable but all too familiar indifference to things spiritual. In America's first European century, then, traditionally thought of as exclusively Puritan, Christian practice not only proved insecure but showed dangerous signs of declining rather than rising.

The religious origins of early Virginia derived from the religious commitments of Virginia Company leaders. Sir Edwin Sandys, long a major Company figure, was the son of the archbishop of York and had studied in Geneva after finishing his college work at Cambridge. Other Virginia leaders shared Sandys's commitment. In seeking funds the Company inevitably mined the gentry and merchant classes, which had deep Calvinist sympathies. Furthermore, a surprisingly strong ministerial presence emerged in the infant colony. Twenty-two ministers served under Company auspices between 1607 and its demise in 1624, and a 1616 report showed four ministers distributed among only 351 settlers, a ratio seldom found in England.[2]

The first Virginia ministers had reforming Calvinist, perhaps even Puritan, credentials. Cambridge-educated Alexander Whitaker celebrated Puritan reform and Virginia colonization simultaneously in a 1613 sermon, *Good News from Virginia.* Robert Hunt, the colony's first minister, Richard Buck, an Oxford graduate, William Mease, who labored in Virginia from 1609 through the 1620s, and Henry Jacob, who died at sea in 1619 while on his way to Virginia and had previously ministered to London's first separatist congregation, all shared reforming Calvinist sentiments. Indeed, Whitaker criticized English colleagues who failed to seize the opportunity Virginia presented. After his arrival he wrote that frustrated reformers who were "hot against the Surplis and subscription" should "come hither where neither are spoken of."[3]

Whitaker and his colleagues promoted a reformed spiritual regimen even as they upheld the liturgical and ceremonial requirements of the *Book of Common Prayer.* In a colony filled with fifteen- to thirty-year-old males, notorious for their spiritual indifference, Whitaker eagerly added catechizing to his Sabbath preaching. He conferred about church matters with "four of the most religious men" in the colony, and he administered communion every month, not just four times a year as was done in most English parishes.[4]

Christianity's institutional importance blossomed after Lord De La Warre rescued the colony from starvation in 1609. De La Warre immediately established Christianity's physical presence in the landscape by constructing a chapel, sixty by twenty-four feet, at Jamestown. William Strachey described it as having a "chancel of cedar and a communion table of black walnut." Two bells called settlers to worship, and public processions confirmed both Christianity's presence in Virginia and De La Warre's hierarchical principles:

> Every Sunday, when the Lord Governour went to church, he was accompanied with all the Councillors, Captains, other officers, and all the gentlemen, and with a guard of fifty Halberdiers in his Lordship's livery, fair red cloaks, on each side and behind him. The Lord Governour sat in the choir, in a green velvet chair, with a velvet cushion before him on which he knelt, and the council, captains, and officers sat on each side of him, each in their place, and when the Lord Governour returned home, he was waited on in the same manner to his house.[5]

Sir Thomas Dale's "Lawes Divine, Morall and Martiall" of 1612 reinforced public Christian practice in Virginia. They demanded the death penalty for "being a Church robber" and for a third offense of blasphemy and disobedience. They ordered colonists to forswear gaming, to attend catechizing, to hear sermons, and to sanctify the Sabbath by "preparing themselves at home with private prayer." They also prescribed the loss of one day's food allowance for a first absence from divine worship and six months in the galleys for a third. Early legislation continued the support for Christianity. In 1619 the first Virginia Assembly prescribed further penalties for immoral, blasphemous behavior, authorized "Ministers and Churchwardens . . . to prevent all ungodly disorders," and, in traditional English fashion, required records kept "of all Christenings, burials, and marriages." The Assembly emphasized the ministers' duty to catechize "suche as are not yet ripe to come to the Communion," and it sanctioned quarterly ministerial meetings with the governor "to determine whom it is fitt to excommunicate." And, of course, it ordered the towns to instruct Indian children blessed "in witt and graces of nature . . . in the first Elements of literature" so they might be prepared for their conversion to Christianity.[6]

By mid-century, however, Virginia was better known for irreligion and indifference than piety. Its religious difficulties were rooted in traditional European spiritual lethargy. Whitaker complained bitterly about the lax Christian practice that continued despite his own energetic preaching and catechizing. Immigration added few colonists who were likely to lessen his worries. Through at least 1650 Virginia remained filled with the young, single males who had long vexed English clerics and who formed the kind of population unlikely to stimulate, much less increase, Christian piety in the colony. Between 1625 and 1640 about fifteen thousand people, mostly servants, arrived in Virginia. Men outnumbered women, sometimes by as much as six to one, and death claimed immigrants so swiftly that in 1640 the colony still contained only eight thousand settlers, among them few women, children, or families.[7]

Institutional Christianity did not lack for immediate support after the Crown assumed control of the colony in 1624. Court records reveal at least four ministers in the colony in that year, and subsequent records document the presence of between five and ten ministers in the next several decades. In 1625 the Assembly reasserted the need to establish public worship and sacralize the landscape in traditional English ways. It ordered every plantation to erect "some decent howse or sittinge roome" for worship, and it demanded that each plantation set aside a "strongly paled or fenced in [place] for the buriall of the dead."[8]

In 1626 the Assembly clarified one additional aim of its regulations. It decreed that "there be an uniformities in our Church kept as neere as may be to the Canons of Englande both in substance and Circumstance." Historians have suggested that the qualification, "as neere as may be," reflected a reluctance to transplant a full state church system to New World soil. But the caution reflected concern about Virginia's rudimentary society, not any rejection of Anglicanism or the state church tradition. In the next decades, the Assembly levied church taxes and ordered settlers to pay ministers in their best tobacco or have poor tobacco "burnte before theire faces," and it ordered the Assembly and Governor's Council to attend quarterly church services at Jamestown. A 1628 Council order about Jamestown's church books and communion vessels revealed the splendor in which Virginians could receive communion at Jamestown—"[a] Communion silver guilt cup, and two little chalices in a cloath of gold cover, one Crimson velvet carpet with a gold and silke fringe, One white damask Communion cloath with buttons [and] Fower divinity books with brasse Bosses." And the Assembly sacralized commemoration of the disastrous 1624 Indian massacre that very nearly destroyed the colony by directing that each March 22 be marked with a special Christian service.[9]

The church-state union did not always proceed smoothly in early Virginia. When Captain William Tucker commandeered the Reverend Rowland Graine's boat for military purposes in 1628, Graine stood his ground as firmly as any New England cleric: "I am going to Administer the Communion," he told Tucker. "God must be served before the King . . . my boate shall not goe of[f] my ground, if the Goeuvnor send twenty war[rants]." Still, at times government and colonists cooperated with vigor and enthusiasm to replicate traditional English Christian practice. In 1628 the General Court successfully wooed Hog Island residents to buy timbers to construct the first church building there, and in 1642 the Jamestown vestry erected a larger church to replace the building ordered by De La Warre in 1609.[10]

Documenting Christian practice among the Virginia laity between 1630 and 1650 is difficult, because no church records and few literary sources have survived for this period. Tantalizing evidence from court records, however, suggests that even Virginia's young males did not lose all their Christian referents. Some residents framed time by the rhythms of the liturgical year and ran contracts from "Christmas" to "Christmas" or identified events as occurring near "St. Johns" or "St. Stephens" days. Ministers published banns to regulate marriages and were encouraged to do so by demographic patterns that made marriages rare, contested, and in need of documentation. Churchwardens cited residents for profaning the Sabbath, such as "Thomas Farley gentleman," who was brought to court by the Jamestown churchwardens for hunting dogs and missing worship for three months. They used worship to implement punishments and laid men "neck and heels during divine service." Women convicted of sexual offenses were made to dress in white gowns, hold white wands, and stand on chairs or stools during worship, a traditional English punishment symbolizing the need and desire for purity. When Ellnor Sprage promised to marry two different men in 1624, the Virginia Council demanded that she acknowledge her transgressions in a way that hinted at disciplinary processes more commonly associated with Puritan worship: "Penetently Confessinge her faltes [she] shall ask god and the Congregations forgiveness."[11]

Christian sentiment also appeared amid a sometimes squalid social life. When Thomas Balby, whom no one described as a gentleman, screamed out, "Lord have mercy uppon us, Lord Jesus receave my soule" after he had been skewered with a knife, his panic at least suggested some catechizing in the colony or in England. When Joan Vincent claimed that seven of fourteen women who attended Kecoughtan Church were Thomas Harris's "whoares" and that Harris once "made faste the [church] doore and would have layne [there] with a woman in the Plantacione against her will," jurors might have convicted her of slander as much because she injured their sense of sacred space as because she impugned the reputation of Kecoughtan's fine colonists.[12]

Yet discrete Christian survivals did not a coherent spiritual life make, and institutional Christianity experienced its own starving time in Virginia between 1630 and 1680. Like its secular counterpart between 1607 and 1609, Christianity's starving time here stemmed from failed leadership, not from Indians or from the wilderness. The principal difficulty was institutional. Until 1689 London authorities failed to place Virginia under English ecclesiastical jurisdiction by appointing any of three available representatives: a major figure like the bishop of London; a suffragan or assisting bishop, who could direct clerical and parish affairs but not hold ecclesiastical courts; or a "commissary," who acted as the bishop's agent. This failure did not occur for lack of suggestions. Proposals to establish direct Anglican episcopal authority in Virginia or other American colonies emerged in 1634, 1636, and 1638 but languished for reasons of domestic politics. A Parliament at odds with the Crown over religion as well as over taxation and legislative authority was not about to enhance royal power through the appointment of an Anglican bishop for the colonies. Yet years later

Anglicans still acted slowly. Although Henry Compton's appointment as bishop of London in 1675 resulted in new attention to the Virginia situation, Compton did not finally name a Virginia commissary, James Blair, until thirteen years later, eighty years after the colony's settlement.[13]

Vigorous religious leadership did not emerge within the colony, either. The 1634 Assembly redefined parish boundaries and formalized churchwarden and vestry appointments in the colony's Anglican establishment, but localities implemented these changes in highly idiosyncratic ways. In the main these reflected the collapsing of several traditional English institutions in Virginia into one until the 1670s. This compression may be best seen in Accomack County on Virginia's eastern shore. There, contrary to English law and tradition, the county court managed parish affairs before 1635. It hired the minister, ordered construction of a church building, and empowered churchwardens to "distrayne" or seize goods in payment of delinquent tithes. The minister, William Cotton, had little influence over the court, which prosecuted sexual and financial offenses but avoided heresy and other charges that required greater theological sophistication. When the court created a separate vestry in 1635 to conform to the new vestry legislation the Assembly had passed, parish operation did not change quickly. The court simply named eight of its current members and one former member to the eleven-member vestry and kept vestry minutes in the court records for a year, drawing a line across the page to separate court and vestry business. For several decades, at least, half or more of the members of the court and the vestry held seats on both bodies.[14]

Other early Virginia vestries, most of them similarly containing many county court magistrates, engaged clerics in long, tough contests over salaries, houses, church lands, servants, and, later, slaves. In 1642 the Virginia Council demanded an end to the "many controversies [that] do daily arise between Parishioners and ministers throughout the colony concerning the payment of their Duties." But the demand had little effect. William Cotton sued frequently for tithes and fees before 1642, and his successor, Thomas Teackle, extended the acrimony well into the 1690s by regularly suing parishioners and vestry alike for salary, debts, servants, slaves, and even slander.[15]

Unlike England, the Virginia landscape failed to receive the strong imprint of Christian institutions. Indeed, by comparison, Virginia's territory underwent a substantial desacralization between 1630 and 1670 despite the promising start on church construction made by the Virginia Company. Accomack County was a notable exception, despite the apparently acrimonious relations between its ministers and vestries. At least four church buildings were constructed there between 1620 and 1668, and they placed most county settlers within reasonable walking distance of a state church structure despite fairly rapid population growth.[16]

But across the Chesapeake, where the land drifted endlessly back into the continent, church building proceeded lethargically. In the major part of the Virginia colony mid-seventeenth-century vestries simply ignored church construction, despite the push of settlers deeper into the country. The original church buildings that were strung out along a few of Virginia's eastern rivers and streams masked a Christian emptiness elsewhere in the expanding colony. Four of the eight shires created when the Assembly restructured the colony's political boundaries in 1634 contained no church buildings, and the available records suggest that the buildings in the other four shires were in sad repair. Construction of the new church at Jamestown in 1642 stirred few other parishes, which added and replaced church buildings only slowly, if at all. The result was a major new cultural pattern: without explicitly rejecting traditional English patterns, English immigrants were shaping an American landscape remarkably free of the church buildings that overflowed the humanly shaped environment at home.[17]

Surry County exemplified the process. Before 1655 most of its residents lived within three to five miles of both the James River and the two church buildings that the vestries had constructed in 1628 and 1650. But this pattern changed in subsequent decades. Although people settling land along Upper Chippokes Creek in the far western part of the county had to journey five to seven miles to attend Sabbath services, the two parish vestries authorized no new church building for the area until 1680. In the 1660s and 1670s settlers claimed even more distant interior lands along the Blackwater River and its adjacent swamps and more than doubled the county's population. Still, the Surry vestries authorized new buildings only slowly. They did not construct a chapel at Seacorrie Swamp until 1700, did not build one at Spring

Swamp until 1725, and did not add others at Cypress Swamp and St. Paul's until 1745, the latter actually replacing the Seacorrie Swamp chapel. As a result, even old Surry County neighborhoods often lacked accessible places for Christian worship long after their original settlement.[18]

Virginia's mid-seventeenth-century clergymen hardly compensated for the accelerating desacralization of the landscape. Between 1630 and 1670 relatively few ministers worked in Virginia. Roger Green's 1661 tract, *Virginia's Cure,* claimed that only ten of the colony's fifty parishes then had ministers. The charge probably was accurate. Despite Virginia's nearly tenfold increase in population from four thousand colonists in 1630 to about thirty thousand colonists in 1670, the number of ministers did not increase from the five to ten men laboring there in the 1640s. When the Lord Commissioners of Foreign Plantations quizzed Governor William Berkeley in 1671 about the "course taken about the instructing the people, within your government in the christian religion," Berkeley disingenuously replied that Virginia took "the same course that is taken in England out of towns; every man according to his ability instructing his children." He said that the colony had forty-eight parishes and that its ministers were "well paid," but he omitted a count of ministers occupying parishes. Instead, perhaps alluding to older Puritan inclinations that were still present, Berkeley claimed that Virginia's ministers would receive even better salaries "if they would pray oftener and preach less." "Thank God there are no free schools nor printing, . . . learning has brought disobedience, and heresy, and sects into the world, and printing has divulged them, and libels against the best government. God keep us from both!"[19]

Nor were Virginia's ministers models of Christian fortitude. Descriptions of doggedly pious clerics in the 1610s gave way to bitter, cynical portraits. In 1632 an Accomack County layman ridiculed William Cotton as a "black cotted raskoll." In 1642 William Durand, a Nansemond County layman and self-confessed Puritan, protested that "if we continue under these wreched and blind Idoll shepards[,] the very bane of this land[,] we are like to perish." In 1656 John Hammond described the colony's ministers as lascivious drunks who had abandoned all vestiges of Christian discipline. They "babble in a Pulpet, roare in a Tavern, . . . [and] by their dissoluteness destroy rather than feed their Flocks." Lionel

Gatford echoed the criticism a year later. He claimed that the ministers were "indecent and slovenly" in their preaching and led "wicked and profane lives." He found their behavior not surprising, because in his view they had immigrated to Virginia because they "were ashamed or afraid, to live any longer here in this Nation."[20]

Actually, Virginia's clergymen were not without redeeming qualities. If nothing else, they were at least as likely to have some college training as most of their English counterparts. About half the known ministers of seventeenth-century Virginia could claim Cambridge or Oxford matriculations, a ratio that compared favorably with English patterns. Finally, despite their reputation among historians, the Virginia ministers were no more immoral or dissolute than ministers elsewhere. Wherever they occurred, drunkenness, immorality, and financial chicanery naturally disappointed parishioners, but these failings were relatively uncommon in both Virginia and New England.[21]

That no *Magnalia Christi Americana* ever celebrated Virginia's clergymen stemmed not from their poor training or dissolute behavior but from the lack of leadership and collective memory that spurred Cotton Mather's New England enterprise. It is all but impossible to recover contemporary descriptions of day-to-day ministerial labor in mid-seventeenth-century Virginia. Even the most generous reading of Virginia's elusive sources on religion hints at little of the colonywide communication that characterized New England clerical labor—there are no known ministerial meetings, records of clerical correspondence, ecclesiastical conferences, not even occasional gatherings to protest isolation or lack of direction. Lacking the instruments of cohesion, even the more active ministers under the Virginia Company never passed into the sort of collective memory that in New England promoted Christian endeavor and shaped a hagiography that, for good or ill, underwrote institutional vitality.[22]

Yet a familiar English localism also produced configurations that ran against the grain of Virginia's general lethargy in Christian commitment. Nansemond and Lower Norfolk counties, south and east of Jamestown, sustained a strong Puritan piety and discipline in the 1640s. Probably originating during the Virginia Company period, these persistent Puritan instincts were led by prominent laymen, including William Durand and Daniel Gookin, and a Calvinist minister, Thomas Harrison. When in 1641 Harrison decided to leave, seventy-one Nansemond adults petitioned the New Haven Puritan minister, John Davenport, to send three ministers to serve what they described as a vital and even expanding religious community to the south of New England.[23]

A letter from William Durand to John Davenport that accompanied the Virginia petition revealed the source and fervor of lay piety in Nansemond and Lower Norfolk. These Virginians were as "Puritan" as the New Englanders to whom they were writing. Durand himself had heard John Davenport preach at London's St. Stephen's Church in the 1630s. Like Boston's Robert Keayne, Durand filled a notebook with substantial summaries of Davenport's sermons. In Virginia, the notebook became "noe little stay to my wreched and miserable condition," Durand wrote. Nor was he alone. Other Virginians had also "lived under the meanes, and bin wrought upon" in England. But now in Virginia, with Harrison's departure imminent, they were "scattered in the cloudy and darke day of temptation, beeing fallen from their first love, and are even as the wife of youth forsaken and desolate . . . for if ever the lord had cause to consume the citties of Sodom and Gomorrah he might as justly and more severely execute his wrath upon Virginia, swoln so great with the poison of sin, as it is become a monster, and ready to burst."[24]

If Governor Berkeley saw rebellion in these Puritans, his response to their challenge also etched the complexity of religious realities in early Virginia. Berkeley expelled the three New England ministers. But he allowed Thomas Harrison, who had not yet actually departed, to remain, after Harrison agreed in a meeting with Berkeley to abide by Anglican church canons. Subsequently Berkeley also allowed two apparently moderate Puritan clergymen to minister in Accomack County: Nathaniel Eaton, a Harvard tutor expelled from Massachusetts for child molestation, and Eaton's successor, Francis Doughty, sometimes identified by historians as a Presbyterian but probably a moderate Puritan or reforming Anglican.[25]

Nansemond's Puritan localism had collapsed by 1647. In 1645 Lower Norfolk vestrymen installed by Berkeley cited Harrison for "not administering the Sacrament of Baptism according to the Canons" and for ignoring the *Book of Common Prayer.* In 1647 the Assembly castigated the agitators as a "schismaticall party, of whose intentions our native country of England hath had and yet hath too sad experience" and relieved all Virginians from paying tithes to such schismatics. When William Durand "sett in the Desk or Reading Place . . . as alsoe the pulpitt" and "preached to the said people," replacing Harrison and presumably drawing on his notes of Davenport's sermons, Berkeley banished both Harrison and Durand. Harrison returned to England, where he supported Cromwell and the Commonwealth. Durand and other Nansemond settlers moved across the Chesapeake to pursue a reforming religious agenda, with equally frustrating results, in Maryland.[26]

Another model of vigorous localism emerged in Accomack County, where Thomas Teackle served as parish priest for more than forty years from 1655 until his death in 1696, a record tenure in seventeenth-century Virginia. None of Teackle's writings or the church's records survive, though the court records do contain one intriguing complaint, made in 1662 without further particulars, that Teackle preached false doctrine. What allows us a glimpse of his work—or at least of the materials with which he worked—is the inventory of Teackle's library, filed by his executors February 11, 1697, with the Accomack County Court. The library would have been important in any seventeenth-century British colony. Its 317 titles made it second in size to only the library of Cotton and Increase Mather. Most important, it offers an unequaled view of the printed materials attainable by a Virginia minister in pursuit of a vital spiritual life.[27]

Much of Teackle's library was thoroughly orthodox. Teackle owned works by standard seventeenth-century Anglican authors—Henry Hammond, John Jervell, John Richardson, Jeremy Taylor, James Usher—and classic works by the Church Fathers commonly possessed by both Anglicans and Puritans. But Teackle failed to include other Anglican favorites—Henry More, Matthew Poole, Symon Patrick, Edward Stillingfleet, Robert Sanderson, and John Tillotson. More interesting, Teackle owned an unusual range of Puritan books. He possessed major works by Puritan authors—William Ames, Jeremy Burroughs, Calvin, John Cotton, William Perkins, John Preston, and Richard Sibbes—and his list of minor Puritan authors was even more impressive: John Barlow, Joseph Caryl, William Fenner, William Greenhill, Henry Hammond, Robert Harris, Samuel Hieron, Arthur Jackson, Edward Leigh, Christopher Love, Thomas Manton, Mathew Meade, Samuel Newman, Elinathan Parr, Thomas Playfere, John Rainolds, Francis Roberts, Richard Ward, Thomas Wilson, and John Yates. And Teackle acquired more than mere snippets. For example, he owned three of John Cotton's major works—the *Brief Exposition of the Whole Book of Canticles, A Practical Commentary . . . upon the First Epistle Generall of John,* and *The Way of Life*—and eight of twelve volumes of Joseph Caryl's *Exposition with Practicall Observations upon the Book of Job,* the most extensive commentary on Job ever written.[28]

Teackle also evidenced enormous interest in books on personal piety. He owned the *Works* of the late Elizabethan Puritan Thomas Adams, whose titles included *Mystical Bedlam, Diseases of the Soul,* and *A Divine Herbal;* Thomas Brooks's *Apples of Gold* and *Pretious Remedies against Satan's Devices;* Anthony Burgess's *Spiritual Refineing;* Jeremy Burroughs's *Rare Jewell of Christian Contentment;* Ralph Robinson's *Christ the Perfect Pattern;* William Jackson's *Celestial Husbandry; or, The Tillage of the Soule;* Mathew Simmons's *The Yearnings of Christs Bowells towards his Languishing Friends;* George Swinnock's *The Christian Man's Calling, Door of Salvation,* and *The Fading of the Flesh;* Ralph Venning's *Mysteries and Revelations;* and Thomas Walkington's *Raboni, Mary Magdalene's Tears.* Teackle's interests also extended to occult and magical works, but those will be discussed in Chapter 3. Even the breadth of these holdings in Calvinist and Anglican works demonstrates that the range of spiritual possibilities in seventeenth-century Virginia extended far beyond the boundaries traditionally drawn by historians.[29]

The 1670s witnessed a significant reassertion of organized religious activity in Virginia, all the more important because of its origins. Evangelical Dissenters did not stimulate this renaissance, despite the importance historians frequently attach to their activity. Quakers claimed several meetings for worship from the mid-1650s on, but they remained isolated and small; Presbyterians did not form congregations in Virginia until the 1690s and then formed only two or three; and Baptists were not active in the colony until the 1720s. Nor did the Assembly display significant leadership, since between 1660 and 1680 it passed only occasional statutes to lay out new parishes, to suppress Quakers, and to proclaim fast days. Meanwhile London and Canterbury authorities continued their disinterest in the colony's spiritual condition. Instead, the first church renaissance in Stuart Virginia stemmed from the remarkable post-1660 economic and political maturation that Bernard Bailyn has described as the origin of the Virginia aristocracy. Vital, competing elites built fortunes and political power within their resident counties and fought for political leverage within the colony in the 1676 Bacon's Rebellion. They also replicated the parish life familiar to county elites at home—vestries, church buildings, church lands, and, of course, resident ministers. This achievement was aided, in turn, by a reasonably plentiful supply of clerics in England. A 1680 report, drawn up for unknown reasons, reveals the extent of this institutional expansion. Though no more than a dozen ministers could be found in the colony in the 1660s and four-fifths of its parishes were empty, in 1680 thirty-five Anglican ministers worked there and two-thirds of its parishes were occupied.[30]

Like the Yorkshire authorities in 1743, Virginia's newly arrived ministers knew that resident clergymen could not guarantee steady Christian adherence. Indeed, the colony's previous half century of erratic localism had already caused a major departure from one important form of Christianization in old England: infant baptism. The colony's earliest surviving records, from York County's Charles Parish, reveal that despite a lack of active Dissenters and the almost unique steady presence of Anglican ministers there, infant baptism remained the exception rather than the rule. Between 1649 and 1670, 111 of 130 Caucasian children (85.4 percent) born in Charles Parish were not baptized. The pattern continued even in the 1670s, when surrounding parishes began to sustain regular public Christian worship: 145 of 169 white children (85.8 percent) born there between 1671 and 1680 similarly failed to receive baptism.[31]

The 1670s expansion of parish activity and Anglican worship, though a hopeful sign for the church, did not seem to recover patterns of English Christianization lost in the previous half century, as the baptismal records demonstrate. But just as frequent baptism had not produced steady Christian adherence in Tudor-Stuart England, neither had its recession completely snuffed out Christian practice in seventeenth-century Virginia. Virginia's state church parishes, revived by secular maturation, recovered opportunities to promote Christianity under a new, more mature alliance of church and state. Virginians knew some of the dangers and illusions of that alliance. But they also knew that because other sources of Christian endeavor, especially English Dissenting Protestantism, were absent, the future of New World Christianity would be even more questionable without it.

The evolution—or devolution—of organized Christianity in Maryland demonstrated how relatively hopeful Virginia's circumstances were, even in its darkest period. In Lord Baltimore's Maryland the collusion of geography, shifting immigration and settlement patterns, and government inaction left most settlers without even the simplest rudiments of public Christian practice between 1630 and 1690. This situation produced a major crisis over the future of institutional Christianity in the colony and the preservation of Christian identity in the population.

Part of Maryland's problem derived from the paradoxical consequences of Baltimore's Catholicism. Catholicism never prospered in Maryland, because Baltimore could not provide enough Catholics to settle there. Catholicism survived among only an elite few in seventeenth-century England, and most of them were sufficiently well off to resist the lure of New World settlement. Instead, most of Maryland's early settlers were poor servants and unskilled laborers who, if not good Protestants and certainly not Puritans, had long since emptied themselves of Catholic sympathies.[32]

Despite its minority position, however, Catholicism offered the only public Christian practice widely available in Maryland before 1640. Maryland's first priests built at least four churches and chapels in the colony, two for English settlers at Baltimore Town and St. Mary's City, the seat of government until 1695, and several to serve the Indians they hoped to Christianize. The priests faced a dilemma, however. They believed Catholicism to be the only true religion, and they knew that Protestant services were seldom available in the colony. At the same time, they dared not proselytize among English settlers for fear of alienating Protestants at home and risking the Maryland charter. As a result, Baltimore enjoined Maryland Catholics to worship "as privately as may be" and "to be silent upon all occasions of discourse concerning matters of religion."[33]

The Catholic paralysis frequently left Maryland without public

Christian worship of any kind. The Baltimores never considered establishing the Church of England, and the Anglicans themselves paid little attention to Maryland before 1690. William Claiborne bought Anglican prayer books and Bibles for Kent Island settlers and paid ministers from Accomack County, Virginia, to make occasional visits in the 1630s, but the practice stopped in the next decade. No Presbyterian or Baptist congregation prospered in Maryland before 1690, and only six Anglican ministers are known to have lived or worked in Maryland before 1690. One returned to England in 1638, others stayed only a few years, and another, John Coode, proved so contentious—he led rebellions in Maryland on at least two occasions—that Protestantism and Christianity might have profited more from his absence.[34]

Anti-Catholicism prospered even if Protestantism did not, however. The Baltimores' Catholicism made Maryland authorities quick scapegoats for local discontent. Every one of Maryland's numerous political upheavals—the Ingle Rebellion of 1645, the "Puritan" revolt of 1654, the Charles County discontent in 1676–77, the Fendall and Coode uprising of 1681, and the Glorious Revolution of 1689—witnessed violent anti-Catholic episodes. Protesters claimed that Catholics conspired to deliver the colony to France or Spain. They arrested Catholic priests, plundered the Catholic chapels at St. Mary's City and Baltimore Town, and abridged Catholic religious and political liberties.[35]

Maryland's anti-Catholic vigilantism soon shaped Catholic practice. Priests proselytized unopposed among Maryland's aboriginal population. But increasingly they emphasized private, family-centered worship among English settlers. Itinerating priests could say Mass quickly and quietly in homes. Church doctrine and morality could be learned in homiletic books accessible to the minority whose literacy outstripped that of most Maryland settlers. But as Catholics kept their faith to themselves and married only fellow Catholics, the constraints that upheld the movement also narrowed it. Late seventeenth-century Maryland Catholicism became tribal, like Stuart Quakerism and New England Puritanism. As a result Maryland's Catholic minority declined even further.[36]

Only English Quakerism found Maryland's spiritual vacuum enticing and even, perhaps, nourishing. The Quaker method of proselytizing deftly avoided the problems that plagued other early

Chesapeake religious groups. Their traveling preachers, "Public Friends," brought quick results in the province. Elizabeth Harris's appearance there in 1655 won some initial converts, and George Fox's 1672 tour of the English colonies, including Maryland, created more. As early as 1658 the Maryland government fined thirty settlers for entertaining Quaker preachers and for adopting their views. By 1672, when Fox visited the colony, Quakers had established five or six worship meetings there, and these grew to at least fifteen meetings on Maryland's western shore and another six or seven on the eastern shore by 1680.[37]

In both Virginia and Maryland Quakerism prospered where reforming Anglicanism had earlier appeared—in Virginia's Nansemond and Lower Norfolk counties, then in Maryland's Anne Arundel County, where some of the Virginia dissidents settled after being exiled by Governor Berkeley. In Maryland, moreover, Quaker doctrines had the advantage of a unique realism. The Quaker rejection of the Anglican liturgy of baptism, marriage, communion, and burial appeared perfectly reasonable in a society where these rites were so frequently unavailable and unpracticed. Quakerism rationalized the Protestant liturgical wasteland that typified the colony between 1630 and 1680.[38]

Yet not even Quakerism overcame Maryland's lay religious indifference. Although Lord Baltimore assured the Privy Council in 1676 that three-fourths of his colonists were "Presbiterians, Independents, Anabaptists, and Quakers, [with] those of the Church of England as well as those of the Romish being the fewest," his estimates were as mistaken or as disingenuous as those Governor Berkeley had made for Virginia. Before 1690 it is doubtful that Catholicism and Quakerism could claim more than three thousand adherents, although the population reached twenty thousand by 1675. One of Maryland's earliest Anglican clerics, John Yeo, offered a more realistic assessment in 1675: "[N]oe care is taken or Provision made for the building up [of] Christians in the Protestant Religion by means whereof not only many Daily fall away either to Popery, Quakerism or Phanaticisme but alsoe the lords day is prophaned, Religion despised, and all notorious vices committed . . . it is become a Sodom of uncleanness and a Pest house of iniquity."[39]

Yeo exposed early Maryland's stunning secularity. The colony, sloughing off both Catholic and Protestant appearances simultaneously as it filled up with young indentured servants, experienced what even by traditional English standards was an astonishing desacralization. Settlers heard few sermons and participated in little liturgical exercise. They received no catechetical instruction. Secular officials performed marriages. Maryland's few children went unbaptized. Kent County records, for example, show only 5 baptisms among 115 white births between 1657 and 1670. Indeed, by 1674 English settlers had become so indifferent to baptism that a French Jesuit reported that they no longer even complained about its absence.[40]

Nor did the landscape compensate for the absent ministers and unsustained worship. The Catholic chapels constructed in St. Mary's City and Baltimore fell prey to vandalism during political turmoil in the 1650s and the 1680s. Quaker buildings sacralized the landscape for relatively few settlers, and in any case those that resembled the Kent County Quaker meetinghouse, built in 1698 and described as looking like a "tobacco house," hardly replicated traditional English sacred architecture. With no sustained Presbyterian or Baptist presence, only Anglicans remained as potential church builders, and they left the land as bereft of churches as of clerics. Although two Anglican buildings may have been constructed before 1670, their existence is as much a matter of conjecture as of fact.[41]

The failure to establish a traditional Christian presence in Maryland and the limited number of dissenting Quakers, Catholics, and Puritans confused Marylanders struggling toward a Christian practice. The 1649 "Act concerning Religion" was indeed the first toleration act passed in the English colonies. But it also constituted a plea for religion or, at least, for Christianity. By prohibiting Marylanders from hurling so many religious epithets at their neighbors—"heretic, Scismatic, Idolator, puritan, Independent, Presbiterian, popish priest, Jesuite, Jesuited papist, Lutheran, Calvinist, Anabaptist, Brownist, Antinomian, Barrowist, Roundhead, Separatist"—Maryland authorities signaled a welcome for almost any kind of Christian practice in the colony.[42]

Maryland's decaying Christian presence revealed itself with particular elegance at death. Maryland settlers shaped their land and society with as little Christian identification for the dead as they provided for the living. The absence of church buildings precluded traditional English common burial grounds, and the absence of ministers discouraged traditional church interments. In contrast to English tradition and even some Virginia practice, Maryland settlers buried the dead in family plots or singly in the woods. Funeral customs solidified this landscape secularization. In England, Anglican rites constrained secular funeral banquets and drinking. But such traditions withered in a colony where death came quickly to its young immigrants and where institutional Christianity was so weak. In Maryland banquets became the dominant public ceremony surrounding death. Meats, fowl, breads, cakes, candies, cider, and as many casks of brandy, rum, and beers as a legacy could purchase were spread among friends and acquaintances. The Charles County Court had to inquire in 1662 "wheather it bee Christian like at the time of a funerall for too or three neighbours to meet togeather and instead of showing a mornfulnes for the los of their frind and neighbour to turne of their bousing Cups to the quantitie of three barrells of beeare to the valew of nine hundered pounds of tob[acco]." In early Maryland life swallowed up death in drink rather than in churches and Christianity.[43]

Colonial New England could hardly have offered a greater contrast to the Chesapeake colony for transmitting English Christianity to the New World. New England's surface and inner textures exemplified a deep Christian religiosity centered on an aggressive, reforming Protestantism. Doubt existed only about Christianity's definition, not its importance. Protestant commitments shaped immigration, settlement patterns, popular and learned religion, government, and secular liberties that included voting and land holding.

New England Protestantism also contained anomalies and contradictions, inherent in its origins and complicated by New England's growth. Calvinist criticism of English society and religion did not produce a clear and uniform vision of society and religion in America. The religious choices available in the seventeenth century, though constrained by Calvinism, stimulated diversity and heresy as often as they generated homogeneity and orthodoxy. Moreover, New England changed between 1630 and 1690. It changed from within, as its own intellectual and social dynamics shifted, and it changed from without, as new immigrants brought new and old values to new and old settlements.

Some New Englanders handled the region's religious and social maturation by imagining a purer, more homogeneous moment earlier in its history from which society should not have departed. Others, less baffled, exercised new choices and created new foundations for a "new" New England. In many ways, they Europeanized New England. They shattered the older Puritan hegemony not through a new-found atheism but through their simple indifference to the Puritan churches that had been the principal means of expressing Christian adherence in this quite remarkable society. The contrast to the Chesapeake region is instructive. There, Christians wondered whether they could even match the level of Christianization then present in Europe. In New England, Puritans wondered whether they could retain what they had achieved in the 1640s and 1650s (or at least what they imagined they had achieved).[44]

As in Virginia, the religion of seventeenth-century New England was shaped by its settlers, and New England's were different from those in the Chesapeake Bay area. The latter were almost all young, single, male, seldom interrelated, and seldom connected to Puritan congregations in England. New England immigrants, from the so-called Great Migration of the 1630s through the 1650s, included the old as well as the very young, children as well as parents, masters as well as servants, and men and women committed to reforming congregations within the Church of England that were then under attack from Archbishop Laud.[45]

The belief of many New England immigrants in spiritual reform quickly expressed itself in the landscape. Massachusetts Bay leaders authorized construction of a church building in Boston shortly after their arrival there, much as Virginia leaders had done at Jamestown two decades earlier. Unlike the Virginians, however, the New Englanders continued the process in many other places and well beyond the 1630s. The residents of Dedham in Essex County, England, left behind a magnificent sixteenth-century stone building. Arriving in Massachusetts in 1637, they raised a wooden church in new Dedham a year later, though it was so small it could have fit inside the old Dedham church. New Haven's first church measured twenty-five by fifty feet and was constructed of wood. Sudbury's measured twenty by thirty feet and was also a wooden structure; a replacement built in 1653 was larger but still of framed wood construction. Indeed, all known

New England church buildings constructed before 1680 were small, built of wood, and different from the buildings even in small, out of the way, rural English parishes. Still, churches could be found in every New England town, something lacking farther south.[46]

New England's swiftly achieved landscape sacralization symbolized a lay adherence to Christianity that thoroughly outstripped old English patterns. From 1630 through the 1660s, church membership, attendance, and baptism reached rates rarely obtained at home. No town sustained an adult church membership ratio of 100 percent, not even in the heady days between 1630 and 1650. But town after town developed church adherence ratios that transcended Tudor-Stuart patterns. In new Dedham, 70 percent of the town's men belonged to the church in the 1650s, and 80 percent of its children received baptism before 1660. Boston achieved remarkably high church membership rates despite its larger, more heterogeneous population. Through 1635, well over half of the town's families were represented through the formal membership of either husband or wife in First Church, and between 1630 and 1640 the church had admitted some sixty young and single household servants, as well.[47]

New Englanders attended the churches they joined. Unlike Virginia authorities, those in Massachusetts Bay did not compel church attendance until 1635; the law did not need to demand what religious inclination and social background invited. The New England laity also worked at its worship. Sabbath services devalued collective chanting and processions and stressed the Scriptures and sermonizing. Ministers read long sermons lasting from forty-five minutes to two hours. For the intensely committed, sermons were only the beginning of their worship. The Boston merchants Robert Keayne and John Hull and the Springfield magistrate John Pynchon were three of the many who summarized sermons in notebooks for later use and tirelessly recounted spiritual struggles in carefully kept diaries.[48]

The religious creativity of the New England laity appeared most obviously in the confessions they made to gain church membership. This was true both in the 1630s, when ministers demanded only an accounting of their scriptural knowledge, and after 1645, when ministers demanded fuller statements of their spiritual struggles and experiences. The confessions reveal remarkable biblical knowledge and doctrinal awareness. George Selement suggests that between 1638 and 1645 the membership confession of the average parishioner in Thomas Shepard's Cambridge church contained twenty-five biblical references and fifteen allusions to Shepard's theology. Yet, as with Virginia's William Durand, the spiritual voices remained unique. The rambling, disjointed statement of a woman identified only as "Katherine, Mrs. Russell's Maid" reveals the laity's potential importance even in seeking religious knowledge. By her own account, Katherine "went on in ignorance and had no means [of] light" until she went "to an aunt who did," rather than to her minister. Gilbert Crackbone's wife interwove Christian concepts of supernatural imminence with a tragic narrative as rich in metaphor as the sermon of any New England clergyman:

> And so I came to New England. I forgot the Lord as the Israelites did and when I had a new house yet I thought I had no new heart. And means did not profit me, . . . And [then,] seeing [my] house burned down, I thought it was just and mercy to save [the] life of the child and that I saw not after again my children there. And as my spirit was fiery so to burn all I had, and then prayed Lord would send fire of word, baptize me with fire. And since [then] the Lord hath set my heart at liberty.[49]

The quest for individual piety also shaped New England society and politics. No single New England town was "typical," of course. But enough typicality emerges from recent town studies to suggest important persistent patterns of religious practice. John Winthrop enjoined challenging goals in his famous sermon aboard the *Arbella* in 1632: "Wee must be knitt together in this worke as one man, . . . wee must delight in each other, make others Conditions our owne, rejoice together, mourne together, labour, and suffer together, allwayes haveing before our eyes . . . our Community as members of the same body." Through "covenants" binding signers to God and to each other, New England towns attempted to suffuse legal corporations with spiritual obligations that might seal existing demographic, familial, and social ties. As they established towns "in the fear and reverence of our Almighty God," settlers variously promised to resolve disputes "according to that most perfect rule, the foundation whereof is everlasting love" (Dedham, 1637), to secure a minister "with whom we purpose to join in church covenant to walk in all the ways of Christ" (Springfield, 1636), to establish principles for land use and allocation (Dedham, Springfield, and most other covenanted communities), and to "receive only such unto us as may be probably of one heart with us" (Dedham again).[50]

Settlers of a different heart also came to New England, however. Some were there from the very beginning. Some came to New England later in the century, when economic attractions supplanted religious ones. Some were made different by their New England experiences. The result transformed New England after 1670. The region's early immigrants had stamped an indelible Christian identity on the institutions and culture of the developing region; whatever its changes and failings, New England would never become a Virginia, much less a Maryland. But New England's "second foundation" between 1650 and 1690 reshaped its lay religious patterns and challenged old ideals and old realities.

Doctrinal heterogeneity belied the New England myth of homogeneous Calvinist orthodoxy. English Calvinists fueled their demand for religious reform with incessant criticism of the Church of England and its archbishop of Canterbury, William Laud. But the freedom won in immigration to America also exposed discontinuities previously masked by the anti-Anglican, anti-Laudian campaigns. By 1650 Massachusetts authorities had grappled with three major religious disputes. Anne Hutchinson revealed dangerous perfectionist impulses lurking within Puritan theology and won a large and prominent lay following when she expounded her views. Roger Williams and Henry Dunster, Harvard's first president, demonstrated how quickly reforming Calvinists might become Baptists, as with Dunster, or pursue more idiosyncratic beliefs, as with Williams. Springfield magistrate, John Pynchon, and minister, Henry Moxon, Socinians who denied Christ's divinity, revealed the persistence of Puritan heterogeneity well past the 1650s and deep into the New England countryside.[51]

Somewhat strangely, especially given New England's long reputation as a theocracy, strong internal constraints limited the suppression of Calvinist dissent and the creation of a homogeneous orthodox theological environment in New England. Governments could and did expel the most vocal dissidents—Anne Hutchinson to Long Island, Roger Williams to Rhode Island, Samuel Gorton to England. But the treason and sedition charges on which they were expelled were difficult to employ against less vocal followers, and the clergy avoided direct confrontations on narrower theological issues or on the larger problem of heterodoxy within the society. Virtually all of Hutchinson's many followers, for example, remained unmolested, if not uncensured, in Boston.[52]

Clerical unity also proved elusive. Reforming Calvinist theory placed ecclesiastical sovereignty in individual congregations and denied it to any nonlocal institution, whether bishop, presbytery, or even ministerial meeting. The result was ironic: ecclesiastical torpidity at the apex of "Puritan" society. Ministers gathered in "consociations" from the 1630s on. But these consociations only advised; they could not dictate. Although a Massachusetts consociation implored Dunster to disavow Baptist principles or at least keep them quiet, it could not force him to do so. He merely resigned his Harvard presidency and moved to the Plymouth colony. The 1648 Cambridge Platform revealed the ministers' languor with special eloquence. Written to provide an order for the New England experiment, it bespoke theological and ecclesiastical heterodoxy among ministers and laity alike and vacillated on major issues such as church membership and sanctification.[53]

In fact, while ministers hedged and towns grew older, the early pattern of unusually high church adherence faded away. A shift from conversion narratives to demonstrations of personal sanctification — what Edmund Morgan calls "visible sainthood" — slowed membership applications from children in old families and discouraged applications in new families and among new settlers. After 1650 most New England congregations and ministers also refused to baptize children born to nonmembers (one parent had to be a church member), and the number and ratio of baptized children fell in a society where it had previously been high. The Half-Way Covenant of 1662 confirmed new, complex, and incomplete church membership patterns. Some residents were "full" church members who had "owned the covenant" by testifying to God's work in their lives; some were baptized adults who had not yet owned the covenant and therefore were "half-way" members; and some were unbaptized sons and daughters of the baptized "half-way" members.[54]

Other New Englanders stood outside the church order altogether. Some settlers moved beyond the effective reach of ministers, congregations, and buildings as they took up new land in far corners of large town grants. Sometimes towns themselves moved, as when in 1642 a majority of Newbury's often disputatious residents moved the town center three miles from its original site, a very long way in a rural society. In other towns, selectmen refused to build new meetinghouses for either separated or abandoned settlers. The effect was the same. New Englanders who could once scarcely escape Christianity's institutional presence now found themselves outside the sphere of collective Christian worship.[55]

After 1650 new immigrants joined churches far less frequently than did earlier settlers. That New England's post-1660 immigrants carried fewer links to Calvinist congregations in England is not surprising, since the English congregations were declining themselves. Although we know little about these immigrants, they appear to have been young, single indentured servants not unlike the settlers of the early Chesapeake. Frequently, they worked as seasonal laborers in the expanding New England countryside and in the older seaport towns of Boston, Salem, and Plymouth. Economic opportunity rather than religion — New England rather than New Zion — attracted them to America. They formed a new, increasingly secular population in an older, highly Calvinistic culture. Together with congregational tribalism and more individualistic settlement patterns, their arrival reshaped lay adherence patterns in late seventeenth-century New England communities.[56]

Boston prefigured the trend. Darrett Rutman reports that in 1645, 293 of Boston's 421 families (69.6 percent) claimed either a husband or wife linked to the town's church, high rates by traditional English standards yet still short of what John Winthrop wanted. But if servants were added to the figures, by 1649 more than 50 percent of Boston's men already stood outside the church. The implication was ominous. As early as 1650 the Boston church was a place for families, especially for those who had arrived first and set the tone of town worship. But servants and new families with weak or peripheral connections to English Puritanism viewed the churches from outside when they arrived and remained there after they settled.[57]

Boston proved to be very much a city upon a hill. Church membership rose in New England after 1660, but not at all in proportion to the region's population increase. Some New England towns equaled the Boston decline. Gerald Moran's study of seven early Connecticut towns reveals only two communities in which roughly half of the men were church members in 1675 or 1680—Middletown (54 percent) and Farmington (45 percent). Four towns—New Haven, New London, Stonington, and Woodbury—reported adult male membership rates of 15 percent. Richard Gildrie reports an equally desolate picture in Salem. Although only a fifth of Salem's men had signed the town's church covenant in 1637, Hugh Peter raised the membership to nearly two hundred men and women, perhaps three-fourths of the adult population, by 1643. But a significant decline set in during the next half century. By 1683, 83 percent of Salem's taxpayers failed to claim church membership even though the congregation began baptizing nonmembers' children in 1679. Even adding Quakers and Baptists, perhaps 10 percent of the town's adults, still leaves about 70 percent of Salem's taxpayers outside the town's Christian congregations in the 1680s.[58]

Salem's decline in church membership mirrored the social and religious interaction in Boston. In the 1640s new church members were members' spouses and children from families already associated with the church; nonmembers were generally newly immigrated families and single individuals. A strong association between landholding and church membership also emerged. Where twenty-five of the thirty men holding between a hundred and three hundred acres belonged to Salem's church through 1650, the same was true for only twenty-nine of the seventy-nine small landholders, who had a half acre to nine acres of land. By the 1680s even wealthy inhabitants were ignoring the church. Only half of Salem's well-to-do selectmen belonged to it in 1683, when the church claimed fewer than 15 percent of Salem's poor and middling sorts. New England's maturity was yielding a meager Christian harvest.[59]

The decline that Increase and Cotton Mather bemoaned after 1680 was real, not imaginary. This did not mean that the Mathers and their ministerial colleagues understood it properly or prescribed effective remedies. They exaggerated the unity of purpose, theology, and work in early New England. They attached too much importance to increasing Protestant pluralism as another sign of declension—first the coming of Baptists and Quakers, then the arrival of Anglicans. They seemed oblivious to New England's changing population patterns and, especially, to the effect of a new immigration. Still, they knew well that New England had changed and that by the standards of the 1640s and 1650s public Christian practice and adherence had fallen significantly.

As the seventeenth century drew to a close, the prospects for the Christian triumph envisioned in the first decades of English colonization remained problematic. Pennsylvania struck the most positive note, at least for those who believed Quakerism was a Christian religion. The colony was flooded with Quaker immigrants. The landscape received Quaker sacralization through the construction of innumerable meetinghouses, though we know little about their replication of regional meetinghouse architecture in England. German sectarians sacralized the earth in different ways when seekers like Johannes Kelpius turned caves along the Wissahickon Creek into holy places in which to await the millennium. Baptists erected church buildings at Pennepek, Welsh Tract, and across the Delaware River in East Jersey, where Quaker buildings also were going up.[60]

But disorder and, among Quakers, decline, followed early settlement in Pennsylvania as well. Quaker political troubles in 1688–89 were succeeded by the so-called Keithian schism of 1692, which pitted followers of a Scottish Friend, George Keith, against an elite of local Quaker ministers and merchants. English and German Baptists fell out over doctrines and rites, then found themselves caught in the backwash of the Keithian schism when Quaker dissenters left the movement to become Keithian Baptists. Newly arrived Anglicans claimed that Quaker authorities inhibited Anglican worship and church construction. Meanwhile the Quakers' emerging system of behavioral standards—including the famous Quaker dress—all too quickly belied lagging internal discipline, especially in moral standards and in marriage to non-Quakers. Nevertheless, Pennsylvania remained a model of religious vitality in comparison with other Restoration colonies.[61]

New York's late seventeenth-century religious life reflected problems of quality as well as quantity. Dutch religious commitments, never strong in America, revived somewhat as expressions of minority Dutch culture and sentiment after the English conquest. The arrival in the 1680s of Huguenot refugees from France and the increasing presence of Jews brought more religious minorities to the colony. By the late 1690s the Jews had built a small synagogue in the city, and the Huguenots had constructed churches in the city and New Rochelle and on Staten Island.[62]

Yet few English New Yorkers were served by Christian congregations. As late as 1695, two decades after full English control of the colony, not a single English church building had been erected outside Fort George, which guarded the entrance to New York City. As in early Maryland, minority sectarian sentiment seemed to anesthetize popular religious sensibilities. In 1687 the governor of New York, Thomas Dongan, himself a Catholic, allowed that although New York housed many religions, most colonists followed none: "Here bee not many of the Church of England; few Roman Catholicks; abundance of Quakers preachers men and Women especially; Singing Quakers, Ranting Quakers; Sabbatarians; Antisabbatarians; Some Anabaptists[;] some Independents; some Jews; in short[,] of all sorts of opinions there are some, and the most part [are] of none at all."[63]

The Carolinas outdid all the colonies in their institutional lethargy. In South Carolina, the only church buildings constructed before 1695 were for refugee Huguenots, whose French-language worship scarcely attracted English listeners. Although some historians have placed an Anglican church in Charleston as early as 1680, no documentary evidence substantiates its existence. Nor does any evidence exist to suggest the presence of an Anglican clergyman to serve it. It is more likely that Charleston's first Anglican church was constructed in 1698. It marked a dubious advantage for either Anglicanism or Christianity, however, since its minister, Atkin Williamson, was all too well known for baptizing bears when he was drunk.[64]

North Carolina rivaled South Carolina's churchless landscape. No Anglican, Presbyterian, or Baptist clergyman made more than occasional visits to the colony before 1700, and not a single Anglican, Presbyterian, or Baptist church building was constructed there before 1700. Not unexpectedly, perhaps, Quakerism found a niche there. George Fox and William Edmundson encountered almost naively curious listeners when they visited in 1672. Settlers had "little or no religion, for they came and sat down in the meeting smoking their pipes." Yet once established, Quakerism advanced no faster in North Carolina than in the Chesapeake Bay area. No regular Quaker meetings sprang up until 1680, and when a Quaker yearly meeting was formed in 1698 its meetings for worship still could claim no more than 5 percent of the colony's English adults as members.[65]

The cities of the late seventeenth century confirmed the crisis of Christian hegemony in England's North American colonies. Boston remained the architectural capital of British New World Christianity, although by the 1690s its church spires had assumed the Old World function of demanding Christian adherence from a lethargic population. The situation was even more grim in New York City and Charleston. By 1690 the New York skyline had scarcely changed from its appearance in Jaspers Danckaerts's sketch of 1679, which offered a highly secular and military interpretation of New York's early cityscape. The largest buildings were still the fort and trading centers erected by the New Netherlands government. The only separate religious structures in the city were the small wood Dutch Church, an even smaller French Protestant meetinghouse, and an Anglican chapel, wholly enveloped within Fort George. Charleston likewise lacked any ecclesiastical splendor. In 1698 its chief architectural characteristics were its walls, behind which residents could find two small wooden church buildings, Anglican and Huguenot, as squat and mean as the Carolina lowlands that surrounded them.[66]

These new patterns scarcely meant that common religious patterns had been forged across the English mainland colonies by 1690. Virginia Anglicans might wonder whether they could sustain the progress suddenly encountered in the 1680s; New York, Maryland, and the Carolinas failed to achieve the Christianization common to European society; New England Puritans and Pennsylvania Quakers wondered whether they were about to lose what they had achieved in the first years of settlement. These divergent crises stemmed from conjunctions of social and institutional causes. In America as in Europe, Christian practice and belief had to be learned. They were not inherent in colonists or implicit in the societies they brought from Europe or created in America, whether in the Chesapeake Bay area, New England, or the diverse new Restoration colonies.

The failure to transfer the English state church tradition left many immigrants to shift for themselves in religion — at least for Christian practice. In the late 1680s, the New World landscape often remained bereft of both traditional Christian practice and traditional Christian symbols. Wilderness often remained wilderness; at least it lacked a Christian signification meaningful to most English colonists. In many colonies settlers found only the most meager church order, and in some they found none. The churches themselves were frequently becoming tribal, first among New England Puritans, then among Maryland Catholics, finally among Pennsylvania Quakers.

The early American spiritual milieu also became more complex in ways only partially complementary to Christianity. Magic, divination, and occultism made the journey to America, and their fate revealed how colonization both retarded and reinforced religious expressions that church leaders found as troubling in the New World as they had in the Old.

MAGIC AND THE OCCULT

3

Historians traditionally describe colonial religion as the story of Old World Christianity in New World society. This usually means, "What happened to English Puritanism in America?" "Why did Dissenting churches prosper in the colonies when state-supported churches failed?" "How did American Calvinism shape nineteenth- and twentieth-century society?" It ought to prompt other questions as well, and questions about magic and occultism should be among them. However seemingly bizarre, the story of magic, astrology, and occultism in early America crosses the major themes in American religious history—the fate of Old World notions in New World societies, the diversity and range of religious belief and practice in Western culture, and the use of the law to support some religious practices and restrict others.

The strong presence of magic, astrology, and occult practice in early modern Europe should have dictated their appearance in America as soon as settlers arrived. Yet the nature of early American society placed major obstacles in the path. The colonizers' aims to plant Christianity in America militated against the rise of occult religious practices and the sociology of immigration further complicated magic's transit. Gentry and family immigration to New England and the youth of the lower-class immigrants to the Chesapeake Bay area both retarded occult practice, the former because their leaders frequently opposed it, the latter because they were too young to have learned it before they left their native land.

The land too militated against the occult. The English countryside abounded with places associated with wonderful and terrifying things, sunk into the memories of those who lived there. Seventeenth-century America necessarily lacked such places, at least for European immigrants, because they were creations of the mind rather than of nature itself. Yet it did not long lack for wondrous events. As intimate, face-to-face settlements emerged, as the social and religious spectrum of settlements widened, and as increasingly complex religious configurations took shape, magic and occultism also emerged in England's North American colonies and became part of the American experience.

Determining how and when colonists turned to occult practice in America is as difficult as it is for England. Such activity was illegal in most colonies and was usually kept from full public view. Its noninstitutional character produced few written records except those its practitioners preferred to avoid: court prosecutions for its practice. Even in the early seventeenth century, however, the record is more full than we might imagine.

Occultism's first notice in the colonies, not surprisingly, involved witchcraft, its most notorious form. It also occurred in Virginia rather than Massachusetts, again demonstrating that colony's broad resonance with important themes in American religious history. Furthermore, its appearance demonstrated not only how community tensions and social interrelationships fed occult practice, fear, and accusation in America as in England but also how magistrates might tolerate beliefs and rituals that were illegal.

In September 1626 the Virginia General Court took depositions regarding alleged acts of magic committed by Goodwife Wright of Kickotan. The depositions were notable for their description of Wright's training in magical folklore in England. According to her Virginia neighbors, Wright first learned magic from her master's wife while working as a household servant in Hull. The training was episodic, not systematic. For example, when someone suspected of being a witch visited the house while Wright was churning butter, her master's wife showed Wright how to deal with the situation. The woman "clapt the Chirne staff to the bottom of the Chirne and clapt her handes across uppon the top of it[,] by which means the witch was not able to stire owt of the place where she was for the space of six howers." Later, when the master's wife fell ill and believed a witch's curse to be responsible for her ailment, she taught Wright how to turn the curse back on its author: "At the coming of a woman, which was suspected, to take a horshwe [horseshoe] and slinge it into the oven and when it was red hott, To slinge it into her dames urine, and so long as the horshwe was hott, the witch was sick at the harte, And when the Irone was colde she was well againe."[1]

In Virginia, where death stalked the inhabitants, Wright soon intrigued, then frightened, neighbors with her foreknowledge. Using insights she "had in her forehead," Wright told Rebecca Gray that she would "burye her Husbande," Mr. Fellgate that he would bury his wife, Thomas Harris that "he should burie his first wiefe" (although the woman was only then "bethrothed unto him"), and a woman with a mean husband that she should "be content for thow shalte shortlie burie him" (according to her accusers, most of these deaths "came to pass").[2]

Wright also wrought harm or "maleficium" by manipulating natural and supernatural fears among neighbors as wise men and wise women traditionally did in England. She brought sickness to a mother and newborn infant after the mother had used Wright's left-handedness (an ominous sign) as an excuse to reject Wright's services as a midwife. Wright prevented a hunter from killing game that was "very faire to shoote at." She threatened to make a recalcitrant servant girl "daunce starke naked." She killed chickens when a neighbor refused to sell them. She cursed Robert Threasher when he asked her to take two hens to Elizabeth Arundle and told him that "Arundle would be dead before the henns were sent over."[3]

Wright knew the cost of her occult reputation. When Alice Bayly asked Wright "whether her husbande should bury her, or she burie him," Wright refused to answer: "I can tell you if I would, but I am exclaimde against for such thinges and Ile tell no more." If the refusal did not save Wright's reputation, it revealed her caution on at least some occasions in occult matters. Oddly, she found similar reticence in Virginia's General Court. Her neighbors' evidence to the contrary, the justices refused to prosecute her for occult and magical practice, probably because she agreed to desist and because nobody linked her directly to witchcraft.[4]

Similar patterns occurred in New England. Elizabeth Goodman of New Haven killed chickens a neighbor refused to sell. Elizabeth Garlick of East Hampton saw death in the face of a neighbor's child. The disputatious John Godfrey spoke all too suspiciously about "the power of witches" as he moved from town to town in Massachusetts and Connecticut. Salem's infamous witch episode of 1692 took root in three decades of disputing over ministers, churches, taxes, and roads that made a mockery of John Winthrop's sermon aboard the *Arbella* and uprooted almost any notion of community, secular or religious.[5]

As in Virginia, New England's witch episodes spoke to issues of desire and power. John Demos's massive study of the early New England witch trials that preceded that Salem affair reveals how commonly accusers blamed witches for using occult manipulation to turn them away from Puritan and English values. He writes that in 1671 Elizabeth Knapp "was alternately tortured and plied with offers of 'money, silkes, and fine cloaths, ease from labor'; in 1692 Ann Foster of Andover confessed to being won over by a general promise of 'prosperity'; and in the same year Andrew Carrier accepted the lure of 'a house and land in Andover.'" Carol Karlsen argues that accusations frequently targeted women who had achieved considerable economic power in a male-dominated society and who, therefore, threatened male authority. A remarkable number of New England's accused witches had amassed property, usually through their husbands' deaths. Worse, they seemed disinclined to remarry, as their peers expected them to do. Their frequent knowledge of medical as well as magical skills only furthered public suspicion. To possess both economic and supernatural power proved very dangerous indeed, and far more dangerous to the possessor than to the possessed.[6]

Protestant theologians considered witchcraft dangerous because it crossed over into boundaries of supernatural manipulation. Puritans believed deeply in God's capacity and desire to intervene in human affairs. Their "worlds of wonder," as David Hall so aptly calls them, extended from colonization to floods, earthquakes, bizarre heavenly sounds, visions, apparitions, and remarkable medical events. The Puritans' "errand into the wilderness" was one such wonder. So too the Boston girl whose "brains stuck out" after an accident yet who "lived to be the Mother of two Children . . . [and] was not by this Wound made defective in her

Memory or Understanding." As Perry Miller describes, God accomplished wonders through "natural instruments, by arranging the causes or influencing the agents, rather than by forcible interposition and direct compulsion." Although these special providences were "not contrary to Nature," the Puritan John Preston wrote, Nature was "turned off its course."[7]

But Puritan theologians and ministers, if not all the laity, did not believe in miracles, that is, in supernatural intervention that changed nature's course by means contrary to nature, and they distinguished them sharply from acceptable wonders. Puritan theologians followed orthodox Reformation doctrine, which held that miracles had ceased with the death of the apostles. Catholic "miracles," in their view, were either fraudulent or diabolical, because they could occur only through evil compacts with the Devil. Puritans often used the term "diabolical miracle" to describe such events. The events themselves betrayed their origins: their very unnatural character proved that they were the Devil's doing, even when no covenant with the Devil could be located or when the accused refused to confess.[8]

This distinction between wonders and miracles underwrote Puritan thinking. Increase Mather's four-hundred-page *Essay for the Recording of Illustrious Providences* (Boston, 1684) described many of the amazing, peculiar, and wonderful things that had occurred in New England since the 1630s. But New England's "wonders" and "illustrious providences" were not miracles. Indeed, Mather used the word "miracle" only three times: once in a book title, once when reminding readers that the Devil was incapable of a "true Miracle," and once when ridiculing Valentine Greatrakes, an Irish healer, as a "miracle Monger or Mirabilarian stroaker."[9]

Salem's 1692 witch trials and the more than two hundred witch episodes that preceded them reveal the extent of occult practice in seventeenth-century New England. The early modern judicial process wove a web of circumstantial evidence around the accused that demonstrates the many ways contemporaries believed they could invoke supernatural power through nonscriptural means. Chadwick Hansen's study of the 1692 Salem trials, *Witchcraft at Salem,* uncovered reference to varied magical practices among the accused. Dorcas Hoar was known as a fortune-teller in the 1680s; her description, given at her 1692 trial, of a manual on chiromancy suggests that she both owned and used it. Goody Bishop possessed rag dolls stuck with pins and could not satisfactorily explain why she kept them. A black or Indian slave named Candy produced rags, grass, and cheese that she used as mediums through which she attempted to harm others. And several witnesses reported that Wilmot "Mammy" Red cursed a woman to prevent her from urinating.[10]

Earlier New England trials produced similar descriptions. As with those offered in Salem, their significance lay in their specificity. In 1655 John Brown of East Haven claimed that he could "raise the Devil," much as the legendary John Dee conjured angels, and he drew horoscopes and invoked jargon ("lords of the second, third, tenth, and twelve houses") that neighbors recognized as astrological. Katherine Harrison, a woman of considerable wealth, admitted that she told fortunes and claimed to have learned it by reading "Mr. Lilly's book," probably Lilly's *Christian Astrology* (London, 1647). Other accused witches had reputations as wise men or wise women; their crafts made them immediate suspects when unexplainable or disastrous events occurred.[11]

Cotton Mather documented popular magical practice in his "Discourse on Witchcraft," published in his *Memorable Providences, Relating to Witchcrafts and Possessions* of 1689. He ruefully acknowledged the commonality of occult practice in New England, including the use of charms, enchantments, and most dangerous of all, witchcraft. Mather also borrowed subtly from the vocabulary of magic to describe Christian defenses against their temptations and effects: "There are three admirable *Amulets* that I can heartily recommend unto you all: *A Fervent Prayer* . . . *A Lively Faith* . . . [and] *A Holy Life*":

> Use these things as the Shields of the Lord . . . Suppose now that any *Witches* may let fly their Curses at you, you are now, like a *Bird* on the *Wing,* in such Heavenward Motions that they cannot hit you. Now the *Devils* and their Creatures cannot say of you, as the *Demon* said of the Christian Woman whom, at a *Stage-play* he took *Possession* of, and being asked, gave this reason of his taking her, *I found her on my own ground.*[12]

The Mathers' collective concerns about non-Christian occultism in New England never abated. Increase Mather's 1684 *Essay for the Recording of Illustrious Providences* described the use of occult remedies to cure disease a decade before the Salem trials. A Boston man displayed an amulet against a toothache "wherein were drawn several confused Characters, and these words written, *In Nomine Patris Filii, & Spiritus Sancti, Preserve thy Servant, such an one.*" Another Bostonian created "a Cure for the Ague," which he "left with another in this Town, as a rare secret." He used five Greek letters and the word "Kalendant," all of which were "to be written successively on pieces of Bread" that were then to be eaten. "In five dayes (if he did believe) he should not fail of cure." In Mather's view, these practices were designed to call forth miracles, not merely wonders, and were dangerous however innocently or desperately men and women sought them out. The danger, he felt, lay in the origins of the effects. Those who recovered from illnesses through occult means could not say, "The Lord was my Healer"; they had to say, rather, "The Devil was my Healer." "Certainly it were better for a Man to remain sick all his dayes, yea (as Chrysostom speaks) he had better die than go to the Devil for Health."[13]

The Salem trials failed to change Cotton Mather's mind on the dangers of occult practice. In *The Angel of Bethesda,* a medical work written about 1720 but never published, he claimed that New Englanders continued to embrace occult techniques and healers despite incessant ministerial criticism of such practices. He knew that colonists consulted occult practitioners because they wanted "some Ease of their Distempers." Mather believed that their action was doubly perverse. Colonists knew well that occult remedies had "no Natural Efficacy for the Cure of Diseases" and that they worked through blasphemous attempts to manipulate supernatural power. The search for health turned New Englanders from a pursuit of wonders to an invocation of miracles and, hence, to the Devil and diabolism.[14]

Magical practice persisted in Virginia as well, beyond the intriguing case of Goodwife Wright of 1624. The evidence is not nearly so rich as that of New England, in part because of the colony's many lost literary and legal records. Still, Darrett Rutman describes the range of Virginia magical practice between 1640 and 1700:

> In sound mind and with clear conscience a Virginian could . . . hold that only the horseshoe over his door protected his sick wife from the evil intentions of a neighbor woman who perforce passed under it on her way to saying black prayers at his wife's bedside (1671), could attribute to a witch the death of his pigs

and withering of his cotton (1698), and, in court, faced with suits for slander, could insist that "to his thoughts, apprehension or best knowledge" two witches "had rid him along the Seaside and home to his own house" (again 1698).[15]

Magic also surfaced in Pennsylvania, where its appearance among Quakers reflected the legacy of a once powerful but now fading religious heterogeneity. Chester County's Quaker meeting and court records reveal particularly widespread occult practices in this farming area just west and south of Philadelphia. In 1695 the county's Quaker leaders demanded that two members of Concord Monthly Meeting, Phillip Roman, Jr., and his brother, Robert, stop using astrology, geomancy, and chiromancy "in resolving questions Concerning Loss and gain with other vain Questions." After some discussion, Phillip agreed. He proudly told the monthly meeting that "he had denied Severall that came to him to be resolved of their questions already." But Robert refused. Although he agreed to abandon some occult crafts, he insisted on practicing others, especially if "it was to do some great good." In response, Quaker leaders disowned him and circulated an epistle to Pennsylvania and New Jersey Quaker meetings denouncing him and other Quakers "who, professing the art of astrology, have undertaken thereby to give answers and astrological judgments concerning persons and things."[16]

The same Quaker leaders then invoked government coercion against Robert Roman's astrological activity. In the process they demonstrated that their rejection of the state church tradition did not preclude governmental action to suppress magic. Quakers who sat as Chester County magistrates indicted Roman "for practicing geomancy" and "divineing by a stick." Another charge verged on witchcraft: that he had used occult means to take "the wife of Henry Hastings away from her husband and children." To support their accusations they named three books found among Roman's possessions: "Hidon's Temple of Wisdom which teaches geomancy, and Scots Discovery of witchcraft, and Cornelias Agrippas Teaching negromancy [*sic*]." Not all these books could have actually supported charges of occult practice. Reginald Scot's *Discoverie of Witchcraft* (London, 1584) denounced witchcraft trials. However, John Heydon's *Theomagia; or, The Temple of Wisdom* (London, 1644) and *The Fourth Book of Occult Magic* (London, 1655), long mistakenly attributed to Cornelius Agrippa, a

Renaissance defender of some occult practices, were standard texts in occult crafts. The magistrates' verdict was scarcely surprising: a fine of five pounds and an order that Roman "never practise the arts but . . . behave himselfe well for the future."[17]

Two additional Chester County court cases offer further evidence of magic practice in the area. In September 1696 the magistrates tried James Woodward for stealing a thimble and bottle of rum from James Swaford. Swaford testified in court that Woodward denied the theft but that the missing goods could be found by consulting an occult practitioner. Swaford alleged that Woodward had told him "he would goe to a wise man a boute them, and After some time his son Richard came to me and would have me to meet him Att a wise man's house and there I should hear of my goods." After giving the proposition some thought—obviously Swaford did not consider the strategy outrageous on its face—Swaford rejected it. "I answered I would not goe."[18]

Who was Swaford's "wise man"? It might have been Robert Roman, the former Quaker. But it also might have been Richard Crosbye, another Chester County resident who claimed occult powers. In 1698 the Chester County magistrates cited Crosbye for contempt after he ridiculed one magistrate's niece as a "whore" and jeered the entire bench as "knaves" and "rogues." During his contempt hearing Crosbye further insulted the magistrates by contrasting their collective ignorance with his own occult wisdom. According to the court clerk, Crosbye claimed that "he and his son knew more of the mathematical arts than any of us all, pretending he could tell fortunes, and who had stole goods and describe where they were." Like Roman, Crosbye was fined and warned against further occult activity; over the next decade he appeared frequently on disorderly conduct charges but never again in connection with the occult.[19]

More learned occultism appeared among scientifically inclined Puritans, who investigated the natural world and alchemy simultaneously. Several were well known in English alchemical circles. Robert Childe and George Stirk both practiced alchemy while in America in the 1630s and 1640s and continued to do so after they returned to England during the Civil War. John Winthrop, Jr., eldest son of the famous Bay Colony governor, brought an enormous alchemical library to America. And Americans not only read alchemy but contributed to its literature as well. Anonymous alchemical works were published in England in the 1670s, under the pseudonym Eirenaeus Philaletha, by a writer who acknowledged his American residence. John Winthrop, Jr., was their most likely author, though the attribution is not a settled matter. Whoever their author was, the works were not only widely circulated in England but were gathered together and published in a Latin edition in Turin in 1695.[20]

At the end of the century Charles Morton, a Harvard tutor, demonstrated that occult views still existed among New England intellectuals. Morton's *Compendium Physicae,* used to tutor Harvard undergraduates in the natural sciences, approvingly cited learned astrology for use in medicine. He wrote, for example, "Complexions are Cheifly handled in Medicine with their proper signs and Inclinations to deseases." Yet he rejected crude, unlearned, popular occultism. He chided astrologers and their defenders, including John Gadbury, Thomas Gataker, and Sir Christopher Heydon, Charles I's unlucky astrologer. Like Thomas Brattle and Increase Mather, Morton also rejected unlearned theories about the "evil eye," which described how witches could cure their victims if the Devil allowed them to do it. "By [their] touch, the venomous and malignant particles, that were rejected from the eye do, this means, return to the body whence they came, and so leave the afflicted persons whole and pure." In Morton's view such notions not only dispensed with God but were based on suspect theories of magical or sympathetic healing.[21]

Occult sympathies among intellectuals in Pennsylvania came from non-English European immigrants who began to arrive in the colonies in the 1680s. Johannes Kelpius's religious community on Wissahickon Creek, formed in 1694, took Christianity as its spiritual focus. But Kelpius's Hermetic interests, links to the secret Rosicrucian movement, acceptance of astrology, and willingness to cast horoscopes for inquiring visitors separated his venture from other Christian groups in the Delaware Valley. His letters to correspondents as far away as Rhode Island and Virginia reflect an occult Christian network that spanned considerable distances. Kelpius's followers subsequently pursued quite different paths. Several became Quakers in Germantown; Daniel Falckner became a well-known Lutheran clergyman in the Delaware Valley; and others later joined the large German communitarian settlement at Ephrata, which was established in the 1740s near what is now the town of Lancaster. Kelpius himself was used as a model in Charles Brockden Brown's *Wieland* (1798), discussed in Chapter 8 (see also Figure 14 there).[22]

Virginia's learned occult milieu was reflected in the books owned by the colony's emerging aristocratic elite. Like the Reverend Thomas Teackle's 1697 estate inventory described in Chapter 2, these lists do not tell us how or why colonists acquired their books, whether occult manuals or Bibles, or what they did with them. But the lists do tell us what Virginians bought and kept. Moreover, they reveal that occult books figured in their libraries with some frequency. Books by astrologer-physicians such as Nicholas Culpeper and William Salmon led Virginia's list of occult favorites, and other books appeared as well. Mathew Hubbard, who died in 1667, owned Joseph Moxon's *A Tutor to Astronomy* (London, 1659), which instructed readers in astrology. A Middlesex County Anglican, Ralph Wormeley, owned two books that attacked occultism—John Webster's *The Displaying of Supposed Witchcraft* (London, 1677) and John Gaule's *The Mag-Astro-Mancer; or, The Magicall-Astrological-Diviner Posed, and Puzzled* (London, 1652)—and several others that defended and advanced occult practices—John Baptiste Porta's *Natural Magick* (London, 1658); the collected works of the German alchemist, Johann Glauber; three works by the Stuart astrologer and vegetarian, Thomas Tryon, including Tryon's *Pythagoras His Mystic Philosophy Revived* (London, 1691); and Richard Mathew's *The Unlearned Alchymist His Antidote* (London, 1692), which described alchemical medical treatments. Richard Lee, who died in 1715, owned Albertus Magnus's alchemical works, Vincent Wing's *Urania Practica* (London, 1649), an astrological and astronomical work, and a Latin edition of Wolfgang Hildebrand's *Magia Naturalis* (Darmstadt, 1611). Edmund Berkeley, a member of the Virginia Council who died in 1718, owned Richard Saunders's *Physiognomy and Chiromancy* (London, 1653), which instructed readers in predicting the future by analyzing facial features (physiognomy) and by reading hands (chiromancy).[23]

The Reverend Thomas Teackle possessed an amazing collection of occult books that rivaled his Puritan works. The range of his library is revealed in the way he followed suggestions made in a book he owned, Samuel Boulton's *Medicina Magica Tamen Physica: Magical, but Natural Physick* (London, 1665). Boulton synthesized

Hermeticism, Paracelsian medicine, and Christianity to bring supernatural and revelatory processes to bear in healing the sick. He suggested that his readers acquire three additional volumes for reference: Oswald Croll's two-volume synopsis of Paracelsian medicine, *Bazilica Chymica* (London, 1670); a frequently reprinted sixteenth-century Italian collection of occult remedies by Levinus Lemnius, *De Miraculus Occultis Naturae* (London, 1559); and Porta's *Natural Magick*. Teackle owned at least the works by Croll and Lemnius and may have owned Porta's, since the 1697 inventory listed "Magica Nature, etc., an old Book with a parchment cover, the Title page torn out," which could have been either the Latin edition of Porta's book or Hildebrand's *Magia Naturalis*.[24]

Like the books of his Virginia counterpart, Ralph Wormeley, some of Teackle's books ridiculed occultism in both religion and medicine. This was true especially of some of his medical books, particularly those by Walter Bruel, Walter Charleton, Robert Sprackling, William Harvey, Daniel Sennert, and Thomas Willis. But more of Teackle's books advocated a Christian-Hermetic-occult healing therapy. These ranged from small, minor works such as Anthony Askham, *A Little Herbal* (London, 1550), to major, lengthy medical tomes by Johannes Beverovicus, Joseph Du Chesne, Johann Baptista van Helmont, Thomas Brugis, Marchamont Nedham, William Simpson, and Johan Schroder. These books did not merely dabble in occult, Hermetic medicine but offered major explanations of its theory and working. William Salmon's *Synopsis Medicinae* (London, 1671) explained astral signs and described innumerable astrologically based medical cures. Salmon's voluminous *Medicina Practica* (London, 1692), which Teackle purchased only three or four years before his death, contained scores of astrologically based recipes, a synopsis of the philosophy of Hermes Trismegistus, and four hundred pages of medieval and early modern European alchemical writings. Marin Cureau de la Chambre's *The Art How to Know Men,* translated by John Davies (London, 1675), gave precise directions for analyzing human passions through astrology, chiromancy, and metoposcopy (forehead reading) and, in its frontispiece, instructed interested readers in the arrangement of a consulting chamber (see Figure 2).

But it was Teackle's collection of Rosicrucian books that demonstrates how closely a Virginian could follow the most obscure of Europe's occult-Christian movements. Rosicrucians believed that

2. *Frontispiece to Marin Cureau de la Chambre,* The Art How to Know Men *(1675).*

Hermetic texts, alchemy, and Christian scripture could be synthesized to unlock Christian secrets and mysterious natural processes, and its followers included major European intellectuals and powerful political figures. The number of Rosicrucian tracts Teackle owned suggests far more than an accidental or peripheral interest. These included Thomas Vaughan's *Magia Adamica; or, The Antiquitie of Magic and the Descent Thereof from Adam Downwards . . .* (London, 1650); John Heydon's *The Rosi Crucian Infallible Axiomata; or, General Rules to Know All Things Past, Present, and to Come* (London, 1660); and Johann Reuchlin's *De Arte Cabalistica* (Haguenau, France, 1517), which was the leading Renaissance exploration of Jewish mystical writings of the Cabala, central to Rosicrucian doctrine. Teackle also owned *Magnes Sirede Arte Magnetica* (Rome, 1641) by Athanasius Kircher, a well-known alchemist, Hermeticist, publisher of Egyptian hieroglyphic texts, and Rosicrucian, and Guilielmus Gratarolus's collection of alchemical writings, *Varae Alchemiae Artisque Metallicae, Citra Aenigmata* (Basel, 1561), another Hermetic-alchemical text, which Teackle's estate inventory well described as "an old book."[25]

Almanacs played a central role in popularizing occult religious concepts in the colonies, much as they had done in England. American historians have often observed that almanacs were the most popular books published in the colonies and outsold the Bible. The significance of this popularity, usually mentioned only as an anecdote, becomes clearer in the context of the broad religious choices available to American colonists. Colonial almanacs closely followed their English counterparts. They provided the astronomical information necessary for astrological calculations in a twelve-month calendar called the "ephemerides," and they also included the "anatomy," the crude male figure encircled by the twelve zodiac signs that were thought to control various portions of the body (see Figure 3). Using the almanac, even semiliterate colonists could plant, bleed, marry, or breed on correct days and, by following its guide to the stars, predict the future.[26]

Colonists demanded that almanacs contain occult material and almanac makers feared to exclude it. Printers sometimes complained bitterly. In his 1728 almanac, Dedham's Nathaniel Ames reprinted a poem that protested the demand for the anatomy from a 1633 English almanac and added his complaint that even his most ignorant readers insisted the anatomy be included. Still,

1 7 2 9.

The Anatomy of Man's Body, and what part thereof is Represented by the 12 Signs of the Zodiack.

The Head & Face

Neck & Throat

Breast, and Stomach

Bowels, and Belly

Secrets

Knees

ARIES

TAVRVS

CANCER

VIRGO

SCORP

CAPRI

GEMINI

LEO

LIBRA

SAGI

AQVA:

PISCES

Arms & Shoulders

Heart & Back

Reins and Loins

Thighs

Legs

The Feet.

The Blackmoor may as eas'ly change his Skin,
As Men forsake the ways they'r brought up in;
Therefore I've set the Old Anatomy,
Hoping to please my Country men thereby,
But where's the Man that's born & lives among,
——— ——— ——— Can please a Fickle throng?

The Vulgar Notes of this Year, 1 7 2 9.

Golden Number	1	Epact	11
Cycle of the Sun	2	Dominical Letter	C.

☞ *Note*, The Planet ♀ *Venus* is Occidental or Evening Star to the Third day of *June*, and from thence Oriental or Morning Star to the Years End.

3. The anatomy from Nathaniel Ames's Almanac *of 1729.*

Ames knew the realities of his market. In his 1728 almanac he also used a poem from Samuel Clough's *New York Almanac* of 1703, which summarized the situation all too well:

> The Anatomy must still be in,
> Else the Almanack's not worth a pin,
> For Country-Men regard the Sign,
> As though 'Twere Oracle Divine.[27]

Almanac makers complained that readers demanded too much in the way of predictions of the future. Pennsylvania's Daniel Leeds complained in 1697 that he dared "not assign and limit" the effects of lunar and solar eclipses "to any particular place" because readers were "too much led astray in these latter Ages by many of their Teachers" and also misused the information. A year later, nevertheless, he defended the argument that lunar and solar eclipses affected world politics. In 1743 a bitter Jacob Taylor described in disgust how families rejected Bibles and prayer in favor of occult recipes to solve personal crises: "Billy and Dicky, Peggy and Molly must see the Man on the Moon, and where the little child cries the great one runs for the Almanack, to bless the House with Peace." To John Jerman, another Pennsylvania almanac maker, the almanac was merely the prisoner of its consumers:

> I During Life a Servant am, and I
> Just one poor Year shall live that I must die;
> Am sold for five pence, and obliged to go.
> A Slave, compelled to serve I know not who.[28]

Protests or no, some almanac makers were obviously adepts, well familiar with the major literature of magic and occultism. Before 1710 Pennsylvania's Jacob Taylor quoted Hermes Trismegistus and Cornelius Agrippa in his almanacs. He even found a quotation from Sir Francis Bacon — "though Fortune be blind yet she is not invisible" — to support the belief that the movement of the heavens predicted human affairs and natural events. At the same time Taylor attacked necromancy, exorcism, and sorcery as beneath the dignity of true occult arts.[29]

Daniel Leeds was even more enthusiastic. His use of astrology in his 1687 almanac and his publication of works by the German mystic Jacob Boehme and the English mystic George Wither resulted in his expulsion from the Quaker movement in 1688. In the next decades Leeds actively supported astrological and occult endeavors in his almanacs. He complained about Christianity's absurd heresies and defended what he felt were true religious principles against corrupt sects and denominations. He equated astrology with theology, quoted Hermes Trismegistus, summarized seventeenth-century astrological predictions of William Lilly and John Partridge, trumpeted Hermetic and Paracelsian medicine, quoted the Book of Psalms to prove that the "first Cause" used stars as "second causes of Effects upon Mankind" much as angels were used as agents, and told readers to gather herbs only "when the Planets that governed them are dignified and friendly aspected."[30]

By traditional accounts, magic and occultism died out in the eighteenth century: the rise of Enlightenment philosophy, skepticism, and experimental science, the spread of evangelical Christianity, the continuing opposition from English Protestant denominations, the rise in literacy associated with Christian catechizing, and the cultural, economic, and political maturation of the colonies simply destroyed the occult practice and belief of the previous century in both Europe and America. Yet significant evidence suggests that the folklorization of magic occurred as much in America as in England. As in England, colonial magic and occultism did not so much disappear everywhere as they disappeared among certain social classes and became confined to poorer, more marginal segments of early American society.

The fate of witchcraft beliefs and witchcraft trials demonstrates how folklorization occurred in America. Although the Salem episode of 1691–92 witnessed the last known witchcraft execution in the British colonies, the end of legal activity against witches did not occur for another two decades. In 1705 two Virginia juries examined Grace Sherwood for witches' marks and reported that her body was "not like them nor noe other woman that they knew of, haveing two things like titts on her private parts." When the court subjected her to the infamous dunking test, she swam ("Contrary to Custom" as the court record put it), and the magistrates therefore bound her over for trial on witchcraft charges. Her fate, however, remains unknown because the remaining court records have been lost.[31]

In 1706 the chief justice of South Carolina, Nicholas Trott, demanded that the Charleston grand jury prosecute witches. Salem's ten-year-old blot aside, Trott refuted two Elizabethan critics, John Webster and Reginald Scot, who criticized justices for prosecuting only deluded old women. "Some Persons that are no great Friends to Religion, have made it their Business to decry all Stories of *Apparitions* and of *witches*." But as Moses, Luke, and the Church Fathers knew, witches existed and should be punished. In Trott's view, Scot and Webster based their objections on mistranslations of biblical texts (Trott was the author of a Hebrew lexicon), and he quoted both the *Discourse of the Damned Art of Witchcraft* (Cambridge, 1608), a work by the early Puritan theologian William Perkins, and Increase Mather's *Cases of Conscience* (Boston, 1693), a book published to defend the Salem trials, to complete his arguments.[32]

Trott's enthusiasm produced meager results, however. In 1707 the Charleston grand jury considered witchcraft charges against one unknown local resident but returned the indictment "Ignoramus." The rebuff alarmed Francis Le Jau, then serving as the Church of England minister at St. James Goose Creek Parish and one of Trott's acquaintances, who wrote London authorities that he was "amazed that the Spirit of the Devil should be so much respected as to make men call open Witchcraft Imagination and no more." Whether the accused felt this way is not known. But the jury's decision apparently annoyed no one else, and witchcraft prosecution fared no better later than it had earlier in South Carolina.[33]

Two episodes, one from New England and another from Virginia, demonstrate how folklorization confused those colonists who remained concerned about magic and witchcraft but who had been abandoned by courts and magistrates in suppressing it. In 1720 Elizabeth Blanchard, an eleven-year-old girl in Littleton, Massachusetts, experienced trances and visions as well as "wounds and pinches and prickings." She tore her clothes, fell in fits, and bit friends and visitors. Her sisters quickly imitated her behavior, and shortly thereafter they accused a town woman of "afflicting them," a progression similar to Salem's. In the absence of any judicial intervention, the case festered for months. Neighbors and minister alike "said that they were under an evil hand, or possessed by Satan"; Littleton's minister, Benjamin Turrell, called it "the general cry of the town."[34]

Littleton's cry turned a modern corner, however. Town residents refused to take vigilante action against the accused witch. Instead, they plumbed their own doubts for resolution. Turrell reported that early in the episode a few townspeople described the girls as physically sick, "underwitted," or merely "perverse and wicked children." Turrell himself wondered about the witchcraft charge. He acknowledged a belief in "spirits, an invisible world, and particularly the agency of Satan." But such things were difficult to establish: "Many things have been dubbed witchcraft, and called the works of the devil, which were nothing more than the contrivance of the children of men."[35]

Littleton's denouement moved culturally backward and forward simultaneously. In almost prophetic fashion, the accused witch became sick and died, the Blanchard sisters became well, and the town crisis passed. But a new ritual followed some eight years later. Apparently bothered by an episode whose intellectual foundations crumbled as she matured, Elizabeth Blanchard confessed that she and her sisters had invented the symptoms and causes and had falsely accused the alleged witch. In the process she transferred responsibility for the affair to herself and her sisters rather than to devils, demons, and supernatural forces. Doing so signaled the approach of modern sensibilities in an obscure prerevolutionary colonial village.[36]

The experiences of John Craig, a Scottish Presbyterian minister, demonstrate how similar tensions filled a far different society to the south. In 1740 Craig settled in Augusta County, Virginia, a community divided by the quarrels that so often underwrote witch accusations. Craig's status and occupation soon drew him into these arguments. In the midst of the dispute, his wife became seriously ill during her first pregnancy. As a midwife delivered the child, Craig began to experience a parallel psychological crisis that resulted in hallucinations, though he "knew not from what reason or cause" they came. Craig's child died four months later, followed by the death of his cattle and horses. Although they were penned with other livestock owned by neighbors, only Craig's animals contracted the deadly sicknesses. The context and result made Craig suspect witchcraft. But, like Turell, Craig found that his lack of respect for witchcraft beliefs left him at a loss. Surely, he wrote in his autobiography, the "Divel had higher Designe than to kill Brutes." Nor could he bring himself to lay the death of his infant child to witchcraft. [37]

Ironically, Craig's neighbors soon made occult accusations against him. The suspicions surfaced when Craig told acquaintances that he believed his cattle had been poisoned and named the culprits. His "enemies" — Craig's word — charged that Craig could have obtained this information only through the use of charms. But unlike the hapless Grace Sherwood in 1705, by the 1740s neither Craig nor his detractors fell victim to dunking or other tests of truth. Although the law still forbade witchcraft and occult practice, Virginia magistrates proved no more willing to hear such charges than town officials in New England or juries in South Carolina. In mid-eighteenth-century Virginia, witchcraft and occult accusations were fodder for gossip and rumor but not something with which the law concerned itself.[38]

The persistence of belief in witches despite judicial indifference signaled the survival of less dangerous but no less vital occult activity in the general population, if not among magistrates and other elites. Perhaps half the almanacs published in the colonies down to the American Revolution continued to print the anatomy, descriptions of the signs of the zodiac, and days when bleeding might be good or bad. Texts in physiognomy and chiromancy were more difficult to find, since few were printed in either England or America after 1680. But one notorious source remained, *Aristotle's Master Piece.* Issued in several eighteenth-century editions and known for its lurid, near pornographic, descriptions of sexual maladies, the 1755 edition contained an introduction to chiromancy and a brief chapter describing "the Powers of the Celestial Bodies over Men and Woman."[39]

One new occult phenomenon was actually created in eighteenth-century America: rattlesnake "gazing." The rattlesnake had intrigued European settlers since their arrival in America. Stories about rattlesnake "fascination" or "gazing" emerged in the late seventeenth century. The first accounts concerned squirrels, which rattlesnakes overpowered "by fixing their eye steadfastly upon them," as the traveler and botanist, John Lederer, wrote in 1672. By the eighteenth century, the rattlesnake's powers extended to man, whom the snake could "gaze" into a stupor that precluded a defense against attack. As Herbert Leventhal has described, Christopher Witt, Joseph Breitnall, and John Bartram all sent accounts of rattlesnake gazing to the London cloth merchant and scientific promoter, Peter Collinson, who used the materials in an account, "Remarkable and Authentic Instances of the Fascinating Power of the Rattlesnake over Men and Other Animals," which appeared in *The Gentleman's Magazine* in 1765.[40]

Rising immigration from the Continent to the British mainland colonies after 1720 introduced new sources of occult practice in America. When the Lutheran churchman Henry Melchior Muhlenberg wrote about occult supernaturalism in the 1750s, he described beliefs and practices far removed from the sophisticated Christian Hermeticism and Rosicrucianism of Kelpius and the German mystics of the 1690s. Muhlenberg castigated the "superstitious and godless notions [that] still prevail among the old, presumptuous people who have had no instruction in their youth." But he also complained that "the new immigrants who are coming annually from various regions [of Germany] are no better; their heads, too, are full of fantastic notions of witchcraft and Satanic arts." Indeed, he concluded that Pennsylvania housed "more necromancers . . . than Christians (if little children are excepted), which is wanton blindness in the light of the Gospel."[41]

Not even Muhlenberg, however, considered occult sentiment an overwhelming threat. He explained away the reputed appearance of a ghost at New Hanover "which made frequent appearances and disturbed the minds of the people" as mere "hocus-pocus." When a parishioner pressed Muhlenberg on the matter of spirits and particularly on why a belief in ghosts might be blasphemous, Muhlenberg patiently explained that such a belief constituted a "sin against the Holy Ghost." Sometimes Muhlenberg could count success in these matters. A 1767 funeral sermon for Simon Graf allowed Muhlenberg to report a victory in suppressing magic in a former adept. Muhlenberg recalled that when Graf came to Pennsylvania, he "found him in error because he dealt in witchcraft and exorcism of devils," though he belonged to a Lutheran congregation. Muhlenberg's strategy was simple: "I . . . excluded him from the congregation until he burned his books and publicly confessed his offense before the congregation." Since Graf "also had a blessed death," meaning that he had confessed his dependence on Christ, Muhlenberg eagerly used Graf's life to make a "good impression upon the congregation since his circumstances were known."[42]

Despite growing cynicism about magic and occultism, "cunning people" also persisted in the eighteenth-century American colonies. The almanac maker Nathaniel Ames, for example, vacillated frequently on the question of predicting the future and warned readers about wise men in a way that assumed their continued presence in New England. "Observe it you may," Ames wrote in his 1752 almanac, "that Cunning Men are not always honest; trust them as you have tried them." To the chagrin of some, colonists found them all too easily, especially in times of trouble. In 1755 the Reverend Ebenezer Parkman registered his disgust with parishioners who resorted to a wise man to find a lost child rather than placing their faith in God. On August 19 Parkman noted that a child "of Mr. Robert Keys of Wachusett [has been] missing Some Days." Parkman's concern rose when, on August 21, "Mr. Keys's Child not found, tho some Hundreds of men were Yesterday and to Day in Search after her." A day later, Parkman reported an even more disturbing event: "Discourse with Mr. Thomas Smith who went to a Wise-Man (Mr. Williams Wood a blacksmith in Scituate nigh Providence) to know where Mr. Keys's lost Child might be found." Parkman never recorded the fate of the missing child, but he did take care to record his strict instructions to his congregation on the dangers of occult practice: "Apr. 27. Read 2 Sam. 4. Preach'd on Josh. 7, 13. P.M. read Isa. 8, and preach'd on number 20 against the foolish and wicked practice of going to Cunning Men to enquire for lost Things. And may God succeed what has been Said!"[43]

Colonial observers sometimes confused personal disdain for popular occultism with the disappearance of such crafts from eighteenth-century society. In the 1780s Yale's Ezra Stiles dismissed occult crafts as mere relics of a vanished society: "In general the System is broken up, the Vessel of Sorcery shipwreckt, and only some shattered planks and pieces disjoyned floating and scatered on the Ocean of . . . human Activity and Bustle." But Stiles's judgment was more accurate in metaphor than substance. Magic and occultism, with their special appeals to direct supernatural manipulation, especially for healing, had largely been folklorized. Stiles himself uncovered evidence of magic's continuing popularity among seamen and ship captains, and he also wrote that "something of it subsists among some Almanac makers and fortune tellers." He personally knew of two, a man in Tiverton, Massachusetts, who cast horoscopes and located lost objects for seamen, and a woman in Newport, Rhode Island, who made urine cakes for use in divining.[44]

Explaining how occultism became folklorized in America is as difficult as explaining how it happened in Europe. Alan Macfarlane first traced the erosion of witchcraft accusations in England to the triumph of the market economy; dissipating village cohesion destroyed the neighborly intimacy that had nourished witchcraft accusations. Yet, in a rare interpretive reversal, Macfarlane discarded this explanation when his subsequent work on the origins of English individualism suggested that English villages were never as cohesive as he had thought and that the seventeenth century witnessed no great rise in individualism to account for the decline in witch trials. Keith Thomas has argued that the decline stemmed from the rise of modern medicine and the expansion of technology. Historians disagree vociferously about the real effectiveness and spread of the new medicine, however, and the technology Thomas emphasizes is limited: improvements in newspaper printing and distribution did not prevent English literacy from remaining notoriously low. And since the notion that a "scientific revolution" erased occult ideas among English intellectuals is now discredited—witness Isaac Newton's alchemy—we are left to find new explanations for occultism's folklorization on both sides of the Atlantic.[45]

Personal discord and intellectual vacillation certainly eroded occultism's credibility. In both Europe and America, astrologers and almanac makers never developed the institutional strength clergymen had behind them. An astrologers' society, formed in London in the 1650s, died out in the 1680s. Only vague hints point toward organization in the colonies among occult practitioners or almanac makers. In a rare autobiographical statement, Jacob Taylor asserted that he had learned astrology and other occult crafts from Pennsylvania's "Sons of Art" in the late 1690s. But not even Taylor suggested anything more than an apprenticeship with one of the colony's older practitioners, and no evidence points to any organization paralleling the institutions subsequently established by Quakers, Baptists, and Presbyterians.[46]

Personal rivalries further exposed occultism's questionable intellectual foundations. Taylor spent an entire career confronting rivals. He battled Daniel Leeds through at least 1710 and belittled William Ball and John Jerman in the 1730s and 1740s. Almanac makers responded slowly to ridicule from critics like Jonathan Swift and Benjamin Franklin. Instead, they withdrew from the fray. They increasingly declined to predict specific political events. Almanacs published after 1720 that included the anatomy sometimes excluded the herbal signs for preparing astrologically based medicines and printed recipes that emphasized natural physical properties of ingredients rather than alleged planetary relationships. Almanac makers were conscious of these changes. Nathaniel Ames wrote in 1751 that when astrology "was caressed by Princes and great Philosophers," everyone defended it. "Now, the Table is turned, they speak against it, and the multitude must follow."[47]

The multitudes were also pushed by vigorous public criticism and legal coercion to reject the occult. Boston's Thomas Fleet, publisher of *The New England Primer Enlarged* (Boston, 1737), tied astrology to Catholicism and replaced the traditional "anatomy" with "the POPE, or Man of Sin." Some adepts turned against their craft. Perhaps in conjunction with one of the visits of George Whitefield to the city, Jacob Taylor apparently underwent a Christian conversion in Philadelphia in 1743 or 1744 and angrily denounced the occultism he had promoted for decades. In an essay scattered through his 1746 almanac, Taylor linked astrology to the "filthy Superstition of the Heathens." He charged that only four of twenty-seven astrologers he had known in Pennsylvania "could write plain English or spell common Words," argued that reputable physicians "never debase their Writings with Fables of Planets and Signs," and used alchemical imagery to deride further William Ball and John Jerman, whose publications were "as remote from Truth as Lead from Silver."[48]

Christian ministers used their institutional authority to attack occultism and the all too popular view that everything was equal in the worlds of wonder. New England clergymen inveighed not only against witchcraft but against sorcery and occult medical practice for fifty years before the Salem trials. In 1723 Quaker leaders renewed the denunciation of occultism and astrology first made during the Chester County episodes of the 1690s. In a new Book of Discipline that codified Quaker institutional procedures, Friends denounced settlers who "by color of any art or skill whatever, do or shall pretend knowledge to discover things hiddenly transacted, or tell where things lost or stolen may be found."[49]

The case of a New Jersey Presbyterian minister, Joseph Morgan, illustrated the collapse of the seventeenth-century accommodation between Hermeticism and Calvinism that John Winthrop,

Jr., had so assiduously pursued in New England. In 1728 the Synod of Philadelphia received a complaint that Morgan had tested judicial astrology before his Scottish congregation in Freehold, New Jersey. The experiment, if that is what it was, only hinted at Morgan's many interests. He corresponded with the Royal Society in London and Cotton Mather and Nathan Prince in Boston about "Fire-particles," cold, and the "Motions of Saturn and Jupiter and the Comets," and published a quasi-utopian apocalyptic novel, *The Kingdom of Basaruah,* in 1715. The Philadelphia synod dealt lightly with Morgan in 1728, and he continued as the minister at Freehold for another decade. But he resigned in 1739 at age fifty-eight and disappeared from all subsequent Presbyterian affairs.[50]

Five years later, in 1744, the Maryland physician, satirist, and traveler, Alexander Hamilton, described what had happened to Morgan. While stopping at a New Jersey inn during a trip to New York, Hamilton described how

> a solemn old fellow lighted att the door. He was in a homely rustick dress, and I understood his name was Morgan. "Look ye here," says the landlord to me, "here comes a famous philosopher." "Your servant, Mr. Morgan, how d'ye?" The old fellow had not settled himself long upon his seat before he entered upon a learned discourse concerning astrology and the influence of the stars, in which he seemed to put a great deal more confidence than I thought was requisite. From that he made a transition to the causes of the tides, the shape and dimension of the earth, the laws of gravitation, and 50 other physicall subjects in which he seemed to me not to talk so much out of the way as he did upon the subject of judiciall astrology . . . I found him very deficient in his knowledge that way, tho a great pretender. All this chat passed while the old fellow drank half a pint of wine, which done, the old don took to his horse and rid off in very slow solemn pace, seemingly well satisfied with his own learning and knowledge.[51]

Institutional Christianity also subtly challenged occultism by paralleling its characteristics in ways that went beyond Cotton Mather's intriguing use of the term "amulet" to describe Christian prayer. To be sure, beyond the case of Jacob Taylor, no conversion of an adept in magic was recorded in the literature of the occasional eighteenth-century American revivals. Yet the occult and Christian ritual sometimes resembled each other in striking ways. Scottish Presbyterians used tokens and small cards that resembled amulets to admit persons to communion. Those used by a eighteenth-century Virginia Presbyterian, Samuel Davies, for example, read:

> Do this says Christ
> 'till time shall end
> In Memory of your dying Friend.
> Meet at my Table and Record
> The Love of your departed Lord.[52]

Evangelical conversion ritual also paralleled occult practice in eighteenth-century America. The laity approached both cunning persons and ministers with numerous fears, doubts, and problems. Wise men and women recast complaints about birth, money, background, and disputes in astrological and occult terms capable of solution through geomancy, chiromancy, metoposcopy, horoscopes, or divination. Clergymen recast these problems in a Christian context. Their inquirers' real problems concerned salvation. Then, in simple sermons on elemental Christian doctrine, they began dissolving listeners' anxieties. They explained Christian faith. If listeners panicked when they discovered that their own salvation was in doubt, the panic only increased the clergyman's authority. After all, only the Christian god knew the future and controlled the world, and the minister, trained in Christian doctrine and—in evangelical circles—having undergone a conversion experience himself, was the proper guide to charting the Christian's future. Much evidence suggests that listeners enjoyed this conversion ritual. At least for a while, colonists went to hear revival ministers in large numbers and enacted rituals of doubt, inquiry, and resolution that paralleled encounters between wise men and clients of an older, now folklorized, occultism.[53]

Intellectual parallels vital in their very crudity further underlined subtle exchanges between evangelical Christianity and occultism. The fatalism inherent in Calvinism's concept of predestination found an occult equivalent in the notion that the stars and planets revealed a future uncontrolled by individual action. Revivalists and occult practitioners also explained catastrophes in similar ways. Believers in occult ideas thought that the coming of comets and eclipses had inevitable, usually disastrous, consequences.

Not even kings and queens escaped their verdicts. Nor did anyone escape Calvin's god, who sometimes displayed his sovereignty merely by consigning model Christians to hell.[54]

Government coercion also contributed to magic's folklorization in America. However poorly or slowly, colonial governments used their authority to make institutional Christianity the only legitimate religion in all the colonies. They banned occult practice and enforced such laws with sufficient frequency to make sure colonists knew that they were assuming dangerous risks if they carried occult religious practice too far or if it challenged Christianity too openly.

English statutes against occult practice, including the famous statutes passed under James I that outlawed white and black magic, also applied in the colonies. Colonial legislatures added to them. As late as 1736, George Webb reminded Virginia magistrates that the colony's laws specifically prohibited witchcraft and the use of occult techniques to find lost goods and provoke "unlawful love." In the seventeenth century, Maryland governors demanded that grand jurors repress witchcraft, sorcery, and necromancy. The 1649 Maryland Act concerning Religion, which pleaded for nearly any kind of Christian practice and protected Puritans and Catholics, offered no protection to sorcerers or wise men. Nor was New England different. Both Massachusetts and Rhode Island demanded execution for convicted witches; whatever their differences on other issues, Roger Williams and John Winthrop shared a common dislike of magic and the Devil.[55]

Blasphemy statutes repressed occult religion by making it illegal to slander Jesus or Christianity either directly or indirectly. They were important because colonial authorities viewed occult practice as a challenge to orthodox Christianity, regardless of the extent to which some men and women tried to synthesize them. Seemingly tolerant Pennsylvania forced officeholders to affirm their belief in the divinity of Jesus, banned blasphemy, forbade Sunday labor, and urged all settlers to attend Christian services on the Sabbath so "looseness, irreligion, and Atheism may not creep in under pretense of conscience." Seven colonies forced settlers to pay taxes to support specific churches—the Church of England in the southern colonies and New York and the Congregational churches in New England. But all of the colonies ordered fines and even death for colonists who blasphemed Christ or engaged in occult activity, and most demanded some kind of public confession of Christian beliefs as the price for entering colonial politics.[56]

Colonial officials enforced these statutes in varying ways. Massachusetts and Connecticut were especially vigilant, and in fact America was more dangerous for accused witches than England had been. The colonial American conviction rate was about the same as the English rate: half of those tried were found guilty. But English courts handed down relatively lenient punishments to proven witches; New England's courts, in contrast, executed fully half of those they convicted. The New England executions occurred after 1649, although English executions had been declining since the 1620s and ended in 1685. But Connecticut and Massachusetts authorities executed twenty-two colonists for practicing witchcraft between 1649 and 1690, and, of course, Salem's executioners hanged nineteen more in 1692.[57]

Eighteenth-century officials only irregularly enforced the laws against less malevolent occult practice. A Boston justice of the peace, John Clark, committed an African servant girl to the house of correction for fortune-telling in 1709. But nearly two decades later, in 1727, a Boston almanac maker, Nathaniel Bowen, complained that officials ignored her successors: "If the wholesome Laws of the Province were duely Executed on such Negro manceres, I would venture to Foretell what would soon be their Fortune."[58]

Bowen's prediction would have been as difficult to test then as now. In early America as in modern society, knowledge of crime comes largely from the very officials whose work the historian wants to assess. Little independent evidence therefore exists to determine whether colonial law enforcement officials actually restricted all known illegal behavior, very little of it, or could do either consistently. It can be said that court records seldom mentioned occult activity other than witchcraft; the cases in Chester County, Pennsylvania, were notable exceptions to this pattern. More often, the law repressed occult activity indirectly. Magistrates used the blasphemy statutes to cite colonists for swearing or for laboring on the Sabbath. Such actions warned colonists where permissible practice ended and illegal religious activity began.[59]

This uneven prosecution became part of occultism's folklorization in a two-part labeling process. First, the written law branded it illegal and therefore illicit. Second, the mere apprehension of individuals for practicing it, without formal charges, trials, or convictions, reinforced occultism's legally sanctioned disrepute. Jack Douglas's description of the process in modern society may be even more appropriate to colonial society, with its extraordinary social intimacy. Arrest becomes "the crucial stage in legal stigmatization" because "arrest, not conviction, makes an individual into a *distrusted outsider* . . . It creates a suspicion in the minds of most members of the society. How are they to check out the charge? Surely the police, who are seen as experts on such matters, know something about [these] activities that warrant such suspicion."[60]

Two cases from Maryland and New York, colonies not customarily associated with early American religious intolerance, illustrated how the labeling process might constrain occult practice, especially among middle- and upper-class colonists. The cases reflected official support for Christianity, suppression of anti-Christian behavior, and the legal equation of magic with blasphemy and, hence, with illicit, illegal religion. The Maryland case involved an otherwise obscure Jewish resident, Jacob Lumbrozo, arrested for blasphemy in 1658. During a dispute with neighbors, Lumbrozo ridiculed Christ's resurrection. Christ's disciples merely "stole him away . . . by Negromancy or sorcery," Lumbrozo said; Christ himself was a "Negromancer" who performed miracles by "the Art Magick." The New York offender was more prominent and the crime perhaps more intriguing. A Queens County justice of the peace, Jonathan Whitehead, was cited in 1701 for equating Christian ministers and occult practitioners. "Religion was onely an invention of cunning Men to gett thaire living by," Whitehead was alleged to have said. The colleague who reported the statement also complained that Whitehead's slur and his all too eager willingness to travel on the Sabbath (seemingly a peculiar charge in New York) "tended to nothing less than Atheism and the discouragement of Christianity." "He being a Justice [he ought] in a particular manner to take care not to give such examples."[61]

Neither Lumbrozo nor Whitehead was ever prosecuted for his alleged offense, and viewed from traditional perspectives on early American church-state relationships, the cases point to a pragmatic, if not theoretical, religious freedom in the mid-eighteenth-century colonies. But viewed from another perspective, the cases illustrate how government and the mere threat of coercion helped shape magic's folklorization in America. As in England, intellectual change, increasing Christian opposition, and government coercion all worked to suppress occult and magical practice in the advancing social elite and to contain it within the rougher segments of early society. Maryland and New York officials feared the occult, and they defended orthodox Christianity in the face of what they regarded as direct challenges from occult opinion. By bringing Lumbrozo and Whitehead before the court and entering their alleged comments in the permanent court record, colonial officials as much stamped the label of deviance on "Art Magick"as on Lumbrozo and Whitehead. Neither trials nor convictions were needed to repress or constrain occult practice, since colonists hardly turned to it comfortably and, certainly, not very publicly when officials arrested settlers, even prestigious ones, for describing Christ as a magus.

Even the many colonists acquitted of witch charges—half were—aided occultism's folklorization. Perhaps they were indeed innocent. No matter. Through the 1690s, at least, the trials demonstrated the authorities' vigilance in suppressing magic. And to fellow colonists—and to subsequent historians as well—the innocent remained *accused* witches. In the process, innocence became guilt and the acquitted became victims of a larger, more important, campaign to repress occult activity in America.[62]

The legal activity against witchcraft demonstrated the broad range of early American religious expression. The persistence of belief in witches after witch trials had ended reflected the folklorization of magic in the twilight of early modern Western society on both sides of the Atlantic. Although upper social classes largely abandoned occultism, other colonists continued to believe in witchcraft, astrology, and the ability of wise men and wise women to find lost objects and cure disease. In this regard, folklorization prevented the complete suppression of occultism and magic. Opponents lacked the means to eliminate it completely, and magistrates and ministers tolerated its minimal expression, in part because such views seemed quaint and in part because they were held by the folk. By the standards of the time, occultism did minimal harm to people of minimal importance. After 1776, however, these people became sovereign, and to the chagrin of some, perhaps many, their less than orthodox notions about the nature of the supernatural world began to assume far more importance than had been true during the century of prerevolutionary American maturation.

THE RENEWAL OF CHRISTIAN AUTHORITY

4

American society underwent momentous change between 1680 and 1760. Crude backwoods settlements became bustling provincial capitals. Enslaved Africans replaced English indentured servants as farm laborers and household workers. Continental European immigration upended the national homogeneity of English America, especially outside New England. Settlers created political institutions and invented political "traditions" that the Crown would later invade.[1]

Religion changed as well. First, the state church tradition that had emerged only fitfully in Virginia but more fully, if peculiarly, in New England experienced a vigorous revival in both areas after 1680. Second, the landscape of eighteenth-century America underwent a major sacralization; this stemmed directly from the reviving state church tradition but had significance that extended far beyond it. Third, eighteenth-century American Dissenters embraced authority and coercion in their own ranks; they created denominational institutions that greatly expanded their own reach into colonial society and, eventually, had a profound effect on American society. This eighteenth-century transformation turned American religious development in new and often unexpected directions. Somewhat surprisingly, it emerged as establishmentarian rather than Dissenting, coercive rather than voluntary, and institutional rather than individualistic. Ultimately, it bespoke an

America not so much fleeing its European past as pursuing it in vibrant, complex ways.

The Anglican effort at colonial religious transformation began in Virginia, where the Church of England had been established by law since 1626 and by practice since 1607. James Blair's appointment in 1689 as Virginia's first Anglican commissary, or representative of the bishop of London, actually capped the secular growth that had already increased parish activity in the 1670s. Virginia had moved from a colony with under a dozen working parishes and fewer than ten clergymen in 1650 to some fifty parishes and thirty-five ministers by 1680. But parishes did not necessarily mean a smoothly functioning state church, or at least not the Church of England, and Blair sought to bring the two into greater conformity in Virginia for nearly five decades. In this period, no one questioned the Church of England's right to legal establishment. Furthermore, Dissenters remained relatively uncommon in the colony and played no significant role in the seventeenth-century debate over Anglican development there. Despite these advantages and Blair's best efforts, however, his plans for ecclesiastical splendor failed.

Although the 1626 law establishing the Church of England "as neere as may be" gave it state support, Virginia law also dispersed parish authority into too many hands, usually those of vestrymen and parish ministers. Blair wanted to centralize ecclesiastical administration, with greater power lodged in the commissary's hands, and he frequently passed proposals for new ecclesiastical statutes implementing his plans to the Assembly. Previously accustomed to promoting minority Anglican interests in Scotland, where Presbyterians emphasized piety and learning, Blair proposed both for Virginia, under Anglican auspices. His plan to found the College of William and Mary and the curriculum he suggested for it were rooted in a dual concern for personal spiritual renewal and local clerical training, not unlike the Puritans' early use of Harvard. Little wonder that in his old age Blair welcomed to Virginia the young George Whitefield, a man whose piety and commitment to Anglican reform might have reminded Blair of his own hopes forty years before.[2]

Blair's centralization scheme failed. The parish clergy resented his personal power and aggrandizing instincts, and his incessant political forays won him major enemies in the aristocracy. Yet his tenure as commissary bore extraordinary and perhaps unexpected local fruit. The number of Church of England buildings in Virginia nearly doubled from about thirty-five in 1680 to sixty-one in 1724. This growth primarily reflected the successful use of the law to establish parishes for new settlements. Although the correlation was never perfect, Blair and the Virginia Assembly effectively advanced the Church of England into every new county formed between 1690 and 1740. The Assembly laid out new parish boundaries, authorized new vestries, levied new taxes, backed new church construction, and watched Blair confirm new ministers to preach in the many new pulpits.[3]

Virginia's Anglican renewal solidified the relationship between the colony's aristocratic elite and its state-supported church. By the early eighteenth century, membership on a parish vestry had become a familiar station for aristocratic sons entering public careers. They learned how to manage public affairs at the local level, where they levied taxes, maintained parish properties, supervised care for the poor and sick, and hired and fired clergymen. Church of England adherence and involvement in parish life and governance became a sine qua non for success in Virginian society and politics from the 1680s until the time of the Revolution.[4]

The Anglican renaissance also thoroughly transformed Virginia's ecclesiastical architecture, while continuing the sacralization of the landscape. This happened in two ways. First, new settlements and new parishes built new buildings. The first Virginia backcountry, between the original tidewater settlements and the fall line, filled up with new churches where none had existed before. The eight built between 1660 and 1669 equaled the number constructed between the colony's founding in 1607 and 1659, and eleven more, nearly all of them brick rather than wood, went up between 1670 and 1700. Second, old parishes replaced buildings constructed from the 1640s to the 1680s and, in the process, destroyed virtually the whole of the colony's seventeenth-century ecclesiastical architecture, including all the buildings constructed during the local revival of the parish system between 1660 and 1680. In all but a few parishes, the small wooden buildings that had gone up between 1620 and 1680 were replaced by major new buildings between 1680 and 1740. York County authorities, for example, built Grace Church in 1696 to replace a building erected in 1642 or 1643. In New Kent County between 1701 and 1703, St. Peter's Church replaced what parishioners had long and probably appropriately called the "Broken Back'd Church," apparently dating from the 1650s, with a more substantial, ornate building.[5]

Virginia's post-1680 churches were suited to the increasingly wealthy, aristocratic society. They were larger, placed on spacious grounds, and almost never constructed of wood. St. Peter's honeycombed English bond brickwork gave it a sophistication lacking in Grace Church's plain exterior. But both churches' interiors displayed the new elegance common to eighteenth-century Virginia Anglican church architecture. Furnishings included hand-carved pews, large windows, royal coats of arms, and massive pulpits cantilevered out into the chancel.[6]

Robert Beverley's *History and Present State of Virginia* (London, 1705) encapsulated the Anglican renaissance even as it proceeded. Beverley confidently asserted that each parish had "a convenient church built either of timber, brick, or stone." It was "decently adorned with everything necessary for the celebration of divine service." Small chapels served settlers "if a parish be of greater extent than ordinary." Ministers were present in most parishes, and settlers were "generally of the Church of England, which is the religion established by law in that country." "No more than five conventicles [existed] amongst them," Beverley said, "namely, three small meetings of Quakers and two of Presbyterians."[7]

Above all, Beverley captured early eighteenth-century Virginia's remarkable and unique Anglican homogeneity. The colony's Anglican renaissance revealed the impotence of English Dissent there before 1740. Despite obvious opportunities to do so, Quakers and Presbyterians failed to expand their minor seventeenth-century inroads, and Baptists did not become active in the colony until after 1740. As a result, Anglican vestries, levying compulsory church taxes, accounted for every one of the colony's new churches constructed between 1680 and 1720. Never again would Virginia be so overwhelmingly Anglican. It was not a golden age, perhaps, but it was surely a unique one.[8]

Virginia's Anglican renewal prefigured the reassertion of the state church in colonial America between 1680 and 1720. Anglicans led this development in the southern and middle colonies by seeking legal establishment of the Church of England. In New England, Calvinist Congregationalists created a new parish system to supplement the already outmoded town church system. The effort produced a new range of church law and, in response to its successful implementation and an advancing economy, a major resacralization of the colonial landscape.

Maryland's desultory seventeenth-century church life made Anglican renewal there all the more notable. As in Virginia, a small advance in Church of England fortunes occurred in the 1670s, and the number of informally established Anglican "parishes" rose from three to four or five. Aided by political changes that gave more power to men interested in strengthening the colony's English ties, the Maryland Assembly in 1692 passed the first of three acts that finally established the Church of England as the colony's state church. The 1692 establishment act, though vetoed, nonetheless became a model for the successful establishment act of 1702. It proclaimed that "the Church of England within this Province shall have and Enjoy all her Rights Liberties and Franchises," and it laid out thirty parishes in the colony's ten counties, with vestries to collect taxes and manage parish business. Maryland authorities immediately established the parishes created by the act, and they operated them in accordance with the act for two years, even after it had been vetoed. As a result the 1702 act changed the actual operation of Maryland's nearly ten-year-old parishes very little.[9]

New York's establishment, accomplished in the 1693 Ministry Act, demonstrated how even weak legislative enactments could create state churches and transform the appearance of institutional Christianity in the colony. The 1693 act authorized salaries for "good and sufficient Protestant ministers" in four of the colony's ten counties—New York, Richmond, Westchester, and Queens. In its own peculiar way, and certainly without any democratic intent, the act provided religious establishment from the bottom up, or at least from the parish up, and it therefore strayed far from traditional English concepts of church establishment. In fact, the act did not mention the Church of England, much less establish it in a way recognizable to an English bishop. It provided for vestries, to be elected by parish freeholders, which would in turn hire the parish ministers. Although the ministers were required to be Protestants, they were not required to be Anglicans. Church of England partisans would have to curry local favor in each parish to control each pulpit.[10]

The 1693 Ministry Act, despite its limitations, significantly advanced institutional Christianity in New York. Its geographical restriction to New York City and the surrounding counties, often puzzling, reflected its concern for Christianity among English settlers. Not surprisingly, Anglicanism proved to be state church Christianity's chief beneficiary in New York. Anglicans won the vestry contests in five of the six established parishes, including New York City, by plying both local and transatlantic political connections, chartering New York City's Dutch Church (whose adherents then voted for Anglican candidates in city vestry elections), and paying salaries (secretly, apparently) to Dutch and refugee Huguenot ministers, also in order to curry their favor in vestry elections.[11]

South Carolina's Anglican establishment act of 1706 followed a bitter, complicated debate. The colony's first establishment bill of 1704 created a traditional territorial parish system and commissary to represent the bishop of London, but it also disenfranchised Protestant Dissenters and created a unique board of lay "church commissioners," thoroughly unknown in the English ecclesiastical system, to counterbalance the new commissary. In a colony already torn by byzantine political factionalism, the bill provoked immediate anger, a transatlantic debate to which the novelist and religious Dissenter Daniel Defoe contributed, and finally a royal veto. Two years later, a more moderate bill enfranchised Protestant Dissenters, reduced the lay church commission to a largely powerless body, and created ten parishes, thereby establishing the Church of England and Christianity in South Carolina law.[12]

North Carolina struggled even more slowly toward Anglican establishment. Vetoed "vestry acts" in 1701, 1704, and 1711 were finally overcome by a successful measure in 1715. As in South Carolina, the North Carolina debate reflected many-sided contests about church power, tax support, and Dissenter toleration. The 1701 act created a parish and vestry system but provided absurdly low clerical salaries and hedged on toleration. The 1704 act guaranteed Protestant toleration but provoked a bitter controversy with North Carolina's Quaker minority that led to the so-called Cary Rebellion of 1711. The successful 1715 act settled for toleration, stated vestry powers more clearly, improved ministers' salaries, added new parishes, and, perhaps most important, capped vestry taxes at "five shillings per poll on all taxable persons in the parish."[13]

As in England, Anglicans paralleled the drive for legal establishment with the creation of powerful voluntary agencies, which further reshaped the eighteenth-century colonial ecclesiastical landscape. The SPCK and SPG publishing and proselytizing societies, chartered in England at the turn of the century, had strong American roots. The experience of Thomas Bray, their founder, as Maryland commissary in the 1690s had led him to worry not merely about Anglicanism but about Christian activity of any kind in the colonies, and he proposed the formation of the societies to improve the lax Christian presence in America. Bray built them on what he perceived to be a strong Dissenting tradition of "voluntary" support for Christianity, especially among Quakers (an irony, given Dissenter lethargy in late Stuart England): "Whilst the Papists, the Dissenters, and the very Quakers have such Societies for the carrying on [of] their Superstitious Blasphemies, Heresies, and Fooleries[,] we have had nothing of this nature yet set up." Hence the foundation of the SPCK for publications and the SPG for ministers, the books and clergymen to be sent to English settlers, not to native Americans or slaves.[14]

SPG and SPCK aid to America followed reforming models of Anglican endeavor. The SPG solicited and furnished clergymen for parishes far distant from universities and bishops, "good, substantial, well studied Divines," to avoid angering "a People so well versed in Business, as even the meanest Planter seems to be." The society augmented the salaries of ministers where the legal establishment provided only meager pay, as was true in South Carolina, for example; it also provided salaries where no establishment would ever be obtained, as in Pennsylvania. By 1720 the SPG had sent more than sixty Anglican priests to colony settlements that usually had yet to see a resident ministry of any kind. For its part, the SPCK sent books. Some one hundred parishes received libraries of more than a hundred volumes each, mainly for their ministers' use, and down to the American Revolution both societies sent thousands of tracts and pamphlets to the colonies for public distribution.[15]

Anglicans also organized congregations in colonies where the legal establishment of the Church of England was impossible and where local authorities resented the intrusion. Their campaign inevitably carried a partisan flavor, but Anglicans justified their demands on the grounds that the king's church was the inevitable and proper choice of increasing numbers of immigrants. In Boston Anglicans capitalized on the creation of the Dominion of New England in 1685 to found the city's first Anglican church, King's Chapel, a year later in 1686. In Philadelphia they took advantage of William Penn's political troubles to muscle through a charter for Christ Church in 1696. Anglicans were all the more pleased about the foundation of these new congregations because they so angered their Puritan and Quaker competitors. But the achievements of the Anglicans also revealed their anomalous place in the American religious configuration. Anglican church charters, wrung from reluctant Massachusetts and Pennsylvania authorities, guaranteed not only Anglican worship but Anglican freedom from government harassment and interference at the Dissenters' direction, certainly an irony for England's state church.[16]

As Anglicans obtained legal establishment for their church in the middle and southern colonies after 1680, New England Congregationalists replaced town churches with a parish system that itself restructured their old church-state relationship. The cause was not Anglican competition, though New Englanders were aware of it. The new system instead represented a major effort to deal with social and material change in the region. Shifting immigration and settlement patterns had created both legal and illegal "squatter" communities, which were far from the sites of the first homes and first churches. Some of the settlers were the original town residents' children, who were taking up backlands on immense town grants. Some were newcomers not connected to the old town, let alone to its values and church. All were now far from the church. Worse, not only did they seldom attend, but they balked about paying town taxes for religious services they did not use. In turn, the towns often refused to let the new settlers form separate, legally established communities or even new congregations. The solution was the parish. Beginning in the 1680s, the Massachusetts and Connecticut legislatures authorized territorial parishes within towns where new settlement patterns placed residents far from the old church buildings, so that these settlers could find legal ways to begin new congregations.[17]

The New England parish system carried the seventeenth-century state church into a more complex, perhaps even a more "modern," society. The creation of the territorial parish, like the creation of a county system and a new court system, were typical of the maturation of eighteenth-century New England society. Together they restructured New England politics and society by opening localities to complex, interlaced elites and to new social and religious realities. The parish contributed to this opening in oblique but powerful ways. Many parishes (and towns as well) became what Michael Zuckerman has called "peaceable kingdoms," island communities that rejected dissent and sent challengers packing to the next settlement. Yet these islands were not identical. The decentralized character of New England's state church precluded effective means of ensuring "orthodoxy" from parish to parish and town to town. Some parishes became avowedly Presbyterian, others remained Congregational, and a few became Baptist. In the process the parishes rationalized modest Calvinist pluralism of the kind that had always characterized New England Puritanism but that had also expanded in the eighteenth century. The shift also allowed a narrower, possibly even sectarian, focus for the congregations. Now they no longer bore the burden of sustaining "community" in the way John Winthrop might have wanted. Through deft maneuvering they could concentrate on narrower doctrinal, liturgical, or ecclesiastical interests without abandoning coercive authority or legal establishment.[18]

The late Stuart revival of the state church in Britain's American colonies found its literary expression in Nicholas Trott's *The Laws of the British Plantations in America, Relating to the Church and the Clergy, Religion, and Learning* (London, 1725). In his preface Trott lamented the colonies' lack of "any General *Laws* to establish religion there, and support for their Ministers, as is usual in other Provinces." Yet Trott found enough provincial legislation to fill a quarto-sized, three-hundred-page volume. Rhode Island took up only two pages. But Pennsylvania required sixteen, New York thirteen, Massachusetts Bay thirty-seven, Virginia forty-eight, and his beloved South Carolina eighty-two. Virtually all the legislation Trott digested and reprinted was the product of the post-1680 state church renaissance, and Trott's work was a massive demonstration of late Stuart creativity in reviving the state church and the use of government coercion and legislation to support Christianity in America.[19]

The drive to reassert the coercive state church tradition in England's American mainland colonies found its most obvious expression in the landscape itself. Places that had never seen the presence of Christian buildings now found them in striking profusion. The Maryland achievement was especially notable. Notorious for its irreligion, Maryland contained only four or five religious structures at the time of the 1692 Anglican establishment act. Within two years, twenty-two Anglican churches had been erected in the Maryland countryside. Moreover, the construction was spread throughout the colony, not isolated in one or two counties. Anne Arundel County lagged furthest behind; boundaries had been laid out for four parishes there by 1694 but no churches had been built. Other counties achieved far better results. Kent counted two parishes laid out and one church built. Calvert counted five parishes laid out and three churches built. St. Mary's had two parishes laid out, one church built, and another "going forward to be built." In Charles there were four parishes laid out, three churches built, and one "agreed to." Dorchester County's Old Trinity Church, constructed about 1692, not only brought an Anglican presence to the area but encouraged traditional English burials around the church in consecrated ground (see Figure 4). Filling the pulpits of the new churches with ministers took longer, of course. But at least now parishes existed to pay and house them and to construct and maintain buildings for Christian worship. A decade earlier such possibilities had been mere dreams.[20]

New York's 1693 Ministry Act also spurred a flurry of church construction. Between 1690 and 1715 Anglican church structures went up in New York City, Staten Island, Westchester, Eastchester, New Rochelle, and Queens. The new structures were the only free-standing English churches yet built in the colony, and they remained so until the 1710s, when small Baptist and Presbyterian churches were erected.[21]

Anglican structures also transformed North Carolina's all but churchless landscape. Although several Quaker meetinghouses had existed in the colony since the 1670s, they were tiny and crude, as in Maryland, and their significance only declined as the Quakers failed to increase their following while the North Carolina population expanded. Three Anglican buildings went up after passage of the 1701 vestry act, even though it was rejected by the Carolina proprietors. When the proprietors approved the 1715 vestry act, Anglican churches were constructed in each of the dozen parishes that the act created. These buildings remained the principal architectural evidence of Christian presence in the colony until the 1740s, when Presbyterians and Baptists finally became active there and began to construct their own buildings.[22]

The Anglican renaissance brought the scale and, sometimes, the style of rural English church architecture to the newly sacralized American wilderness. Especially outside Virginia, the rural buildings were usually small and reflected modest establishment acts and smaller, less well developed communities. South Carolina churches provide a good example, especially in their interiors. Unlike the brick buildings frequently found to the north, the South Carolina structures at St. Andrews (1706), St. James Goose Creek (1708), and Strawberry Chapel (1725) possessed severe stucco exteriors, though the pink coloration of the church at St.

4. Old Trinity Church, Dorchester County, Maryland, ca. 1692.

James Goose Creek smoothed the starkness. The interiors of all three buildings proclaimed the sovereignty of both Christ and the king of England through superb craftsmanship and gently assertive design. Wooden wall plaques displayed Bible verses. Hand-carved royal coats of arms painted in vibrant reds, blues, and gold proclaimed church support for the Crown. Canopied pulpits of carved and polished mahogany or oak projected priestly occupants above the congregation as they read the Scriptures and preached.[23]

New England also experienced a major resacralization of the landscape after 1680, which created the "colonial" New England church known to tourists today and resulted in the destruction of all of the region's first church buildings of the seventeenth century. As in Virginia, this happened in two ways. Old towns with modest and crude seventeenth-century buildings supplanted them with far larger, more opulent, buildings. New parishes and towns—some detached from old towns, some crossing old town boundaries, some representing new settlements in new areas—created new church buildings.

The new proved quite unlike the old, even in New England. The 1681 Hingham meetinghouse stood at the crossroads of seventeenth- and eighteenth-century New England church architecture. Its exposed and unpainted interior structural beams, which have long reminded viewers of a ship's innards and prompted its name, the Old Ship Meeting House, represented the simpler, cruder seventeenth-century New England church building style. Its exterior, with its Georgian formality and two-story height, and its pulpit, with its fine wood and extraordinary breadth, signaled the far larger, more formal, and more finished buildings typical of eighteenth-century New England. (See Figures 5 and 6.)

The new Hingham church heralded the triumph of a post-Puritan materialism and a new, more expressive, religious aesthetic in the region—a New England rococo, at least by seventeenth-century standards. Pulpits became more massive as designers and carvers responded to the sharply increased size of the buildings, and they were centered on platforms that sometimes stretched across the full width of the sanctuary. Platform and pulpit together increased the grandeur of the eighteenth-century buildings. The result reflected both the constraints and the expansiveness of post-Puritan society. The vast, empty, undecorated spaces of these larger, bulkier buildings bore the imprint of seventeenth-century Puritan severity. But the details crowding in at the edges expressed New Englanders' increasing pleasure in fine craftsmanship and expensive things, not unlike the choices of their compatriots to the south. Finely polished pews, detailed decorative carvings, and weighty mahogany communion tables reflected a society of rural and urban elites that was both more affluent and more formal, where church membership remained "tribal" and family centered and where ties to the locality implied a broader county and even regional perspective — no longer merely a town or a "community" view.[24]

The aural landscape changed too. As churches went up, bells arrived, the first church bells ever heard in many colonies. In the

5. Exterior, Old Ship Meeting House, Hingham, Massachusetts, 1681.

new rural churches most bells were hung from platforms placed to the front or side; bell towers for the most part appeared only later in the century. The bells were widely noticed. They cut through the thickened forests to call the half-interested to ritual, and they spread their sound out across steadily growing urban areas. In the cities, bells went up with the great Anglican churches constructed in the late 1690s and early 1700s, all of which had bell towers, but they were not always added to the smaller Dissenting churches constructed later. In New York City both Trinity Church and the new Dutch Church incorporated bell towers into their design. In Philadelphia only the Anglican Christ Church and apparently the Presbyterian church had bells. For two decades they served all the city's non-Quaker Protestant congregations, for they were rung together to signal the start of Protestant Sabbath services, and in

6. Interior, Old Ship Meeting House, Hingham, Massachusetts, 1681.

the 1740s the Philadelphia City Council and the Protestant vestries cooperated to purchase three additional bells.[25]

Even Boston had bells. They appeared at the Third Church as early as 1669, when the congregation paid £18 for a bell, and the Anglican King's Chapel added one in 1689. New churches built after 1700, such as Old North Church, from whose bell tower Paul Revere hung his famous lantern, nearly always had bells. Still, it is not clear that Bostonians knew quite what to do with them. When the city's French Protestant minister, Andrew Le Mercier, published his *Church History of Geneva* in 1732, he took some care to explain the ritual of bell ringing in Calvinism's Old World capital. Le Mercier was at that time the only Boston cleric who had ever been to Geneva, and he explained how the seeming cacophony of one-, two-, and three-ton bells, themselves a weighty reminder of the church's increasing wealth, still might be turned to pious uses in this aging post-Puritan society.[26]

Bells did not become ubiquitous, however. Gottlieb Mittelberger noted that rural central Pennsylvania remained largely bereft of bells at mid-century, even though it was filling up with German settlers and some German Lutheran and Reformed congregations: "The whole year long one hears neither ringing nor striking of bells." Similarly, bells were sufficiently unique to Ebenezer Parkman, who ministered at Westborough, Massachusetts, that when he visited Boston in October 1742 he could write in his diary that he "gratifyed my Curiosity at the Chiming of the Ring of Bells at Dr. Cutler's Church—viewed the ells—the Organ, Vestry, etc."[27]

Landscape sacralization also brought with it the first religious graffiti in the colonies. The indefatigable Ezra Stiles first noticed these displays in the 1770s and traced them to the late 1720s. On a rock overlooking Brenton's Point, five miles southwest of Newport, Rhode Island, he found a rock inscription dated 1728, with the words, "BELEVE IN CHRIST & LIVE IN NO SIN" (see Figure 7). Another carving, also dated 1728, on a rock at Price's Cove, east of Newport, proclaimed, "GOD PRESARVE ALL MANKIND." The messages were meant to command the attention of Rhode Island fishermen, although Stiles ruefully reported that when he saw the words they were "dayly trodden upon." Residents attributed them to the Reverend Nathaniel Clap, who began his ministry in 1695 and died in 1745, though because Stiles could not believe that such "illy spelled" inscriptions could have been the work of an ordained clergyman, he thought a local layman, Mr. Brenton, must have been responsible.[28]

The late Stuart resacralization also transformed colonial American cityscapes into dramatic assertions of the demand for Christian adherence traditional in European cities. This proved especially important in prerevolutionary America, where cities of real urban complexity, sophistication, and economic prowess quickly became entrepôts of cultural maturation. Again Anglicans took the lead in sacralizing the urban landscape outside Boston, and Boston too eventually experienced a changing religious skyline, redrawn by Anglicans and Congregationalists.

Between 1695 and 1705 three of the four major colonial cities constructed Anglican churches that dwarfed all others. New York offered a particularly dramatic example of a shifting religious cityscape stimulated by Anglican activity. As late as 1695 the city still possessed the skyline of the old Dutch period (see Figure 8). The

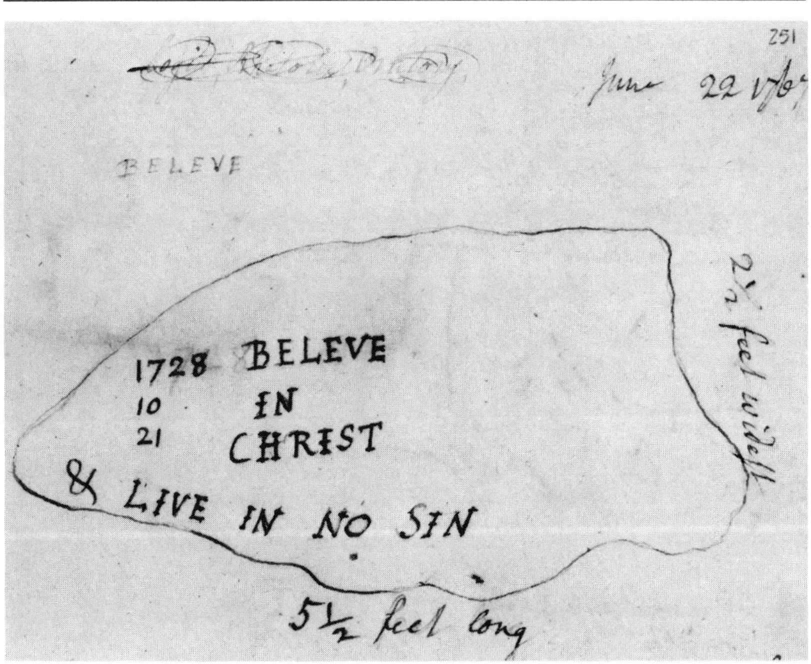

7. Rock inscription at Brenton's Point, Rhode Island, 1728, copied by Ezra Stiles in his itinerary, 1767.

Anglicans' construction of Trinity Church in 1696, however, stimulated construction of a new French church for Huguenot refugees in 1704 and of Dutch and Presbyterian churches in the 1710s. By 1730 the changing skyline expressed the shift in the city's spiritual vista (see Figure 9). Residents walking west down a narrow, crowded Wall Street suddenly encountered an open three-block area, containing Trinity Church and a clear view of the North River carved from the dense tangles of one- and two-story buildings that already typified the city. Dutch leaders achieved much the same effect in 1729 for their own new church and, as it happened, for the 1704 Huguenot church as well, when they carved out an unobstructed view of both buildings amid the ever more crowded urban undergrowth around them. If New Yorkers still ignored Christian worship, certainly it was not because they did not notice its availability.

Charleston and Boston underwent similar transformations. In 1700 Charleston was a town with only the small meetinghouses of the Anglicans and French Protestants. In 1722, comparatively late, the Anglicans abandoned their meetinghouse to build the

8. View of New York City, from the east, ca. 1679–80. Drawing by Jaspers Danckaerts.

most impressive church yet constructed in the mainland colonies — St. Philip's — which still dominated the Charleston skyline down to 1752, when the construction of St. Michael's Church gave Charleston two major Anglican churches. In Boston, King's Chapel challenged Dissenting competitors not only with its existence but with its stone construction, a sharp contrast to the old wooden Congregational buildings, and also with the fact that patrons doubled its size in 1710. In the next thirty years, new construction by the old Puritan congregations brought forth larger, taller buildings, nearly all with bell towers.[29]

Colonial America's urban Anglican churches capped the increasing display of material opulence in worship. Here, in sacred settings, were even more impressive hand-carved wooden pews, massive pulpits, velvet seat cushions, hanging lamps, two-ton bells, and silver chalices and plates for communion rites. Neither budgets nor available skills could produce all these objects in-

9. View of New York City, ca. 1730. The spires or towers of (from left to right) the Trinity Church, Lutheran Church, New Dutch Church, French Church, City Hall, Old Dutch Church, Secretary's Office, and the church in Fort George can be seen. Engraving by I. Carwitham.

stantly. Communion silver was obtained from London through the 1720s and then increasingly purchased from American-trained silversmiths; organ building, however, remained a relatively rare craft, dominated by European-trained craftsmen down to the Revolution. But Anglicans—as well as Congregationalists, Presbyterians, and even Baptists (at least in New England)—pressed on, refining, enlarging, rebuilding, refinishing, and enlarging again, each time conveying the importance of public Christian display in a wealthy, hierarchical, increasingly differentiated society.[30]

The growing splendor of the late Stuart churches intertwined with the rise of an informal social and political aristocracy. Though not always obvious in rural congregations, it was blatantly so in urban ones. Everywhere, members of the burgeoning imperial aristocracy contributed to Anglican church construction. Usually they were joined by current and would-be members of the local merchant elite who sought to signify their support for the monarchy and their readiness for government contracts. The range of the contributors was impressive. In Boston donors to Anglican construction included Congregationalists and Presbyterians; in New York they included Dutch Reformed, French Huguenots, and Jews; and in Philadelphia they included Quakers and Presbyterians.[31]

The construction of churches empowered institutional Christianity in the New World as much as in the Old. So too did the creation of disciplinary bodies to define and exercise authority within the Christian denominations active in early America. Like the sacralization and resacralization of the colonial landscape, this too largely occurred between 1680 and 1760, not earlier.

In both New England and the Delaware Valley around Philadelphia, Dissenters established disciplinary institutions to strengthen their denominational organization. Though these efforts occurred simultaneously with the Anglican campaign, important differences separated their efforts. The Anglican campaign was a truly broad effort that extended from Massachusetts to South Carolina. Dissenting institutions created between 1680 and 1720, in contrast, were regional and extended beyond their original boundaries only after 1740. The Anglican campaign involved direct financial help from London. Dissenters built on Old World organizational models but derived little monetary aid from England, where most Dissenting groups were in decline. Yet by the 1760s, the law and early church construction to the contrary, it was Dissenters, not Anglicans, who prospered. Dissenting denominations established the disciplinary institutions that characterized American Christianity for three centuries. England's state church never completed its own institutional maturation before the Crown it supported lost the colonies it served.

New Englanders moved only slowly toward vigorous, collective denominational institutions, even after 1680. In theory, outside ecclesiastical bodies could not exercise authority over an individual congregation. As a result New England's clergy—the "theocrats" against whom historians used to rail—met only in "consociations," which were largely fraternal clerical gatherings in which ministers discussed common problems but exercised no authority over those who attended, much less over congregations. The fragility of the two major seventeenth-century documents that came out of ministers' meetings, the Cambridge Platform of 1648 and the Half-Way Covenant of 1662, was demonstrated by the fact that half or more of New England's congregation ignored them.[32]

By the 1680s, however, New England consociations were becoming ministerial associations. The first was organized in Cambridge, Massachusetts, in 1690. Its model was English, quite literally. Charles Morton, serving as clerk, took a record book he had used in the 1650s to keep minutes for the ministerial association in Cornwall, turned it upside down, and began the minutes of the new Cambridge Association at the other end. Over the next half century other ministerial associations emerged in New England, and there were perhaps as many as six or seven by 1750. Most called themselves associations; some used the name "presbytery," as did the Presbytery of New Londonderry, formed in the 1740s. In comparison to the institutions that emerged in the Delaware Valley among Quakers, Baptists, and Presbyterians, they remained relatively powerless. They certified ordination candidates, but ordination and hiring remained in the hands of town and parish authorities. Similarly, though the associations regularly offered advice in congregational disputes, legal establishment protected individual ministers. It was extremely difficult to discipline wayward colleagues, especially in the face of unwilling town and parish majorities. Most associations were reluctant to promote proselytizing or sponsor the formation of new congregations, because both often challenged existing town and parish structures. Those looking for theocracies in the eighteenth century would have to look past Puritan New England.[33]

It was the Delaware Valley that became the citadel of denominational authority in prerevolutionary America. This achievement involved the transplanting of older, sometimes weakening, institutions among English Dissenters. Alongside Philadelphia's splendid Christ Church, Dissenters formed denominational meetings of such power that the region all but replaced Boston as the capital of Dissenting Christianity in Britain's New World colonies. By 1740—indeed, as early as 1710—Boston could claim little that rivaled the authority, prestige, and institutional sophistication of the Quakers' Philadelphia Yearly Meeting, the Presbytery and, later, Synod of Philadelphia, and the Philadelphia Baptist Association.

The success of Quaker settlement in Pennsylvania in the 1680s and 1690s occurred as Quakerism itself changed. George Fox, its founder, died in 1691. The movement, always disputatious and containing many unharmonized tensions, faced schisms, including one led by William Rogers as Penn sailed for America in the fall of 1682. Early Quaker radicalism, symbolized in part in Fox's miracle working, gave way to Penn's "quietism," which stressed greater inward contemplation and outward peaceableness. Immigration too challenged Quaker discipline. The very success of Pennsylvania created an influx of settlers whose numbers overwhelmed Quaker leaders. Gone were the old face-to-face communities that had reinforced theological commitments. Thrown together in the New World, many Quakers were now strangers even if they also remained Friends.[34]

Pennsylvania Quakers moved more swiftly than Virginia Anglicans and New England Puritans to establish a centralized institutional structure. The first "monthly meeting" for business was put in place in January 1683, and a quarterly meeting appeared a month later. Quakers constructed meetinghouses, purchased record books, and registered certificates from the English meetings that were flooding in. By 1684 the Philadelphia Friends had smoothed out differences with earlier settlers in Burlington, New Jersey, and had established the Philadelphia Yearly Meeting, exercising institutional authority across all Quaker meetings in Pennsylvania and East and West New Jersey.[35]

The Quaker meeting system in Pennsylvania followed the hierarchicalism of its English predecessor. Business meetings were small. In Philadelphia the monthly meeting was attended by no more than seven to ten people. This was also the size of the monthly meeting in rural Chester County, though there were at least four times as many Philadelphia worshipers as Chester County worshipers. "Public Friends," who were, in fact, preachers, dominated both quarterly and yearly meetings. Although George Fox criticized them for not forming a separate ministerial meeting immediately, he needn't have worried about their control of Delaware Valley Quakerism. After founding their separate organization in September 1685, they long exercised a double authority over Friends in the colony. They dominated worship when they appeared to preach, and they constituted virtually the entire membership of the Philadelphia Yearly Meeting, which they also advised in their separate gathering as the Philadelphia Meeting of Ministers and Elders.[36]

This hierarchicalism and ministerial dominance prompted criticism. By 1690 the Scottish Friend, George Keith, complained that the Public Friends in the New World were altogether too powerful. He formally asked the Friends—actually the ministers themselves—to develop a formal Quaker creed, to require statements of "what God hath wrought in them" (not unlike the Puritan practice), and to include all newly tested members in business meetings. The result was another Quaker schism, this one occurring in the New World. It attracted support from farmers and small merchants, from modest Friends distressed by ministerial haughtiness, and from Scottish Friends who resented English Quaker dominance. The rout of the Keithians revealed the power of institutional authority within an infant New World Quakerism. Keith called the ministers "fools, ignorant heathens," and "infidels." With the help of supporters, he tore down the special galleries where the ministers sat in Philadelphia's Quaker meetinghouse. Violence proved no match for disciplinary rigor, however. Although Keith drew about a quarter of the Delaware Valley Friends to his side, the Philadelphia Yearly Meeting disowned Keith in September 1692, under the Public Friends' guidance, and the London Yearly Meeting did the same in September 1694. Some of Keith's followers became Baptists, and others became Anglicans, as did Keith himself, who scoured the Delaware Valley for converts after returning to America as an Anglican missionary in 1701.[37]

Ironically, the Quakers soon broadened their leadership and made it oligarchic if not democratic. Beginning in the late 1690s, the Delaware Valley Friends invested prestigious nonministering Friends with more authority. In 1695 the Philadelphia Yearly Meeting ordered the appointment of two "weighty" Friends or "overseers" for each monthly meeting, to inquire into personal behavior such as "tattling, tale-bearing, backbiting, whispering, and meddling in other men's business." Within a decade the overseers were sitting with ministers in Public Friends' galleries at meetings for worship; one meeting ordered all worshipers "to sit with their faces toward the galleries." Quakers also conducted more "retired" meetings for worship, which were carried on in silence and without sermons from the Public Friends. These subsequently came to typify Quaker worship.[38]

New meetings and new regulations paralleled the oligarchic broadening of the Quaker ecclesiastical system. Special quarterly meetings for young people appeared in 1696, although they apparently did not continue long into the eighteenth century. About 1700 "preparative" meetings, in which overseers approved subjects to be discussed at both quarterly and monthly meetings, began to precede quarterly meetings. The Philadelphia Yearly Meeting began enjoining specific kinds of behavior and habits. Slavery came in for brief condemnation, although the yearly meeting readily created separate worship services for Africans (in 1700) and refused to condemn slaveholding until the 1750s. Instead, the yearly meeting focused more tightly on dress and formal behavior, forbidding "vain, needless things," public pipe smoking, Quaker attendance at non-Quaker funerals, and children's dress, concerns that typified the Quaker approach to religion and life for a half century.[39]

Baptist settlement in the Delaware Valley occurred at a dispiriting moment in English Baptist history. In 1690 only a third of the English congregations existing in the 1660s still survived, and virtually every one of them was smaller than it once had been. The Baptist national assembly formed in 1689 had collapsed in 1692, and the declining congregations were divided theologically, among Calvinists, Arminians, and Sabbatarians, and ethnically, Welsh Baptists maintaining a separate organization from their English counterparts.[40]

In the Delaware Valley, Baptist denominational order emerged in a three-stage process. In the first stage Baptists in small, widely separated congregations cooperated to share ministers and congregational life. A congregation at Middletown, New Jersey, organized in the 1690s by English Calvinist Baptists, managed its own affairs. A congregation at Pennepek, north of Philadelphia, formed a complex, four-part church with worshipers in Pennepek, Philadelphia, and at Burlington and Cohansey in West New Jersey, among whom it rotated a minister for Sabbath services. A second stage centered on solving ministerial and liturgical problems among an increasing and increasingly diverse number of Baptists in the area. After the unexpected death of its second minister in 1702, the Pennepek congregation proved so unable to choose among two competing elders for the post that it proposed to cast lots "to see which god would Chuse to be our pastor," although one of the elders finally withdrew from consideration, allowing the other to be named minister. Tensions over the rite of "laying on of hands" in baptism increased ethnic tensions among English and Welsh Baptists and prompted a meeting in June 1706 to resolve the differences. In May 1707 Baptists in both New Jersey and Pennsylvania agreed to meet yearly to "consult about such things as were wanting in the Church and set them in order."[41]

The Philadelphia Baptist Association, founded in September 1707, emerged as archetypically English. It was a regional association and only slowly drew constituent congregations from beyond Pennsylvania, New Jersey, and the Delaware Valley. It was also ministerial, though in typical Baptist fashion it defined the ministry broadly: it included "deacons" and "elders" as well as preaching ministers, and association meetings were carried on "in the work of the public ministry and by whom the public ministry of the word should be carried on." Its first major task was the examination of preaching credentials and a prohibition on preaching by strangers who lacked recommendations from England.[42]

As early as 1710 the association successfully solved major disputes at Pennepek and Middletown. In the next decade it worked to promote ministerial labor. In 1722 it secured funding from a wealthy London Baptist, Thomas Hollis, to finance clerical education in England for promising Delaware Valley youths, though no students were ever sent. A year later it laid down rules for examining newly arrived English and Welsh ministers and for preaching when no ordained minister was available. Misconduct in Piscataway, New Jersey, demonstrated how the association solidified its authority and power. In 1728 or 1729 the Piscataway congregation ordained Henry Loveall as its minister, despite an association suggestion that they wait until Loveall had preached to them for a trial period. After ordaining him, the congregation discovered that Loveall was an impostor named Desolate Baker who had changed his name to hide a bigamous second marriage, sexual liaisons with slaves and Indians, and even a case of syphilis. The association used Piscataway's predicament to shame it into acknowledging the association's authority. Nathaniel Jenkins, the association's correspondent, flippantly observed that Desolate Baker's alias was all too well suited to "one who loves so well the Black, the swarthy and the white." But he found no humor in the congregation's behavior: "As persons Infatuated you have Rushed on without rule or presidence to Ordain a Man for the Ministry that is hardly fit to be a Common or private member." Why had they only accepted advice about Baker from an uninformed visiting minister from South Carolina, Jenkins asked. "Were there no ministers belonging to your own Association? . . . Consider the reproach you have brought on your profession hereby. I am ashamed of it. I could have told you."[43]

Over the next forty years, the Philadelphia Baptist Association continued to sustain the Baptist ministry and solve congregational problems through its exercise of denominational authority. This frequently occurred in providing answers to congregational queries. The exchanges of 1745 were typical. The association was asked whether unordained persons could preach publicly (yes, but only under the most limited circumstances), whether unordained deacons and ruling elders could exercise their offices (only if they were being tried to determine their fitness for the office), if women could vote in church matters (a long answer: no, but women, "as members of the body of the church, [have] liberty to give a mute voice, by standing or lifting up of the hands" just as they must be able to "discharge their conscience and duty towards God and men" in confessing their faith or defending themselves against malicious accusations), whether congregations should associate with congregations that restricted communion to their own members (everyone should cooperate), and whether persons who would not qualify for communion could serve as association delegates (no).[44]

Thus, though the association wrote in 1749 that it was not a "supreme judicature" but consisted of "independent churches," which had "a complete power and authority from Jesus Christ," its activities belied its words. It exercised authority and power not in principle but in practice, and the association expanded as it did so. By 1762 it contained 25 congregations and 1,318 baptized adults as members. By 1776 those numbers had increased about 80 percent to 42 congregations and 3,013 baptized adult members. Statistics themselves became a major sign of Baptist institutional sophistication. Baptists took considerable interest in numbers and by the 1760s counted not only baptized adult members but five other kinds of people as well: newly baptized adults, members received from other congregations, those dismissed to go to other congregations, persons excommunicated, and the dead. The figures reflected far more than empty bureaucratic formalities. A religious people renowned for precision and institutional propriety were creating ways to manage church adherence in a vigorously mobile New World society.[45]

The origins of the Presbytery of Philadelphia reveal the full dimensions of the Dissenting denominational achievement in the middle colonies after 1680. Looking back from the twentieth century, the founding of the presbytery appears perfectly natural: what could have been more inevitable than the emergence of Presbyterian churches and synods among the largely Scottish settlers of the Delaware Valley? In fact innumerable obstacles hindered creation of any Presbyterian synod in Philadelphia, much less a powerful and successful one. First, as Ned Landsman has demonstrated, before 1720 Scots came from a variety of religious backgrounds, Quaker and Anglican (the Church of Scotland) as well as Presbyterian, and many belonged to no group, much like the immigrants from England. Second, as Marilyn Westerkamp has shown, the potential members of a presbytery were divided by ethnic, national, and ecclesiastical differences; even in Scotland and northern Ireland major disputes separated those claiming the Presbyterian label. Third, immediate models for presbyterian order and activity were absent, desultory, or irrelevant. No other presbyteries existed in the colonies, the 1691 union of Congregationalists and Presbyterians in England had disbanded by 1694, and the Scottish presbyteries were frequently concerned with church-state issues of little meaning in the American and immigrant context.[46]

The Presbytery of Philadelphia originated in 1706 as a ministerial, not a congregational, organization. Francis Makemie, one of its founders, wrote that it was formed "to consult the most proper measures, for advancing religion, and propagating Christianity" and to improve "Ministeriall ability" by hearing and criticizing sermons. These fraternal instincts blossomed, but the Presbytery of Philadelphia and the larger Synod of Philadelphia that succeeded it in 1716 became far better known for exercising authority over congregations than for promoting fraternal relations among ministers. Their authority stemmed from three sources: traditional Christian regard for the ordained clergy, a commitment to hierarchical notions of church government, and the incorporation of lay elders from local congregations in the presbytery's meetings. The admission of the lay elders empowered presbytery and synod ministers, not the laity. It symbolized the congregations' assent to presbyterian authority, much as the existence of the parliament symbolized the people's acquiescence to royal authority in both England and France. But unlike in England and, later, in France, the lay elders never used their admission to the presbytery and synod to usurp power from the ministers or to dominate the presbytery.[47]

The laity did not triumph in Delaware Valley Presbyterianism. Ministers were the permanent members of the presbyteries and synod, and lay elders were transitory, dependent visitors. In theory laymen could outnumber ministers at presbytery and synod meetings, because each congregation could send two elders with its minister to the denominational gatherings. Yet this happened only once during the entire colonial period, when eight lay elders and seven ministers attended the 1714 meeting. Indeed, the gap between ministers and elders grew. In 1765 forty-three ministers and seventeen elders attended the Synod of Philadelphia, and in 1775 twenty-five ministers and five elders came. Elders attended presbytery meetings only in the presence of their ministers, moreover, and exceptions were usually caused by a minister's sickness or other indisposition. Although after 1760 elders began to sit on some of the presbytery and synod committees, they never chaired them. Presbytery and synod clerks, the presiding officers, were always ministers, and the ministers enjoyed the privilege of having their names recorded as absent if they could not attend, while the absence of the elders went unnoticed.[48]

The Presbytery of Philadelphia sustained its authority and extended its power by in effect guaranteeing the work that ministers did. It tested orthodoxy and quality by controlling the ordination process. It approved candidates' education and examined their knowledge and doctrines. It sought ministers through Scottish presbyteries as early as 1708, and it sought financial help from an influential London Dissenter, Sir Edmund Harrison, in order to compete with Anglican proselytizing and church building. It arranged for visits to congregations without a minister by neighboring clergymen. It guided ministers in answering "calls" from congregations looking for permanent ministers, and it only forwarded calls from congregations that accepted its authority and promised to pay ministers regularly and well. It restricted balloting for calling a minister to "those that shall contribute for the maintenance of him," but it tried to smooth relations between more prosperous and poorer worshipers by requiring that "the major vote" of all contributors "shall be determinative." Like the Philadelphia Baptist Association, the Philadelphia presbytery and synod also settled disputes. They censured congregations that hired unqualified ministers without its supervision. The presbytery's lecture to one such congregation uncannily echoed the Philadelphia Baptists' treatment of their wayward Piscataway congregation: "We could have wished you had taken better advised steps for your provision."[49]

The Philadelphia presbytery's tough, well-honed denominational order accounted for much of its continuing growth. When it split its membership into three subordinate presbyteries and created the Synod of Philadelphia in 1716, it contained 27 ministers and 30 congregations. The new synod supervised the work of the presbyteries, and its membership already stretched beyond the Delaware Valley as far as New York and Maryland. This process of numerical increase and institutional subdivision typified its subsequent growth in America. By 1740 the synod had 6 presbyteries and 50 ministers. By 1770 it counted 9 presbyteries and more than 120 ministers, now spread from northern Virginia to New York.[50]

Other, more recent immigrants from the European continent also turned to authoritative, coercive institutions to discipline congregational order in their New World settlements. The German Calvinists or German Reformed, as they were frequently called, organized a Coetus in 1747, and German Lutherans established the Lutheran Ministerium of Pennsylvania a year later in 1748. Both were ministerial organizations, and their actions were similar to those of the English Baptist association and the Presbyterian synod. They extended their power by governing through service, providing orthodox and decorous ministers to congregations in exchange for acquiescence to collective ministerial authority. In 1745, even before the ministerium was formally organized, Henry Melchior Muhlenberg forced the lay elders of a new congregation at Tulpehocken to submit to the judgment of the Lutheran ministers in Pennsylvania as their "spiritual guides and shepherds, investing them with full authority to watch over our souls in whatever manner they see fit, and by whatever agency, and for as long [a] time as may be agreeable to them."[51]

Disputes revealed the full importance of coercive institutional authority among Delaware Valley Christians in the mid-eighteenth century. For a half century members of the Philadelphia synod argued over the adoption of the Westminster Confession, the disciplining of ministerial misconduct, and most dramatically, standards for ordination, including a requirement that candidates should demonstrate their own religious experience. The disputants carried on their arguments within the presbyterial arena precisely because the presbyteries' authority and power made the outcome significant. None of the disputants rejected the principles of institutional order, authority, and coercion; rather, they fought over them. Their arguments, which threatened Presbyterian cohesion, were eloquent testimony to the institutional authority that Presbyterians had created in the previous fifty years.[52]

Quakers, despite major changes in their movement, demonstrated a similar attachment to institutional prowess. Between 1750 and 1770 the Pennsylvania Friends accomplished what Jack Marietta has called the "reformation of American Quakerism." Quakerism shifted from a churchlike group, in which membership had become increasingly innocuous and which made allowances for frequent violations of behavioral rules, to a sect requiring separation from society. Quakers tightened discipline, censured most transgressors, disowned others, and withdrew from politics in a colony they had once thoroughly dominated. This reformation deepened the introspection, pacifism, abolitionism, charity, and educational reforms for which nineteenth-century Quakerism became known. Most important, the reform was accomplished from the top down by an elite of Public and weighty Friends who enforced their demands through the Quaker meeting system. Yet though the reformation cost Pennsylvania Quakerism from a third to perhaps as much as a half of its following, no schism occurred. Even minor resistance was uncommon; backsliders drifted away rather than rebelled. In the process mid-eighteenth-century Quakerism transformed itself almost as smoothly as it had planted itself sixty years earlier, and functioned in both periods with a coercive institutional structure.[53]

Ironically, it was the Anglicans who failed to achieve disciplinary rigor and authority in prerevolutionary America. Put simply, their capacity to erect buildings was never matched by success at building authoritative institutions. Worship, churches, ministers, and books did not make a church — at least not the Church of England. The SPG had sent over six hundred ministers to the colonies by the time of the Revolution. The SPCK had sent thousands of books. The Anglican campaign of 1680–1720 brought one hundred churches to the colonies, and the effort did not stop. Between 1760 and 1776 another one hundred Anglican churches were constructed in the colonies, often in the new frontier areas created by accelerating westward movement.[54]

But ultimately the Church of England failed in America because it was forced into compromises Dissenters avoided. No bishop was ever appointed for America. The commissary system failed, more fully in some colonies than in others, but with sufficient consistency to allow no significant success anywhere. Ministers met occasionally in clerical gatherings, but these meetings failed to develop even the fraternal cohesion characteristic of New England's weak consociations and presbyteries, much less the disciplinary stature of Dissenting institutions elsewhere. Parish clergymen provided Sabbath services for congregations without their own minister but in the main found such labor as unpleasant in America as they had in England. The result was the supreme irony of early American denominational development: the failure of the

Anglican church in Britain's American colonies, a failure caused not by its inability to adjust to American individualism but by its inability to transplant its institutional authority in the ways the Dissenters did so successfully.

The years between 1680 and 1760 marked a thorough revolution of colonial America's seventeenth-century religious patterns. The state church tradition was firmly if not perfectly replanted. Cities became centers of ecclesiastical splendor. Rural areas received churches, bells, and ministers where there had been none. Dissenters fashioned sophisticated, complex, and authoritative denominational institutions. In pursuing these achievements, Europeans in America did not flee their past; they embraced it. They moved toward the exercise of authority, not away from it, and they understood that individual religious observance prospered best in the New World environment through the discipline of coercive institutional authority.

But as Anglicans, Baptists, Congregationalists, German Reformed, Lutherans, Presbyterians, and Quakers drew on institutional authority to sustain and expand their own religious traditions in the New World, other residents of the colonies, forced there against their will, encountered quite different results of the spectacular transformation of institutional Christianity in eighteenth-century America. For them, the embrace of authority, so positive for English settlers and religious groups, proved voraciously destructive.

SLAVERY AND THE AFRICAN SPIRITUAL HOLOCAUST

5

Between 1680 and 1760, slavery transformed the American colonies. All the southern colonies — Maryland, Virginia, North and South Carolina, and Georgia — and many northern ones — especially New York, Pennsylvania, and Rhode Island — exploited a captive, coerced labor force that had been used only rarely in previous decades. The enslavement of Africans originated in the colonists' desire for cheap labor and in English prejudice, first against "heathens" — despite their own highly erratic church adherence before 1680 — and then against persons of color.[1]

The great rise in slave ownership by colonists paralleled the resurgence of institutional Christianity in the colonies after 1680. However accidental their interaction, Christianity and colonial slavery shaped each other in powerful ways. After 1680 Christianity molded the *kind* of slavery that touched so much in American society of the eighteenth century and later. Led by Anglicans and later powerfully reinforced by Presbyterian, Baptist, and Methodist leaders, clergymen articulated a planter ethic of absolute slave obedience that ran thoroughly counter to contemporary English political and social theory and became a principal foundation of American slavery's distinctive paternalism, violence, and sentimentalism in late colonial and antebellum society.

Those who molded and imbibed slavery also produced the

single most important religious transformation to occur in the American colonies before 1776: an African spiritual holocaust that forever destroyed traditional African religious systems as *systems* in North America and that left slaves remarkably bereft of traditional collective religious practice before 1760. The supreme irony of this holocaust was that it paved the way for a remarkable post-1760 slave Christianization, whose first appearances more closely resembled European expressions of Christianity than might ever be the case again. Together the rise of Christian absolutism and the creation of an African spiritual holocaust demonstrate how and why, despite its vagaries, renewed Christian activity in eighteenth-century America could powerfully reshape New World society, European and African alike.

Understanding how Christianity and slavery interacted in eighteenth-century America requires a preliminary look at several secular matters. One concerns a disjuncture between law and social practice. Although slavery had emerged by 1650, it did not become economically or socially significant until the period between 1680 and 1760. By 1660 the law in each colony established slavery's most elemental forms: the owner possessed the slave, the slave's labor, and the slave's progeny. Yet beyond the island colony of Barbados, this newly legalized slavery meant relatively little. Before 1680 most mainland colony planters used English indentured servants as laborers. Slaveholding remained uncommon, even in Maryland and Virginia. Down to 1680 Africans made up less than 10 percent of the Maryland and Virginia population, and even then between 10 and 20 percent of the region's Africans were free rather than enslaved.[2]

This early slavery was quite different from its post-1680 successor, moreover. Early slavery was certainly slavery. As T. H. Breen and Stephen Innes have demonstrated for seventeenth-century Virginia, planters owned Africans in perpetuity, harvested their labor and progeny, and permitted them few legal rights and liberties. But early slavery was also more informal and less brutal than its successor. The fledgling institution generated relatively few reports of violence against slaves. It also tolerated and perhaps even encouraged surprising numbers of manumissions. Between 1650 and 1680, free Africans worked, prospered, and even owned slaves themselves in Virginia. The Africans' freedom was limited, of course. Whites were suspicious of them, and their social boundaries were far more circumscribed than was true for British settlers, including indentured servants. Still, early Virginia and Maryland slavery was not nearly as oppressive as its eighteenth-century counterpart.[3]

Slaveholding underwent explosive growth in the mainland colonies after 1680. Its demographics outline the story. In Maryland, the proportion of Africans in the population stood at 13 percent by 1700, 18 percent by 1710, and 30 percent by 1762, and after 1750 slaves made up nearly half of the population in several Maryland counties. Virginia experienced a similar growth in slaveholding, although its lack of censuses makes it impossible to chart the expansion as closely as in Maryland. South Carolina, founded in the 1670s by English West Indian planters, outstripped both Chesapeake Bay colonies. Slaves formed a third of South Carolina's population by 1700, half by 1708, and over 60 percent through the 1790s; as early as 1740, slaves made up as much as 90 percent of the population in some South Carolina counties, and this pattern held true into the early nineteenth century. Nor was slavery confined to the South. Slaves in Rhode Island, New Jersey, and Pennsylvania accounted for between 6 and 9 percent of those colonies' populations after 1700. In New York, slaves were between 12 and 18 percent of the total population between 1700 and 1770 and as much as 25 percent of the population of New York City and its environs, a figure that rivaled the slaveholding record of many southern counties.[4]

On the surface, Christianity's role in shaping American slavery might seem to have been minimal. Moses Finley has observed that most ancient, medieval, and modern religious systems supported slavery, and that Christianity was no exception to this rule. Whether in ancient Greece and Rome or in early modern Spain, pagans and Christians rationalized slaveholding in ways that satisfied owners, if not slaves. Richard Dunn and Gary Puckrein have documented that in the English West Indies, slavery's astonishing growth occurred without any significant push from Christianity. Indeed, the West Indies furnished a ready model for mainland colony slavery, especially when the West Indies planters turned to the Carolinas to expand their plantation empires in the 1670s and 1680s.[5]

Yet several considerations prompt a further look at the relationship between Christianity and slaveholding in colonial America. First, mainland colony slavery did not follow the West Indian model. West Indian slavery was even more harsh and cruel than its mainland counterpart. Slaves quickly came to outnumber English settlers by mammoth margins that exceeded the population disparity characteristic of slavery in South Carolina. West Indian slaves died rapidly and those that survived reproduced themselves only fitfully throughout the colonial period. West Indian plantations were extremely large; many planters owned a hundred slaves and some owned several thousand.[6]

Mainland colony slavery had some quite different characteristics. Gross population imbalance occurred in only a few places. Slaves began to reproduce themselves in the Chesapeake Bay area by the 1730s and simultaneously experienced a significant decline in mortality rates. The native-born slave population was longer-lived and more capable of asserting at least some control over its immediate environment. And mainland colony slavery was relatively intimate. Most slaveholders owned from ten to twenty slaves between 1680 and 1760, and few owned more than fifty.[7]

Second, if anything, the English associated Christianity and especially Protestantism with freedom rather than with enslavement. Certainly they knew far less about Christianity's support for ancient slavery than do modern historians. To the extent that the English thought about it, they credited Christianity with the abolition of the medieval institution of villeinage. As the Elizabethan writer Sir Thomas Smith put it, villeinage declined because Christians would not "make or keepe his brother in Christ, servile, bond, or underling for ever unto him, as a beast rather than as a man." Smith's probable historical errors on villeinage aside, he articulated widely held views about the relationship between Protestant Christianity and individual freedom. If anything, these views might have inclined English colonists to worry that their own or their slaves' Christianity might preclude slaveholding, which was otherwise economically attractive.[8]

Even in slavery's earliest years and certainly before 1720, mainland colonists voiced fears about slave baptism and conversion that were strongly reminiscent of Smith's comments on villeinage. Despite the meager presence of institutional Christianity in the early Chesapeake Bay area, the small number of slaves, and the near total absence of slave conversions to Christianity, colonists viewed Christianity as a real bar to slaveholding and, certainly, to effective slave management. The Maryland and Virginia assemblies felt obliged to assure potential slave owners that slave baptisms would not abolish the servitude and labor they expected to reap from their Africans. It was Christianity's potential social effects, not its theology, that concerned prospective slaveholders. Christianization empowered slaves, just as it empowered the English—as the latter were beginning to notice in an age of rapid parish development and church building. Christianized slaves not only became "proud" but "irascible," "uppity," and "saucy"—words whose recitation assumed an almost ritual lilt among slaveholding planters and farmers even before 1720.[9]

Planter complaints about slave conversion did not abate until the 1750s and in fact never really ended. As late as 1770 Anglican and Dissenting clergymen were still assuring listeners that slave baptism did not compromise slave ownership. Colonial legislatures passed and repassed earlier legislation that denied freedom to baptized slaves. Winthrop Jordan points out that some legislatures denied the ability of slaves to become Christians. The Virginia Assembly determined in 1699 that the "Gros Barbarity and rudeness of their manners, the variety and Strangeness of their Languages and the weakness and Shallowness of their minds" made conversion impossible, or so the legislators hoped.[10]

Equally striking, colonists' worries about slave Christianization reflected a complex mix of theological uncertainty and ethical anxiety about growing problems with slaves and slaveholding. Planters almost never quoted Scripture or cited doctrine to buttress their rejection of slave baptism, and their complaints remained theologically uninformed throughout the colonial period. Two South Carolina Anglican ministers, Francis Le Jau and Robert Maule, traced planter concern to the results of their obvious religious indifference. "I really believe they speak so unwisely through ignorance," Le Jau lamented. Yet planters often exhibited a remarkable guilt about slaveholding, and this guilt seems to have been unconnected to the very modest advances of Christianization among either themselves or their slaves. Planters regularly denied to others that slavery was vicious, mean, or cruel; they constantly claimed that their own slaves were well fed, well treated, and fairly employed even if other slaves were not. At the same time, they avoided slaves in situations that tested their own ethical and religious principles, especially when the test was public. Communion offered such an occasion, even among planters learning and relearning Christianity. Without at all implying that he believed his slaves were inferior to him, one South Carolina planter told Le Jau that he had "resolved never to come to the Holy Table while slaves are received." Another worriedly asked a simple, telling question: "If any of my slaves go to Heaven, . . . must I see them there?"[11]

The possibility that Christianity could shape the dramatic post-1680 expansion of slavery in America was further underlined by the slaveholding options available to late seventeenth- and early eighteenth-century English planters. These options were real, not moot. Even in the late seventeenth century, not all slave systems were the same. Orlando Patterson's study of contemporary world slave systems, *Slavery and Social Death,* reveals the great variety of slaveholding practices not only in ancient times but in early modern times as well. Some systems were lenient and relatively flexible. They enslaved adults only, excluded children and progeny, offered legal protection from wayward owners, and provided for swift and easy manumission. Other systems were vicious, some extraordinarily so. They enslaved captives of all ages, refused to recognize family units, denied all legal rights and liberties, restricted or refused manumission, and often used slaves as sacrificial offerings to the gods. Only the last characteristic did not typify slaveholding in British America.[12]

Variety thus impelled choices, and the law demonstrated how British colonists turned slavery away from some forms of development to embrace others. Colonial assemblies that limited wage labor performed by slaves for others, sometimes for the slaves' profit and sometimes for the profit of owners, rejected a more pliant, malleable slave economy which was already advancing among them but which some viewed as threatening to the owners' authority. Similarly, the magistrates and planters who skewered the severed heads of rebel slaves on poles erected at prominent places after New York City's slave rebellions of 1712 and 1741 and in South Carolina after the Stono Rebellion of 1739 (they had first disemboweled the slaves and then hanged them) deliberately chose to stress the violence permitted to owners and governments in suppressing threats to slaveholding and in upholding slavery as a cultural artifact. As slavery evolved from a minor curiosity to a major determinant of American culture, these choices, not surprisingly, also involved conceptions of authority. The rising number of clergymen in the southern colonies soon found themselves addressing increasingly important questions of obedience, obligation, and punishment, and they did so with a thoroughness and breadth not found in any other contemporary source. We can never know how American slavery would have emerged without the ministers' contributions, but we can know how those contributions shaped the slavery that did emerge in the colonies.[13]

The unique Anglican domination of Christian institutional life in the late seventeenth-century southern colonies dictated Anglican dominance of public comment on slavery. These discussions emerged not only quickly but with acute awareness of the choices facing American planters and society. This was most obvious in the sustained comment of William Fleetwood, bishop of St. Asaph, reforming Anglican, SPG activist, and political Whig, whose complex and important discussion of slavery appeared in 1705, only four years after the entrance of SPG ministers into the American colonies. At 495 pages, *The Relative Duties of Parents and Children, Husbands and Wives, Masters and Servants,* was not a work for the typical colonial family. But it was a book for those who shaped opinion and society in England and America, and it reflected a remarkable sensitivity and even anxiety about potential difficulties in American slaveholding.[14]

Fleetwood's *Relative Duties* came to slaveholding only after discussing more traditional English servitude in the context of Paul's advice to the Corinthians (1 Cor. 22–24), "Servants, obey in all things, your Masters according to the Flesh." Of course, like all Whigs who supported the Glorious Revolution of 1688, Fleetwood immediately qualified Paul's words. "Neither Father, Husband, nor Master, nor any Superiour whatsoever, is to be obeyed *in all things,*" he wrote. "Obedience in that Restriction or Reserve, belongs to no Mortal Man," since the "Laws of the Land" and the "Commands of God" preceded the wishes of masters. Indeed, servants were not only permitted to confront and disobey masters in certain situations but were obligated to do so. "Where the case is plain and evident, and the execution of the Command must certainly be hurtful to them, as opposing some Command of God, there they must needs dispute and disobey . . . No body excuses them for acting by Authority, for no one has Authority against Justice."[15]

No one except slaveholders. Immediately after investing servants with obligations to disobey errant masters, Fleetwood suddenly distinguished between those who were "captives and downright Slaves, and others [who were] only Servants by agreement." "All are not alike Servants," he cautioned. Then he asked a simple question. Did Paul really mean to say the same thing to each and to place the same obligations of disobedience on "captives and downright slaves" as on those who were "Servants by agreement"? Fleetwood's answer took a crucial step toward developing the ethic that shaped planter concepts of authority, obedience, and punishment. Fleetwood reinterpreted Paul and thereby solved the dilemma created by Whiggish morals in an expanding slave society. Although Paul "said the same Words" to all servants, Fleetwood believed he said them "in different Senses, according to the different condition of their Servitude."

> To the slaves and Captives [Paul] would say, "Obey your Masters in all things, as becomes your sad Condition, and make your Chains as easie as you can, by your Compliance and Submission"; but to the hired Servants he would be understood to say, "obey your Masters in all things, according to your Contract and Agreement, behave your selves as diligently and faithfully, as you have promised them to do, or by the Custom of the Place are presum'd to have promised them."[16]

Fleetwood's dialogue depicted a Paul far more verbose with contractual servants than with slaves. Paul's words to contractual servants used the language of covenants, described promises, and invoked the "custom of the Place" by way of limiting masters' authority. But Paul's words to slaves only lamented their "sad Condition," suggested that easing their chains hinged on their obedience rather than on their masters' goodness, and concluded with a reaffirmation of their obligation for "Compliance and Submission" before masters. In all this Fleetwood denied that he had introduced or articulated new distinctions. "Here is no new Servitude induc'd, nor old one abrogated," Fleetwood claimed. "Servants are left by Christianity just in the State it found them; their Condition is not at all alter'd; but not [made] for the worse, to be sure." As a practical—or impractical—matter, Fleetwood even imagined that servants might refuse "the labour of the Gallies, if their Masters should command them thither," a reference to Louis XIV's notorious use of common criminals and imprisoned Protestants to row French naval vessels, but he remained silent about the tasks slaves might resist.[17]

The sermon Fleetwood delivered at the annual meeting of the SPG in London in 1711 enunciated principles regarding slaveholding and planter ethics that the SPG followed for the next half century in America. Fleetwood gave his sermon in the context of rising SPG concern over slavery's spectacular advances in the colonies and its implications for colonial American religious development. Like earlier speakers before the group, Fleetwood acknowledged that the society's original charge was to Christianize English settlers. But new social realities demanded major new missions to the rapidly increasing slave population as well as to the Indians. Fleetwood condemned owner resistance to slave conversion. Their behavior suggested that the society's old charge had only been compounded by the rise of slavery: "What do these People think of *Christ?*" Fleetwood asked, when questioning their refusal to baptize slaves. The answer was, of course, that too many of them thought not at all about him.[18]

That Fleetwood's sermon came at a unique and early stage in English thinking about slaveholding is clear from his frankness about the conflicts between national economic policy and English and Christian ethics in regard to slavery. To some extent, Fleetwood's interest in both slave and planter conversion complicated the problem of Christianity's relationship to slavery. Fleetwood came down firmly on the side of those who accepted the Africans' full humanity. They were not inferior beings. Fleetwood described the slaves as "equally the Workmanship of God . . . endued with the same Faculty, and intellectual powers; Bodies of the same Flesh and Blood, and Souls as certainly immortal." This view led, in turn, to openness about English choices in national economic policy and to more tightly structured views of owner privileges than those outlined earlier in *The Relative Duties*.[19]

In a forthright argument, Fleetwood declared that Christianity might indeed handle English slaveholding in ways different from current practice. "In an Age so free and fruitful of Laws as ours," Fleetwood said—a reference both to late Stuart activity in economic planning and to the 1689 Toleration Act, passed in the aftermath of the Glorious Revolution—Christianity might, "by the favour of Laws, and by the Indulgence of Princes[,] immediately emancipate and free all Slaves receiving Baptism." But Fleetwood chose slavery over freedom. "I would not have any one's Zeal for Religion (much less my own) so far outrun their Judgment in these matters," he concluded: "We are a People who live and maintain our selves by *Trade;* and that if *Trade* be lost, or overmuch discouraged, we are a ruined Nation; and shall our selves in time becomes as very *Slaves,* as those I am speaking of, tho' in another kind."[20]

Awareness of the potential conflict between Christianity and burgeoning American slaveholding pushed Fleetwood to sharpen the distinction between servitude and slavery made six years earlier in *The Relative Duties.* In his 1711 SPG sermon, Fleetwood turned to Luther's restrictive doctrine of "Christian Liberty" to heighten the claims for slave obedience and planter authority further. Luther's doctrine had emerged from his denunciation of the German Peasants' Revolt of 1524–25 and its incipient social radicalism. Fleetwood echoed Luther's warning. Christian liberty did not free slaves "from all former Engagements." Fleetwood, like Luther and Augustine before him, argued that the "Liberty of Christianity is entirely Spiritual." Baptism "left Men under all the Obligations and Engagements that it found them, with respect to *Liberty* or *Bondage.*" It did "not exempt [anyone] from continuing in the same State of Life he was before." In his reference to "before," of course, Fleetwood adopted an additionally narrowed horizon. He meant Africans as previously unbaptized slaves rather than as previous participants in the native societies from which they had been taken.[21]

In America the emerging Anglican understanding of slavery fitted with uncanny precision the elaboration of slave codes and social behavior that increasingly specified the degraded condition of captive Africans after 1680. As A. Leon Higginbotham has observed, the law that guaranteed liberty to English men and women became the seal of slavery for Africans. More important, like Anglican sentiment on slavery and servitude, the law "itself created the mores of racial repression." It did not idly ratify social convention but played a major role in shaping it. The codes primarily addressed planters, not slaves. Winthrop Jordan has argued that the laws were passed "for the eyes and ears of slave-owners."

"They aimed, paradoxically, at disciplining white men . . . the law told the white man, not the Negro, what [he] must do." The effect was both profound and subtle. The codes instructed owners on their rights against slaves. They advised them of their duty, rather than mere permission, to punish, and reminded them of their rights in court against slaves, of their obligation to hunt down runaways, and, especially, of the absolute necessity to execute rebels. They also instructed owners on the poverty of their slaves' legal rights, and quite unlike the situation with regard to indentured servants, hired laborers, or apprentices, they accomplished this through silence rather than through positive denial.[22]

The Anglican ministers who were flocking to Maryland, Virginia, and the Carolinas at the same time that slaveholding escalated after 1680 rationalized, deepened, and thereby extended the doctrines emerging in the slave codes of the early eighteenth-century southern colonies. One major means was the Anglicans' promotion of slave Christianization. The SPG circulated thousands of copies of Fleetwood's 1711 sermon to missionaries attempting to convince slaveholders of the obligation and benefits of slave proselytization. Two tracts extended Fleetwood's themes in subsequent decades. Bishop George Berkeley's SPG sermon of 1731 stressed the interrelationship of planter religious observance and slave conversion: "The likeliest step towards converting the heathen would be to begin with the English Planters," a reminder that the rapid rise of slaveholding only increased the necessity to promote Christianity among English planters. Thomas Secker's 1741 SPG sermon stressed the utilitarian value of slave conversion for owners. Secker took Mark 6:34, "They were as sheep not having a shepherd: and [Jesus] began to teach them many things," as his text and argued that Christ's principal teaching concerned the subjection of subordinates. Rather than "making any Alteration in Civil Rights," the Gospels taught "that every Man abide in the Condition wherein he is called, with great Indifference of Mind concerning outward Circumstances." Secker was sure this relieved slaves of their rebellious instincts. Christianity made slaves' "Tempers milder, and their Lives happier," taught them "Dutifulness and Loyalty," and helped "create some Dependance in point of Interest." If Africans would agree "in the same Faith and Worship with us," surely, Secker believed, slaves would imbibe "an everlasting Motive to civil Unity."[23]

Yet the Anglican literature that instructed slaves proved even more important to planters. What was written to convey lessons to one group conveyed equally powerful messages to another. Indeed, it was the literature addressed to slaves that became the major instrument through which a planter slaveholding ethic emerged in the mainland British colonies. These writings circulated in enormous numbers. Missionary book orders suggest that Anglican ministers distributed more of these tracts through the southern colonies than any other single type of religious literature. Works such as Edmund Gibson's *Three Addresses on the Instruction of the Negroes* (London, 1727) and Thomas Wilson's *Knowledge and Practice of Christianity Made Easy to the Meanest Capacities* (London, 1741) provided general guidance for slave instruction and sample lessons for both ministers and owners. These tracts ratified all the lessons regarding subjugation and obedience enunciated in the Fleetwood, Berkeley, and Secker sermons (Wilson's manual reprinted Secker's sermon). Wilson particularly stressed lay instruction for slaves; he set out lessons on Christianity and slave obedience that were as instructive to the owners as to the slaves they were teaching.[24]

Anglican clergymen working in America provided the second major means of Anglican instruction to planters. Ministers seldom spoke before slaves alone, in part because owners distrusted the practice and in part because the ministers themselves disliked it. Instead, the ministers nearly always spoke to slaves and owners in each other's presence, and evidence suggests that planters listened attentively to the ministers' strictures on slave obedience. Francis Le Jau provides a telling example. He was a former Huguenot, trained at the University of Dublin but working among English planters in St. James Goose Creek Parish, where slaveholding had rapidly expanded. To handle the sometimes awkward perceptions of Christianity among the English planters, Le Jau invented a new public ritual for use in slave baptism. He gathered the newly converted slaves, owned by the few masters who would allow slave proselytization, and placed them at the front of his new and finely fitted St. James Goose Creek Church (see Figure 10). Before he baptized them and in the presence of attending slaveholders and slaves, he required the candidates to repeat an oath he had prepared especially for the occasion: "that you do not ask for the holy baptism out of any design to free your self from the Duty and

Obedience you owe to your Master while you live." After the slaves repeated this oath, he baptized them. The planters understood the significance of Le Jau's action. Le Jau worried that the slaves viewed their oath cynically. For planters, however, Le Jau's rite offered visual and aural proof of Christianity's practical application for slaveholding and brought them at least partially inside a newly enriched world of Christian doctrine and ritual.[25]

It is true that Fleetwood, Berkeley, Secker, Gibson, and Wilson all implored owners to treat slaves well, citing the planters' responsibility to care for all servants. Ministers working in the colonies were no less concerned. Le Jau frequently criticized planters for their "unjust, profane and Inhumane practices." One planter couple burned a slave to death in retribution for setting fire to their house, and Le Jau took no little pleasure in recording their own death by drowning six months later. Le Jau also protested the South Carolina law that required castration for runaway men

10. St. James Goose Creek Church, South Carolina, ca. 1708.

and the amputation of ears for runaway women. He told the SPG in London that the statute violated "the law of God," specifically Exodus 21:26–27, which "setts a slave at libertty if he should loose an Eye or a tooth when he is Corrected."[26]

But imploring was not commanding, especially among planters whose attachment to Christianity was itself ephemeral. Assertions of planter responsibility reinforced expansive conceptions of planter authority. Although Fleetwood demanded that Christian "Mercy and Compassion be shewn to *all the World* alike," the demand faded before his eagerness to ease planter worry. He wrote, for example, that planters could not "be oblig'd to use [baptized slaves] with *less Rigour,* than the nature and necessity of their Service will admit." Christian ethics had to recognize what Fleetwood now described as the rudimentary realities of slavery.[27]

By the 1740s, Maryland's Thomas Bacon, another Anglican minister, put the matter starkly. In a series of sermons given before both slaveholders and slaves and subsequently published in London in several editions, Bacon encapsulated what he and his ministerial colleagues had shaped as the dominant slaveholding ethic of the colonial South. He knew well that he could only implore masters to show kindness and act with good behavior toward slaves, and the resignation with which he faced the problem revealed his implicit answers to the rhetorical questions he asked: "If our servants neglect or refuse to give us that which is just and equal, the law hath given us power to correct and force them to do it. But if we refuse them that which is just and equal, where is their remedy?" The remedy lay only with the planters, and the question highlighted their powers without delineating their responsibilities.[28]

Lodged within Bacon's sermons was a fully formed doctrine of *absolute* obedience, founded in the ministers' developing understanding of Christianity's relationship to slaveholding. Using a term made even more meaningful by its importance in colonial slavery, Bacon told the slaves—and their owners, of course—that masters were "God's overseers." Slaveholders could expect much from slaves because slaveholders were God's agents. Slaves ought to "do all service for *them* as if [they] did it for *God* himself," Bacon thundered, and owners could expect that slaves would not complain about the "behaviour of your masters and mistresses." Slaves must obey commands that "may be [for]ward, peevish, and hard."

They must even obey commands that forced them into illegal and immoral acts. Even to these commands, disobedience constituted "faults done against God himself." It was not for slaves to object to these acts. God would forgive them in the next world; in this world obedience took precedence over moral courage.[29]

The Anglican contribution to a slaveholder ethic of absolute authority was all the more notable because it so directly rejected other possible modes of handling slaves and slaveholding. Anglicans worked out their new doctrines in a society alive with controversy about obedience and its limits, and two sources held especially potent alternative ways of thinking. After the restoration of the monarchy in 1660, Anglicans frequently argued that citizens should passively obey and should refuse to resist an illicit sovereign because rebellion only produced civil war and regicide. A second source came from high Tories, who rejected the Glorious Revolution of 1688, refused allegiance to William and Mary, and adopted a theory of nonresistance to rationalize their behavior. These Tory doctrines of passive obedience and nonresistance were both politically inexpedient and culturally charged. They were politically inexpedient because most SPG supporters and colonial Anglican ministers supported the Glorious Revolution and rejected high Toryism. They were culturally charged because the doctrines of passive obedience and nonresistance assumed full intelligence and moral virtue in its practitioners. They implied that subjects, servants, or slaves made conscious and informed choices, that such choices were theirs to make, and most important, that they possessed a capacity and even a right to disobey that they merely happened to bypass in this case, perhaps for their own good, perhaps for society's good, but that they might not bypass in the future. In contrast, a doctrine of absolute obedience implied no such choice or capacity in slaves and placed all power with owners. Slaves might or might not be intelligent. They might or might not be moral. Such questions were irrelevant. In this world they simply obeyed.[30]

The doctrine of absolute obedience articulated in the Anglicans' colonial pulpits was important in its own right. But it also became the foundation of the distinctive planter paternalism that gradually characterized American slavery in the colonial and antebellum periods. Eugene Genovese, in his massive study of antebellum slavery, *Roll, Jordan, Roll,* suggested that this paternalism originated in the "close living of masters and slaves" that differentiated slaveholding in the mainland colonies and states from its Caribbean and South American varieties. Alan Gallay has argued that it emerged out of evangelical revivalism, which became common in the colonies in the 1740s. But in fact its origins antedated the 1740s revivals. It emerged in the way colonists shaped the "close living" of slaveholders and slaves, a close living that turned social circumstances into cultural imperatives. Paternalism took root not in an absence of authority but in its overweening presence. Only a "master" possessed of truly extraordinary powers could voluntarily interject the kindnesses and caresses that typified paternal authority on the American farm, and no group or body more clearly articulated those concepts of authority than did the Anglican clergymen and SPG missionaries flooding into the southern colonies at the very time that slavery itself was becoming a meaningful social force.[31]

Anglican ministers moving back and forth from parish to plantation shaped a paternalistic ethic among planters that not only coalesced with the doctrine of absolute obedience but made it all the more palatable and attractive as it made it less stark and ominous. First, the clergymen helped planters explain slave "misbehavior" in ways that solidified the masters' prejudices about slave degradation. The Anglican clergymen transformed planter views about laziness, lust, and lying among slaves into powerfully detailed pictures of African depravity. Within this perspective paternalism and later racism flourished in the eighteenth- and nineteenth-century South. Le Jau's allusions to sexual looseness among slaves echoed all the more loudly with his planters because they knew him to be a vigorous critic of planter society. Similarly, when Charles Martyn complained as late as 1752 that baptized slaves too frequently became "lazy and proud, entertained too high an opinion of themselves, and neglected their daily labor," he solidified planter convictions about slave untrustworthiness precisely because he and his clerical colleagues had so long pressed for slave instruction and baptism.[32]

Anglican parish ministers forged a maudlin, self-pitying rhetoric about awesome and burdensome responsibilities that formed another crucial characteristic of American planter paternalism. Maryland's Thomas Bacon praised masters before his assembled congregation of slaves and owners. He pointedly asked slaves,

"Do not your masters, under God, provide for you?" Slaves who intimated that planters skimped on their slaves' care and profited by exploiting their condition as well as their labor prompted denunciations pleasing to all owners who listened. From this perspective slaves enjoyed "a great advantage over white people." Planters had to care for themselves, for their slaves, and for tomorrow. They bore these burdens endlessly until death, which was the length of the slaves' service. But slaves were carefree. They did not even have to worry about old age. After all, planters provided for them even when they could no longer work in the fields. "You are quite eased from all these cares, and have nothing but your daily labour to look after, . . . when that is done [you can] take your needful rest."[33]

Anglican emphasis on absolute obedience had crucial implications for slave punishment. Finley notes that in ancient slavery, Christian criticism of slave mistreatment nearly always attributed unwarranted violence to wayward owners rather than to slavery itself. Early Anglican ministers followed the same course. Even before 1720, when American slaveholding was most malleable and susceptible to alteration, Anglican clerics in Maryland, Virginia, and the Carolinas treated owners' abuse of slaves as merely an episodic phenomenon. It was rooted in particular situations, owners, and slaves rather than endemic to the institution. Le Jau's criticism of South Carolina's law on slave castration prompted no broad attack on slavery itself, despite the fact that the castration penalty was unknown both in Europe and in other American colonies.[34]

An episode involving the small number of Baptist Dissenters in early Charleston demonstrated how the developing Anglican view of toleration for planter misdeeds quickly became the general English view of such matters. In 1710 some members of Charleston's Baptist congregation refused to worship with a member who had castrated a slave in accordance with the colony's law on runaways. To heal the breach, the congregation sought help from England. The answer of the Devon Baptists kept attention on the slaveholder's faith rather than on his actions. His doings would be abhorrent "if he doth it without the law of the Majestrate, or in a Spirite of revenge, or obscenely like that forbiden, . . . or if he aimeth by it at his Slaves death." But since the "gelding" was done in accordance with South Carolina law and for the purposes of discipline, no objection could be raised. Rather, "may we not Se[e] Some mercy mixt with this Brother's Cruelty?" A non-Baptist might have done the same "for the Sake of filthy lucre[,] . . . might have been more severe and after that have ruled over him with greater rigour." More important was the return of a "healing Spirite" to the congregation so that its worship and spiritual development could continue.[35]

The advancing paternalism rooted in a doctrine of absolute obedience reinforced the growing violence of eighteenth-century slaveholding. It encouraged owners to excuse nearly all discrete instances of violence toward slaves. Ironically, paternalism loaded owners with obligations that were difficult to fulfill in a competitive, erratic economy where there were few effective restraints on the owners' treatment of their labor. Even "ethical" owners mistreated slaves. Worse, both "ethical" and unethical owners could readily agree that slaves disobeyed. A rigid doctrine fostered rigid responses. The stress on absolute obedience turned minor infractions of planter authority into major confrontations, and the result brought forth the first fixing of an indelible image in American race relations—the perpetually disobedient black. Blacks were not Sambo—the soft, docile, lethargic slave—but had become rebellion personified, and their "insolence" was all but guaranteed by the doctrines that demanded absolute rather than conditional obedience first rationalized by Anglican ministers in the colonies. In the process, the meanings of blackness and disobedience had already begun to converge.

And of course slaves did disobey, as a host of studies have demonstrated. Planned rebellions occurred in New York in 1712 and 1741 and in South Carolina in 1739. On farms and plantations, slaves resisted owners in intimate and personal ways. They refused to work, acted insolently, or labored so lethargically that they became a liability in the fields. The result was a dramatic impasse, particularly for slaveholders taken with what was now Christian absolutism. By their account, they treated their slaves with love (in the nineteenth century, some would even say that they *loved* their slaves). Surely the slaves would return that love, would work diligently, and would behave honestly.[36]

This emerging Christian absolutism ravished slaves and transformed English culture in the colonial South. Slaveholders who approved of African Christianization treated slaves as cruelly as those who did not. Le Jau's account of one such episode was more gruesome than most but exemplifies the general problem. In 1713 Le Jau found himself appalled by the behavior of an overseer who had encouraged a slave to be baptized but later punished him viciously for losing a bundle of rice. The overseer starved the slave, then put him "into a hellish Machine . . . [in] the shape of a Coffin where he could not Stirr." After the slave had spent several days in the coffin, one of his children slipped him a knife and he committed suicide. Within three years the overseer had destroyed four more slaves in the same way, and even Le Jau admitted that he was only one of all too many owners who found neither their own Christianity nor that of their slaves a bar to the most monstrous cruelties.[37]

The emergence of absolutist, paternalistic, and violent slavery gave Christianity as thoroughly different a cast as Christianity had given to slaveholding. Christianity's interpretation of social behavior and religious ethics produced a distended emphasis on sentiment, charity, and love utterly uncharacteristic of the society in which it was propounded. In a collection of sermons published in 1750, the Charleston Anglican minister, Samuel Quincy, stressed the mutual love needed in a Christian society. Love meant "fulfilling . . . the Law," not merely obeying it. Quincy also stressed mundane piety rather than "miraculous gifts" because the former healed the real wounds of society, while the excesses of the latter, especially those associated with ecstatic, visionary religion, only worsened social problems. Also in 1750 a Maryland Anglican, William Brogden, extolled the beauties of freedom and love before the colony's Freemasons, most of whom were planters, confirming their wealth and status in a new fraternal association. Brogden played on the dark, developing meanings of slavery to celebrate enlightenment in his own society. "By Nature," Brogden wrote, "every man is a *Slave* in the spiritual Sense . . . The Selfish man is in truth a Slave to a wretched tyrannizing Master." But the "well ordered *Society*" was "cemented together by mutual Help and Love." Its members "lighten each other's Burthen, and constitute one undivided well-compacted Edifice." Masonic, Christian, and Maryland ideals all coincided in a paean to friendship, the ultimate cement of the thoroughly integrated society, though Brogden did not spell out which of these applied to whites, which to Africans, and which to masters and slaves together: "Lovely, peaceful

Friendship! joining Hands, uniting Hearts, covering Secrets, reproving Errors, and giving one Heart and one Tongue to all its Votaries."[38]

By mid-century, Christians of all kinds — Anglicans, Presbyterians, Congregationalists, even Quakers — played out a dichotomous moralizing that masked black-white relationships in the South and became typical of both social and religious analysis in America for more than two centuries. Ministers who set strict limits on the obedience planters might give in politics eschewed such limits in slaveholding. Josiah Smith, Charleston's Congregationalist minister, wrote in *Duty of Parents to Instruct Their Children* (Boston, 1730) that though children should recognize proper authority, absolute authority as well as the "doctrine of unlimited Passive Obedience is but a Chimera" — but he did not consider the implications of this thought for slaveholding. The Maryland Anglican, John Gordon, celebrated the defeat of the Catholic Stuart pretender at the Battle of Culloden in 1746 as Britain's "Deliverance from Oppression and Slavery." Britons must "despise and detest the absurd and slavish doctrine of *unlimited Submission, Non-Resistance,* and *hereditary Right.*" The Charleston Quaker, Sophia Hume, severely censured her society in her *Exhortation to the Inhabitants of the Province of South Carolina* (Philadelphia, 1750). The colony's "Masquerades," "Musickgardens," and "theatrical Entertainments" symbolized the sins of luxury, hedonism, and moral vacuity. Adults allowed children "a Superiority over Servants" and failed to keep them "in Subjection and Order." As a result, children learned "a Lesson in Self-Will, which many never unlearn all their Lives after." If this was a criticism of slaveholding, however, the term "slave" never entered Hume's lexicon, and it was the only comment that even approached the topic in a three-hundred-page social and religious criticism.[39]

It could be argued, of course, that the Anglican and Dissenting failure to advance widespread church adherence severely limited the importance of institutional Christianity in shaping eighteenth-century southern slaveholding. Ministers in longer-settled areas complained of rising numbers of laypeople who neglected communion and Sabbath services. In 1743 the Charleston grand jury complained publicly about the unwillingness of magistrates to enforce laws "against Irreligion, Deism, and a licentious Ridiculing [of] the Holy Scriptures and Matters of a Sacred Nature." At mid-century Thomas Bacon described the Maryland colony's religious state in stark terms: "Religion among us seems to wear the face of the Country; part moderately cultivated, the greater part wild and savage." A decade later the Anglican itinerant, Charles Woodmason, described his backcountry Carolina and Virginia listeners as assembling "out of Curiosity, not Devotion." Indeed, they seemed "so pleased with their native Ignorance, as to be offended at any Attempts to rouse them out of it."[40]

Ironically, Anglican clergymen and their Dissenting counterparts may have experienced more success in shaping slavery than in securing church adherents in the half century before the American Revolution. Two developments attest to this transformation. First, especially after 1730, increasing numbers of planters allowed slaves to be baptized. Although most slaves still rejected Christianity before 1760, the number of complaints about planter resistance to slave baptism from either Anglican or Dissenting ministers declined significantly after 1730. Some Anglican clergymen actually began to object to the owners' easy willingness to bring slaves into the churches, because the owners expected no more of their slaves' religion than they expected of their own. John Lang, Anglican minister at St. Peter's Parish in New Kent County, Virginia, complained in 1726 that white parishioners who were themselves "supinely ignorant in the very principles of Religion and very debauch't in Morals," were also "fond of bringing their Negroe Servants to Baptism," though afterward both owners and slaves lived "in common without marriage or any other Christian decency's as the pagan Negroes do who never entered into the Church membership." Whatever their own failings, owners thus satisfied themselves that Christianity presented no bar to slaveholding and increasingly allowed slave proselytization. As we will shortly see, it was the slaves who proved indifferent, a behavior that, on the surface, did not differentiate them from many owners but whose substance and cause may have been quite different indeed.[41]

Second, a dramatic and significant demonstration of Anglican success in shaping lay attitudes about Christianity and slaveholding occurred during the unique campaign to abolish slavery in postrevolutionary Virginia. In 1784–85 the Virginia Assembly seriously entertained proposals to abolish the state's most important labor system. The proponents ranged from aristocratic and middle-level planters concerned about the inconsistency of slavery and revolutionary principles of freedom to citizens worried that slaveholding would retard economic diversification in a state now frozen out of traditional British markets. But these agitators were soon met with petitions supporting slavery signed by thousands of backcountry Virginians.[42]

The Virginia proslavery petitions revealed the importance of both Anglican and Dissenting rhetorical support for slaveholding. Some petitions used secular revolutionary rhetoric to support slavery; they noted that the Revolution was fought to preserve property and that slaves were among the most important and valuable properties owned by the state's planters and farmers. But others used religion to support slaveholding, in ways that had been unthinkable in 1700. The petitioners charged that though the antislavery campaign was being led by individuals "pretending to be moved by Religious Principles," their attack on slavery only revealed their incorrect knowledge of true religion. "Slavery was permitted by the Deity himself," the petitioners trumpeted. Christian history itself supported slavery, since it had survived "through all the Revolutions of the Jewish Government, down to the Advent of our Lord." Indeed, "Christ and his Apostles hath in the mean time, come into the World, and past out of it again, leaving behind them the New-Testament, full of all instructions necessary to our Salvation; and hath not forbid it: But left the matter as they found it, giving exhortations to Masters and Servants how to conduct themselves to each other." If the Anglicans wanted testimony about the effectiveness of their labor in Virginia, these petitions could not have spoken more loudly.[43]

Anglican education of the planter slaveholders suffocated the abolitionist sentiment that appeared among some revolutionary-era Baptists and Methodists in the South after 1780 and helps explain the weak antislavery record of all major Dissenting groups except the Quakers in the southern colonies and states. When evangelism turned evangelical in the southern colonies after 1750, the Christian record on slavery shifted relatively little. Evangelical and Dissenting criticism of slavery proved weak or short-lived, although historians have sometimes emphasized the few such impulses that came to light in this period. John Thomson, a Presbyterian, may have alluded to slavery in his *Explication of the Shorter Catechism* (Williamsburg, 1749), when he wrote that children "under the jurisdiction of professing Christians, [and who] depend on them for Education, have a right to Baptism." But it is not clear whether Thomson meant white or black children, and he ignored slavery when he discussed Christian moral values. Revivalists like George Whitefield and Samuel Davies and the South Carolina layman Hugh Bryan criticized the treatment of slaves. Still, like other clergymen, they were at least as ambivalent about Africans as about slaveholding or, as in Bryan's case, were willing to abandon their antislavery diatribes in exchange for the privilege of seeking individual Christian conversions among slaves, thereby leaving the institution itself unchallenged.[44]

The Virginia Baptists' short-lived antislavery campaign suffocated for lack of support among the Baptist laity. John Leland questioned slavery as part of his general attack on Virginia's Anglican aristocracy. By the early 1780s, Virginia's statewide Baptist association condemned slavery as antiscriptural, the group's first major attack on the institution in thirty years of activity in the state and colony. But this impulse waned. Most Virginia Baptist congregations ignored the antislavery resolution, and by 1790 denominational leaders had dropped the campaign. Slavery was a "political," not a religious, problem. Methodist acquiescence to slavery after 1790 closely replicated the Baptist experience. A few Methodist preachers working in the South opposed it, as did others in the North. But as among Baptists, their listeners had long been trained in a different tradition regarding the relationship between Christianity and slaveholding. In a movement that consciously appealed to the integrity of those who needed saving and who were so frequently slaveholders themselves, antislavery agitation faded quickly.[45]

If Christianity clearly shaped slaveholding, in what ways did it shape slaves, at least in their religious expression? By most accounts, slave religion in America reflected the deep persistence of African religious forms and practices. Mechal Sobel describes the persistence of a generalized African sacred cosmos among slaves that may even have informed both Afro-American and white Christian evangelicalism in the nineteenth century. John Blassingame describes how antebellum slaves feared witches and sorcerers of African extraction not only because they believed in them but because such persons existed on numerous plantations.

W. E. B. DuBois placed the African conjurer at the very center of black slave culture: "[He] early appeared on the plantation and found his function as the healer of the sick, the interpreter of the unknown, the comforter of the sorrowing, the supernatural avenger of wrong, and the one who rudely, but vividly, expressed the longing, disappointment and resentment of a stolen and oppressed people."[46]

Antebellum slave cemeteries contained dramatic visual evidence of African practices. These are confirmed in the antebellum slave narratives, with their references to voodoo, amulets to ward off disease, and conjurers to settle disputes. Black medical practitioners ministered to both whites and blacks in the antebellum South, one of many testaments to the complex relationships between Afro-American culture and planter society. Indeed, such influences persisted into the twentieth century, when they were rediscovered and reinvigorated. According to Gilbert Osofsky, in the 1920s Harlem abounded in "'spiritualists,' 'herb doctors,' 'African medicine men,' 'faith healers,' 'dispensers of snake oils,' 'layers-on-of hands,' 'palmists,' and phrenologists who performed a twentieth-century brand of necromancy there." Osofsky stressed that the crafts of these practitioners were well rooted in the slave and African past.[47]

But when and under what circumstances did African religious practice, including non-Christian rites and rituals, first emerge in America? Nearly twenty years ago, Gerald Mullin argued that historians had too frequently treated slavery and Afro-American culture as a static topic and had lost sight of the way they changed, especially between 1619 and 1800. The issue is especially important in the study of slave religion. Scholars have long insisted that African religious practices were important to Afro-American society in antebellum America. But we have been less successful in tracing an evolving relationship between religion and Afro-Americans between 1619, when the first Africans arrived in Virginia, and 1865, when the Civil War ended. In the same years, British colonists witnessed enormous changes in the substance and meaning of religion in their lives and in their culture. What changed in black religious practice?[48]

Discussions of Afro-American religion usually describe it as profoundly shaped by the survival of African religious practices under slavery. Sobel argues forcefully that neither black nor white southern Christian evangelicalism can be understood without reference to African religious concepts. Blassingame states that the "strength and longevity of conjurism and voodooism among the blacks illustrate clearly the African element in their culture." In a still highly controversial 1941 study, *The Myth of the Negro Past,* Melville Herskovits advanced the idea that African "survivals" made Afro-American culture, and hence religion, possible. Similarly, though Eugene Genovese has dismissed the argument about African survivals as unsolvable, he has insisted that the "spiritual experience of the slaves took place as part of a tradition emanating from Africa."[49]

But when? Did African religion survive from the very beginning of slavery in the seventeenth century to prosper in the nineteenth? Did religious practice among Africans change across the centuries, perhaps in remarkable ways, as we would assume would have been true among other peoples in parallel or even in different circumstances? Is it possible that the religious practices of Africans in America shifted significantly as slavery evolved, so that both the substance and dynamics of Afro-American religion might have been far different between, say, 1680 and 1760, than they were between 1810 and 1860?

These queries can be answered affirmatively through a three-part model of emerging religious practice among African slaves in America. First, between 1680 and 1760, African slaves in the British mainland colonies experienced a spiritual holocaust that effectively destroyed traditional African religious *systems,* but not all particular or discrete religious practices. Second, collective religious practice of both Christian and African sorts emerged after family life and kinship systems had been redeveloped among surviving slaves. This would date the emergence of a significant sustained collective religious life for most mainland colony slaves at about 1760, although regional variations might place the date as early as 1730 or 1740 in the Chesapeake Bay area and as late as 1770 or 1780 in the Carolinas. Third, through the end of the colonial period, the effect of both previous developments engendered a collective Christian practice among slaves more fully European in its character than would ever subsequently be true, as slave and free black Christianity became increasingly Afro-American *after* rather than before 1800.

One important exception to this model existed in the New England colonies. There the relatively small number of slaves and their dispersion throughout the society created a significantly different dynamic of cultural and religious development among enslaved Africans. Pulled into different households, separated by long distances, usually owned by relatively well-to-do settlers who were themselves church members and not infrequently clergymen, the press for Christian conversion was intense. Slaves isolated in the countryside often joined Christian congregations, just as the slave owned by Boston's otherwise obscure Huguenot clergyman, Andrew Le Mercier, applied for membership not in Le Mercier's declining congregation but in the city's North Church. By mid-century Africans in New England celebrated their own festival days, but their significance was secular rather than religious, and many, if not all—perhaps a higher percentage there than elsewhere in the colonies—had become attached to Christian congregations.[50]

It is perhaps controversial to argue that slaves experienced an African spiritual holocaust in America before 1760. Genovese correctly observes that "little is known about the religious beliefs of the slaves during the seventeenth century or most of the eighteenth century." Moreover, anthropological literature based on largely "functional" models of religion's role and character asserts the ubiquity of religion in human societies and particularly in West African societies. As a result historians have often simply assumed the persistence of traditional African religion among enslaved Africans in the colonies between 1680 and 1760. In the renewal of slavery studies in the past twenty years, scholars have almost universally asserted the resilience of Africans in the face of capture, Atlantic transit, and enslavement and have applied this argument to African religious expression as well.[51]

It is true that we still lack a great deal of information about slave life and religion in colonial America. Yet we have learned much about the slaves' secular life before 1800. We have uncovered the shape of slave imports (negligible before 1680, extremely heavy between 1680 and 1750), sex ratios and age distributions (most imports were young adult males), chances for survival (slim before 1740, much better afterward, when African importations were also declining), and African origins (from diverse cultures, but with a bias toward the area of modern Angola). Slaveowners' letters and diaries reveal much about the daily texture of life for plantation slaves before 1800—work habits, field banter, dress, marriage, sexual practices, and language. Yet these same studies have proved largely unrevealing about slave religious practices before 1800. The lack of reference to Christian practice is easy to understand, because by both contemporary and modern historians' accounts slave Christianization did not advance significantly until well after 1760. But the lack of evidence about African practice remains more puzzling and, perhaps, more troubling.[52]

Some evidence does suggest that Africans persisted in their traditional religious practices as slavery evolved in late seventeenth- and eighteenth-century colonial society, despite the difficulties of cultural transfer and public expression. Blacks planning New York City's slave revolt of 1712 supposedly received powder from a free African sorcerer, which they spread on their clothing to make them invulnerable to their owners' weapons. The conspirators also allegedly sucked blood from one another's arms to forge a ritual bond among themselves. South Carolina planters sometimes complained of "rites and revels" among recently imported slaves, some of whom had come directly from Africa (not the usual pattern), and throughout the eighteenth century southern planters often referred to their slaves as "heathens" and "pagans" even as they also refused to Christianize them. Finally, Mechal Sobel's evidence of discrete African cultural survivals, from house styles to beliefs about witches and magic, suggests the possible persistence of traditional African belief systems in mainland colony slave societies.[53]

Yet especially before 1740 and in some places as late as 1770, English colonists were vague when they described slave religious practices. Gossipy white planters, such as William Byrd II and Landon Carter, chattered endlessly in their letters and diaries about nearly all aspects of their slaves' lives but said little or nothing about religion. When they did comment on religion, they were vague and formulaic. Their slaves were "heathens" and "pagans," just as parish clergymen said they were. But the planters did not elaborate on the meanings of the labels.[54]

The contrast to colonists' fascination with religion among native Americans is intriguing. Both Robert Beverley at the beginning of the eighteenth century and Thomas Jefferson at its end offered extensive comments on religion among American Indians. Their descriptions, as well as those written by scores of other colonists, have furnished crucial sources for our knowledge of religion among native Americans before 1800. But neither Beverley nor Jefferson nor any of their contemporaries wrote anything substantial about religious practices or beliefs among slaves. Jefferson's failure is especially striking. The philosopher who otherwise took an interest in "natural" religion and mined both the classics and the New Testament to uncover universal religious precepts wrote nothing about slave religion. In his only book, *Notes on the State of Virginia,* the chapter entitled "The different religions received into that State" ignored African religion.[55]

Colonial slave revolts also seem to have been bereft of religious motivation. Outside of the 1712 slave rebellion in New York City, no colonial slave rebellion before 1760 appears to have had religious roots, though most colonists gave the causes little notice. South Carolinians traced the 1739 Stono Rebellion to secular discontent among slaves, not to religion. New Yorkers laid the alleged 1741 slave plot to Catholic agitators sent from French Canada, not to African sorcerers living and working in the city. In contrast, America's nineteenth-century slave rebellions all had significant religious connections. As Gerald Mullin observes, Gabriel Prosser might have succeeded in his 1800 revolt in Virginia had he only accepted the support tendered by black occultists working in the slave quarters. Denmark Vesey and the plotters of Charleston's 1822 slave revolt all belonged to the city's African Methodist congregation. Nat Turner, leader of the bloody Southampton, Virginia, slave revolt of 1831, was a Baptist preacher who read the Scriptures differently than did Martin Luther, William Fleetwood, or Virginia's postrevolutionary Baptists and Methodists.[56]

The question is not whether Africans in America were religious but how and under what circumstances Africans might have engaged in their traditional individual and collective religious practices in America. Uncovering individual religious opinion among eighteenth-century slaves is especially difficult. In colonies where historians have only recently explored the range of religious heterodoxy among English settlers, it is not surprising that the range of religious opinion among individual slaves is almost thoroughly unknown. Caution is our surest guide, and through 1760 at least it would be wise to leave open the question of religious commitment in individual slaves. We ought not assume secure religious interests among slaves any more than we would do so among their masters. Nor should we assume an irreligiosity in slaves. Like Europeans, slaves came from complex societies that tolerated wide ranges of secular and spiritual opinion and whose suppleness and social malleability preclude any easy categorization of religious commitment in individuals.[57]

A significant body of surviving evidence, however, points up a holocaust that destroyed collective African religious practice in colonial America. Between 1680 and 1760 African slave capture, the rigors of slavery, and even the active opposition of Anglican and Dissenting clergymen suppressed and decimated traditional African religious systems in the mainland colonies. This African spiritual holocaust differed significantly from the Jewish holocaust of the twentieth century. It occurred as a by-product of slaveholding rather than as a direct result of efforts to destroy an entire people; it did not stem from a carefully planned program; and it was not a step in the promotion of a master race. Still, it stemmed from violence and repression as well as from an open contempt for different religious beliefs, and it resulted in a cultural destructiveness of extraordinary breadth, the loss of traditional collective religious practice among the half-million slaves brought to the mainland colonies between 1680 and the American Revolution. No other religious event of the entire colonial period, including the evolution of Puritanism or the emergence of American evangelicalism, so shaped a people's experience of religion in America.

The African slave trade initiated what Albert Raboteau calls the "death of the African gods" in America. The slave trade was religiously deselective. Africans possessed of special religious roles and knowledge were not sought out for enslavement. If they were valuable, they were valuable for their physical rather than their spiritual labor. The complexities of slavery exacerbated this religious deselectivity. The nineteenth-century slave Charles Ball recalled in his narrative, *Fifty Years in Chains,* that in the 1740s his eighty-year-old grandfather "retained his native traditions respecting the Deity and hereafter" in Maryland but kept these traditions to himself, in part because "he was an African of rank in his native land" who only "expressed contempt for his fellow slaves."[58]

Social and demographic factors further suppressed traditional African religious practice among slaves. Mainland slave settlements were far more dispersed than the more dense settlements in Brazil or Hispaniola. Even large plantations, such as those in the Carolinas, contained many slaves from many societies whose languages and national religious traditions were as different from each other as those of European colonists. Mortality among newly arrived slaves was extremely high, especially before 1740, and mortality only climbed higher through frequent suicides.[59]

Coercion and labor discipline also constrained collective African religious practice in the colonies. Abundant evidence suggests that planters denied collective African religious practice as a way of maintaining labor discipline. Throughout the colonial period planters worried about collective slave activity of any kind, religion included. Clergymen reflected that concern. In 1709 South Carolina's indefatigable Francis Le Jau worried that he had not yet fully suppressed African "feasts, dances, and merry Meetings upon the Lord's day," which he reported were "pretty well over in this Parish, but not absolutely." To remedy the situation among baptized slaves, he threatened to cut them off from communion. A year later he happily reported that "the Lord's day is no more profaned by their dancings, at least about me." The law aided this suppression. In some colonies it tolerated only Protestant Christianity, sometimes only certain of its forms; nowhere did it protect or recognize Ashanti or Yoruba religions.[60]

The devastating "middle passage" from Old World to New, the prospect of early death in America, the humiliation and resulting anomie produced by the introduction to slavery, and the reality of limited population reproduction in male-dominated slave quarters all took their toll on the early slaves. Contrary to much of the theorizing about the ability of crisis and trauma to reinforce religious commitment, the devastating experience of early slavery, together with the direct suppression of the slaves' public religious activity by planters, clergymen, and the law, reshaped the religious practice of Africans enslaved in America's colonies.[61]

The most obvious result of the American circumstances was the destruction of traditional African religious systems as *systems* in the mainland colonies. The comparison with Europe is telling. Whatever the difficulties and anomalies of colonization, a broad range of religiously inclined Europeans — Puritans, Scottish Presbyterians, German Lutherans, Dutch Reformed, Quakers, and Jews — not only survived in America but often eventually prospered, both individually and spiritually. But the rich religious systems of Akan, Ashanti, Dahoman, Ibo, and Yoruba societies — to name only some of the major sources of African religion in America — collapsed in the shattering cultural destructiveness of British slaveholding. All were breathtaking in their expanse of world view, causality, and supernatural vitality. All were distinctive, certainly as distinctive as the English, German, or French versions of Protestantism or Catholicism. Like Christianity, the African religious systems took public activity as a major measure of their vitality and had used it as a major instrument of propagation. By 1760, all had been destroyed in the mainland colonies.[62]

What survived, then, were not African religious systems but discrete religious practices that crossed African cultural boundaries and had individual rather than collective connotations. One form centered on healing. As early as 1710 Thomas Walduck described the work of an Obeah man in Barbados who used diabolical magic to injure other slaves and another, later called a Myal man, who cured diseases. Walduck compared them to English witches and cunning persons: "Their manner of bewitching is the same we read of in Books." Walduck also argued that their skills were found not among Barbados's few American-born slaves but only among recently imported Africans, "chiefly the Calamale Negros." Evidence of slave healers, conjurers, sorcerers, and witches in the mainland colonies before 1760, however, is slim, despite their subsequent ubiquity and their appearance in histories of nineteenth- and twentieth-century Afro-American culture.[63]

Death rituals and burial practices were the second form of collective religious practice to survive among American slaves. Again, the earliest and most extensive evidence comes from Barbados and Jamaica rather than from the mainland colonies. Richard Ligon reported in his *True and Exact History of the Island of Barbados* (London, 1657) that the colony's first slaves believed in their resurrection and return to Africa, and this perception continued among English planters and visitors through the eighteenth century. Griffith Hughes recorded traditional slave burial rites in his *Natural History of Barbados* (London, 1750), and modern archaeological studies by Jerome Handler and Frederick Lange have confirmed Hughes's comments. As in European burials, body orientation in African burials on Barbados from the seventeenth through the nineteenth centuries was almost wholly of an east-west orientation. However, most east-headed burials date from seventeenth- and early eighteenth-century burials, which did not use coffins, while most burials dated after 1750 were west-headed. Handler and Lange speculate that the former probably were burials of African-born slaves and that more of the latter were Barbadian-born. Most important, the archaeology confirms careful burials. Bodies were laid out in fully articulated form; they were carefully placed in common burial grounds; objects of African, European, and American origin were frequently placed with the body. The care suggests sustained, coherent ceremonies surrounding death, even if the precise meaning of those ceremonies cannot be ascertained from the physical evidence.[64]

Unfortunately, archaeological excavations have involved antebellum rather than colonial plantations and have shed little light on religion. The extant literary sources, however, hint that colonial planters felt unwilling to intrude directly into slave burial rites even though they suppressed other African religious practices. Planters' letters and diaries of planters described their slaves' deaths without any comment beyond occasional notices of the slaveholders' sorrow, and baptized slaves appear to have received Christian burial, though not necessarily in the same burial ground with whites. This may account for the fact that burial rites constitute one of the most important examples of persisting African religious forms found among American blacks into the late nineteenth and even the twentieth century. It is not easy, however, to determine whether specific practices in burials and other religious rites constituted colonial survivals or represented relatively recent African imports.[65]

The turn to Christianity among mainland colony slaves, then, followed rather than preceded the development of an indigenous secular slave culture, however intertwined such relationships subsequently became in antebellum society. This first Afro-American culture emerged out of redeveloping family and kinship systems among slaves. It occurred in different places at different times, around 1740 in the Chesapeake Bay area, for example, but perhaps not until the 1760s or 1770s in the Carolinas. Slave mortality declined, the sex ratio normalized, the number of children and conjugal families increased, and labor systems became routinized. As a result farm and plantation life changed for mainland colony slaves in ways that soon proved hospitable to collective religious expression. Second- and third-generation slaves now had families to raise, children to teach, and old and new cultural inheritances to transmit and create. In this setting of relative personal and cultural optimism and despite the still important brutalities of slavery, significant slave Christianization first emerged among mainland colony slaves.[66]

Slave Christianization in the South largely remained under Anglican aegis until the 1760s, though historians often emphasize more fleeting efforts by evangelical Dissenters. The Anglican efforts ranged across the century, from the development of the first mainland colony school for slaves in New York City in 1704, led by the former French Huguenot, Elias Neau; to the SPG emphasis on slave catechization by Anglican parish ministers; to the formation of the Associates of Dr. Bray, organized in 1731 to sponsor slave schools in America; to the SPG's inheritance of the Codrington plantation in Barbados and its effort to develop it as a "model" plantation. Like planters, slaves first learned the rudiments of Christian principle and practice through the state-supported church, and this meant that the Anglican parish was the most likely place for slave catechesis and baptism. There, slaves underwent baptism, including Francis Le Jau's peculiar version of it, took communion, and underwent burial. In contrast, Baptists and Presbyterians seldom proselytized among slaves until the 1760s and did not begin major campaigns for slave conversion to Christianity until after the Revolution.[67]

Early slave Christianity in the mainland colonies also remained strikingly isolated from African influences and closely tied to white sponsorship, probably more so than would ever be the case again. Before 1760 and, in most places, even up to 1800 and beyond, Christian worship among slaves was conducted with and among white planters. Where slaves had been Christianized and where Anglicans, Baptists, and Presbyterian congregations could be found—in Virginia's tidewater by the 1760s, for example—whites and blacks worshiped together. After 1770 evangelicals and Anglicans began to manage slave worship differently, both with regard to Anglican practice and with regard to limits and opportunities among evangelicals themselves. But that was a different matter with different causes, to be discussed in the context of religious creativity in early national and antebellum society.[68]

Slave Christianization before 1760 reflected no golden age of integration and racial harmony. Christian congregations were only mixed, not integrated. Slaves remained slaves, and the number of free blacks to be found in such gatherings was infinitesimally small, whether in Anglican or Dissenting and evangelical congregations. Among Anglicans and Presbyterians, preaching remained a wholly white phenomenon. Blacks listened. Although before 1770 Baptists permitted slave preaching, the occasions were limited and rare. Thus, both in comparison with previous African practice and in comparison with antebellum developments, a distinctively African element in colonial slave religion was far less common than it would be later. Even minor differences are difficult to decipher. Although historians have sometimes argued that slave evangelicalism did not engender the guilt about sinfulness exhibited in white evangelicalism, it is impossible to confirm such comparisons before 1760 or even before 1790.[69]

In the end, late colonial slave Christianity retained principally English characteristics, even among evangelical Baptists. The sermon, the liturgical sparseness, the ostentatiously uneducated clergy, the attack on aristocracy and privilege, the emphasis on collectivity, and the emotionalism, all of which seem endemic to southern white-black Baptist worship between 1760 and 1790, are most sensibly accounted for by English rather than African inheritances, especially given the obvious English influence in the governance and dynamics of Baptist congregational development. That this would not be the case in subsequent decades and in a variety of religious communities only testifies to the dynamism and creative potential continuously evident in the developing American religious environment.[70]

The eighteenth-century contribution to the shaping of slave religion and society thus proved significant. Slavery's destruction of African religious systems in America constituted not only wholesale cultural robbery but cultural robbery of a quite vicious sort. If we assume that African religions, like Christianity, were especially helpful in times of stress and danger, the loss was acute. Slaves were robbed of more than their lives; they were robbed as well of traditional collective means of comprehending life and loss. This destruction had immense implications for American society and culture. For slaves, it precluded the development of the autonomous synthesis of African religions that typified slavery in so many other places, including the West Indies, Brazil, and Hispaniola. At the least, such a system or systems would very likely have competed successfully for the spiritual loyalty of second- and third-generation slaves and of the continuing imports arriving from Africa long after the American Revolution ended. They would also very likely have changed slaveholding. In their absence, and amid the slowly rising Christianization of slaves, colonial and antebellum slaveholders took for granted at least superficial religious relationships between themselves and their slaves. To the extent that slaves themselves chose to be religious, the destruction of traditional African religious systems channeled slaves to the most complete religious system available to them — Christianity. The African spiritual holocaust also consigned discrete African religious practices to the status of "survivals" within a new religion that, at least for the moment, retained strongly European characteristics. The configuration of religious practices among Christianized slaves did not remain static, however, and their spiritual resilience was well measured in their subsequent capacity to reshape the spiritual legacy first offered them in the guise of absolute obedience.[71]

THE PLURAL ORIGINS OF AMERICAN REVIVALISM

6

The slaves of eighteenth-century America might have contrasted their own spiritual holocaust with the broadening stream of Christian spiritual expression that overran European settlement in the eighteenth-century colonies. This widening diversity forever altered the European religious configuration of colonial America. Two such streams were especially important: the establishmentarian Anglican and Congregationalist traditions and the explosion of efforts at religious renewal and revival. Neither of these traditions produced church adherence or membership rates equal to twentieth-century American practice. But they laid out new and powerful forms of religious practice and activity that influenced organized Christian endeavor for more than a century after their first appearance in the colonies.

Historians usually focus on the "Great Awakening" of the 1740s as the principal religious occurrence of prerevolutionary American society. Since its first elucidation in Joseph Tracy's *The Great Awakening,* which was published in 1841 to provide historical support for America's nineteenth-century revivals, its interpretative significance has multiplied a thousandfold. In the 1970s and 1980s, various historians have seen in it nothing less than the first unifying event of the colonial experience, the origins of the American evangelical tradition, and a major source of revolutionary antiauthoritarian and republican rhetoric.

This emphasis on the "Great Awakening" may say more about subsequent times than about its own. The term was not contemporary, nor was it known to the historians of the revolutionary and early national periods. Nowhere in George Bancroft's magisterial history of the United States can a single reference to this "event" be found. Although Tracy coined the term, he limited his history to New England and wrote only fleetingly about revivals elsewhere in the 1740s. Internal descriptive and analytical inconsistencies belie the event's importance and even its existence; it is difficult to date, for example, because revivals linked to it started in New England long before 1730 yet did not appear with force in Virginia until the 1760s. Its supporters questioned only certain kinds of authority, not authority itself, and they usually strengthened rather than weakened denominational and clerical institutions. It missed most colonies, and even in New England its long-term effects have been greatly exaggerated. On reflection, it might better be thought of as an interpretive fiction and as an American equivalent of the Roman Empire's Donation of Constantine, the medieval forgery that the papacy used to justify its subsequent claims to political authority. More important, an obsessive concern with it distorts important historical subtleties and obscures other crucial realities of eighteenth-century American religious development.[1]

For better or worse, the state church tradition, rather than Dissenting evangelicalism or voluntaryism, gave Christianity its primary shape in eighteenth-century colonial American society, at least through 1740. The state church tradition took its power from three major characteristics: coercion, territoriality, and public ceremonialism. Different varieties in different colonies used these means in very different ways. But they produced a remarkably similar product, especially when viewed from the perspective of the laity whose religious needs and desires they sought to direct.

The principal task of congregations enjoying the benefits of legal establishment was to construct an effective parish life. This was true of all the colonial state church systems, whether in the Anglican middle and southern colonies or the Congregationalist commonwealths of Massachusetts and Connecticut. The territorial parish designated the physical boundaries within which clergymen exercised their ministry. The parish minister assumed responsibility for propagating and maintaining Christian practice and belief among the entire population, not just among a few knowledgeable and loyal believers. Indeed, the state church minister rightly assumed that evangelism—spreading the Christian gospel—was the major obligation of his ministry. Even where the state church minister might reach for saints, he ministered to everyone.

For the Church of England, a central premise guided ministerial work: successful Christian adherence intersected and informed community life. Such a premise underlay Bishop Gilbert Burnet's *Discourse of the Pastoral Care,* a 1692 tract that was typical of reforming Anglican sentiment about the role of the clergy. Burnet criticized lazy "Mass-Priests," who, like their Catholic counterparts, merely manipulated symbols before a gullible and uninformed populace. "Parish-Priests" were Burnet's ideal, and they fused Christian teaching to a vital parish social life. Parish priests would "be well instructed in their Religion, lead regular Lives," and would gain their living from the parish in which they ministered, thus avoiding the notorious evil of "multiple benefices," through which clergymen increased their income from parishes in which they never or seldom served. "Parish priests . . . almost perpetually employ[ed] themselves in the several parts of their Cures." They led Sabbath services, performed marriages, conducted funerals, preached, catechized, visited the sick, and heard confession throughout the length and breadth of their jurisdictions.[2]

The public ceremonialism so bitterly criticized by Dissenters was crucial to the work of the parish priest. Burnet argued that the effective parish priest ministered "under the constant obligation of the *Breviary,*" the *Book of Common Prayer,* which laid out the schedule of Christian ritual that characterized Anglican worship. The central claim of the *Book of Common Prayer* was that its rituals conveyed the truths of the early Christian church. Its central attraction was regularity. The *Book of Common Prayer* furnished stability amid the confusion engendered by new landscapes, new settlements, new economies, new elites, new labor, and new forms of government.[3]

Burnet's parish priest ideal guided Anglican parish work in eighteenth-century America, stereotypes and Dissenting critiques aside. South Carolina's Francis Le Jau wore himself out in ten years of labor in his lowland parish. His was an unending stream of visits, processions, sermons, baptisms, catechizings, and conferences, all squeezed into the schedule of ritual activity set out in the *Book of Common Prayer*. Nor was Le Jau unique. A half century later Charles Woodmason tramped the backcountry of North and South Carolina, spreading the gospel as an Anglican itinerant, instructing listeners in proper liturgical manners, baptizing not only children but their parents, because none of them had yet received baptism, and in some cases marrying the parents as well, because not even that rite had yet been performed.[4]

In the main, legal establishment turned Anglican parish churches into vital centers of colonial community life. In Virginia especially, but also in other colonies with Anglican establishment, the Sabbath emerged as a day of intense and quickly mingled sacred and secular ceremonies—the gathering of the laity for worship, the reading of the ceremonies prescribed for worship in the *Book of Common Prayer*, the spreading out of the worshipers across the church lawns as listeners broke up into small knots of conversation after the service, and sometimes more social activities, such as horse racing, which might continue into the afternoon. Vestry meetings followed parallel patterns. The vestrymen often met on court days, in part because some also served as magistrates, and the collection of so many prestigious and economically active men together in a single place provided a common focus for the conduct of secular business. Before and after the vestry had decided on building maintenance, ministers' salaries, or poor relief, they and other parish residents were busy with transactions of many kinds—land, goods, and increasingly after 1700, slaves.[5]

The collusion of secular and sacred in the Anglican parish ministry reflected the Anglican understanding of religion in society. Long past the great age of Calvinist influence in the Elizabethan church, Anglicans adopted an unabashedly moderate stance on the question of religion. They criticized Dissenting negativism about human nature. As Thomas Barton, an SPG minister in Pennsylvania, put it in 1770, "Instead of instructing the people to 'serve the Lord with *gladness*' and to have 'joy in the Holy Ghost,' these miserable teachers advance a gloomy and dreadful religion which has . . . made many [listeners] fitter objects for a *Hospital* than a *Church*." Anglican theology typically combined rationalism, moralism, and piety. Within limits, the world was comprehensible. The principal problems faced by most individuals were doing good and conforming to Christian moral precepts. A modest piety taught men and women to inspect their own actions in order to understand both the world and the God who had made it. Morbid, pathological urges were better left to Dissenters.[6]

Anglican clergymen became catechists and liturgists, not field generals warring against society. They taught reading and writing with an eye for moral lessons useful among a reasonable people. In large parishes they hired catechists or tutors because it was educationally sound and freed the clergymen to perform their other numerous duties. They distributed enormous numbers of tracts obtained from the SPG and the SPCK, and their sermons were as much or more the occasion for catechetical instruction as for explication of difficult, sophisticated theological issues.[7]

Anglican parish life upheld the modern social structure by honoring establishmentarian concepts of deference and social prestige. The South Carolina commissary, Gideon Johnston, always placed the most prominent communicant at the top of his communicant list at St. Philip's Church in Charleston in 1711 and 1712: Judge Nicholas Trott, on Whitsunday, May 20, 1711; Colonel William Rhett and Madame Rhett, followed by the customs official Colonel Robert Quarry, on August 5; Governor Charles Craven on Easter Sunday, April 20, 1712. When prestigious men's wives took communion alone, as Madame Rhett frequently did, Johnston always placed their names ahead of less prestigious male communicants.[8]

Anglican ceremonialism accompanied a rising secular ceremonialism in eighteenth-century America. For elites rising out of an expanding colonial economy came installation ceremonies for public offices, silver maces for magistrates' courts, engraved seals for commissions, and duplication of English court and legal ceremonies. Anglicans frequently occupied center stage in these rituals. As early as the 1680s and certainly by 1710, Anglican clergymen regularly preached before the assemblies in colonies where the Church of England was established. They heard confessions from convicted murderers and preached public execution sermons for the condemned containing messages — rhetorical and ritual — designed for the living.[9]

Anglican ceremony did not imply a "high church" tradition in the colonies. In the context of English religious life the colonial Anglican church emerged as decidedly middle of the road, although this guaranteed it no more adherents in America than it did at home. Although Anglican ceremonialism sometimes verged on the pompous in colonial cities and in Virginia, the physical intimacy of Anglican churches, especially in rural areas, exposed the elite in all their glories and failings; squalling children and sullen slaves were unique to no social group. Not even city churches were immune from such inclusiveness. Both the pious Elie Neau, originator of New York City's school for slaves, and New Jersey's governor, Lewis Morris, quickly and bitterly complained to London officials when the New York governor, Lord Cornbury, paraded in women's clothes on his balcony on the Sabbath services and wore them at his wife's funeral, to the disgrace of Neau and Morris, though perhaps to the amusement of others.[10]

Parish labor solidified Anglicanism's middle-range ethos. Anglican ministers performed religious rituals for everyone in the society, not merely for the well-churched few, and their frequent status as the only easily available clergymen brought them many marriages, baptisms, and funerals from a wide clientele. During Charleston's smallpox epidemic of 1711 and 1712, Commissary Johnston married 20 couples, baptized 22 children, and conducted 150 burials. Johnston had not seen a single one of them as a communicant in the previous year, though he assured the SPG in London that most of the smallpox victims he counseled "promised to be constant Com[munican]ts and made Solemn promises to lead new lives, Should God be pleased to restore them to their health." If most of Johnston's clients seem to have been unchurched, among the deceased were also 20 Presbyterians, 5 Baptists, and 2 French Huguenots. Johnston interred them because the city's Dissenting minister was "afraid to Venture himself amongst them for fear of the Small Pox." An Anglican commissary could not afford such a luxury.[11]

The Anglican laity always included a wide spectrum of contemporary social classes. The church enjoyed strong aristocratic support, in part because it was established by law, in part because Crown officials were at least tacit Anglicans, and in part because it was the king's church. But modest men and women formed its adherents in most parishes. Though Johnston began his communicant lists with the names of the socially prestigious, he concluded them with the names of the unknown and the obscure. "Mr. and Mrs. Hitchcock" appeared last on all but one of Johnston's lists; they were Johnston's most loyal communicants, and at least one of them appeared at each communion between September 1711 and May 1712.[12]

Parish life and ministry in New England's state church establishment simultaneously paralleled and differed from its Anglican counterparts. The perception and reality of decline was one major difference. Unlike Anglicans, who could look upon growth and expanding institutional vitality in the eighteenth century, most New England Puritans viewed the century at best with equanimity, at worst with fear. Declension that reduced church membership to no more than 10 to 15 percent of the adults in towns like Salem before 1700 was accompanied by expanding denominational pluralism after 1700. Competition from Quakers, Baptists, and Presbyterians escalated even as many potential listeners drifted away from churches altogether. Adherence patterns also became more complex. Gender was the most striking point of difference. Between 1680 and 1740 a new spiritual couple emerged in New England, the member wife and the nonmember, or delayed-member, husband. Women made up the majority of members in most New England established churches in the 1680s. By the 1720s women dominated membership in virtually all known New England congregations. In one regard, this development was a product of the seventeenth-century Puritan emphasis on the woman's role in family religion. In another, however, it reflected a shift in the timing and, perhaps, in the substance of male spiritual awakening. Women continued to join churches in their twenties, just before or just after marriage. Men increasingly delayed church membership until their thirties or forties. Single men seldom became full members at all, and married men often undertook full membership only before assuming local political office, something that usually happened after they passed their fortieth birthday.[13]

Towns reacted to these changes in a variety of ways. Before 1740 not a single New England town, parish, or provincial leader called for abolishing the state church system, despite New England's increasing religious and social complexity. In the "peaceable kingdoms" Michael Zuckerman describes, a religious majoritarianism defined orthodoxy at the expense of any vocal minority. But given the lack of a centralizing church power, these peaceable kingdoms varied widely from one town to another. Some churches adhered to the Half-Way Covenant, some did not; some required religious testimonials for full membership, some did not; some held to Congregational principles, some to "Presbyterian" or even Baptist ones. Other towns and parishes quietly gave in to the increasing variety of opinion and, as in Salem, grudgingly accepted the inevitability of Dissenting worship in their communities. It must be added, however, that the variety present in eighteenth-century New England can be exaggerated. It constituted only a shallow preview of modern American pluralism because most of it, Quakerism aside, circled a narrow Calvinist orbit.[14]

Like their Anglican counterparts, New England's town and parish churches attempted to evangelize by providing a major ritual and ceremonial focus for community life. Their Erastian tendencies—placing the authority for religious order in the hands of the state—aided this effort. Ultimate authority for the operation of the state-supported churches rested with locally elected selectmen and vestries, who exercised primary responsibilities for hiring and paying ministers. Towns and parishes could keep ministers on edge for years, picking and choosing exactly whom they wanted, paying meager and marginal salaries, refusing raises, criticizing doctrine, sometimes refusing to renew a minister's yearly contract. It was partially in response to these conditions that ministers turned to each other and, after 1690, increasingly joined the ministerial associations that paralleled the more powerful Dissenting denominational institutions formed in and around Philadelphia in the eighteenth century.[15]

Town and parish concern about ministerial matters bespoke the clergyman's central role in the religious life of the community. Although the law allowed civil officials to perform marriages and allowed the laity, including midwives, to perform baptisms, ministers performed most such ceremonies in New England. But many parish and town ministers baptized only children born to members, though some indeed baptized more widely. Ministers also conducted funeral ceremonies and preached constantly when cycles of sickness produced deaths in large numbers. And of course ministers buried the dead in the consecrated and fenced burial grounds found in most New England towns, but relatively uncommon in the middle and southern colonies even after the rise of Anglican worship in the eighteenth century.[16]

The principal ceremonial function of ministers in eighteenth-century New England towns was distinctive — delivering the sermon. Other regions knew what sermons were, of course. But they did not experience them with the frequency common in New England. Sabbath sermons were most important for those New Englanders who patronized their town and parish churches. There listeners learned about Scripture and salvation. As Harry Stout explains, early eighteenth-century New England Sabbath sermons "signaled [an] enduring loyalty to *Sola Scriptura.*" Listeners were told again and again to return to God's word as the primary instrument of their faith. That they were subsequently instructed on what those words really said and meant only confirmed the intent, if not the practice, of depending on the Bible as the source of Christian doctrine. Salvation was the object of that endeavor. What was typical of its discussion in New England sermons between 1690 and 1730 was its commonplace exposition. Preachers did not terrorize. Nor did they ignore. They simply assumed that their listeners should hear about the necessity of salvation and proceeded to tell them in thoroughly mundane ways.[17]

For popular evangelizing, weekday sermons were even more important. They might be preached on fast days, declared to proclaim public humiliation or to seek divine blessing for New England society, on thanksgiving days, on election days, and on military occasions, such as sermons delivered before militia units or to confirm election of militia officers, and, most ominously, at executions. The occasions held immense ceremonial importance. Here were unparalleled opportunities to speak to a broad range of men and women in local society, not just church members. Not surprisingly, town and parish ministers whose position to speak was sanctioned by the state in both theory and practice frequently used weekday sermons to comment on public as well as religious affairs.[18]

The style of weekday sermons confirmed their role in public and state evangelizing. In them New England's ministers preached with more drama than in Sabbath sermons. Their estimation of the audience seems to have produced the change. Implicitly speaking to the unconverted, they spent more time describing disasters, listing sins, and fixing blame. If on thanksgiving days they spoke more of New England's religious foundations, they also warned about losing them. On days of humiliation they excoriated the population about its failings. On election days they warned about the dangers of political principles detached from proper religious foundations. And at executions they warned about sin while still holding out the hope of salvation to everyone, including the person about to die. In all this ministers thundered out the word of God through the authority of the state, using state functions as a pulpit from which to reach those who had long since left the meetinghouse.[19]

While state ceremonial functions of New England's established churches persisted, disciplinary functions tended to decline. Edward Taylor, the poet and minister, justified congregational discipline to the newly formed frontier church at Westfield, Massachusetts, in 1678 on the grounds that even well-tested believers were "not all Spirit but part flesh." "Sensures of the Church," Taylor said, would take the "Captive out of the hand of the Adversary" and "keep the Holy Place Clean from being defiled by unclean ones." But strict discipline scarcely followed his stern words. In the next three decades Taylor's congregation heard only four disciplinary cases—that of John Mawdsly for coveting land, of Thomas Dewy for wrecking a dam and hiding tools, of Joseph Pomery for embezzling town funds, and of Rebecca Ashley for committing adultery. Other towns followed a similar path, in part because parishioners felt comfortable with a less than rigorous "discipline." In 1749, when Northampton's Jonathan Edwards attempted to increase discipline by reversing the open communion that his grandfather, Solomon Stoddard, had instituted in the 1690s, his parishioners balked, then fired him. However brilliant, however evangelical, Edwards found himself stonewalled by intense local resistance to an emphasis on conversion. His new theology was unfamiliar and unhistorical. Better to expound it in the wilderness among Indians.[20]

Like the Anglican parishes of eighteenth-century Yorkshire, New England Congregational parishes patrolled the edges of unchristian and immoral behavior. They censured a few parishioners and excluded one or two others, usually unmarried couples involved in fornication or illegitimacy cases, but they seldom pursued immorality everywhere they found it. It was more important to announce the possibility of censure than to pursue every accusation, especially in churches established by law and erected at considerable local expense with taxes levied from most local property owners.[21]

A striking pluralism of Christian expression soon supplemented the state churches of eighteenth-century America. This pluralism provided an astonishing variety of European religious traditions in a maturing, increasingly complex society. Although eighteenth-century American religious pluralism most likely did not exceed that found throughout Europe as a whole, by 1760 it probably had no equal in any single European society. As important as its existence was its effect. It soon underwrote a wide variety of ways to support religious renewal in prerevolutionary society and laid down complex patterns of revival that would persist into the nineteenth and even twentieth centuries.

Institutional proliferation became a major sign of eighteenth-century colonial religious pluralism. The diversity of individual opinion long characteristic of English settlement from Boston to Virginia in the seventeenth century took on institutional expression after 1680. This was most obvious, of course, in the rise of the great Dissenting denominational institutions organized in and around Philadelphia between 1685 and 1710 and extending into other colonies in later decades of the eighteenth century. Baptists, Presbyterians, and Quakers all had appeared in New England by the 1670s but gained significance through their persistence across the next half century. In the case of the Quakers, this occurred despite the execution of three Public Friends from England in 1658 and jailings of Quaker leaders in Salem. Less well known groups, descended from the region's complex Puritan history, further complicated the New England mosaic. "Rogerenes," former Seventh Day Baptists who followed John Rogers of Newport, Rhode Island, combined Baptist and Quaker principles with a belief in miraculous healing and attracted adherents in both Rhode Island and Connecticut, usually from among well-to-do rather than poor settlers. Seventh Day Baptists themselves sustained small but persistent congregations in Rhode Island and Connecticut. Finally, of course, Anglicans enjoyed the fruit of SPG proselytization, especially in Connecticut. As elsewhere, Anglican appeal was broad, not narrow. Often they attracted poorer settlers squeezed out of dominant parish and town churches. At the same time, by mid-century, Anglicans enjoyed their own favor among new elites in new and changing towns and began to hold public office in numbers out of proportion to their numbers in society.[22]

The middle and southern colonies offered even broader examples of Christian pluralism. As in New England, some of this pluralism descended from English Baptist, Presbyterian, and Quaker sources. Increasing ethnic pluralism soon engendered further religious variety. French Protestants (Huguenots) and Sephardic Jews who arrived in the 1680s and 1690s were joined in the next half century by settlers from Scotland, northern Ireland, a wide variety of German states and principalities, and Switzerland.

The new ethnic mix brought with it an even richer variety of religious groups. This was first noticeable among Scots. The first Scottish immigrants settled largely in West New Jersey and were Quakers, but they were quickly followed by Scottish Anglicans and, of course, by Presbyterians. German-speaking immigrants settling in Pennsylvania provided even greater variety. The first group, arriving in 1683 from the Rhine town of Krefeld, reflected both the vibrancy and the complexity of late seventeenth- and early eighteenth-century German pluralism. Most of the Krefeld immigrants had only recently become Mennonites, followers of the sixteenth-century reformer Menno Simons, and though they expressed an interest in Quaker principles in indicating their desire to emigrate to Pennsylvania, they had not yet joined the Quaker movement. In fact, most never did. In Germantown, just outside Philadelphia, they were joined by visionary Lutherans and more than a few avowed sectarians, some led by the mysterious Johannes Kelpius.[23]

Between 1695 and 1740 Christian pluralism exploded in the middle colonies. The Keithian schism among the Quakers stimulated a flurry of sectarian groups. Keithian Quakers became Keithian Baptists who, in turn, became Calvinist or Particular Baptists only to watch others become Anglicans and even Presbyterians. Kelpius's Wissahickon settlement disintegrated before 1710, after which a few followers traveled west. Near Lancaster, with newly immigrating German Seventh Day Baptists, they formed a new settlement at Ephrata (meaning "fruitful"), renowned for its seeming prefigurement of nineteenth-century

American communitarianism. It was characterized by antiworldly sectarianism, division into male and female segments, and a special musical regimen that prompted Thomas Mann to model one of his principal figures in *The Magic Mountain* after Ephrata's mid-eighteenth-century leader, Conrad Beisel. "Dunkers," the derisive name applied to the adherents of the Church of the Brethren, were antipaedobaptists who believed in complete immersion during adult baptism. Followers of the reformer Kaspar Schwenkfeld arrived in Pennsylvania in 1734, and in 1741 Count Nicholas Zinzendorf arrived in Philadelphia, bringing a major group of Moravian settlers to the colony.[24]

Although the southern colonies could not compete with the spiritual jangle heard in Pennsylvania, its landscape was by no means silent. As in Pennsylvania, some of its pluralism came through Continental sources. Followers of Jean de Labadie, a former Jesuit, formed a communitarian settlement in Maryland in 1683, and in 1728 Schwenkfeldian refugees who had fled Silesia settled in Georgia, where they were followed in the 1730s by Moravian immigrants. Older Quaker meetings persisted but did not expand. More important was Dissenter activity. The Presbyterians experienced considerable growth in the 1750s as the result of Scottish and Scots-Irish immigration. Especially in Virginia, Baptists expanded after 1750, though usually at Anglican expense. They challenged Anglican hegemony in the colony, both figuratively and literally, and lured Anglicans into foolish contests over preaching and taxes that the Baptists could not lose.[25]

International cosmopolitanism accompanied this growing eighteenth-century American religious pluralism. Cotton Mather maintained an extensive European correspondence, particularly with Pietists. Charleston's French Protestant minister, Paul L'Escot, corresponded with two theologians in Neuchâtel and Geneva, Jean Frederick Ostervald and Jean Alphonse Turrettini, sending Turrettini rattlesnake skins. Henry Melchior Muhlenberg kept up an enormous correspondence with Lutheran leaders in Halle and elsewhere in Germany from the 1740s until his death in 1787. Quakers in Pennsylvania, New England, and the southern colonies used the "transatlantic connection" with traveling or Public Friends to keep the movement spiritually cohesive before 1750 and to promote religious change and reformation after 1750. English Seventh Day Baptists in New Jersey, Pennsylvania, and

Rhode Island kept in close touch both through correspondence and through frequent emigration from one colony to the other. Even a settlement like Ephrata, physically far removed from the challenge of a city like Philadelphia, maintained a remarkably cosmopolitan theology, fusing together diverse elements of German pietism, anabaptism, and social experimentation in its communitarian setting.[26]

This burgeoning pluralism and its broad public acceptance was perhaps best displayed in New York City in August 1763, when the governor proclaimed a day of thanksgiving to celebrate the British victory over France in the French and Indian War. The city's two Anglican clergymen were joined in their sermons by their Dutch, French, Presbyterian, Baptist, and Moravian counterparts. Even the "hazan," or prayer chanter, at Congregation Shearith Israel, Joseph Jesuron Pinto, delivered a thanksgiving sermon, taking for his text Zechariah 2:10: "Sing and rejoice, O daughter of Zion: for lo, I come, and I will dwell in the midst of thee, saith the Lord."[27]

The increase in religious pluralism provides an important clue to understanding the attempts at religious renewal in eighteenth-century America. It was the breadth and diversity of these efforts—not their cohesion or their limitation to the 1740s—that solidified their significance. Even in New England, Perry Miller described efforts at renewal and revival as episodically persistent. They appeared as early as the 1670s, and reappeared in major forms in the 1680s, the 1730s, and the 1760s, with a major peak between 1740 and 1745. Middle colony religious renewal began tumultuously with the rise of "singing Quakers" on Long Island in the 1680s and continued with efforts to create a piety of suffering among French Huguenots in the 1690s, with Dutch revivals in the 1720s in New Jersey, and with Presbyterian and German revivals (the latter largely failures) in the 1740s in Pennsylvania. In the southern colonies efforts at religious renewal appeared for short periods in both South Carolina and Virginia in the 1740s, stimulated by the preaching of the Anglican itinerant, George Whitefield, but met with more sustained growth there and in North Carolina after 1760, when Presbyterian and Baptist activity increased.[28]

Although religious revival missed many colonies, it usually attracted notoriety and charges of political radicalism when it occurred. Alexander Garden of Charleston and Charles Chauncy of Boston both charged that the religious "enthusiasm" of the 1740s was modeled on the behavior of London's infamous "French Prophets" of the 1710s, who raised followers from the dead, prophesied Christ's imminent return to earth, and used female preachers. The charges of radicalism actually pointed up the relative modesty of what was taking place. Some prerevolutionary colonial revivals allowed and even encouraged emotional outbursts as a sign of true conversion. Jonathan Edwards apparently permitted such episodes in the early revivals he encouraged, and James Davenport brought them to a climax when he and his New London, Connecticut, followers burned books written by their opponents. Yet heightened emotionalism characterized only some revivals. The revivals in the New Jersey Dutch churches led by Bernardus Freeman and Theodore Frelinghuysen emphasized personal discipline rather than emotion as evidence of conversion, and Baptist revivals in both New England and Virginia defined success more in terms of the listeners' sober reception of the new doctrine that was propounded than in displays of emotional excess.[29]

Doctrinal diversity also characterized eighteenth-century religious renewal. Calvinism clearly dominated New England revival. But it had been preceded in the 1710s by a major interest in German Pietist doctrines, circulated through the writings of a Halle reformer, August Herman Francke, with whom Cotton Mather had begun an intensive correspondence in 1709. In the 1750s revivalism incorporated Wesleyan Arminianism, brought to America through the example of John Wesley's English Methodists. In the middle colonies, not surprisingly, Calvinism was important in the Scottish Presbyterian revivals. But quite different doctrines spurred religious renewal among other communions. Frelinghuysen's and Freeman's disciplinary revival among Dutch Reformed colonists was encouraged by a Dutch renewal tradition with strong seventeenth-century origins. Among Germans, efforts at religious renewal took root in reformed Lutheranism, in a distinct German Calvinist tradition quite unlike that found in New England, and in a Pietism of great breadth and eclecticism. As espoused by immigrants like Christopher Sauer, this Pietism could easily involve Lutheran sacramentalism, Hermetic Rosicrucianism, and universalist Freemasonry. And the spectacular growth of the Baptists in Virginia and North Carolina used Arminian doctrine as its fuel.[30]

Colonial revivals nearly always reflected regional and local conditions. In New England they flourished amid tensions stemming from religious, social, and economic maturation, which had brought increased disparities of wealth, social stratification, and sometimes incomprehensible social diversity. Middle colony revivalism was more narrowly circumscribed and often took root in efforts to articulate ethnic dimensions in religious observance, both Scottish and German. In Virginia, Baptist revivalism prospered alongside the inability and even the refusal of established Anglican churches to comprehend broadening religious needs in the colony, particularly among poorer, less literate settlers.[31]

The peculiar, seemingly contradictory, mix of provincialism, regionalism, and internationalism became especially obvious in the labor of revival and religious renewal. George Whitefield's colonial appeal fed on his English and Scottish success and on the news of that success spread by colonial newspapers and theological sympathizers. Private letters from ministers to each other, read at public occasions on both sides of the Atlantic, created a "concert of prayer" that made the revivals of the 1740s and 1750s seem even more momentous than they were. And the exchange was more than one-way. Thomas Prince's weekly newspaper, *The Christian History,* published in both Boston and Edinburgh in the 1740s, brought as much news of America to Europe as of Europe to America. George Whitefield, moreover, publicly acknowledged very early colonial models for his mid-century reform work. When he visited Northampton, Massachusetts, in 1740, he expressed more interest in Jonathan Edwards's grandfather than in Edwards himself: "After a little refreshment, we crossed the ferry to Northampton, where no less than three hundred souls were saved about five years ago. Their pastor's name is Edwards, successor and grandson to the great [Solomon] Stoddard, whose memory will be always precious to my soul, and whose books entitled 'A Guide to Christ,' and 'Safety of Appearing in Christ's Righteousness,' I would recommend to all."[32]

In general, revivalism embraced conservative rather than radical or egalitarian approaches to the question of authority. It is true that revivals frequently produced schisms that threatened the old order. In New England, revivals in the 1740s produced more than two hundred schismatic congregations that split away from old churches, and several "New Light" Congregationalist and "Separate" Baptist denominational organizations. In the middle colonies Presbyterian revivalists withdrew from the Synod of Philadelphia to form the Synod of New York. Yet these schisms usually occurred because proponents demanded more, not less, authority from their churches. This became particularly obvious during the Presbyterian schism of the 1740s. Usually interpreted as an attack on authority—as "antiauthoritarian" and as perhaps a preface to the American Revolution—it was actually proauthoritarian. Its instigators, Gilbert Tennent and the ministers of the evangelicals' so-called Log College, had long objected to disciplinary laxness in the old Synod of Philadelphia. When the synod refused to raise its disciplinary standards, the Log College ministers walked out, not into the heady air of antiauthoritarian freedom but to New York. There they created new presbyteries and finally another synod—the Synod of New York—to exercise effective coercive authority over "true" Presbyterian ministers, ministerial candidates, and congregations.[33]

Colonial revivals also raised, rather than lowered, the status of the ordained ministry and did little to increase lay authority within either local congregations or their denominational institutions. Revivalism prompted many ministers to change their style of preaching. Many turned to extemporaneous preaching more frequently than they had before, accelerating a tradition that can be dated back to at least the 1680s. Isaac Backus, the New England Baptist leader, noted that revivalists used sermons to "Insinuate themselves into the affections" of the people and even induced opponents to incorporate more "emotion" and "sentiment" in their sermons. At the same time some sermons were clearly more "extemporaneous" than others. Some itinerant ministers, especially Whitefield, memorized sermons and interchanged sections to suit particular moments and audiences. Since they preached without notes their listeners believed these sermons to be products of immediate inspiration.[34]

Revivalists upheld important distinctions between ministers and laypeople. Ministers had rights, the laity had duties. Jonathan Edwards acknowledged, in *Some Thoughts concerning the Present Revival of Religion in New England,* that "some exhorting is a Christian duty" for a few of the converted. But Edwards was quick to protect clerical privilege. "The Common people in exhorting one another ought not to clothe themselves with the like authority, with that which is proper for ministers." Gilbert Tennent spoke even more adamantly. His infamous 1740 sermon, *The Danger of an Unconverted Ministry,* was taken by many as a siren of antiauthoritarianism, and historians have frequently treated it as a prelude to the rhetoric of the Revolution. Tennent attacked "unedifying" ministers who could not lay claim to a conversion experience. They were "Pharisee-shepherds" and "Pharisee-teachers." He argued that listeners and even parishioners had a duty to turn to the sermons of other clergymen if misfits persisted in their office. But Tennent never attacked the ministry itself or suggested that anyone with a conversion experience should begin preaching to others. Only ministers properly ordained by legitimate denominational bodies preached, and only preaching brought men and women to Christ. As early as 1742 Tennent thundered against lay preachers. They were "of dreadful consequence to the Church's peace and soundness in principle . . . [F]or Ignorant Young Converts to take upon them authoritatively to Instruct and Exhort publickly tends to introduced the greatest Errors and the greatest anarchy and confusion."[35]

Revival ministers often took more paternalistic attitudes toward their listeners than did their less enthusiastic colleagues. Regenerate ministers saw themselves as true shepherds, who brought their sheeplike listeners to religious conviction they would likely never experience except under proper, inspired guidance. In the 1740 Presbyterian revival at New Londonderry, Pennsylvania, James Blair's "soul exercises" transformed the congregation. His instructions on relating their experiences with God set limits and forms for their spiritual exercises. He constantly exhorted his listeners to "moderate and bound their passions." He warned them against excesses through which they might misconstrue God and, in turn, have their doings misconstrued by others. Finally, he withheld judgment concerning his listeners' state of grace, a proper Calvinist practice that also broadened and extended rather than constrained his authority.[36]

Itinerancy likewise solidified ministerial authority. Although some itinerants lacked formal education, none of those who were active in the American colonies are known to have been illiterate.

The century's most famous itinerant, George Whitefield, took an Oxford degree in 1736, and its most infamous, James Davenport, stood at the top of his Yale class in 1732. Itinerants opposed settled ministers only selectively. They bypassed local churches when the minister opposed their work and preached in them when the minister was favorable. Nearly all itinerants wore the protective badge of clerical ordination. When he was charged in Virginia with being an unlicensed minister, the evangelical Presbyterian, Samuel Davies, defended his orthodoxy by pointing to his ordination by the Presbytery of New Castle. Only Davenport ventured into the colonial countryside lacking ordination, with just his high-flown spirituality and his Yale degree to protect him. But only Davenport was judged by a court to have been crazy.[37]

The complexities of religious renewal in eighteenth-century America are revealed with almost ironic fullness in the careers of the Tennents of New Jersey and Whitefield. The Tennents — the father, William Sr., and his four minister sons — Gilbert, John, William Jr., and Charles — were one of the best-known ministerial families in the colonies, and Whitefield, aside from Britain's monarchs, was arguably the best-known Englishman of the mid-eighteenth century. Yet the Tennents and Whitefield revealed the different means by which eighteenth-century revivalist clergymen probed lay religious understandings. These differences centered on the issue of charisma. In Max Weber's definition, charisma involves three characteristics: leadership, demonstrations of supernatural intervention, and social validation of the leader's claims by followers. Hermits thus cannot exhibit charismatic leadership, because charisma is implicitly social; nor can atheists and humanists, because charisma takes root in supernatural belief and invocation. As another sociologist writes, charisma is "not a personality attribute" but "the social recognition of a [supernatural] claim."[38]

The Tennents emerged from a Scottish society redolent of intense popular supernatural expression, but by no means fully Christianized, much less Protestantized. Early modern Scotland exhibited magical expressions, including sacred places, healers, and amulets, as vivid as those found in England. And Scotland too was riven by strong regional differences, stark economic disparities, and major religious conflicts. Scottish Quaker, Anglican, and convenanting and nonconvenanting Presbyterian colonists to the Jerseys and Pennsylvania brought these divisions to the New

World. William Tennent, Sr., reflected this complexity in his own career. Sometimes called the father of American Presbyterianism, Tennent was a Scot who, living in northern Ireland, received Anglican ordination in the Church of Ireland in 1704 and served Anglican parishes there until he left for America. Only after applying for membership in the Presbytery of Philadelphia in 1718 did he recant his Anglican principles, before a suspicious presbytery.[39]

The Tennents cultivated community, Christianity, and Presbyterian adherence through long-term residential ministries. After ten years in New York, William Sr. served a fifteen-year residence with the "Scotch-Irish" community at Neshaminy in Bucks County, Pennsylvania. John and William Jr. monopolized Presbyterian preaching for forty years in the Scottish settlement at Freehold, New Jersey, where Joseph Morgan had earlier entertained and appalled the congregation with his astrological experiments. Gilbert Tennent served two congregations in thirty-eight years in his career at New Brunswick, New Jersey, and Philadelphia (the Second Presbyterian Church).[40]

Catechization and regeneration formed the Tennents' principal theological interests. William Sr.'s surviving manuscript sermons avoid millenarianism altogether, and Gilbert discussed it only perfunctorily during the French and Indian War, when many other ministers turned to the theme as well. Instead, the Tennents catechized. They stressed elemental Calvinist and Christian doctrine to a heterogeneous and disputatious people. It was no accident that Gilbert described his brother John as a "keen disputant" and "expert Casuist." The Tennents also stressed personal regeneration, meaning spiritual rebirth occurring as a result of a conversion experience. Their emphasis on regeneration was itself a proselytizing tool. Christian adherence would reshape the life of the individual and, ultimately, of the community.[41]

Such evidence shows the Tennents to be evangelical — not charismatic. But though the Tennents Christianized and Presbyterianized Scottish immigrants by emphasizing doctrine, regeneration, and community, they also probed popular, quasi-Christian Scottish supernaturalist sentiment. They did so by manifesting supernatural power in their own bodies. Theirs was not a cold, austere Calvinism that adamantly rejected popular culture. Nor was it a Calvinism in which "ministers and their flocks held a theology in common," as historians recently have described New England.

Rather, here was a Calvinism that simultaneously tapped and disciplined yearnings for supernatural intervention, through clergymen who were not only prophets of God's Word but holy men.[42]

Three of the Tennent sons — Gilbert, John, and William Jr. — became living exemplars of supernatural, even miraculous, intervention. Their experiences took three principal forms — supernatural possession, apparition, and miracle. Supernatural possession occurred in the form of God-induced sicknesses, radical personality shifts, and ecstatic behavior. All of them attributed divine causes to the severe sicknesses they endured in their early days as ministers. Gilbert developed a debilitating illness that gave him an "affecting view of eternity," and he likened his recovery to the raising of Lazarus, a point he was not at all ashamed to make before his congregants: "After I was raised up to health, I examined many about the grounds of their hope of salvation." After John's own conversion experience, he cast off his bitterness and anger, then began to experience frequent weeping and sighing. "In his private Studies," Gilbert wrote, "he often took the *Bible* in his hand, and walked up and down the room, *Weeping,* and *moaning* over it."[43]

Divine apparitions occurred in both religious and secular settings. John pleaded for and received visions of Christ during the sickness that dogged him in his early ministry at Freehold. "O brother, the Lord Jesus has come in mercy to my soul. I was begging for a crumb of mercy with the dogs, and Christ has told me that he will give me a crumb," he reportedly said. The apparitions increased as death approached a year later, and after John had been buried, Gilbert wrote of the perfect union of body and soul that death engendered. More mundane apparitions saved William Jr. from a perjury conviction. In a bizarre occurrence not unlike the early modern French episode recounted in Natalie Davis's *The Return of Martin Guerre,* which involved a clerical impostor, a stolen horse, and perjury charges, William Jr. was saved from conviction in part if not wholly by a Pennsylvania couple who dreamed he was in trouble and traveled to New Jersey. They corroborated Tennent's testimony in the case and freed him from the perjury charge.[44]

William Jr. also exemplified the miraculous both by being raised from the dead and by later losing all the toes on one foot for no known reason. The resurrection occurred during the illness he endured while taking his ordination examinations, a period during which his brother John, also ailing, received visions of Christ. William's condition worsened, and he died. His brother Gilbert came to comfort family and friends and to supervise the funeral arrangements. Three days later, however, after William had been "laid out on a board" and his funeral had been announced, his eyes opened, he groaned, and he was nursed back to health under Gilbert's guidance. Some years later, William awoke in the middle of the night to discover that the toes on one foot were missing. He could find neither the toes nor any instruments or animals that he could imagine might have effected their removal — knives, rats, even cats — and he traced the loss to the Devil: a miracle, to be sure, but one demonstrating God's power through the work of his nemesis.[45]

The Tennents explained what happened to them as demonstrations of God's direct intervention in human affairs, and their experiences set them apart as holy men, not mere expositors of God's written word. Such explanations were only reinforced by popular belief in supernaturalism. Gilbert acknowledged that his brother John eagerly evidenced his weeping and moaning "to almost all that came near him." His public spectacles validated his identity by affecting others: "Even some Strangers who came to see him, were much affected therewith; the *Tears* trickling down their Cheeks like *Hail.*" In the 1740s Gilbert described his own God-induced sickness and Lazarus-like reprieve from death in a letter about religious revivals in the Presbyterian congregation at New Brunswick; it was circulated on both sides of the Atlantic in *The Christian History.*[46]

Not all evangelicals felt comfortable with claims of direct supernatural intervention, much less miracles. Jonathan Edwards distrusted them as Devil-induced and as easily mistaken for faith and grace itself. Presbyterian antirevivalists made the intriguing claim that the revivalists' pretenses about religious experiences crossed over into magic. David Evans, a conservative Presbyterian minister and reputed author of *The Querists,* likened Gilbert Tennent to an astrologer and fortune-teller. Could Tennent really ascertain "Men's *inward Feelings*"? If so, "Must not Mr. T have some cunning Art, beyond what is common to Man[?]" Pennsylvania wits joined in. A critique appearing in Benjamin Franklin's *General Magazine* compared both the Tennents and Whitefield to conjurers and

"Holy Necromancers" and traced their lineage to Munster radicals and Commonwealth Ranters, some of whom claimed miraculous powers.[47]

George Whitefield's long public career reveals significant and surprising differences with that of the Tennents. Whitefield came closest to the Tennents' style in claiming parallels with Christ in his conversion experience. He unashamedly noted that both he and Christ had been born at inns (Whitefield did not claim a manger). His early religious struggles had produced bodily manifestations, including "unspeakable Pressure both of Body and Mind" and "an uncommon Drought and a disagreeable Claminess in my Mouth," which Whitefield compared to Christ's experience on the cross "when *Jesus Christ* cried out, 'I thirst.'" Whitefield also preached on miracles to considerable public effect. The manuscript diary of Daniel Rogers, a Massachusetts minister who followed Whitefield to New York in 1740, reveals that in his first New York sermon, Whitefield preached "upon the miracle of the woman healed of the bloody [flux]," all to "great power . . . one or two women cryd out loud."[48]

But Whitefield stopped far short of the Tennents. He never claimed to have experienced apparitions or to have accomplished or benefited from miracles. He criticized John Wesley for tolerating trances and convulsions among listeners in England; there might be "something of God in it," but "the devil . . . interposes." Like Edwards, he worried that such enthusiasm would "take people from the written word, and make them depend on visions, convulsions, etc., more than on the promises and precepts of the gospel." Whitefield had similar feelings about wonders and miracles. His journals reported wonders, such as deliverance from storms at sea and peculiar occurrences, with some frequency. But like the Mathers before him, Whitefield saw them as demonstrations of God's awesome powers in nature, not as miracles. The age of miracles had passed, and modern claims for their performance were fraudulent.[49]

Whitefield's evangelicalism also differed from that of the Tennents. Whitefield and the Tennents all preached on original sin, election, and regeneration. But Whitefield emphasized original sin and election while the Tennents emphasized regeneration. Whitefield made and sustained his reputation on his ability to convince men and women of God's sovereignty, the reality of original sin, and the doctrine of election. Listeners reported that their primary reaction to Whitefield lodged in their understanding of his great question, "Are you saved?" Since Whitefield usually convinced them that the answer was no, they took home an overwhelming sense of guilt and failure. Whitefield hoped that this guilt would result in their surrender of their lives to Christ. In contrast, the Tennents spoke about Christian regeneration and the creation, building, and sustaining of faith.[50]

This subtle difference in preaching intersected differences in pastoral labor. Whitefield traveled all his life and never labored in a settled ministry. In thirty-two years, between 1738 and 1770, he made seven tours of English America, the shortest lasting seven months (1738), the longest lasting three and a half years (1744–1748). Whitefield announced his grand themes to strangers. He made his reputation and exercised his ministry among people he had never met, quite unlike the Tennents, most of whose listeners knew them intimately. Whitefield's death dramatized the difference. In 1770 thousands of spectators crowded into Newburyport for Whitefield's funeral. No settled minister could have created such a stir. Even sympathizers thought the focus on the man, rather than on his message, was unseemly and excessive. Ezra Stiles, then Congregational minister at Newport, Rhode Island, carefully calculated the dimensions of Newburyport's Presbyterian church just to confirm his suspicion that the claims for the numbers of Whitefield's mourners were greatly exaggerated.[51]

The tumult at Whitefield's funeral points up the frequent attempts of his followers to create a charismatic relationship despite Whitefield's careful reluctance about such matters. The public often interpreted his behavior charismatically and attempted to treat him as a holy man. Nathan Cole's description of Whitefield's appearance in Middletown, Connecticut, in 1740 offers one such instance: "When I see Mr. Whitfeld come upon the Scaffold [at Middletown], he looked almost angellical—a young, slim, slender youth before some thousands of people, and with a bold, undaunted countenance. And my hearing how God was with him everywhere as he came along, it . . . put me in a trembling fear before he began to preach, for he looked as if he was Cloathed with authority from the great God."[52]

Portraitists emphasized what was apparently a facial tic, which made Whitefield appear cross-eyed and which his followers associated with divine blessing. A satirical cartoon, published in London in 1760, lampooned their fascination with his problem. The cartoonist could not resist disparaging the sexual appetite of Whitefield's listeners — one says, "I wish his Spirit was in my Flesh" — and he also ridiculed the significance they attached to Whitefield's crossed eyes — "His poor Eye Sparkles with Holy Zeal," says another (see Figure 11).[53]

Whitefield's corpse also became an object of attention. In 1775, a revolutionary chaplain, with a group of officers that included Benedict Arnold, entered Whitefield's tomb in Newburyport (see Figure 12). They viewed the body, then removed the evangelist's clerical collar and wrist bands to pass among their soldiers. Such viewings, usually by evangelical ministers rather than military men, continued into the nineteenth century at a rate that suggests a kind of cult of Whitefield's body. In 1789 Jesse Lee and two other Methodist ministers entered Whitefield's tomb. "Removing the coffin lid, [we] beheld the awful ravages of 'the last enemy of man,'" Lee wrote. "How quiet the repose, how changed the features." In the 1820s Abel Stevens, also a Methodist minister, visited the tomb and "took his skull into my hands, and examined it with great interest." By the time David Marks, a Freewill Baptist minister, visited the tomb in 1834, "the coffin was about one third full of black earth, out of which projected a few bones. The skull bone was detached from the rest, and was turned over."[54]

George Whitefield probed popular culture, but not in the ways the Tennents did. Among other things, he probed it for questions, not answers. He used common concerns about life and death as a vehicle for demonstrating the truth of Christianity and the necessity of adherence to its doctrines. His constant preaching on God's sovereignty and original sin responded to yearnings for transcendent descriptions of the world even as it challenged contemporary cynicism and religious indifference. Although his message was often catechetical, he taught rudimentary Christian doctrine with drama and spectacle. Whitefield's performances were not charismatic, however. They focused attention on his figure, his face, his voice, his demeanor, and even his notoriety, as when a Delaware Anglican confronted Whitefield with the rumor that the orphan traveling with him was actually a concubine. But they did not involve claims to divine intervention either in his life or in his body.[55]

Ultimately the Tennents and Whitefield expressed two different

11. Satirical cartoon of George Whitefield, 1760.

evangelical styles common in American revivalism in the nineteenth and twentieth centuries. The Tennents were simultaneously more traditional and more radical. They were more traditional in their willingness to satisfy popular desires for direct supernatural intervention. They tapped a supernaturalist tradition deeply rooted in older times that continued to flower in America through figures who manifested direct supernatural intervention, such as Anne Lee at the end of the eighteenth century, Joseph Smith in the nineteenth century, and Father Divine, A. A. Allen, and Oral Roberts in the twentieth century. At the same time, the Tennents were more radical in their willingness to offer demonstrations of supernatural activity in the contemporary world. Through their very bodies, they revealed the power of supernatural authority and its capacity to change lives in ways that resembled nothing less than Christ's resurrection from the dead.[56]

12. George Whitefield's casket and crypt, First Presbyterian (Old South) Church, Newburyport, Massachusetts.

In contrast, Whitefield proved to be more modern. He did not pursue people and their culture through charisma. He pursued them through popularity. In Whitefield, the self became an object of its own fascination rather than a vessel of supernatural exposition and intervention. Unlike the Tennents, Whitefield worked outside traditional denominational channels. He never abandoned the Church of England, though he criticized it bitterly. As a result his legacy was personal, rather than institutional. Followers sometimes established nondenominational congregations to promulgate Whitefield's message locally. Andrew Crosswell founded such a church in Boston in the 1740s, a Philadelphia meetinghouse opened to evangelical preachers of all kinds in that same decade, and a "Tabernacle" opened in Salem in 1770 after Whitefield's death to carry his message into the next century. But all three had collapsed by the 1780s. Whitefield's nondenominational, noncharismatic revivals thus prefigured another tradition in American revivalism, exemplified in the careers of Charles Grandison Finney, Billy Sunday, Billy Graham, and Robert Schuller. Such evangelists thundered out the message of God's sovereignty and stressed their own popularity at the expense of any denominational loyalty, but they did not pursue claims to charismatic authority.[57]

The reinvigoration of the state church parishes in New England and in the southern colonies, the expansion of European religious diversity, and the rise of a pluralistic evangelical revivalism kept prerevolutionary rates of church adherence from sinking further in many places, if not everywhere, and improved them in some. At mid-century New England exhibited the greatest range in church adherence rates. Highs in rural membership rates varied from two-thirds of the adults to less than a fifth of the eligible adults, and in Boston Samuel Mather admitted in 1780 that "not one sixth" attended public worship. In New York some rural congregations contained between 40 and 60 percent of eligible adults, but others contained far less, and New York City's church adherence rate probably did not approach 15 percent.[58]

Anglican records suggest some gains early in the century followed by some losses after 1750. The well-known 1724 survey of Anglican congregations ordered by the bishop of London exhibited large and suspicious gaps between attendance as reported by parish ministers and the record of actual communicants. Clergy frequently claimed congregations of between a hundred and two hundred at most Sabbath services but recorded only twenty to forty communicants. Statistics drawn from long series of yearly reports by SPG ministers in the middle colonies suggest both considerable variation in the ratio, depending on location, and in some places, a widening gap between the two figures as the century wore on. At Radnor, Pennsylvania, Anglican ministers reported about 20 percent of the area's eligible nonsectarian, English-speaking residents as communicants; adding Quakers and Welsh Baptists probably brought the church adherence, attendance, or affiliation rate up to as much as 40 percent of the area's adults in this period. In contrast, at Apoquimminy in Delaware, where Anglicans were the largest single Christian group, communicants accounted for no more than 10 to 15 percent of the area's nonsectarian English-speaking residents between 1743 and 1752. At Newcastle, Delaware, the communication rate among potential Anglicans actually declined between 1744 and 1776, from between 15 and 20 percent of the eligible communicants in the 1740s and early 1750s to between 8 and 12 percent between 1760 and 1776, with no known increase in other Christian congregations to account for the difference.[59]

The result was a mixed record for both state churches and Dissenting evangelicals in eighteenth-century America. On the one hand, the renewal of state church activity in both the northern and the southern colonies, the rise of the Dissenting denominations and their vigorous efforts to promote ministerial labor and discipline, the increase of religious groups from the Continent, and the proliferation of a wide and sometimes surprising range of efforts at renewal all probably saved the public expression of Christianity from the kind of collapse that already seemed imminent in many colonies, led by Maryland and the Carolinas, in the 1680s. Without these new expressions of Christian activity and form, moreover, this weakened Christianity would also have been narrowly English and would have alternated between only middle-of-the-road Anglicanism and increasingly middle-of-the-road Dissenting groups. Instead the colonies were filled with astonishing varieties of Christian expression, which only increased as ethnic and national heterogeneity accelerated.

On the other hand, the statistics regarding church adherence, meager and frustrating as they are, provide little evidence to reject Hector St. John de Crèvecoeur's judgment that in later eighteenth-century America, "religious indifference is imperceptibly disseminated from one end of the continent to the other." Crèvecoeur put a happy face on this situation. He bypassed the suppression of African national religious systems in the colonies, and found persecution and "religious pride" all but absent from America. He eagerly traced American religious indifference to sectarian pluralism and wilderness spaciousness and ignored the European heritage of erratic lay adherence to institutional Christianity. "Zeal in Europe is confined; [but] here it evaporates in the great distance it has to travel; there it is a grain of powder inclosed; here it burns away in the open air and consumes without effect." Still, however poorly Crèvecoeur understood the causes of American religious indifference, his vivid, enduring metaphors rightly fixed its existence.[60]

What would happen to these conflicting patterns in the Revolution? Though a wide range of eighteenth-century changes salvaged Christianity from some of its seventeenth-century difficulties, they scarcely guaranteed the future. And, worse, the causes, experience, and course of the Revolution all too quickly began to expose the insecurity of Christianity's place in American society.

A REVOLUTIONARY MILLENNIUM?

7

British colonists wrought momentous changes in America between 1760 and 1800. They confronted, then overthrew, the government they had known since colonization began. They established new governments and, some hoped, a new society as well. They were not wrong to trumpet their handiwork as "the new order of the ages." Nor were they wrong to worry about what they had accomplished. Benjamin Franklin warned his countrymen in 1776 that their republic would survive "if you can keep it." Part of the challenge, perhaps the most important part, lay in determining what kind of republic Americans intended.

The revolutionary era held immense consequences for religion in America. The advance of organized Christianity after 1680 could not mask the low and erratic levels of church adherence on the eve of the Revolution. Clerics well knew that their hold on the laity was tenuous and that the colonists were dissolving political allegiances far older than any religious allegiances they then held. The only Christian denomination spread with reasonable thoroughness throughout Britain's mainland settlements was the Church of England, headed by George III; other denominations typically counted strength in only one or two regions and were absent elsewhere. And the emphasis on authority, power, and obedience in eighteenth-century American religion, together with the tension that sometimes accompanied religious renewal, only increased the potential for religious instability during the revolutionary crisis.

At its heart, the Revolution was a profoundly secular event. The causes that brought it into being and the ideologies that shaped it placed religious concerns more at its margins than at its center. Yet organized religion not only survived the revolutionary era but probably prospered from it, both because of the nature of the crisis and because of the deft way the denominations handled it. Despite their early hesitation and continuing anxiety about the process, the churches lent their weight to the American cause in a way that paid immense dividends in coming decades. Later, as new tensions arose in the new configuration of politics, society, and religion, the denominations moved to sacralize independence much as they had earlier sacralized the landscape.

Religion has not always interested historians of the American Revolution. Both David Ramsay and George Bancroft saw the Revolution as a thoroughly secular event, and their views represented the dominant opinion of their time. Antebellum revivalism and the approaching Civil War prompted some change in this perspective, though largely among historians of religion. Much as Joseph Tracy sought historical justification for antebellum revivalism in his work, *The Great Awakening*, by mid-century religious activists began to search for models that could be used to guide clerical activity in the North-South conflict. John W. Thornton's *Pulpit of the American Revolution* (1860), Frank Moore's *Patriot Preachers of the American Revolution* (1862), and Joel Headley's *The Chaplains and Clergy of the Revolution* (1864) interpreted the revolutionary era in a way that fit the needs of the 1860s. Aware of the novelty of their view, they proceeded cautiously, however. The "religious element . . . did not give shape and character" to the Revolution, Headley admitted. Still, he noted, "he who forgets or underestimates the moral forces that uphold or bear on a great struggle, lacks the chief qualities of a historian."[1]

More dramatic claims for religion's importance in the Revolution emerged a century later. Carl Bridenbaugh's *Mitre and Sceptre* (1962) drew attention to the "bishop question," in which Dissenters denounced alleged Anglican plots to install a colonial bishop while colonial assemblies were fighting off taxes and the escalation of imperial authority. Alan Heimert's seminal *Religion and the American Mind from the Great Awakening to the Revolution* (1966) substituted Calvinist evangelicalism for theological liberalism as the Revolution's principal theoretical foundation. Since then many historians—Gary Nash on the colonial cities, Rhys Isaac on eighteenth-century Virginia, Harry S. Stout on the New England sermon, Patricia Bonomi on denominational antiauthoritarianism—have stressed the importance of evangelical "style" in shaping the Revolution. In these accounts, evangelicalism underwrote economic discontent, fostered new modes of public address, and provoked confrontations with the standing order that eroded public confidence in the established government and played a substantial role in turning protest into rebellion. In the main, however, these accounts' view of the principal religious force that might have shaped the Revolution is unnecessarily narrow in their focus on evangelicalism. They bypass other religious issues and traditions that influenced revolutionary political discourse, exaggerate religion's general importance to the Revolution, and slight the difficulties that the Revolution posed for the American churches and that they ultimately overcame.[2]

The Declaration of Independence provides clear-cut evidence of the secondary role that religion and Christianity played in creating the revolutionary struggle. The religious world invoked in the Declaration was a deist's world, at best; at worst, the Declaration was simply indifferent to religious concerns and issues. The god who appears in the Declaration is the god of nature rather than the God of Christian scriptural revelation, as when Jefferson wrote of "the laws of nature and nature's God." In other allusive appearances this god emerged as "the Supreme Judge of the world," to whom Americans would appeal "for the rectitude of our intentions," and as "Divine Providence," on whom they would rely for protection. Elsewhere, all was secular: taxes, troops, tyranny. Despite its length, not a single religious issue, including the dispute over the Anglican bishop, found a place in the "history of repeated injuries and usurpations" that closed the Declaration and that established the Revolution's most authoritative list of offensive British actions in America.

Yet the Declaration's remarkable silence on religious issues should not obscure the importance of religion in secondary issues. The bishop question, for example, carried significant long-term implications for revolutionary discontent because it undermined trust in British politicians and their motives. The dispute actually acknowledged the institutional progress that Anglicans had made in the eighteenth century. Dissenters feared a bishop, traditionally required for a full presence of the Church of England anywhere, precisely because they knew how well Anglicans had fared without one. When Dissenters counted, they found Anglican congregations in astonishing numbers: there were some four hundred by 1776. They knew all too well that these congregations were important not only in the colonial cities, where their presence had been visually commanding for many years, but especially in the countryside, where most colonists lived. The Anglicans, in turn, took Dissenter strength seriously. They wanted a bishop to complete their institutional emigration, a journey that Dissenters had finished a half century earlier. When Henry Caner, an Anglican minister in Massachusetts, described the need for a bishop in 1763, he cited Dissenting institutional strength, rather than Anglican ecclesiastical theory, to justify his demand: "We are a Rope of Sand; there is no union, no authority among us; we cannot even summon a Convention for united Counsell and advance, while the Dissenting ministers have their Monthly, Quarterly, and Annual Associations, Conventions, &c., to advise, assist, and support each other." Anglicans asked for a "suffragan" or assisting bishop, whose powers were limited to ordination and confirmation, rather than a regular or full bishop, whose powers at least theoretically included the convening of ecclesiastical courts, including the kind that had been used to attack Puritan reformers in England. The call for the suffragan bishop suggests that American Anglicans recognized colonial realities. Still, Dissenters pressed the issue anyway, ignoring the distinction and accusing Anglicans of hoping to monopolize institutional Christianity in America.[3]

The Anglican-Dissenter contest over a bishop for America escalated transatlantic political tensions for years. The controversy first appeared in the 1710s, abated until it flared in the 1750s, then flared again in 1761 when Anglicans purchased an extraordinarily large home in Cambridge, Massachusetts, which Dissenters gleefully named the "bishop's palace." After 1763 the Dissenters' argument was joined to the colonial protests against taxes and other English efforts at imperial centralization, and it climaxed in protests against the Quebec Act of 1774, through which the English government recognized the Catholic church in the conquered French territories of Canada.[4]

Dissenters consistently linked the bishop question to the English debate on tyranny, a sensitive term in a society that had beheaded one monarch in 1649, overthrown a second in 1688, and defeated a pretender in 1745. Jonathan Mayhew not accidentally chose the 101st anniversary of Charles I's execution to excoriate the Anglicans for demanding a colonial bishop. English history, he said, demonstrated all too well how civil and ecclesiastical tyranny intertwined; hence, the need for constant vigilance: "People [will] have no security against being unmercifully priest-ridden but by keeping all imperious bishops, and other clergymen . . . from getting their foot into the stirrup at all." In case listeners and readers missed the point, Mayhew used the word *tyranny* incessantly, sometimes four or five times on a single page. Nor were Dissenting ministers alone in manipulating the bishop question. The New York City Whig, political agitator, and nominal Presbyterian, William Livingston, specifically emphasized Anglican "usurpation and tyranny" to the city's Dutch, Presbyterian, and Quaker congregations. He thought even Anglicans might well recognize how an elevated episcopal authority threatened to "rob you of an *equal* Share in the Government of what *equally* belongs to all."[5]

The charge of tyranny in the bishop controversy evoked a constellation of images important to the Revolution. Tyranny stemmed from conspiracies that sought to veil their participants' evil motives. The SPG was thought to lead the cabal. How else to explain its massive budget and secret business in London? It sought to destroy Dissenters. How else to explain the society's establishment of so many congregations in New England, where Congregationalists, Presbyterians and Baptists were already active, when it could have ministered instead to settlers on the frontier and to Indians? SPG ministers were agents of repression. How else to explain their half century of whining about bishops?

The Quebec Act called forth another image: secret Catholicism, associated with every attempt at tyranny in England since the 1640s—the reigns of Charles I and James II and the rise of the Pretender in Scotland in 1745. The charges resonated clearly in a society where anti-Catholicism had been a staple crop for two centuries, even among Anglicans. Paul Revere expressed those fears in a superbly crafted engraving in 1774 (see Figure 13). In it the

Devil, Anglican bishops, and England's most notorious politicians, Lord North and Lord Bute, form a cabal to effect their ultimate and long secret objective — Catholicizing the American colonies.[6]

Protestant Christianity also reinforced the Whig political convictions that lay behind early revolutionary rhetoric. Whig sentiment extended throughout the colonies, where it was descended from eighteenth-century English political culture generally rather than from more narrow sources in revivalism or New England Calvinism. Religious support for the Whigs was thus not limited to New England or to evangelical Dissenters. The basic Whig texts — Locke's *Second Treatise of Government,* Benjamin Hoadley's *Origin and Institution of Civil Government Discussed,* and John Trenchard and Thomas Gordon's *Cato's Letters* — were disseminated throughout the colonies, and reached more than evangelicals. Thomas Cradock, a Maryland Anglican, knew them well as a member of Annapolis's prestigious literary society, the Tuesday Club. When the Anglican John Gordon preached against tyranny in his *Sermon on the Late Rebellion* in 1746, his text sparkled with allusions to the Whig literature. Whiggism did not guarantee homogeneity. More than minor subtleties separated the Whiggism

13. "The Mitred Minuet," engraving by Paul Revere, 1774.

of Cradock and Gordon from that of Jonathan Edwards, George Whitefield, Boston's Andrew Croswell, New London's James Davenport, or South Carolina's Hugh Bryan. All were Whigs, yet all were different, and the political as well as religious implications of their Whiggism was not nearly so clear on the eve of the American Revolution as it on occasion has been to modern historians.[7]

Political Whiggism appeared in colonial sermons in two especially important ways. First, the sermons reinforced the emphasis on virtue and morality that pervaded secular political discussion in eighteenth-century colonial and English society. Indeed, it was the very breadth and perfunctoriness of clerical allusions to politics that made the sermons useful in the political debates of the era. Listeners and clergy together, in a vast number of denominations and congregations, *assumed* that liberty proceeded from a virtuous citizenry. It was the ministers' duty to make sure that this virtue was a Christian virtue, of course. As Thomas Cradock wrote, "The life of every sincere Christian is a warfare against a great number of Enemies, some of them very potent, and others very politick. Virtue is a rich Prey rescued narrowly out of the Fire, the purchase of Labor and sweat of Care and Vigilance. We are too liable to loose it by our own Sloth and Treachery."[8]

Systematic public discussion of virtue and morality came more frequently from ordained Christian clergymen than from any other single source. Especially outside New England, morality served as the most common focus of sermons, and even New England churchgoers heard more than doctrine. From the time of John Cotton's seventeenth-century Boston sermon on Judas (he was a bad man) to Devereaux Jarratt's moralizing about personal behavior in Virginia (mirth and dancing were bad) to Sophia Hume's lay critique of eighteenth-century South Carolina (a bad place to raise Christian children), clergymen and lay exhorters spoke incessantly about the need for, and character of, moral rectitude.[9]

When John Cleaveland of Chebacco Parish in Massachusetts preached on Matthew 3:10, "And now also the axe is laid unto the root of the trees: therefore every tree which bringeth not forth good fruit is hewn down, and cast into the fire," he stressed both original sin and his listeners' duty to honor "the commandments of God and of Jesus Christ the Son of God"—good works, as historian Christopher Jedrey points out. Marylanders heard much the same from Cradock. If his virtue was not as somber as Cleaveland's, it was no less serious. Like Cleaveland, Cradock regularly discussed moral behavior in his sermons, and his parishioners heard much from him about death, murder, fraud, wealth, and parents and children.[10]

The clerics' constant emphasis on virtue, responsibility, and, especially, morality helped make sense of revolutionary rhetoric about corruption and evil among English politicians and society. The French and Indian War of 1758–1763 offered some Americans all too intimate a view of that immorality. The behavior of British "regulars" sent from England to fight in America repelled John Cleaveland, who witnessed their antics when he served as chaplain to Massachusetts's Third Regiment. "Profain swearing seems to be the naturalized language of the regulars," he wrote. Their "gaming, Robbery, Thievery, Whoring, bad-company-keeping, etc.," epitomized the evils he and other ministers lamented Sunday after Sunday. Harvard's president, Samuel Langdon, repeated the accusation in more highly charged circumstances in 1775. Considering rebellion to be imminent, Langdon sanctioned action against a society and government driven to evil policies "by its public vices." It had "wage[d] a cruel war with its own children in these colonies, only to gratify the lust of power and demands of extravagance!"[11]

Second, as protest escalated, some ministers discussed Revolution politics specifically. This could occur in Sabbath sermons. But especially in New England it more often happened during midweek fast day and thanksgiving sermons, as best fitted the state church tradition. Just as they had spoken before other, perhaps smaller, audiences in earlier decades, the ministers excoriated the unchurched, criticized the British, and promoted the quest for salvation. But now they also brought Christianity directly to bear on the revolutionary crisis. Samuel Webster told fast-day listeners that the crisis stemmed from their own immorality: "It is for a people's sins, when God suffers this [evil] to come upon them." Ministerial support for the Revolution extended beyond New England. Despite some probable exaggeration in his report that Philadelphia ministers "thunder and lighten every sabbath" with anti-British sermons, John Adams was not alone in remarking on the local clergy's political involvement. Patricia Bonomi notes Jefferson's comment that in Anglican Virginia "pulpit oratory ran 'like a shock of electricity' through the whole colony" and that "Landon Carter's minister 'did very Pathetically exhort the people in his sermons to support their Liberties . . . and in the room of God save the king he cried out God Preserve all the Just rights and Liberties of America.'"[12]

Both ironically (in view of the Revolution's frequent appeals to liberty) and surprisingly (in view of historians' recent emphasis on evangelical Dissent), the most common denominator among pro-Revolution ministers was a state church pulpit. Middle colony Presbyterians and Virginia Baptists formed the most important exception to this pattern, and Anglican loyalism, furthermore, demonstrated that a state church pulpit did not guarantee revolutionary support. Yet tax-supported Anglican ministers also supported the Revolution in significant numbers. Though virtually all Anglican ministers in the northern and middle colonies, where Anglicans often had to act the role of "dissenters," became loyalists, a third of the Anglican clergy in Virginia and Maryland, where Anglicans held tax-supported pulpits, backed the Revolution. Elsewhere, prorevolutionary sentiment among ministers also coincided with a legally established, tax-supported ministry. In most colonies the Revolution pitted a colonial political establishment against an expanding imperial administration, and the colonial clergy often owed more to the former than to the latter, even if the clergy involved were Anglican. The kind of politically active colonists who led protest against British policy after 1763 usually supported the locally established congregation in colonies with state church systems; the established, tax-supported minister supported the Revolution. Moreover, like the colonial political elites who used local government as a base from which to launch revolutionary-era protest and rebellion, ministers in the state churches used their fast and thanksgiving day sermons in the war against British policies. In this way establishmentarian coercion, rather than Dissenting antiauthoritarian voluntarism, underwrote much of the American ministerial promotion of liberty and attack on Toryism.[13]

Most colonial ministers, however, remained silent about politics during the upheavals of the 1760s and 1770s. It has always been known that this was true of Pennsylvania's German Reformed and Lutheran clergymen. Their reticence, as well as that of Scots-Irish clergymen serving frontier settlements, has customarily been attributed to their minority status and frequent tension with the provincial elites who led the Revolution in Pennsylvania. But in fact their concerns were broader. For the German Reformed Coetus, for example, the Revolution threatened both Christianity and America. In May 1775 its ministers told congregants that they lived "in precarious times, the like of which, so far as we know, has never been seen in America." "The Lord knows what He has in store for us, and especially for our beloved Church." In 1777 the Coetus still described the Revolution as a "sad war" that had uprooted "many a praiseworthy observance . . . especially in regard to the keeping of the Sabbath Day and Christian exercises in the families at home."[14]

Clergymen in English denominations shared this fear of revolutionary upheaval. Most members of the Synod of Philadelphia refrained from public comment on the impending conflict. This was all the more notable since a few Presbyterians agitated widely for the Revolution. John Witherspoon, president of the College of New Jersey, not only wrote against the British but attended the Continental Congress, and George Duffield and Abraham Keteltas wrote in support of the revolutionary cause, which they described as a battle between God and the Antichrist. But most Presbyterian ministers simply did not participate in revolutionary politics. The Philadelphia synod reflected both their reticence and the tension that the Revolution produced. In a pastoral letter to its congregations in 1775, the synod acknowledged that "it is well known . . . that we have not been instrumental in inflaming the minds of the people, or urging them to acts of violence and disorder." Indeed, its ministers could not remember when "political sentiments have been so long and so fully kept from the pulpit." They meant sentiment supporting rebellion, of course. The demand for obedience was as strong among colonial Presbyterians as it was among Anglicans, and the Presbyterian commitment had been tested only shortly before the Revolution. During the so-called Regulator Movement in North and South Carolina in the late 1760s, backcountry Presbyterian ministers, supported by German Lutheran and Anglican pastors, had not hesitated to use their pulpits to denounce rebellion against colonial governments dominated by tidewater planter elites and to cite the traditional Pauline texts in doing so.[15]

The Presbyterians' 1775 pastoral letter reflected the conflict that Scottish ministers felt in regard to prerevolutionary protest. The ministers conceived of the contest as a "civil war," a phrase they used three times in their epistle. Scots, of course, had good reason to fear such contests. They had defeated the Catholic pretender, Charles Stuart, in the bloody Battle of Culloden only thirty years before, a battle so savage that even its victors found their success difficult to savor. The Scottish Presbyterians thus knew all too well how "civil wars are carried on with a rancour and spirit of revenge much greater than those between independent states."[16]

In their 1775 letter the members of the Philadelphia synod ultimately both instructed the Presbyterian laity on loyalty to George III and voiced support for Whig political principles. They expressed their "attachment and respect to our sovereign King George"; they also expressed their regard for "the revolution principles by which his august family was seated on the British throne." Still, as violence swirled around them, obedience preceded rebellion. The ministers explicitly upheld their allegiance to "the person of the prince," not merely to monarchy in the abstract. They believed that he may have been misled, but they also rejected "such insults as have been offered to the sovereign" by American protesters.[17]

The Presbyterian statement suggested why loyalism so frequently had a dual religious foundation and extended beyond the ranks of Church of England ministers, two-thirds of whom departed for England after the Revolution began. One reason concerned the traditional emphasis on authority and obedience in colonial preaching. Loyalist clergymen could be found in every colonial denomination: most Anglican clergymen; various New England Congregationalists, including Jonathan Ashly, Mather Byles, Eli Forbes, John Hubbard, David Parsons, Ebenezer Parkman, and Benjamin Stevens; a Philadelphia Baptist leader, Morgan Edwards; and a Swiss Presbyterian in Savannah, Georgia, John Joachim Zubly. These individuals could not repudiate the sermons and catechetical lessons that they had been propounding for years. As protest turned to independence, previously abstract fears that the flight from authority and obedience would turn everything upside down became a reality. The mild-mannered Samuel Seabury, who subsequently became the first Episcopal bishop in the United States, described a world truly revolutionized. Royally appointed authorities had been displaced by "delegates, congresses, committees, riots, mobs, insurrections, [and] associations." Justice was dispensed by "half a dozen fools in your neighborhood." Seabury was as appalled as the old Commonwealth Puritans who had fought to keep "swines and dogs" from the communion table. "If I must be devoured," Seabury wrote, "let me be devoured by the jaws of a lion [the king] . . . not *gnawed* to death by rats and vermin."[18]

A second reason centered on religious discrimination. The political elites who guided the Revolution in so many places also had frequently mistreated religious minorities in earlier times. Scottish and Scotch-Irish Presbyterians in North and South Carolina, English Baptists in Virginia, German Lutheran and German Reformed groups in Pennsylvania, and Anglicans in New England, together with small groups such as Wesley's Methodists or a sect like the Sandemanians of Rhode Island, had all experienced religious and political discrimination before the Revolution that ranged from minor annoyances to legal persecution. Most found the patriots' anti-Parliament protests ironic and even hypocritical. Some groups, like the Virginia Baptists, supported the Revolution anyway. But backcountry Presbyterians, German Lutheran and German Reformed settlers, and middle and northern colony Anglicans often found themselves drawn to loyalism not only out of political and religious principle but because of antagonisms with settlers who had earlier used the government and the law against them.[19]

The experience of William Tennent III, a Presbyterian minister in South Carolina and a son of New Jersey's charismatic William Tennent, Jr., revealed the difficulties of linking religion to the Revolution and the intriguing techniques some ministers might use to do it. In August 1775, the South Carolina Committee of Correspondence sent Tennent and William Drayton, a Baptist layman, to the Carolina backcountry to convince former Regulators to support revolutionary agitation. Backcountry settlers remained unmoved. They told Tennent: "No man from Charleston can speak the truth, and . . . all the papers are full of lies." Tennent's techniques demonstrated his willingness to use religion to affect politics. Sometimes he preached, after which Drayton "harangued" on politics. Sometimes Tennent preached and then did the haranguing himself. On August 20 he "spoke to the people on the state of America," but two Baptist ministers opposed him, and his listeners backed away from supporting the committee. Two weeks later, better prepared and less naive, Tennent arranged a visit by a Baptist minister from Charleston, Oliver Hart, but still apparently met with only mixed success.[20]

Tennent's "harangues" reflected his awareness of his listeners' eclectic, erratic religion. His summary of a two-and-a-half hour sermon at Little River mixed images of folk occultism and Christianity: "I conjured them by all that was sacred, that they would not give themselves up to be dupes of ministerial artifice, . . . and, by God's help, so touched their minds." Occult images remained on his mind a day later when he sought to explain how backcountry support for the Revolution eluded him once again: "A certain Justice Anderson, who formerly was a friend to American freedom, but receiving the magic touch from the other side of the river, suddenly changed his note, and by every artful method has since disaffected his acquaintance."[21]

The Revolution also shaped American religion, of course, and it did so in complex ways. This complexity emerges even in the story of Christian denominational decline and growth. The most serious erosion occurred in the Anglican congregations, which were often most numerous where other denominations were weakest and whose members had initiated the resurgence of public Christian worship at the beginning of the century. In parish after parish, Anglican ministers left because they openly supported the Crown, because they could not endure abuse by local patriots, or because they were no longer being paid by either the SPG or their vestries. Fifty Anglican priests were working in Pennsylvania, New York, and New England before the Revolution; only nine remained afterward. About 100 of the 150 priests in the southern colonies also fled to England. As a result 75 percent of the Church of England parishes, built up so carefully in the previous half century, lost their clergymen and, with them, their principal leadership in sustaining public Christian worship.[22]

Statistics kept by the Baptists and Presbyterians reveal the vagaries of religious experience during the revolutionary period. Between 1761 and 1776 the Philadelphia Baptist Association grew from 29 congregations with 1,300 adult members to 42 congregations with 3,000 adult members. But the association's congregations quickly felt the sting of war. By 1781 the association had lost the membership gains and institutional growth achieved in the previous fifteen years. Its congregations declined in number to 26, and its membership from 3,000 to 1,400 adults. Many congregations disbanded; even surviving congregations lost a fifth of their members. Between 1776 and 1781 average church membership declined from 71 to 55 adults.[23]

Yet in other settings Protestant denominations advanced during the Revolution. South Carolina's Charleston Baptist Association experienced significant growth. In 1775 it counted 9 congregations, 7 ministers, and 529 members; in 1779 it counted 12 congregations, 12 ministers, and 890 members; and in 1783 it counted 13 congregations, 9 ministers, and 966 members. Presbyterian statistics described similar growth after, though not before or during, the Revolution. In 1774 the Synod of Philadelphia reported 139 ministers, 153 churches with ministers (some serving more than one congregation), and 180 vacant pulpits. By 1788 the Presbyterians were experiencing significant growth. They then counted 177 ministers, 215 congregations with clergymen, and 206 congregations without.[24]

Denominational statistics conveyed only part of the story, however. Methodism had the fewest difficulties, in part because it had the least to lose. Methodist missionaries had worked in America less than a decade, and all of them except Francis Asbury returned to England at John Wesley's command. Anglicans suffered most because they had the most to lose, in terms of both ministers and buildings. The physical destruction loosed on Anglican churches was reminiscent of sixteenth-century English anti-Catholic depredation. In parish after parish supporters of the Revolution stripped Anglican churches of their royal coats of arms, although usually they left the buildings and other fittings intact. By 1783 the only building known to have escaped such ransacking was the church at St. James Goose Creek in South Carolina, shown in Figure 10, where Francis Le Jau had proselytized both the English and their African slaves between 1706 and 1717; the reason for its survival, however, was probably due more to the building's increasing isolation after seventy years of population shifts than to any deference to royal politics, religion, or art in the state.[25]

Patriots attacked more than buildings. Isaac Backus noted the apparent murder in November 1776 of Ephraim Avery, a supporter of the Crown and the Anglican minister at Rye, New York. Those responsible contrived to make his death look like a suicide, an adroit move in a colony where loyalist sentiment ran high. Pennsylvania Quakers also experienced significant harassment for their pacifism and neutrality. Their numbers were already greatly reduced by the disciplinary renaissance of the 1750s, and they faced a real schism from "Free Quakers," who both supported the Revolution and rejected pacifism. As a result "orthodox" Friends found themselves hunted down in a colony they had founded and long governed. In May 1776 a stone-throwing mob forced Philadelphia Friends to observe a fast day that the Continental Congress had proclaimed. A Berks County mob shackled and jailed Moses Roberts, a Quaker minister, until he posted a $10,000 bond guaranteeing his "good" behavior. Philadelphia patriots also exiled seventeen Friends to Virginia in 1776 for nearly two years so they would not interfere with revolutionary activities. Patriots celebrating the surrender of Cornwallis in October 1782 ransacked Quaker homes that had not displayed victory candles.[26]

Even patriot ministers spoke in ominous tones after the war began. From 1774 through 1783 the Philadelphia synod regularly designated fast days to commemorate "the dark and threatening aspect of our public affairs, both civil and religious." Some of the danger came from Britain. British troops burned three Presbyterian churches in New York, two in Connecticut, and five in New Jersey, including the church in Princeton where John Witherspoon preached. At Huntington, on Long Island, they dismantled the stone church building and used tombstones as oven floors; funereal inscriptions appeared in newly baked bread crusts.[27]

Other dangers came from within patriot society. Clergymen who had struggled for a half century to advance Christian adherence could see much of their work lost in the turmoil of war. The Philadelphia synod continuously appointed fasts to relieve the "low and declining state of religion among us." Its letters spoke of "gross immoralities," "increasing decay of vital piety," "degeneracy of manners," even "want of public spirit." This feeling was not confined to English-speaking Americans or to the old middle colonies. German Reformed ministers, largely from western Pennsylvania, complained that the Revolution increased citizens' "vanity" and decreased their humility; they "indulge[d], without shame and decency, in the most abominable vices." Baptists in Virginia and South Carolina decried advancing sin and immorality amid the Revolution, and Isaac Backus worried deeply about morality in New England, something he too attributed to decline rather than to more persistent indifference to things moral and religious.[28]

The religious tensions generated by the Revolution appeared with special force in the revolutionary army, where chaplains and soldiers were forced to reconstruct their lives and their religion outside of their normal settings. Chaplains were a traditional part of British military and political culture in both England and America. Colonial militias and British troops appointed chaplains during the French and Indian War, and some of these men served again during the Revolution. From a military perspective, chaplains were present primarily to promote discipline and only secondarily to preserve faith. During the French and Indian War, George Washington described a good chaplain as a "gentlemen of sober, serious and religious deportment, who would improve morale and discourage gambling, swearing, and drunkenness." Washington and other revolutionary commanders expected chaplains to serve the same ends, and the Continental Congress quickly approved chaplains for the army when it designated Washington commander-in-chief.[29]

Chaplaincies revealed the clergy's ambivalent position in the revolutionary war. The coercive, state church affiliation that encouraged clergymen to support the Revolution also propelled them toward chaplaincy service. Approximately two-thirds of the one hundred Continental army chaplains had occupied Congregational or Anglican pulpits in New England or Virginia, where their salaries came from taxes levied on all in their parishes, not merely their voluntary listeners. Most of the remaining Continental army chaplains (nineteen of thirty-six) were Scottish or Scotch-Irish Presbyterians, whose Old World heritage was linked both to the state church tradition and to anti-English sentiment.[30]

Yet the chaplaincies also thrust clergymen into unfamiliar and uncomfortable new settings. At home drunkenness, bawdyness, and even aggressive irreligion could be explained away as the idiosyncratic behavior of peculiar individuals. But such behavior loomed larger in the army camps, where it seemed both more widespread and less explainable. Ammi Robbins, a New England chaplain, had been with his troops in Albany only a day in March 1776 before he termed the city "wicked." The Sabbath was "a high play day." Away from his own community, Robbins quickly felt adrift. "It don't seem like Sabbath Day, but I can't forget it[;] none seem to know or think any thing about it." Indeed, only by leaving his soldiers—and entering the wilderness—did he find a sign, disturbingly idealized, that traditional village Christianity was prospering somewhere. After a long walk, Robbins came upon a house "where I found a woman reading to her husband. It did me good to see any lady serious and [honor?] in any degree the Sabbath." Robbins's isolation—and anomie—also raised his concern about his social status, a problem common among eighteenth-century New England clergymen whose subtle competition with lawyers and merchants was not helped by a Revolution steeped in talk of Parliament and taxes. Robbins was unusually attentive to his treatment by officers: "Much respect [is] shown me as chaplain by all the officers with whom I live." But his nervousness about tea with General Richard Montgomery in July 1776 triggered some guilt about his quest for status: "May I be more concerned to please God and less to please men," Robbins wrote in his journal.[31]

The Revolution produced no new models for chaplains' activity. Sermons reflected a traditional mix of Christianity, patriotism, and invective toward enemies. William Emerson, of Lexington, linked patriotic service and God directly. In January 1775, three months before the skirmish at Lexington and Concord, Emerson preached on the topic "To see thy power and thy glory" before a session to enlist Minutemen. In June 1775 he preached on the topic "And shall not God avenge his own elect." His text in July 1775, Isaiah 19:20, was even more blunt: "for they shall cry unto the Lord because of the oppressors, and he shall send them a saviour, and a great one, and he shall deliver them."[32]

Chaplains used their pulpits to promote Christianity. Robbins, worried that the Revolution undermined hierarchical conceptions of society, substituted a Christian monarchy for a secular one when he talked about sovereignty with troops: "What a consoling thought," he wrote in his journal, "that the Lord, he is our King." Benjamin Trumbull told New York soldiers to follow the examples of Nehemiah and David and to fight "for the Churches of Christ and for their Brethren in Christ Jesus when unjustly invaded." Amos Farnsworth, of Groton, Massachusetts, heard ministers liken the revolutionary war to "spiritual warfare." Republicanism versus tyranny paralleled God versus the Devil. Valley Forge chaplains used the hardship and filth of the camp as a platform from which to stress personal regeneration and spiritual cleanliness as spurs to revolutionary victory.[33]

But war, at least this war, stimulated no more enthusiasm for religion than had peace earlier. Chaplains sometimes preached before large crowds. William Emerson preached to seven hundred men after the Lexington-Concord skirmish, and Robbins reported that a thousand people had attended his prayers in March 1776, in "wicked" Albany. Yet indifference proved as persistent in the camps as it had in the chaplains' villages. Soldiers tired of sermons during the 1776 Quebec campaign and there, as later, officers had to command them to attend. Robbins viewed the results of the coercion happily — "more like a Sabbath-day than any I have seen in the army" — but whether the soldiers listened to or followed his injunctions he did not say.[34]

A secular patriotism reinforced by wartime experiences sometimes competed with Christianity for the soldiers' attention. A Valley Forge observer noted that social standing seemed to inhibit religious participation, especially among officers who found it "unbecoming a Gentleman in the Camps to attend upon any religious exercises." Robbins hesitated before intruding upon the quickly developed military ritual used in officers' funerals: "There is something more than ordinarily solemn and touching in our funerals, especially an officer's; sword and arms inverted, others with their arms folded across their breast stepping slowly to the beat of the muffled drum. I endeavor to say something that will lead to meditation, but only a word."[35]

Indifference sometimes turned to hostility as camp conditions worsened. Disease and battle, rather than bonding soldiers to chaplains, strained their relationship. Sorrow and hopelessness constrained religious inclinations and stimulated bitter criticism of the chaplains. Lieutenant Isaac Bangs reported that a Rhode Island Baptist chaplain "made out miserably" when he preached on John 14:6. Another soldier reported the soldiers' delight when Samuel Spring returned home during the Quebec expedition, because they were tired of his harangues; ironically, Spring was the minister who had tried to raise their morale by removing the collar and sleeves from the jacket on George Whitefield's corpse in 1775 so officers could distribute pieces of them among the troops. Soldiers criticized chaplains for theological obtuseness, and when Robbins noted a clerical conference in his diary, it concerned only a fussy theological discussion—"subject between Mr. McCauley and myself about the accomplishment of the promises, differ a little about the millennium."[36]

Perhaps work with the soldiers was more depressing than chaplains had expected. Military service seldom celebrated health, life, or even victory. Robbins offered a brave rejoinder to the camp physician who warned him not to enter the hospital area. "If a physician goes, why not a minister of the great Physician?" But Robbins himself was poorly prepared to act upon his question. He had not experienced miracles, as had New Jersey's William Tennent, Jr., nor did he perform healings, as did George Fox. Robbins knew what he and the chaplains should do: "Encourage [the soldiers] when doing their duty, attend and pray for and with them when sick, and bury them when they die." But it was draining. If chaplains were not wasted by one of the diseases that raged through the camps, the soldiers' conditions struck them low. "Their sorrows take hold of me," Robbins lamented. One soldier put it more bitingly. Frustrated by the chaplains' helplessness, he ridiculed them as being "as destitute of employ in their way as a person who is dismissed from their people for the most scandalous crimes." With sentiments like these, religion and Christianity scarcely faced a secure future in America.[37]

Between the signing of the Declaration of Independence in 1776 and George Washington's death in 1799, American church and denominational leaders renewed efforts to stamp Christian values and goals on a now independent society. Three of these attempts proved especially important: powerful Christian explanations of the Revolution and of the proper political order that ought to govern American society; attacks on irreligion, especially on skepticism and deism; and the creation of new religious groups, which evinced principles that for the first time might be called distinctively American.

The association of society and government with Christianity was traditional in colonial political culture. But the Revolution strengthened the demand to associate society with Christianity in several ways — by revealing the previously shallow foundations of the association, by stressing a particular form of "republicanism" in government and society, and by stimulating a strong sense of cultural optimism that fitted certain religious themes, particularly American millennialism.

Dark concerns about America's religious future extended far beyond the chaplains working in the army camps. The destruction of church buildings, the interruption of denominational organization, the occasional decline in congregations and membership, the shattering of the Anglican church, and the rise of secular pride in revolutionary accomplishments all weighed on American religious leaders. Even as the Revolution advanced, denominational leaders often bemoaned rather than celebrated America's moral fiber. In 1780 the Synod of Philadelphia expressed dismay at the "decay of vital Piety, the degeneracy of Manners, want of public Spirit and prevalence of Vice and Immorality." In the same year the Philadelphia Baptist Association received letters from congregations "complaining in general of great declension in religion and vital piety" and "of amazing prevailing stupidity."[38]

Republican political ideology heightened concern for moral and religious foundations. Republican principles had enormous importance for American religion because, though they were often vague and elusive, they placed great authority in the very laypeople with whom the clergy had long struggled. The "public," for revolutionary-era theorists, seldom included women, enslaved or free Africans, or poor whites. Yet even with these omissions, republican theory gave sovereignty to a remarkably extensive citizenry. In England sovereignty lodged in a Parliament whose House of Lords contained bishops and a hereditary aristocracy and whose Commons was elected through a narrowly drawn franchise. In America, by contrast, sovereignty rested in an electorate as numerous as it was diverse. And though the American scheme was celebrated, it also gave rise to concern, even among its ardent defenders, about tumult and rabble.[39]

Contemporaries agreed that a successful republican society and government, by definition, depended on "a virtuous people." This sentiment did not take root in a reborn Puritanism but in more modern eighteenth-century principles. Episcopal ministers like William White, Lutherans like Henry Melchoir Muhlenberg,

Scottish-born Presbyterians like John Witherspoon, and Baptists like John Leland and Isaac Backus all equated republican longevity with widely inculcated moral virtue. The whole of society, not merely some of its parts, constituted the bedrock of the future. The contrast was particularly noticeable in Massachusetts. John Winthrop's Puritan society had been ordered by means of hierarchical responsibilities assigned among the people, "some highe and eminent in power and dignitie; others meane and in subjection." The 1780 Massachusetts constitution, however, rested order on a broader foundation: "The happiness of a people, and the good order and preservation of civil government, essentially depend upon piety, religion, and morality." It did not mention the "highe and eminent" or "others meane and in subjection."[40]

Optimism fueled the new republic. In celebration of Washington's inauguration, Charles Wilson Peale fitted Grey's Ferry Bridge across the Delaware River with Roman arches proclaiming "The New Era." Artists of all kinds chose Washington as their subject. Academies trumpeted the arts as a vital instrument in the creation of an independent American culture. A host of publications—the *United States Magazine*, the *American Monitor*, the *Columbian Magazine*, the *American Museum*—commissioned new verse, rediscovered colonial literature, and transformed both into a national literary heritage.[41]

Much of the postrevolutionary optimism was openly secular, not religious, and reflected the Founding Fathers' Enlightenment convictions. This was especially true of those whom Pauline Meier has called the "old revolutionaries." Franklin, Washington, Jefferson, Madison, and Hamilton all professed beliefs in the supernatural: they were not willing to risk identification as atheists. But their references to the supernatural were vague and ethereal, and their views of religion were far different from those of the Congregational, Baptist, Presbyterian, and Episcopalian clergymen who backed the Revolution. Franklin's god was a god of ethics and production, not theology and revelation. As for Christology, the old revolutionaries had even less to say. If Christ was divine, it was because his morals were true to the dignity of mankind rather than because they were divine. Christ took his place beside Socrates, Plato, and the Stoics, none of whom might be his equals but all of whom were moral compatriots nonetheless. Washington was utterly disinterested in theology, and nineteenth-century freethinkers were not without warrant in claiming him as their own. South Carolina's Christopher Gadsden quoted Juvenal, Pope, and Plato (the *Laws,* not the *Republic*) rather than Milton and Christ. Even John Adams, the "Puritan" revolutionary, believed that the argument for Christ's deity was an "awful blasphemy," best discarded in a new, enlightened age.[42]

Progressive conceptions of time rooted in a secular, rather than a supernatural, view of life underwrote much of the new American optimism. "The Muses have crossed the Atlantic," John Adams wrote. The Massachusetts *Centinel* described the result: "England was in the days of yore, the seat of philosophy . . . but now it is become the asylum of vagabonds and imposters." Thomas Paine's arrogantly titled *Common Sense* called for independence based on a belief in a nonsupernatural inevitability. Americans (and Britons too) had been thrust into independence despite themselves — "the *time hath found us,*" Paine wrote. Their cultural maturation over the previous half century had sealed their fate — "We are not the little people now, which we were sixty years ago." Therefore, he continued, "it is repugnant to reason, to the universal order of things, to all examples from the former ages, to suppose, that this continent can longer remain subject to any external power." Like Machiavelli, who warned Florentine humanists about the difficulties of mastering Fortune, Paine warned Americans to seize the moment. "It might be difficult, if not impossible, to form the Continent into one government half a century hence . . . the *present time* is the *true time.*"[43]

American religious leaders responded vigorously to these frequently contradictory stimuli. Their most important responses attempted to absorb and redirect the secular optimism. However frustrating their army service, chaplains glossed over their camp failures when they moved back into their town pulpits. Between 1763 and 1799 they published hundreds of sermons given before militia and army units both before and after the war. The complications of army life dissipated as their printed words floated out across the literate landscape. Their readers could concentrate on the chaplains' messages, efforts that were now joined to increased numbers of other commemorative sermons. Some, like those given with almost universal occurrence on July 4, simultaneously celebrated victory and independence. Fast and thanksgiving day sermons continued and even increased. Everywhere a torrent of ministers' words proclaimed American independence and Christianity together.[44]

If claims measured God's approval, the clergy put the new nation in good stead. Providential rhetoric fixed God's sovereignty over the Revolution. Some clergymen described the struggle in Manichean terms. Abraham Keteltas, the New York Presbyterian, termed it "the cause of heaven against hell." Elhanan Winchester, a South Carolina Baptist, described British actions as motivated by "Rome and Hell." Joel Barlow asserted in his epic poem of American destiny, *The Vision of Columbus*, that Heaven approved independence as much as it had guided America's discoverers—"America" meaning the old mainland British colonies, of course, not the whole of the Western Hemisphere. Timothy Dwight proclaimed that only Israel had "experienced more extraordinary interpositions of Providence."[45]

Millennialist rhetoric predicting Christ's return to earth also expanded. Millennialism thrived on dramatic events, such as the episodic colonial revivals or the French and Indian War, and the Revolution proved an efficient incubator for yet another cycle. Providential rhetoric revealed God's approval of the Revolution, but millennialist rhetoric located it in sacred time. Thinking that Christ's second coming would occur in a specific historical setting, Ebenezer Baldwin, a Connecticut clergyman, thought that the Revolution was "preparing the way for this glorious event." Samuel West, a New Hampshire minister, described the Revolution as fulfilling Isaiah's millennialist predictions. Some clergymen went further and suggested that the Revolution was a precursor to the beginning of the millennium and, perhaps, the "sixth vial" described in the Revelation, which would destroy the Antichrist when it was emptied and usher in Christ's reign.[46]

Yet the very ubiquity of such predictions produced a bewildering variety of styles. No single millennialist vision emerged in the early national period. As Ruth Bloch has noted, proponents variously predicted the coming of true liberty and freedom, a rise in piety, American territorial expansion, and even freedom from hunger. Many propagandists hedged their predictions, just as their predecessors had done in the 1740s and 1750s. The few who provided definite dates for specific events usually developed different and sometimes exotic chronologies. As Americans experienced political, social, and economic setbacks after independence had been won, others turned to darker visions of the world and the new nation's place in it. New Hampshire's Samuel MacClintock warned against "luxury, and those other vices." New Jersey's Jacob Green foresaw "contentions, oppressions, and various calamities." New York's "Prophet Nathan" wrote that crop failure resulted from Americans' greed and disunity.[47]

Despite, or perhaps because of, its inconsistencies, millennialist rhetoric performed important functions in revolutionary society. Above all, Christian millennialism played a significant role in rationalizing popular secular optimism, which it transformed more often than it confronted. Rather than make extensive critiques of secular optimism, millennialist propagandists offered a vision of optimistic progress that was made more understandable by Christian teleology. This progress took root not in man, whose imperfections were all too visible even amid the Revolution, but in God, whose perfection was highlighted by invisibility.

At the same time, apocalyptic thinking generally declined in the revolutionary period. "Millennialism" had previously always had two important components: the destruction of the world, which would precede Christ's return (the apocalypse), and Christ's return and his thousand-year reign (the millennium). Before the Revolution, Jonathan Edwards and other commentators were as much interested in the apocalypse as in the millennium. But the Revolution's success and the desire to increase Christian adherence suppressed apocalyptic digression while raising millennialist speculation. Apocalyptic speculations tended to be negative and even violent in tone. Millennialist speculations were usually hopeful and roseate. With the success of the Revolution, millennialism suited the American temperament better than apocalypticism did, and in this regard the Revolution profoundly shifted the colonial millennialist tradition. The Revolution was an event whose character and outcome seemed to have signaled the beginning of Christ's thousand-year reign, thus making the apocalypse either history or irrelevant.[48]

Millennialism also had important political implications. Millennialist rhetoric secured an unwilling and often perplexed society to the Christian plow with the harness of Christian time. It demanded lay adherence in a society where the people were now sovereign. When New Englanders sought a unicameral legislature and an elected executive on the ground that "the voice of the people is the voice of God" (the view of the *New England Chronicle*), the rhetoric largely benefited the advancement of Christianity: a legislature that spoke for God should also listen to those who articulated Christian theology, morals, and ethics.[49]

The millennialist incorporation of secular optimism in the revolutionary period was paralleled by equally adamant campaigns against irreligion in its intellectual disguises of skepticism, atheism, and deism. Before the Revolution clergymen had often endured derogation steeped in the doubts of the Enlightenment. The sometimes ribald proceedings of Annapolis's Tuesday Club and the satirical "Dinwiddinae" letters circulated in Virginia in the 1750s punctured religious pomposity with an ethic that took man for its measure. The Revolution removed one source of this activity by stripping away the imperial elite of governors, magistrates, and other officials who frequently supported, or were thought to support, such Enlightenment skepticism. As late as the 1830s Virginia's Episcopal bishop, William Meade, complained about the damage done by a degenerate, imperially connected colonial elite: "The grain of mustard-seed which was planted at Williamsburg, about the middle of the century, had taken root there and sprung up . . . the roots shooting deeper into the soil." But skepticism survived nonetheless, as American clergymen knew all too well. Its most prominent representatives — Franklin, Jefferson, Madison, and Washington, among others — seemed the apotheosis of the Enlightenment. Their support for Enlightenment discourse revealed a tolerance of skepticism, perhaps even irreligion, altogether dangerous in a new republic.[50]

Deism became a chief object of attack in the war against irreligion. The choice proved particularly clever, not least because it clothed a familiar specter in new dress. Attacks on popular immorality were not novel, and atheism, meaning a sustained denial of the supernatural, was too rare to foster a believable campaign against it. Deism had the attraction of being relatively new yet suspiciously commonplace among the new nation's political and social leaders. The word itself dated only from the seventeenth century and had achieved a place in common vocabulary only in the early eighteenth century. Most important, deism offered extraordinary opportunities to its critics to demonstrate the need for real religion, meaning orthodox Christianity, in the new republic. This was possible because, to its critics, deism was the epitome of hypocrisy. It masqueraded as religion but was thoroughly irreligious. Deists admitted the justice of religious claims, but they made religion irrelevant to contemporary life. The deists' god was dead. At best, signs of his existence were found only in the distant past, not in the present.[51]

As Americans turned from war making to nation making, clergymen turned to deism to explain their postrevolutionary failures and crises. Deism served as a new and dangerous label under which a broad list of evils, old and new, could be assembled. Thomas Paine's *Age of Reason,* published in 1794, was denounced far more than it was read. In 1798 Jedidiah Morse described why the deism Paine promoted should be so feared: "The existence of a God is boldly denied. Atheism and materialism are systematically professed. Reason and Nature are deified and adored. The Christian religion, and its divine and blessed author, are not only disbelieved, rejected and contemned, but even abhorred."[52]

The eagerness to uncover deism produced two major campaigns of religious paranoia. One scare involved the so-called Bavarian Illuminati, rationalist compatriots of the Freemasons. The campaign encapsulated all the important themes common to later nineteenth- and twentieth-century American nativist crusades. The Illuminati were foreign, anti-Protestant, atheistic, secret, conspiratorial, and perverse. They were seen as having turned Masonic Christianity inside out, and as having hidden behind the respectability of the Freemasons, a group already worrisome to some evangelicals but not subject to massive attack until the 1830s and 1840s. Acting in concert with the French (who surely were atheists, Jesuits or both), the Illuminati would sacrifice any principle for power and, therefore, would subvert both independence and Christianity.[53]

Thomas Jefferson's try for the presidency in 1800 brought out a second antideist campaign. It was particularly important because it focused on the potentially intimate relationship between a president's personal religious views and the fate of the American republic. Jefferson's actual religious views were complex. He was, indeed, a deist, and he also expressed a quiet regard for Christ and Christian ethics. But he rejected Christ's divinity and criticized religious coercion with a vigor that made some suspicious of his real religious views, despite the fact that evangelicals had long supported him for his efforts on behalf of religious freedom. Federalists linked Jefferson to anticlericalism and atheism in the by then notorious French Revolution; in their vocabulary, "Jacobin" meant atheist as well as democrat. Many ministers denounced Jefferson from their pulpits and decried the fate of the nation in the hands of a red-haired deist, an obvious agent of the Devil.[54]

The campaign to advance Christianity after American independence was not wholly negative. Amid the anger directed against deism, skepticism, and rationalism, other Americans again sought religious renewal, reform, and revival. The most immediately impressive form of that quest emerged from rationalist liberal circles. Developed largely from what Henry May calls the "moderate Enlightenment" and centered in what would come to be called the Universalist and Unitarian movements, rationalist liberalism found itself an early beneficiary of the kind of revolution that had already reshaped American political life. Its principal doctrines — a largely positive view of man, universal salvation, rejection of the Trinity, fascination with science, and a trend toward systematization — closely fitted the political optimism of the times. Among a people simultaneously sweeping away the encrustations of the past and forging new constitutions to bring new states and a nation into being, an emphasis on simple, universal religious principles held considerable appeal. Religious reformers sought to locate Christianity's essentials in a few themes and doctrines, to dispense with the excess baggage of historical theology, and to embrace the new science, all in order to advance mankind and Christianity in a new society and a new age.[55]

Unitarianism played a critical role in retaining Christian adherence among a critical segment of the new nation's political and cultural leadership. It was criticized by its contemporaries and subsequently by some historians for simplifications that seemed to strip away religious fervor. But this criticism, which generally reflects an evangelical conception of Christianity, also exposes the source of Unitarianism's importance in postrevolutionary America. As late as the 1790s it attracted more intellectual than popular attention. Between 1800 and 1830 as many as half of New England's tax-supported Congregationalist churches adopted Unitarian principles, sometimes after bitter local schisms that forced losers out of the old town or parish church. Unitarianism's admittedly elite following of literate, well-bred, and relatively affluent adherents, imbibing an abstract, distant theology, connected a significant Christianized element of the older colonial past to the more rambunctious, if not necessarily democratic, future. With little apparent sympathy for sectarian, disciplinarian, and revivalistic religious traditions, this element might easily have drifted into a far more aggressive secularism, perhaps not unlike that both publicly and privately expressed by so many of the Founding Fathers. However much evangelicals opposed Unitarian aloofness, Unitarianism kept a crucial elite moored to a Christian dock, no mean accomplishment in decades when enormous numbers of Europeans — including Europeans soon to be revolutionaries — abandoned Christianity altogether.[56]

Emotion-laden revivals also emerged in postrevolutionary America. They came with a breadth, swiftness, and persistence that make it difficult to separate them from the so-called Second Great Awakening that allegedly began in Kentucky in 1805 and lasted into the 1820s. Indeed, as in the case of the first "Great Awakening" of the 1740s, historians' emphasis on a "Second Great Awakening" of 1805–1820 obscures important religious revivals that began as early as the Revolution. A dramatic "New Light Stir" reshaped religion in New England's upland hill country between 1776 and 1783 and was accompanied by both indigenous and imported religious groups that prefigured important features of antebellum religious eclecticism. New York experienced steady congregational growth from the end of the war well into the 1790s. Baptist revivals persevered in Virginia and the Carolinas in the 1780s and 1790s, and in these decades they were accompanied once again by Methodist revivals, Methodist missionaries having returned immediately to the American fields after the war's end despite John Wesley's Toryism.[57]

The late eighteenth-century revivals exhibited three important characteristics linked to the Revolution. One was a marked tendency toward a reductionism and antitheologicalism, if not anti-intellectualism, which paralleled Unitarian rationalism but not Unitarian spiritual aloofness. Devereaux Jarratt, Virginia's evangelical Anglican who could never bring himself to become a Methodist, expressed the extremes of this trend. In 1800 he wrote a friend that although "*Calvinism* and *Arminianism* . . . divide[d] the Christian Church," he "profess[ed] neither *this* nor *that*" and was "united to *one* as much as to the *other*." New England's Freewill

Baptist movement, founded by Benjamin Randel in the 1770s, rejected Calvinist predestination theology and stressed universal salvation and a strong Christology. The sources of this theological reductionism were sometimes ironic. Elias Smith, a former Baptist who founded a short-lived ecumenical "Christian" movement in 1802, found an important source for his effort in the theology of Jean Frederic Ostervald, an early eighteenth-century Swiss theologian whose works had been an SPG favorite and whose English translations had been almost wholly sponsored by the SPG.[58]

Second, revolutionary and postrevolutionary American revivalism had a tendency to involve dreams, visions, apparitions, and physical manifestations of divine intervention seen in some earlier eighteenth-century revivalism. The best-known example was that of the Shakers. Jesus had first appeared to Ann Lee, their apparent founder (and second manifestation of Christ on earth), and her associates in England, and in 1772 visions prompted them to emigrate to New England as the site of Christ's second kingdom. They arrived in New York in 1774. The Revolution only enhanced their millennialist visions, and the rightness of their celibacy came "to be transparent in their ideas in the bright and heavenly visions of God." For Shakers as well as for American revolutionaries, heaven began on earth.[59]

The Shaker emphasis on dreams and visions was commonplace, not unique. Benjamin Randel confirmed religious truth through out-of-body experiences and dreams: "I never could tell whether I was in the body or not . . . I saw a white robe brought down and put over me, which covered me, and I appeared as white as snow." Freeborn Garrettson and James Horton, Methodist itinerants, unashamedly shared accounts of their own divine dreams with their listeners, who in turn described equally compelling occurrences. In June 1779 a woman told Garrettson "many things that seemed strange," including knowledge of "when she was to dye and what death she was to dye." In February 1780 Garrettson himself reported being "transported" with visions "of the night [and of] many sharp and terrible weapons formed against me." If he did not experience miracles he dreamed of them, for "as soon as [these weapons] came near me they were turned into feathers, and brushed by me as soft as down." Elias Smith believed that divine providence led him to find tables, bibles, and psalm books "in the same place where I dreamed they were" and eagerly attributed divine significance to a dream in which an angel instructed him to preach on the topic of Jacob's ladder: "The next day in the pulpit, I told the people of Jacob's dream and my own and was happy in having [an whole?] Saviour to preach to every creature."[60]

In addition, postrevolutionary revivalism extended the fusion of indigenous and transatlantic dynamics that had been common to prerevolutionary Christian reform and revival. The "New Light Stir," Randel's Freewill Baptists, and even the emergence of the Unitarian movement reflected strong local dynamics whose importance only increased in the new republic. Transatlantic influences, too, pervaded postrevolutionary revivalism. Though the Shakers actually worked out their identity in the New York and New England wilderness, they did so by enhancing the millennialist, apocalyptic, and visionary themes they had earlier imbibed in England. Baptist revivalism throughout the southern states emerged as part of a vigorous Baptist revival that also occurred in late eighteenth-century England. The *Baptist Annual Register*, a London publication, advanced transatlantic revivals that involved blacks as well as whites in both the new states and the remaining British colonies in the Caribbean. Methodist itinerants similarly moved back and forth from England to America immediately after the Revolution, and their great success quickly produced a separate denominational structure that further invigorated the Methodists' national dynamism even as it deepened their transatlantic connections.[61]

In all, Christianity recovered from the American Revolution with remarkable alacrity. The churches, though buffeted by a revolution whose battlefield and army camp experiences exposed the tenuousness of popular Christian adherence and reinforced the vigorous secularity of its political principles, emerged with renewed vigor in the 1780s. They sought to sacralize the Revolution and American society through a Christian rhetoric that pulled secular optimism within a Christian orbit. They experienced surprising growth in the 1780s and even greater growth in the 1790s. They found increasingly indigenous resonances in new religious movements, ranging from Unitarian rationalism to Baptist, Methodist, and Shaker ecstasy. In less than two decades, they demonstrated that religious groups that had not initiated the Revolution could nevertheless survive it. In the next half century, they would begin to master the new American environment by initiating a religious creativity that renewed spiritual reflection and perfected institutional power, all to serve Christian ends.

TOWARD THE ANTEBELLUM SPIRITUAL HOTHOUSE

8

In 1798 Charles Brockden Brown, frequently called the father of American literature, published *Wieland; or, The Transformation.* The story concerned the religious demise of the Wieland family, which lived on an isolated estate overlooking the Schuylkill River outside Philadelphia. The religion of the Wielands was not evangelical Christianity or even Quakerism, however. It was an ecstatic, highly individualized, personal spirituality whose followers were obsessed with manifestations of divine intervention. Spirits communicated messages through the deceased. Dreams and visions offered premonitions of the future. Ultimately, the religion destroyed the entire family. Wieland's father was consumed by flames emanating from a mysterious divine light he could not resist, and Wieland murdered his own children during a religious frenzy. At the conclusion of the novel, Wieland's sister, Clara, the narrator and the family's sole survivor, fled America for France. Only in the Old World could she escape the gothic religious horror that had destroyed her family in America.[1]

Wieland was remarkable for its rich allusions to colonial America's complex religious heritage. It was not a mere "Puritan" novel, nor was it a narrow response to the Bavarian Illuminati crisis of the 1790s, as literary scholars have sometimes asserted. Instead, *Wie-*

land looked back to the American religious past even as it pointed forward to the American religious future. Wieland's father began his religious education—and his slide toward spiritual destruction—by reading a history of the Camisards, the radical "French Prophets" of London who were frequently believed to have inspired English and Continental religious radicalism and colonial American revivalism. Wieland's mother followed the teachings of Count Nicholas Zinzendorf, the German pietist and Pennsylvania immigrant. Wieland and his father both bore striking resemblances to Johannes Kelpius, the German mystic who had settled in Pennsylvania in the 1690s (see Figure 14). Kelpius's "temple" had been dug out of the steep hills of Wissahickon Creek, which flowed into Schuylkill River. Although Wieland, unlike Kelpius, was married, both were "frugal, regular, and strict in the performance of domestic duties." Also like Kelpius, Wieland and his father preferred their own worship to that of other sects because they "perfectly agreed with none," a sentiment that was familiar to many Americans and encouraging the growth of new postrevolutionary religious groups deemphasizing doctrine and complex theology, such as the Unitarians and the Freewill Baptists.[2]

Wieland also offered a provocative vision of antebellum religious enthusiasm and eclecticism to come. To be sure, Brown was a novelist, not a prophet. His condemnation of individual religious enthusiasm failed to measure its permanent contribution to the American religious tradition, and his focus on aristocratic religion failed to anticipate the importance of the broader, more rambunctious religious enthusiasm typical of the Jacksonian era.

Still, *Wieland* tapped an extraordinary range of religious interests already evident in the twilight of the Federalist period. It articulated a fascination with divine interventionism in dreams, visions, and ghosts that increased in the next decades. It uncannily stressed the explosive religious proclivities evident in bourgeois families. It pointed toward broad middle-class interest in supernatural phenomena and in Swedenborgianism, Freemasonry, Mesmerism, and spiritualism. Ultimately, it pointed to a dramatic American religious syncretism that wedded popular supernaturalism with Christianity and found expression in antebellum Methodism, Mormonism, Afro-American Christianity, and spiritualism. *Wieland* would have been believable as history had it been written in 1848, the year Leah, Margaret, and Kate Fox initiated

14. Johannes Kelpius, model for Charles Brockden Brown's Wieland. *Portrait attributed to Dr. Christopher Witt.*

the spiritualist movement. That it was published and widely read in 1798 only points up how after the Revolution Americans turned their attention to spiritual issues that transfixed antebellum society for decades.

The persisting belief in witchcraft signaled the tenacity of popular belief in magic, the occult, and other forms of supernatural intervention in America after the Revolution. The most dramatic evidence of this tenacity occurred in Philadelphia on the eve of the Constitutional Convention. In May 1787, a mob attacked a woman for practicing sorcery. Two months later, after city authorities refused to prosecute her and a heat wave further exacerbated popular anger over the episode, neighbors pelted the woman to death with stones. The Philadelphia press condemned the incident. In a society that had "emancipated itself from the superstitions of authority" and where delegates were then shaping the nation's political future, witch executions seemed anomalous indeed. The press was not the public, however. The only person subsequently charged with aiding the mob and causing the witch's death defended her actions on highly traditional grounds: "her only child sickened and died, under the malignant influence of a *charm*" supplied by the alleged witch; since authorities refused to prosecute the witch, she and other residents had taken the matter into their own hands.[3]

Formally educated Americans generally deplored popular witch beliefs. Yale students debated the witch issue until the end of the century and usually concluded that witches and miracles had been confined to the biblical period. In *Wieland,* Clara condemned "dreams of superstition" and "witchcraft," with "its instruments and miracles," as "monstrous and chimerical," even though she affirmed the existence of other "conscious beings, dissimilar from human, but moral and voluntary agents as we are." Isaac Backus dismissed as an example of confused or mistaken opinion the report of a man who believed himself bewitched or possessed by devils in 1789.[4]

Yet belief in witches continued. The folklore scholar Richard Dorson has traced witchcraft beliefs virtually everywhere in antebellum America, including New England, New York, Pennsylvania, the South, and even the West. The memoir of Brantley York, a nineteenth-century Presbyterian minister, provides graphic detail of witch belief in the early national South. York described a childhood in the 1810s in Brush Creek, North Carolina, that was shot through with witch stories. Witches could transform themselves into animals, "creep through a key-hole, by the magic of a certain bridle called the witch's bridle," and change humans into horses. Such stories, told throughout the new nation, became the social foundation of the supernaturalist literature of Irving, Poe, Hawthorne, Melville, and James that typified American letters throughout the nineteenth century.[5]

The widespread use of the divining rod underscores the breadth of early national supernatural practice. Although long associated with German culture, the divining rod was found in all regions of the new nation by at least 1800. Americans used it to detect underground water (such use was also called "water witching" and dowsing") and to locate valuable objects, including metal ore and buried treasure. As with astrology, its theoretical and theological underpinnings could be exceptionally elusive. Its effectiveness was variously attributed to "natural" sympathies between water and the metal or wooden rod, secret properties of the rod, secret knowledge possessed by the practitioner, or ritual magic utilized by the practitioners but not always under their control. The sociology of its use was equally complex. Practitioners usually came from marginal segments of society, but users cut a far broader social path. Most were middle-class landowners seeking good locations for wells, which were expensive to tap even under the best of circumstances; the transient and the poor had little need for such a service.[6]

Fortune-tellers also made the transition from colonial to independent America and even from rural to urban society. American novelists frequently mentioned astrologers and other "mediums," especially after the rise of spiritualism in the late 1840s. D. Michael Quinn has described a formidable American literature available in earlier decades on occult crafts. Erra Pater's *Book of Knowledge,* a standard eighteenth-century text with crude and even lurid descriptions of medical and occult procedures, received at least thirteen American printings between 1790 and 1810; Ebenezer Sibley's *New and Complete Illustration of the Occult Sciences* also appeared in thirteen editions between 1780 and 1830; and American printers issued *The Complete Fortune Teller* in at least five editions in the same period. A Lutheran minister in New York, Frederic Quitman, protested in a *Treatise on Magic,* published in 1810, that occult nonsense was running wild in the state and that the "government out to stop such fatal practices, whereby the lives of many are put in jeopardy." Not all agreed; one Robert Scott of Poughkeepsie quickly issued a tract to defend occult speculation and practice against Quitman's attack.[7]

York offered a vivid description of rural North Carolina fortune-tellers. "They could tell a young man the color of the hair, eyes, skin and many other minutiae, of the girl who was to be his wife, and describe with much exactness the kind of man that each girl would have for a husband," he remembered. His own parents entertained a traveling fortune-teller in their own home and saw no conflict with their Baptist principles in doing so. In practicing his art the man provided them with an exotic experience. Neighbors filled the house "to its utmost capacity" and witnessed "fortune telling, breaking witchcraft, and removing spells." When York's parents asked their visitor to tell their son's fortune, they heard an exciting tale indeed. "This is no ordinary boy," he said. The child would "be a ringleader, but a leader to all kinds of wickedness, such as card-playing, horse-racing and every species of gambling . . . finally he will end his career on the gallows."[8]

Astrology also remained popular after the Revolution. Some almanacs eschewed astrological information, especially the anatomy and the signs of the zodiac. But others did not. New York almanacs published between 1790 and 1820 offer an excellent sample of contemporary American publication of the anatomy and astrological lore. The *Federal Almanac* of 1797 omitted both the anatomy and the zodiac, and *Gaine's New York Pocket Almanac* of 1796 contained no anatomy but did print the zodiac signs. In contrast, *Hutchins Improved,* a 1797 New York almanac, included both the anatomy and the zodiac, as did *Isaiah Thomas Jr.'s . . . Almanack* between 1804 and at least 1818. Even church-related almanacs printed astrological information. The *Clergyman's Almanac* for 1810 included the signs of the zodiac without comment, and *The Christian Almanac,* begun by the American Tract Society in 1821, included the zodiac signs and daily locations of planets, though it excluded the anatomy.[9]

Treasure-seeking fused supernatural belief with American materialism. Treasure-seeking had colonial origins; Benjamin Franklin had ridiculed it in 1729. Its popularity exploded after the Revolution. New England was alive with treasure-seekers between 1790 and 1850, as Alan Taylor has demonstrated. York reported them in North Carolina, and Joseph Doddridge described them in Virginia and Pennsylvania. An 1825 Vermont newspaper claimed that some five hundred persons were digging up the Green Mountains in search of treasure. Others described a countryside pockmarked with gaping holes dug up to find secret treasures.[10]

Dreams, divining rods, and "peep stones" (cylindrically shaped rocks with holes for viewing) revealed elusive treasures. In Taylor's list of forty-eight treasure-seeking episodes between 1695 and the 1870s, divining rods were the most popular means of recovering treasures (used in twenty-five episodes), followed by seer stones (nine episodes), dreams (five episodes), seances (three episodes), and one episode each involving astrology, conjuring, cat sacrifice, visions, and a ball. Since devils, ghosts, and witches kept seekers from their treasures, failures also could be attributed to supernatural forces. Of course some treasures, such as Captain Kidd's already mysterious fortune, had purely secular origins. But in a society where individual expectation often outran contemporary economic prosperity, it is not surprising that seekers attributed other treasures to divine action, part of the supernatural's influence on the world.[11]

Folk medicine manifested themes of supernatural healing and persisted in the face of the rising practice of "scientific" medicine in the nation's early medical schools and hospitals. One of the most telling examples is a 1784 manuscript, the Joshua Gordon "witchcraft book." Its compiler arranged its contents with ritual-like care. Two pages of charms common to the English magical tradition opened and closed the volume. The phrase "Behold him Seized Malicously Abused" was copied seven times to fill the first page, and the phrase "Your Saviour Sweeting Blood wch is yours," repeated nine times, filled the second page. The same phrases, copied again to fill the manuscript's final pages, linked popular conceptions of supernatural power to Christian practice. They compared the pharisees' seizure of Christ to the Devil's seizure of persons in witchcraft and reminded users that men and women could redeem themselves through Christ's blood.[12]

The cures in the Gordon manuscript invoked divine intervention, and some reflected the syncretism of Christianity and popular magic that still worried clergymen. The more vigorously magical recipes were based on the traditional European notion of sympathetic attraction. Animal feces and human urine cured "old soars," preserved cattle from witchcraft and mysterious disorders, and unmasked malevolent persons. The remedies for warding off evil visitors assumed that offenders were neighbors, not strangers, as had colonial witchcraft accusations: "You must not lend any manner of thing off for the Space of 3 Days [from] your plantation. The person or persons guilty will assuredly come wanting to Borrow Something But by no means Lend; otherwise, you lay open a gain to thir malies [malice], which will be more desperate then Before." Several cures turned Christian ritual into magical rites. "A Cuar for gun that is Speld" required a frustrated hunter to "lod your gun in the name of the father, Son, and holy ghost and put the point of the tung [of a dead deer] down next the powder . . . When you discharge your gun do it in the name of the father, son, and holy gost." A cow losing milk could be cured if its owners would "take a heather belonging to a box Iron, put it in the fire, and make it Red hot[,] take the milk of the cows thats hurt[,] power [pour] on the hot iron repeating the names of the blessed trinity."[13]

South Carolina was not alone in its manifestation of supernatural healing practices. Doddridge described western Virginia "witchmasters," who cured diseases "which could not be accounted for nor cured" and which therefore were "usually ascribed to some supernatural agency of a malignant kind." York wrote of North Carolina neighbors who patronized "witch-doctors" who, "by certain mysterious operations," relieved them "from the influence of the much dreaded witch" and protected them from lead shot.[14]

European immigrants continued to bring magical and supernatural lore into early national and antebellum society, much as they had done in the colonial period. Two students of the early eighteenth-century Philadelphia physician and alchemist, Christopher Witt, practiced their arts around Philadelphia between the Revolution and 1810, and George Dresher and Paul Heym apparently used folk techniques brought from Europe in the Pennsylvania countryside in the same period. Several "powow books" and a nineteenth-century German language text, *Das Sechste und Sie-*

bente Buch Mosis (The sixth and seventh book of Moses), combined Christian prayer with non-Christian magic. Supernaturalist healers even appeared in the federal censuses. Surveys of the massive mid-nineteenth-century Philadelphia censuses have uncovered three German healers and a black astrologer in the 1850 Philadelphia census and two phrenologists, one black and one white, and three herb doctors, all of them black, in the 1860 census.[15]

Manuscripts and books describing supernatural healing also exhibited the first incorporation of native American spiritual curing into European practice, something that seems not to have occurred earlier in the colonial period. The Gordon manuscript included "An Indian cure for the reipture [rupture] in children" and the nineteenth-century Pennsylvania "powow books" included allegedly Indian cures among their medical recipes. Whether these cures actually derived from native American culture is as yet unknown. Their authors, in any case, took care to convince their readers that they did. This new development was not entirely surprising. Magical adepts had long believed that supernatural truth was available to men and women everywhere, irrespective of status, wealth, and inheritance.[16]

Alchemy also persisted into early nineteenth-century America. John William Gerard De Brahm, a German or Dutch surveyor and naturalist who became surveyor general for the southern colonies in 1764, published four mystical works with alchemical significance before his death in 1799 and worked continuously on a major manuscript, never published, which synthesized alchemical, Rosicrucian, and Christian millennial beliefs. Yale's president, Ezra Stiles, exemplified the ambivalence that even observers sympathetic toward alchemy and other revelatory parallels to Christianity had. In a statement penned in his literary notebooks, Stiles denied knowledge of alchemy or even a substantial interest in the topic. Yet he patrolled many of the obscure borders between Christianity and less orthodox supernatural thought and belief. Stiles read works by the medieval mystic Dionysius the Areopagite. He studied angelology and schemes outlining the celestial hierarchy, and he improved his Hebrew by reading Cabalistical texts. He admired the alchemical knowledge of several New Englanders, including Samuel Danford, a Massachusetts jurist, whom he described as "deeply studied in the writings of the Adepts." He did, however, express considerable irritation at a

New Haven physician, Aeneas Munson, who dogged Stiles about alchemy despite Stiles's protest that he knew nothing about it and was not an adept himself.[17]

Swedenborgianism and Mesmerism also crossed the Atlantic to early national America. The Swedenborgian movement, based on the doctrines of the eighteenth-century Swedish mining engineer and religious ecstacist Emmanuel Swedenborg, believed in direct spiritual intercession with God. Swedenborg's descriptions of intense spiritual introspection recalled more radical moments in seventeenth-century Puritanism. In turn, his direct conversations with God, his "seances" with the deceased, and his complex doctrines about the millennium (he believed it had already started), the heavens (much like those of Dionysius the Areopagite), and "correspondences" (which called for the reconciliation of the "inner" and "outer" person) prefigured central themes in antebellum Mormonism, spiritualism, and Christian Science.[18]

Although Swedenborgians were present in America by at least 1784 and at least one Swedenborgian congregation existed in every major American city by 1800, Swedenborg's books, many published in English in London, accounted for his principal influence in America. Stiles was fully aware of Swedenborg's theological daring and termed him "the learned Visionary [who] had a species of Insanity." More favorable assessments came from Philadelphia's literary and scientific elite (the latter also impressed with Swedenborg's writings on mining) and members of the Virginia aristocracy like Robert "Councillor" Carter and the Fairfaxes. It is interesting that Carter, who left Anglicanism in the 1770s to become a Baptist, reportedly attempted to communicate with spirits three years before his conversion to Swedenborgianism in 1790. Carter then abandoned his Virginia plantations, freed his slaves, and moved to Baltimore. There he preached in the city's Swedenborgian congregation while continuing to investigate many other forms of religious expression, until his death in 1802. Swedenborgianism's appeal was not restricted to America's educated and propertied elites, however. After Carter's death, poor tradesmen and artisans increasingly patronized Baltimore's Swedenborgian congregation, which was the third poorest in the city in 1804 and second poorest in 1815.[19]

Theories of animal magnetism, called Mesmerism after their Austrian expositor, Franz Anton Mesmer, probed the boundaries of popular religion, medicine, and science. Animal magnetism attracted widespread interest after Mesmer calmed lunatics in Paris in the 1790s by supposedly aligning their individual magnetic forces with universal ones. Outside France and especially in Britain and the United States, adherents often cast Mesmerism in religious terms. Mesmerism was the first of what Sydney Ahlstrom described as America's great "harmonial" religions, "those forms of piety and belief in which spiritual composure, physical health, and even economic well being are understood to flow from a person's rapport with the cosmos." Mesmerism's emphasis on reconciling individual and universal forces, on healing, and on dreams, visions, and spiritual introspection found sympathetic resonances in an increasingly romantic, impulsive, willful America. Mesmerism's attraction to those at the edges of Christianity also demonstrated the undisciplined energy of spiritual creativity in the early national period. Swedenborgian congregations censured members who participated in Mesmerist experiments or acknowledged belief in Mesmerist principles. But the Swedenborgians also gained converts through Mesmerism. Although the confusion upset Swedenborgian leaders, Mesmerists found it thoroughly innocuous, probably because they never developed a "church" about which to be concerned.[20]

American Freemasonry demonstrated the appeal of secret and magical beliefs to middle- and upper-class men in the antebellum era. Between 1790 and 1840 perhaps as many as a hundred thousand men joined Masonic lodges in the United States, and historians have often documented Freemasonry's thoroughly bourgeois character. It was a movement of middling and affluent merchants, businessmen, and farmers seeking social and political solidarity in a freewheeling materialistic society. Freemasonry's mystical and occult appeal, however, is less well known, at least in American history. Frances Yates has described the movement's seventeenth- and eighteenth-century alchemical and Rosicrucian roots in Europe. Many antebellum denominations from Presbyterians to Freewill Baptists condemned Freemasonry as heretical, in part because its universalist sentiments denied the uniqueness of Christian revelation and in part because it reeked of magic. The Masonic texts and rituals that did express reverence for Christ appreciated his figure more than his doctrine, and they mixed that figure with Pythagorean or mathematical mysticism and alchemy.

These were expressed in elaborate and secret rituals that invoked magic, mathematics, and alchemy simultaneously and that proved attractive to antebellum men, sometimes more so than the rituals of Christian congregations.[21]

The fervently spiritual atmosphere gathering across early national society found direct institutional expression in four major antebellum religious movements: Methodism, Mormonism, Afro-American Christianity, and spiritualism. Each expressed vivid outbursts of popular spiritual syncretism. They reinforced and expanded the syncretistic religious impulses that had been emerging in the colonies on the eve of independence. None combined the same elements, and their internal dynamics differed remarkably. In some groups, syncretism occurred early but waned as the movements matured. In others, syncretism became more powerful as the movements grew. In all of them, the ability to meld seemingly eclectic religious traditions empowered them as much as did their eagerness to create powerful institutional traditions. They tapped themes of supernatural intervention long evident in the American, European, and African pasts and once again demonstrated the breadth of supernatural expression in American religious practice.

American Methodists absorbed and then redirected volatile elements of popular culture and life toward a more narrowly conceived Christian and middle-class movement. Somewhat surprisingly, early American Methodism did least with supernatural healing. This theme had long been important in radical British Protestantism and had fascinated the Methodist founder, John Wesley, as well. Wesley's medical manual, *Primitive Physick: An Easy and Natural Way of Curing Most Diseases* (London, 1747), underwent twenty-three printings in his lifetime, and Wesley frequently asserted the spiritual roots of sickness. He attributed diseases to demons, publicized claims of miraculous healing, maintained a strong belief in witchcraft, and believed that sin brought on the first human sickness. Yet Wesley and the early American itinerants pursued healing only metaphorically. Rather than emphasizing miraculous cures, they stressed the wholeness that followed death and salvation. "Faith healing" did not emerge as even a minor theme in Methodism until the late nineteenth century, and then it developed under outside influences rather than through a re-reading of Wesley.[22]

Syncretism in early American Methodism instead revolved around the figures of its itinerant ministers, who manifested divine attributes in their being, bearing, dreams, and rituals. Especially before 1820, the Methodists' itinerancy was that of "holy men," not unlike the ministry of the Tennents of New Jersey. The itinerants manifested Christian truth in their appearance and demeanor and developed rituals that drew on both Old Testament happenings and revolutionary war experiences. Methodist itinerants made a near ritual of their strong collective identity. They traveled about alone or in company with itinerants, but not with others. They rested at what one itinerant, Henry Smith, called "Methodist harbors" and what Lorenzo Dow more provocatively termed "Methodist taverns." There, Smith remembered, "they could *rest awhile,* and get their clothes washed and mended; or, as Mr. Asbury used to call it, 'get refitted.'" Their "fittings" emphasized their separation from the world. A Congregationalist minister in Connecticut warned George Peck's parents about the "strolling Methodists" they would meet in upstate New York, who would "go about with their sanctimonious looks and *languid* hair, bawling and frightening women and children." When Freeborn Garrettson dreamed about visiting "sanctified Christians," he knew he had received the "faith to believe" by the clothes he received. "In a moment my spotted garments were gone; and a white robe was given me." Yet as an itinerant minister, Garrettson wore black, a dress signifying the doom that awaited those who refused to acknowledge God's sovereignty and pursue their salvation.[23]

In fact early Methodist itinerancy in America bore an intriguingly Catholic character. It was largely celibate, apparently at the insistence of Francis Asbury, who may have had some personal antipathy toward both women and marriage. Asbury constantly warned itinerants about the dangers of consorting with women, and in 1803 he secured the agreement of the Philadelphia Annual Conference to oppose the use of married men on Methodist circuits, though his sometime rival, Thomas Coke, favored married itinerants. "To marry is to locate," Asbury quipped. The Methodist laity also often called early Methodist itinerants "Father." The names "Father Abbott," "Father Vredenberg," and "Father Horton" resonate through the memoirs of the early ministers. Benjamin Abbott, who was an itinerant in the 1790s, described a typical encounter: "Then a young woman came to me and said, [']Father Abbott, pray to God to give me a clean heart.[']" Another woman encountered Abbott later in even more colloquial fashion: "She then said, [']O Daddy Abbott! how can I live?[']" Revealing the power of the itinerants in shaping the Methodist movement, one minister explained the title by observing that the laity viewed the itinerant ministers as the fathers of their religious experience.[24]

Methodist itinerant preaching deliberately used theatricality to promote conversion. George Peck, an itinerant, recalled Jonathan Newman's 1804 discourse on "Nine and Twenty Knives" as only "very loud" but that of another itinerant, Benoni Harris, "a chubby little man with a mighty voice," as loud, entertaining, and effective. Looking "as if he had once been a man of full stature and size" who "had been pushed together like a spy-glass," Peck described how Harris once delivered a sermon while standing on a hogshead barrel. "In the midst of an impassioned deliverance [while] emphasizing his words with a vigorous stamp, he broke in the head, and in an instant almost disappeared. Still, not in the least disconcerted, he continued his sermon as if nothing had happened, the congregation [heard] the steady roar of his wondrous voice, but [saw] nothing of him but the shiny top of his bald head bobbing about, and his hands stretched up, gesticulating wildly."[25]

Early Methodist itinerants invoked the dream-world images already endemic in postrevolutionary society. Dreams had long presented Christian theologians with difficult problems in interpreting God's presence in the world. Some saw them as authentic spiritual expressions. Others, including most major Protestant figures, deemed them utterly unreliable. Though it was thought that dreams reflected individual idiosyncrasies, it was also expected that they conform to the religious truths authenticated in the Old and New Testaments.[26]

The early national Methodist involvement with dreams quickly raised the interpretive problem faced by other Christian groups. It was addressed directly in Freeborn Garrettson's *Experiences and Travels,* published in Philadelphia in 1791:

> Some suppose that we ought not to put any dependence in dreams and visions. We should lay the same stress on them in this our day, as wise and good men have done in all ages. Very great discoveries were made to Peter, Paul, and others in their

> night visions. But is there not a danger of laying too much stress on them? We are in danger from a variety of quarters: let us therefore bring every thing to, and try it by the standard; taking the Spirit for our guide, and the written word for our rule, we shall without doubt go safe.[27]

Garrettson's critique belied the importance of dreams to early American Methodism and especially to the itinerant ministers. Dreams proved especially significant in both their lives and their work. Dreams predicted salvation, death, and the realities of hell. Garrettson paid a flying visit to heaven in a dream. Garrettson ascended "a great height, . . . was over-shadowed with a cloud as white as a sheet" and "saw a person the most beautiful that my eyes had beheld." A dream carried George Peck to hell at age thirty-three, and he saw "nothing but devils and evil spirits, which tormented me in such a manner, that my tongue or pen cannot express."[28]

Methodist itinerants had great faith in the ability of dreams to predict the future. A dream of Benjamin Abbott's correctly foretold that the itinerant who had converted him would soon turn to playing cards and drink. A dream also predicted Abbott's own ministry. Abbott dreamed that Jesus called him to preach in the place of an absent itinerant. "You must speak for me," Christ said. Abbott's wife, however, dismissed the dream with some levity. "You are always dreaming about preaching," she told him, and Abbott deferred his ministry. But when she died only a few years later, in 1788, Abbott quickly went through Methodist ordination and took his place in the Methodists' itinerant and celibate ministry.[29]

Most notably, Methodist itinerants Garrettson, Abbott, and Peck described their dreams openly and enthusiastically when they preached to their audiences. Published Methodist memoirs also were often filled with dreams. "What a glorious time we had reading the Life of Benjamin Abbott," Peck remembered. Abbott's memoir, first published in 1807, turned to his sacred dreams by page three and detailed them throughout the book, offering tempting descriptions of God's many ways of speaking in antebellum society.[30]

The ritual of Methodist conversions soon sacralized additional elements of early national culture. The carefully chosen language, the emphasis on participatory hymn singing, and the very boisterousness all reflected the plebeian culture from which early Methodists sought converts on both sides of the Atlantic. After 1785, despite John Wesley's Toryism, American Methodists appropriated even the Revolution to their own sacred uses.

Abbott's memoir described the Methodist sacralization of the Revolution with special clarity. Like other itinerants, Abbott experienced and sought physical evidence of Christian conversion. During Methodist "love-feasts," some participants fainted. Others entered trancelike states for as long as three hours. One "continued so long, that his flesh grew cold, and his blood was stagnated to his elbows." This episode actually frightened Abbott. "I concluded to go home, and not proceed one step farther, for killing people would not answer." But the man did not die and, like others, was physically revived and spiritually reborn. "He began to praise God for what he had done for his soul," Abbott recalled. Early on, Abbott himself interpreted these episodes as ritual evocations of Lazarus's miracle, and he was careful to observe that they were triggered by God, not by himself. "This is the Lord's doing, and it is marvellous in our eyes."[31]

In the 1790s Abbott added new elements to the ritual while he was preaching on Maryland's eastern shore, an area that had seen some but not constant revolutionary action. He increasingly stressed military imagery. "I arose and gave them an exhortation, and the Lord . . . sent the word with energy, *like a sharp two-edged sword,* to their hearts: and they fell before the Lord, like Dagon before the ark, or like men slain in battle." By 1794 Abbott regularly described his listeners as "slain" by the spirit. Soon Abbott's conversion scenarios resembled a revolutionary military tableau. The gore and sacrifice of the war experience was now made even more sacred in the service of evangelical Methodist conversion: "Friday, August 1 [1794], I gave out a hymn and went to prayer, and the Lord poured out his Spirit and slew them as men slain in battle. Some lay in the agonies of death, some were rejoicing in God, others were crying for mercy, . . . he met with many to the joy of their souls, and his dear children were built up in their most holy faith."[32]

This ritual was more than entertainment. It introduced what earlier French and English religious radicals called "sacred theater" into postrevolutionary American Methodism. Methodist itinerants performed the gospel as much as they proclaimed it. Listeners played important roles in this theater as well. Laypeople acted out figurative revolutionary battlefield scenes, where their wounds, physical and spiritual, could be transcended in salvation and independence simultaneously. Nor were the Methodists to perform this theater alone. Christine Hyerman reports that by 1805 backcountry Carolina Baptists had developed even more richly evocative replications of the revolutionary army experience to stimulate revivals among second-generation Americans, who had never undergone battlefield experience.[33]

The Methodists' distinctive and popular syncretism faded after 1820. As early as the 1810s Methodists breached Asbury's demand for celibate clergy and required married itinerants. By the 1830s sharp tension separated the first itinerants, committed as they were to what one contemporary called "old batchelorism," and younger itinerants, whose marriages and children encouraged a far different and less expansive itinerant labor. Disappearing with the original itinerants were Methodism's fusions of popular and mainstream religious notions. Memoirs of second-generation itinerants say little or nothing about dreams. Methodist revivals of the 1830s paled in comparison to those that Abbott led in the 1790s.[34]

One measure of the change was the notoriety attached to Lorenzo Dow, so well known as a Methodist itinerant that it was commonly said parents named more children after him than after any other figure except Washington. Through the 1830s Dow encouraged listeners and readers to trust the supernatural revelations contained in dreams. He encouraged them to believe that he could locate lost and stolen objects, raise the Devil, and perhaps cure disease (Dow did sell his own medicine, just in case his spiritual healing proved insufficient). He was "crazy Lorenzo Dow," and in the minds of many the label confirmed rather than denied his religious calling. Other, more "orthodox," early itinerants acquired at least part of Dow's image; in the 1810s James Horton was not at all embarrassed to report a listener who referred to him as "crazy James Horton." But second-generation itinerants eschewed such labels and the behavior it connoted. A new, middle-class Methodism, guided by newfound prosperity, mammoth numbers, and a wider following among middling and affluent Americans who had long since turned frontier into settlement and settlement into society, emerged in the antebellum era. This too represented syncretistic impulses, but syncretism of a very different kind from that found in early national Methodism.[35]

* * *

Mormon syncretism borrowed from even broader religious sources and recast the movement in relatively conservative Christian garb, a process not completed until the early twentieth century. Mormonism, like early Christianity, was controversial, of course, and part of its controversy revolved around charges of magic. Within two years of the publication of the *Book of Mormon* in 1830, critics charged its translator, Joseph Smith, with heresy as well as with fortune-telling and treasure-seeking. Such controversies have not only continued into modern times but have even, in the past few years, become murderous. The sensationalism of the magic charges surrounding Joseph Smith encouraged an avaricious Mormon, Mark Hoffman, to forge letters offering additional evidence of Smith's magical practice. But in 1986, by his own admission, Hoffman killed two of his associates who threatened to expose his scheme, which had netted him enormous profits not only in the Smith forgeries but in forgeries of Egyptian papyri and many other "early" Mormon letters.[36]

The *Book of Mormon,* first given to Joseph Smith on gold plates by the angel Moroni in 1827, reflected much in the American religious tradition. One influence was New England evangelicalism, not all of which pleased Smith. Smith and his parents were well-known religious malcontents who were thoroughly disgusted with denominational competition—with "priest contending against priest, and convert against convert." Yet this same denominational wrangling raised Smith's interest in the conversion experience, Scripture, and religious truth, indelible features of New England evangelicalism and central to Mormonism as well.[37]

The *Book of Mormon* sacralized the nation's landscape by directly incorporating it into the Mormon Scripture. The sacred battles of the *Book of Mormon* occurred in America, rather than in the Middle East. This new scenario enabled the Mormons to transcend the Protestant denominational rivalries that had so repelled Smith. The *Book of Mormon* offered American readers a wholly fresh, wholly novel, and—most important—wholly innocent new Scripture. In it there were no theological schools and no theological wrangling. A new Mormon revelation made possible the recovery of ancient spiritual truth that had been hobbled by the corruptions of time and imperfect Christian practice.[38]

Other forms of supernatural intervention preceded and followed Smith's receipt of the golden plates in 1827. In the earlier part of the 1820s and later in the 1830s and 1840s, Smith unashamedly reported receiving divine communication in dreams much as itinerant Methodist ministers had done in the 1790s and early 1800s. Many early accounts of Smith's revelations described them as emanating from dreams. Smith's supporter, Martin Harris, eagerly acknowledged that Smith "had been visited by the spirit of the Almighty in a dream." Subsequently, the angel Moroni appeared in Smith's dreams and revealed the location of the "Golden Bible," which Smith later translated as the *Book of Mormon.* Smith's accounts of additional angelic visitors closely paralleled those of Garrettson, the Methodist itinerant. An angel in a "loose robe of exquisite whiteness" offered instructions in religious truth and guided each man through additional religious experiences.[39]

Smith exhibited a strong interest in manipulating supernatural forces and in securing divine intervention both before and after the 1827 visit by the angel Moroni. There is abundant evidence that Smith practiced treasure-seeking throughout the early 1820s, and that he used occult means to do so. In an 1838 interview in a Mormon newspaper, *Elder's Journal,* Smith acknowledged his "money digging," though he claimed that "it was never a very profitable job to him, as he only got fourteen dollars a month for it." Early Mormon detractors used Smith's reputation as a fortune-seeker to disparage Mormonism, and they buttressed their criticisms with claims that Smith had used occult means in seeking treasure. His mother, Lucy Mack Smith, perhaps unwittingly substantiated these claims. As early as 1825 she described Smith as possessing "certain keys, by which he could discern things invisible to the natural eye," including hidden treasures, and in her autobiography, published in Liverpool in 1853, she offered additional descriptions of her own and her son's intimate acquaintance with magic and occult practices; these descriptions embarrassed Mormon authorities and led them to attempt to suppress the book.[40]

Smith's involvement in the occult intertwined directly with the *Book of Mormon.* The toads or salamanders Smith described as guarding the golden plates before he acquired them commonly appeared as purveyors of divine messages in the English and Continental occult literature that ranged from Henry Cornelius Agrippa in the sixteenth century to Emmanuel Swedenborg in the eighteenth century. As D. Michael Quinn has demonstrated, Smith and other Mormons openly acknowledged that the "Urim" and "Thummin" that Smith used to translate the golden plates and, thereby, produce the *Book of Mormon* was a brown seer stone, or peep stone, of a kind often used in treasure-seeking. The stone, known to many of Smith's successors, has long been stored in the vaults of the Mormon First Presidency in Salt Lake City, and no photograph of it is known to exist. In the 1840s, however, Brigham Young casually remarked that it was not unique and that Smith actually owned five such stones through which he received Mormon revelations. One of the stones, shown in Figure 15, was obtained by Smith in Pennsylvania prior to his visit by the angel Moroni; Smith used it to receive several of the pronouncements later published as the *Doctrine and Covenants,* which set forth basic positions on Mormon doctrine. Smith also possessed a dagger inscribed with the kind of astrological symbols for Mars and Scorpio that European and American adepts commonly used in magic ceremonies, and the Smith family owned a parchment, or lamen, inscribed with magical symbols, that was also a common feature of learned magic in the European occult tradition.[41]

15. Joseph Smith's green seer stone (approximately four inches long).

The early Mormons also tapped radical Christian notions of divine intervention by performing miraculous healings between 1831 and 1835. This was, apparently, controversial from the very beginning, and by 1835 Smith and the Mormon elders determined that it was "not the design of Christ to Establish his gospel by miracles." Smith may have had the abandonment of healing miracles forced on him. He described the decision as originating in an unplanned and heated discussion. By his own account, the discussion only began when, in visiting his father, Smith found "some of the young Elders . . . engaging in a debate, upon the subject of Miracles." They talked about the subject for three hours, apparently with some difficulty, and though Smith described the resulting agreement to discontinue miracles as a "righteous decision," he never elaborated upon it or explained precisely what prompted either the discussion or the decision.[42]

Mormon and non-Mormon sources alike suggest that miracles were both frequent and central to early Mormon proselytizing. The memoir of a Freewill Baptist itinerant named Nancy Towle, published in 1832, only two years after publication of the *Book of Mormon,* described miracles, including "healing the sick, raising the dead, [and] casting out Devils," as one of Mormonism's three most salient features. Towle's assessment proves to be more than an effort at anti-Mormon propaganda. Early Mormon letters and other evidence reveal both the commonality of miracles among them and certain peculiarities in their practice. Miracles did not figure as strongly in the *Book of Mormon* as they did in the Old or New Testament. At the same time, Mormons did not merely receive the benefit of miracles, as had the Tennents earlier, but actually took credit for performing them. The first occurred in 1830, when Smith cast a devil out of Newell Knight. Smith reported that when the Devil left the room, "visions of heaven were opened to my view."[43]

Mormon miracles were not limited to Smith, even in these early years. Both Towle and a Methodist itinerant, Tobias Spicer, reported numerous alleged Mormon healings in Vermont and New Hampshire. Mormon sources confirm the accounts. In May 1832, twenty-one-year-old Orson Pratt, who had only recently been converted to Mormonism by Smith, healed the mother of a boy named Winslow Farr. Like George Fox in the 1670s, Pratt discovered that his reputation for performing miracles brought him eager listeners. After he healed Mrs. Farr both she and her son became Mormons, the miracle having been the catalyst for their conversion.[44]

Pratt was not alone. In 1833 Smith wrote a letter describing David Patten's tour of northern New York: "Many were healed through his instrumentality[.] Several cripples were restored[;] as many as twelve that were afflicted came at a time from a distan[ce] to be healed[.] He and others administered in the name of Jesus and they were made whole." Patten himself subsequently requested prayers from Smith for his wife "that she might be healed," and Smith performed at least six healings in 1835, sometimes acting alone, sometimes in conjunction with other elder Mormons.[45]

The tension over miracles accompanied other debates about the meaning of Mormonism. As Jan Shipps has noted, Smith and early Mormon converts often expressed contradictory notions about the movement's purpose and character. Some saw it as a wholly new religious movement that would transcend Christianity, a view that seemed to be confirmed by the mere existence of the *Book of Mormon.* Others viewed Mormonism as a "restorationist" movement, one of several promoted to restore true Christianity in antebellum society, but surely the only true one. Still others viewed it as a perfectionist movement meant to fulfill Christianity in ways that paralleled eighteenth- and nineteenth-century American millennialist movements.[46]

Amid the debate over Mormonism's identity and purpose, the early syncretism of occult and Christian elements declined. The shift was subtle but substantial. Through the 1890s, older Mormons continued to hold magical and occult beliefs. Astrology attracted some Mormons throughout the century, and Orson Pratt included the signs of the zodiac and other astrological lore in his *Prophetic Almanac* published in 1845. Brigham Young directly criticized both astrology and Mesmerism as leading people "astray" when Salt Lake City Mormons proposed an astrological society in 1855, but he changed his mind later and supported the appearance of astrology in William Phelps's *Desert Almanac* in the 1860s. Joseph Smith's descendants kept various artifacts to which both Smith and they attributed divine powers. These included several of Smith's seer stones and healing handkerchiefs. Heber Kimball, a member of the First Presidency and a Mormon missionary in England, emulating Smith, used his own handkerchief and canes as healing objects, for which he claimed healing powers and the ability to cast the Devil from possessed persons.[47]

Early Mormon syncretism of the occult and Christianity gave way to stronger tendencies channeling the movement toward conservative Christianity after 1870. After first- and second-generation Mormon leaders died, their successors exhibited little interest in seemingly esoteric crafts and practices. If anything they became embarrassed by them and eventually, in the middle of the twentieth century, began active efforts to suppress not only their modern remnants but evidence of their early practice in the 1820s and 1830s. Mormonism also moved closer to mainstream Christianity. Mormon missionaries began to stress Joseph Smith's "first vision," rather than the *Book of Mormon,* because the first vision was relatively innocuous and conflicted less with traditional Christianity. Mormon leaders divided the *Book of Mormon* into chapters and verses so that it more closely resembled long-standard editions of the Old and New Testaments. Church officials adopted conservative political views that distanced them from Mormonism's radical challenge to antebellum American religious, sexual, and economic values—a challenge confirmed in Joseph Smith's assassination in 1844 at the hand of an anti-Mormon mob. As happened among Methodists, these changes constituted new forms of syncretism that reflected significant alterations of Mormon views on crucial issues of both religion and culture.[48]

The evolution of Afro-American Christianity presented a third face of spiritual syncretism in antebellum society. Its dynamics reversed the patterns common to Methodism and Mormonism and accelerated as it matured. Afro-American Christianity's syncretism made it among the most creative of all religious movements in antebellum American society, all the more remarkable for the support it developed among a people once thoroughly alienated from it.

Like the myth of homogeneous Puritan convictions among seventeenth-century New Englanders, a parallel myth also exaggerates the attachment of American blacks to Christianity in antebellum society. Enslaved and free blacks not infrequently stood aloof from Christianity. Some rejected it outright. Some were indifferent to religion altogether, as were many Europeans. Some resented the suppression and loss of traditional African religious systems in New World society.

Still, neither the complexities of individual religious choice among enslaved and freed Africans in America nor the African spiritual holocaust of the seventeenth and eighteenth centuries should overshadow the importance of the Afro-American conversion to Christianity after about 1760. From the eve of the American Revolution to the Civil War, Afro-Americans in enormous numbers formally adopted and re-adopted Christianity as their principal collective expression of supernatural ideals. By 1800, baptisms had been performed for thousands of enslaved and free blacks. By 1820, perhaps as many as seven hundred separate black Christian congregations existed in the United States in both slave and free states. By 1860, black Baptist and Methodist congregations easily outnumbered what the contemporary historian Robert Baird described as the "small sects and denominations" in the United States, including such groups as Mormons, Catholics, Jews, and other American religious minorities.[49]

American blacks who adopted Christianity took it unto themselves, much like Methodists, Mormons, and Puritans. Where owners and European proselytizers, including evangelicals like George Whitefield, demanded obedience in slaves and even "Christian" love of the owner, slaves who became Christians found a different god in the Scriptures. Here was a god of compassion, a god of deliverance, and ultimately, a god of freedom. Whether they were Virginia and Carolina slaves who flocked to hear Baptist and Methodist itinerant evangelists or free blacks in cities like Philadelphia, New York, and Boston who found themselves the object of attention from Christians ranging from Episcopalians to Quakers, blacks celebrated freedom as Christianity's primary message. In a universe where God was truly sovereign, slavery's evil was all the more visible and Christianity's deliverance all the more vital.[50]

The Afro-American Christian emphasis on freedom emerged early, between 1760 and 1810, in the relative absence of Christian-African syncretism. In these years Afro-American Christianity paralleled its white counterpart far more closely than would ever be true again. Although sparse records probably mask at least some forms of Christian-African synthesis in slave and free black congregations, the available evidence nonetheless suggests a significant degree of European modeling for early Afro-American Christianity. Reports of sermons reveal that slave preachers, of whom there were many by the 1790s, followed largely European patterns of preaching. Thus "Black Harry Hosier," a preacher active among Methodists in the 1790s, frequently preached to white audiences with no apparent attenuation of speaking style. Religious emotionalism among American blacks is equally difficult to establish as uniquely African. The evangelical origins of so much Afro-American Christianity makes transatlantic patterns of emotionalism among English and Scottish evangelicals a powerful contender for a major if not an exclusive role in shaping exuberant emotionalism among Christian blacks in America. Abbott's memoir of his Methodist itinerant career in the 1780s and 1790s suggests no significant difference in black and white Methodist emotionalism; both were full, vivid, and, in some eyes, already notorious for their excesses. European modeling affected even hymn singing among black Christians in America. American blacks learned European hymns in both evangelical and nonevangelical American churches, and they modified them slowly rather than rapidly as large-scale conversions occurred after 1760. When mid-Atlantic black Methodists formally rejected white religious leadership to form the African Methodist Episcopal denomination in Philadelphia in 1816, they closed the meeting with the traditional English hymn, "Praise God from Whom All Blessings Flow," rather than with a new American hymn or an African song turned to Christian uses.[51]

The European modeling of early Afro-American Christianity had roots both in white paternalism and in the effects of the African spiritual holocaust of the eighteenth century. Slave owners, whether on plantations or farms, and northern urban whites largely held paternalistic views of black Christian worship. Blacks ought to obey in Christianity as much as they ought to obey in the fields. When Philadelphia's African Church first opened in 1794, Samuel Magaw, the minister of the Episcopal St. Paul's Church, delivered the inaugural sermon in what Gary Nash calls "a perfect display of white paternalism and Christian prejudice." Although many Philadelphia blacks had lived in America as long as or longer than had many of Philadelphia's whites, Magaw emphasized the heathenism and ignorance of the African societies from which they or their forebears had come. He urged them to show gratitude to their white benefactors for their Christian proselytizing and demanded passivity in their attitude toward slavery.[52]

In addition, the second-, third-, and fourth-generation blacks who were the principal converts to Christianity in America before 1800 acquired their Christian faith not in a milieu of cultural freedom but after traditional religious systems had been suppressed and shattered. Neither collectively nor, in the main, individually did they have fully functioning traditional religious systems to integrate with Christianity. As we have seen, North American slaves experienced extraordinary, perhaps unique, constraints that made it difficult to shape new religious systems before 1820 in the way that seemed to be happening in the Caribbean or Brazil or that would occur in a different setting as Christian missionaries began to proselytize in nineteenth- and twentieth-century Africa. The slaves' secular life reinforced the pattern in religion. The new family and kinship systems that emerged after 1740 reflected the impress of a society dominated by English and European patterns of language and culture; Africanisms survived, of course, but as discrete items rather than as symbols of transplanted African cultural systems flourishing in New World society. That these patterns resulted before 1820 in an Afro-American Christianity *relatively* untouched by African spiritual forms and traditions is therefore not surprising.

As Afro-American Christianity matured, its syncretism of traditional African religious elements and Christianity accelerated, for two reasons. First, the relationship to white Christianity changed. Blacks increasingly took control of their own congregational life. The process was subtle and often incomplete in the southern states. There, blacks accustomed to standing along the walls or sitting in balconies slowly separated from the mixed but not integrated congregations, usually with white approval. They began listening to black preachers and, where possible, soon formed their own congregations. The process was less subtle in northern cities like Philadelphia, where blacks first demonstrated their aggressiveness by naming churches and other organizations "African" rather than "colored." Under Richard Allen's leadership, black Christians resisted segregated seating, opened their own congregations, and finally withdrew from white sponsorship and oversight to form independent black denominations (see Figure 16).[53]

Second, African religious forms continued to be imported into America. These forms became ever more useful to a people increasingly insistent on developing their own cultural forms of power and dignity. African importations continued in America not only after independence but long after the prescribed end of the slave trade in 1810. New Africans brought with them fresh knowledge and skill in African religious practice. They renewed lingering desires for such practices among native-born blacks. Most important, it is after 1810 that evidence about selected African religious practices in American society begins to appear with frequency. Beyond Christianity, Voodun, or voodoo, brought to Louisiana after the revolution on Saint Dominigue, began to command increased loyalty from the region's expanding population of free and enslaved Africans, and later mixed in powerful and persistent ways with the region's strong Catholic traditions. Christianity exhibited similar tendencies. The slave spiritual blossomed

16. St. Thomas African Episcopal Church, Philadelphia. Lithograph by David Kennedy and William Lucas, 1829.

in the antebellum period. As early as 1819 a white Methodist, John Watson, complained that even in Philadelphia "the coloured people get together, and sing for hours together, short scraps of disjointed affirmations, pledges, or prayers, lengthened out with long repetitious *choruses*." The "shout," which took various forms but which usually included highly rhythmic singing, dancing, and clapping, came to distinguish black religious services. Finally, black ministers shaped a new and complex theology that drew from the story of Moses's escape from Egypt a long, dramatic commentary on the slaves' forced departure from Africa and stressed the final freedom that Christianity promised them both in life and after death.[54]

As a segregated Christianity solidified in both northern and southern white churches, a powerful, syncretistic, distinctively Afro-American Christianity thus also emerged in antebellum society. With the exception of Voodun in Louisiana, collective black religious expression remained centered in Christianity after 1760. Blacks incorporated African elements into a Christian structure that had itself been reinterpreted first in terms of the slave experience, then in terms of the African heritage. Yet by 1860 Christianity among American blacks had a more African identity than was true in 1820 or 1760. Its sermons, its music, its liturgy, its social setting, and its politics all testified to a syncretism that had merged both American and African elements into a religious system that slaves and freed blacks called their own and that whites were already observing from a distance.

Paradoxically, perhaps, and certainly in spite of its reputation then and now, the spiritualism initiated by the Fox sisters in their "rappings" of 1848 appears almost anticlimactic and among the less daring attempts at religious syncretism and creativity in antebellum society. The history of earlier occult religious practices by no means guaranteed spiritualism's rise. Its popularity, evident in the enormous crowds drawn to spiritualist demonstrations, at least equaled that of earlier syncretistic movements in early national and antebellum society. Like its predecessors, it too tapped secular tensions. Political and social divisions fractured America despite two decades of Jacksonian reform. "Scientific" medicine, which delivered far less than it promised, only increased popular interest in supernatural medical regimens, especially those that seemed to combine divine revelation, science, and "nature" as modes of curing. Secular optimism and evangelical millennialism created demands for breakthroughs in spiritual life that spiritualist communication with the dead seemed to satisfy.[55]

Spiritualism had an international flavor, as did Methodism, Mormonism, and the emerging Afro-American Christian tradition. Although most historians emphasize spiritualism's uniquely American character, spiritualist periodicals like the *Shekinah* and the *Spiritual Telegraph* eagerly reprinted articles from continental Europe about spiritualist demonstrations abroad. But like the Puritan alchemy practiced by John Winthrop, Jr., American spiritualism also taught. In the 1850s, American spiritualists proselytized in Europe. They frequently toured England to help the infant spiritualist movement there and arranged to have their works reprinted by English publishers. The *Spiritual Telegraph* summarized much in spiritualist as well as American religion generally when it headlined a letter on foreign spiritualist activity in 1858 as "The Ocean, a Spiritual Teacher."[56]

Despite its notoriety, however, American spiritualism was far more conservative and cautious than, say, American Mormonism. However much opposed by mainstream and sectarian Christian groups, American spiritualism largely remained within the broad spectrum of New World Christian experience. Before 1870, at least, it was not a self-consciously "alternative" religion like the nontraditional Eastern and "Zen" movements of nineteenth- and early twentieth-century America. True, mainstream Protestant clergymen waged a bitter fight against spiritualism. They ejected spiritualists from their congregations, conducted active lecture campaigns against the movement, and attempted to secure state legislation prohibiting spiritualist activities. But the men and women, including former ministers, who joined the movement usually described it as an extension or fulfillment of Christianity. Spiritualists never claimed large numbers of conversions from among unchurched Americans. Most spiritualists came from American Christian groups, usually mainstream denominations. Episcopal, Presbyterian, and Methodist laypersons adopted spiritualist views because they believed spiritualism represented the most perfect expression of Christianity yet revealed.[57]

It was no accident that a portrait of Jesus served as the frontispiece of the first volume of the *Shekinah* in 1852 and that spiritualist periodicals frequently printed articles on Christian predecessors such as Jacob Boehme, George Fox, and Emmanuel Swedenborg, whose theologies seemed to anticipate spiritualism. Here nineteenth-century American spiritualism reasserted the familiar seventeenth- and eighteenth-century occultist claim that the receipt of their previously secret knowledge would lead to the creation of a true and perfect Christian society. In doing so they denied, in the most obvious way, the charge that they had adopted an "occult" religion. The contrast with English spiritualism was especially great. English adepts frequently stressed links with Christianity and particularly with Christ. But unlike its American counterpart, English spiritualism also contained strongly anti-Christian, even atheist, elements who stressed the movement's "scientific" rather than religious principles.[58]

Spiritualist syncretism also proved far less adventurous than did either Mormon or Afro-American syncretism. American spiritualists narrowed the formerly broad American occult tradition. They focused tightly on the single issue of spirit communication, and they cast aside enormous segments of occult and magical tradition and practice found, for example, in Mormonism. From 1848 to the 1870s spiritualism evidenced little interest in alchemy, astrology, or even fortune-telling. When they borrowed, they more frequently borrowed from America's burgeoning scientific language. Observers at seances heard as much about scientific "laws" as about revelations. What this emphasis said about the realities of science and religion in antebellum society is not nearly so interesting as what contemporaries believed it said. Scientists and seers all searched simultaneously for universal truths; they all exhibited their truths through public experiments and demonstrations; they all brought men and women to richer, fuller lives.[59]

Yet, unlike Methodism, Mormonism, and Afro-American Christianity, American spiritualism offered strongly positive roles to women. Women always made up a majority of spiritualist "mediums." Moreover, to the extent that spiritualism was an organized movement — and frequently and ultimately it was not — the same women also dominated the spiritualist leadership. Men never were able to compensate for their numerical insufficiency as they did in most of the Christian denominations, except the Quakers. Even as strong a figure as Andrew Jackson Davis, whose notions about spirit communication preceded the Fox sisters' rappings and who was extraordinarily well known among spiritualists both before and after the Civil War, attained no greater position within the movement than did a phalanx of women mediums.[60]

Still, the development of American spiritualism after 1848 demonstrated how syncretism, emphasis on divine intervention, and yearning for direct and ecstatic religious truth no more united the country than did evangelical or mainstream Christianity. Certainly spiritualism was a national phenomenon. Spiritualist lectures drew enormous audiences in America's rapidly expanding cities, and spiritualists found eager followers in small-town America as well. In 1853 Warren Chase, a midwestern spiritualist lecturer, reported in the *Spiritual Telegraph* that Lake Mills, Wisconsin, could claim a medium named Augustus A. Ballow; that Waterloo, Iowa, contained two mediums, one "psycologic," the other "healing"; and that Watertown, Wisconsin, also had two mediums, a "writing" medium and one with no specialty.[61]

But spiritualism, like Christianity, never transcended the barriers of class and race in antebellum America. Even in its mature stages, it remained a movement of white, mostly Anglo-Saxon, middle- and upper-class former Protestants. No significant relationship developed between white spiritualists and black occultists until the late nineteenth century, when spiritualism's principal energies had been lost and it had become a cultural curiosity. This separation was illustrated in the work of Thomas Wentworth Higginson, the literary critic, abolitionist, and Unitarian minister who in the 1850s became a spiritualist. Higginson's political commitments led him to command a black regiment for the Union Army. His account of their exploits remains a major source for mid-nineteenth-century Afro-American culture, particularly in music. Yet Higginson's *Army Life in a Black Regiment* evidenced little interest in Afro-American religious syncretism, much less voodoo and occult conjuring, even as a matter of historical interest. Black religion had long since become a separate matter, even for a Unitarian turned spiritualist commanding black troops in the great American war against slavery.[62]

By the 1850s religious syncretism and creativity extended across antebellum society and easily rivaled the American ingenuity and adaptability evident in exploration, politics, and technology.

White and black, rich and poor, literate and illiterate — Americans of all kinds, if not yet all Americans — brought forth religious movements astonishing in their variety, numbers, and vitality. Most of them took Christianity as their focus and some, like Afro-American Christianity, emanated from people who might have been expected to turn their spiritual concerns in quite different directions. Though originating in parallel processes and shared interests, however, antebellum religion reflected the complex and layered quality of antebellum society. Region, class, and especially race all constrained the flow and dispersion of America's rising religious currents, and Americans who shared a common religiosity did not yet share a common religion.

Still, antebellum religious syncretism and creativity permanently solidified the reality of religious pluralism in America, despite the external constraints and internal limitations that slowed pluralism's progress and limited its effects. American religion had never been monochromatic, not even in the colonial period, and the extraordinary spiritual creativity of antebellum society captured and extended that diversity. It guaranteed that to be religious in America was not only to make choices, but to choose among astonishing varieties of religion created in America and duplicated nowhere else.

CHRISTIAN POWER IN THE AMERICAN REPUBLIC

9

Christianity's pursuit of institutional power and authority in America expanded as dramatically as the expression of Christian and non-Christian belief broadened between 1790 and 1840. Most historians have stressed that developments in religion in the early republic obliterated important legacies of the colonial past. Freedom seemed to replace state church coercion. Revivalism fostered a romantic, individualistic ethic. Republican political ideology compromised hierarchical denominational authority. Christianity became simultaneously American and popular. At the least, it emerged as remarkably different from the European models fostered under British colonial rule.[1]

American Christianity changed between 1770 and 1840, but perhaps not in the ways we have traditionally or even recently imagined. Between 1790 and 1860, Americans shaped new and complex understandings about the relationship of religion to government and society. They witnessed the decline but not the thorough uprooting of the colonial state church pattern. They substituted a vocabulary of religion and denomination for church and state and set in motion disagreements regarding government, religion, and individual freedom. They empowered denominational institutions by building on the institutional foundations laid down in the colonial period and reaching into segments of antebellum society that would otherwise have remained largely without an institutional Christian presence, much as had happened in the seventeenth century. That these changes occurred in an expansive, complex, and tendentious nation whose secular order and society was itself only just coming to being (and was to shatter by mid-century) made America's postrevolutionary institutional transformation in religion as important as its burgeoning spiritual creativity.

The First Amendment to the Federal Constitution, passed in 1791, signaled two important changes in the relationship between government and religion in America: the erosion of the traditional colonial church establishment system, and the redefinition of the term "religion" in public discourse. The first change did not come easily, and the second has often been ignored. Neither was a natural consequence of the Revolution, and both proved to be somewhat less authoritative than they might have been. Certainly the First Amendment did not settle the question of religion and government in America. Instead, it opened a long dialogue—sometimes a heated argument—that has lasted now for almost two centuries. Why this might be the case is suggested in one of the amendment's anomalies. Although it dispensed with the religion question in only sixteen words, the two words that are most commonly used in discussing it—"church" and "state"—are found nowhere in its text.[2]

The persistence of traditional church-state relationships after 1776 suggests that the First Amendment did far more than codify a "natural" reversal of colonial laws regarding government support for Christianity. It is true, of course, that the Church of England quickly lost privileges and its coercive power, despite the surprising support of parish clergy for the Revolution. Georgia, South Carolina, North Carolina, Virginia, and Maryland ended the Anglicans' exclusive right to government coercion within two years of the Declaration of Independence, and in 1777 New York abrogated the 1693 act that had given Anglicans effective control of the colony's religious establishment.[3]

But even some of the colonies with Anglican establishments moved quickly to support Christianity generally or to create multiple establishments to replace the previous exclusive establishments. Maryland's 1776 constitution authorized "a general and equal tax, for the support of the Christian religion." Georgia's 1777 constitution authorized government support for Protestant denominations. South Carolina's 1776 constitution remained silent on Anglican disestablishment, both because the parish system was the foundation of local government there and because its Anglican church was unusually well developed; not surprisingly, then, though the 1778 constitution ended the Church of England's monopoly on government support, it authorized multiple Protestant establishments in the state. Virginia too did not formally disestablish the Church of England in 1776 for reasons similar to those in South Carolina. It revoked statutes that empowered specific church actions, however, and began a complex debate on the church-state question that ultimately led to the rejection of multiple establishments as well.[4]

Progress toward ending the colonial establishments was even slower in the northern colonies. Connecticut, Massachusetts, and New Hampshire refused to abandon the old state church tradition immediately. Despite vitriolic criticism from Baptists and milder complaints from Anglicans (who now were becoming Episcopalians), these colonies retained their establishment of state churches. The 1780 Massachusetts constitution authorized "towns, parishes, precincts, and other bodies politic" to levy taxes "for the institution of the public worship of God, and for the support and maintenance of public Protestant teachers of piety, religion, and morality." Reminiscent of an earlier century, it even authorized legislation demanding compulsory church attendance, although it stipulated "no subordination of any one sect or denomination to the other." Connecticut also authorized taxes for the support of Christian churches, and New Hampshire rationalized previous local practice by providing a constitutional authorization for local levies to support "Christian" churches, without preferring one denomination over another.[5]

As Leonard Levy has demonstrated, the appeal of the state church after 1776 rested on its already significant departure from the European pattern of exclusive church establishment. The complex colonial pattern of state churches encouraged revolutionary leaders to broaden but not to discard government support for religion in northern and southern colonies alike. The new establishment schemes in Massachusetts, Connecticut, and New Hampshire allowed some Christian dissenters to escape parish taxes but denied exemptions for atheists and the unchurched. Even Baptists could find government coercion useful. Although Isaac Backus and other Baptist leaders bitterly criticized New England's coercive church establishments, individual congregations sometimes used the courts to collect dues from nonpaying members just as Congregational and Presbyterian congregations did. They found the century-long custom of coercive government support for Christianity more persuasive than abstract principles against it.[6]

The Revolution slowly encouraged some Americans to think broadly about the question of religion and the state and to go beyond older, narrower debates. The state church issue was inherent in all the debates over Anglican or Congregational disestablishment. But in every colony the intellectual center of the debate quickly shifted from the relatively narrow problem of church to the more elusive problem of religion, specifically, the relationship of the new governments toward America's religious and moral foundations and the possibility of direct and indirect support for Christianity. Speaking before the South Carolina legislature in 1778, William Tennent, the Presbyterian minister who had failed to convert backcountry "Regulators" to the Revolution in 1776, charged that the old Anglican establishment had not only produced an "infringement of Religious Liberty" but violated American principles of equality. "Why does the law thus favour one and bear hard upon every other denomination of Christians?" But when Tennent was informed that the legislature was actually considering a multiple establishment that might include many "orthodox" Christian groups, including his own, he found a new meaning for equality. Now he supported the multiple establishment bill, because it "opens the door to the equal incorporation of all denominations" and to a new, more creative relationship in which "Christianity itself is the established religion of the State."[7]

The larger concern for religion rather than the church helps explain the immediate postrevolutionary inclination to support Christianity generally. The multiple establishment authorized by Georgia, South Carolina, Maryland, Connecticut, Massachusetts, and New Hampshire paralleled the support other states gave Christianity in different ways. Most outlawed blasphemy, which they defined as attempts to besmirch Christianity. They allowed legal incorporation of "Christian" congregations and denominations but frequently denied it to others, sometimes even to Jews. Religious groups seeking legal incorporation in South Carolina were required to ratify a five-point Christian creed. Some states, including "tolerant" Pennsylvania, prescribed oaths of office that required public officials to swear to a belief in Christianity. Sometimes, as in Georgia, they limited officeholding to Protestants and excluded all others.[8]

Once again, Baptists demonstrated the complexity of contemporary thinking on the relationship between government and Christianity. Isaac Backus's protests against church taxes did not preclude his support for a coercive government role in religious matters in a new and fragile society. Backus placed the churches in the service of the state both before and after the Revolution. From the 1770s until his death in 1806 he regularly preached on thanksgiving and fast days decreed by the colonial and later the state governments. Such occasions exemplified the "sweet harmony" that it was thought properly characterized relations between civil authorities and Christianity. In Backus's view, such harmony also obligated the government to protect Christianity. In September 1790 he joined other New England Baptists and Congregationalists to urge the Congress to "take such measures as the Constitution may permit, that no edition of the Bible, or its translation may be published in America, without its being carefully inspected, and certified to be free from error."[9]

Yet after 1800 neither multiple nor general establishment characterized American church-state relationships. Especially after passage of the Bill of Rights in 1791, the government faded as a primary repository of religious authority in the early republic. Perhaps not surprisingly, Virginia became the center of this post-revolutionary transformation. Virginia's Anglican establishment had been the most successful in the colonies. Its strength, if not its wisdom, had encouraged the effort to suppress rising Baptists in the 1760s and 1770s, part of the fulfillment of traditional prerogatives in an exclusive, European-style, state church system. Yet Virginia was also the home of revolutionary America's most vociferous and imaginative evangelical movements. The Baptists expanded rapidly there on the eve of the Revolution, and the Methodists, whose leaders' Toryism halted the early gains of the 1770s, prospered once again after the Revolution. Virginia's nominally Anglican political aristocracy, moreover, was at least as well acquainted with Enlightenment political, philosophical, and religious thinking as the elite of any other state and was certainly surpassed by none. It was a minority of the population, of course, but with Jefferson, Madison, and Washington among its members, it was deftly placed to influence public opinion on both religious and political matters.[10]

Like other states with exclusive religious establishments, Virginia initially moved toward multiple establishment after the revolutionary war. The 1776 constitution blandly guaranteed "free exercise of religion," and the 1776, 1777, and 1778 Assemblies suspended religious taxes but did not disestablish the Anglican or Episcopal church. By 1779, however, a two-sided contest had emerged. A "Bill concerning Religion" created a multiple establishment, apparently modeled on South Carolina's 1778 constitution. In contrast Thomas Jefferson offered his bill "for Establishing Religious Freedom," which, among other things, forbade tax levies for "any religious worship, place, or ministry whatsoever." Neither mustered a majority, and the old Anglican church remained formally established by default until 1784, when Patrick Henry offered a general establishment bill backed by at least some Virginia evangelicals, especially Presbyterians, who looked with favor on its declaration of equality among Christian denominations. Despite the bill's apparently considerable popular support and its proponents among the Assembly, James Madison won a postponement of its consideration until after the state elections in 1785 and then wrote his "Memorial and Remonstrance against Religious Assessments" to open the public campaign against a multiple establishment in Virginia.[11]

The Virginia debate of 1784–85 attracted enormous public interest and transformed the American dialogue on religious establishment. It is obvious that the debate assumed the complete collapse of the exclusive state church tradition. No one supported such aid at all, whether for the old Anglican establishment or for potential evangelical Baptist or Methodist challengers. More important, the debate stopped the rise of the trend toward multiple establishment that had emerged in postrevolutionary America. After the election, petitions containing over ten thousand signatures, most of them opposed to the multiple establishment bill, flooded into the Assembly. The debate brought forth vigorous criticism of government activity in religion. Evangelical dissenters took absolutist positions scarcely matched before or since. Because "religion and all of its duties" were of "divine origin," Rockbridge County petitioners declared, they "ought not to be made the object of human legislation." Cumberland County evangelicals observed that Christ had propagated Christianity "for several hundred years without the aid of a civil power," but when Constantine introduced Christianity into the Roman Empire, corruption followed. The lesson of this history? "Religious establishment has never been a means of prospering the Gospel."[12]

The debate also brought crucial redefinitions of religion into wide public view. Madison's "Memorial and Remonstrance," written in the summer of 1785, was the bellwether of this change. Madison exhibited little phenomenological interest in religion but a great deal of interest in mankind's understanding of it, and his discussion centered on religion in the abstract. His "creator" remained undefined and unidentified. Neither God nor Jesus inhabited the "Memorial and Remonstrance." Religion was "the gift of nature," and therefore it "must be left to the conviction and conscience of every man." It was yet another "unalienable right" whose interpretation could not be usurped by others or by the state: "the opinions of men, depending only on the evidence collected in their own minds, cannot follow the dictates of other men."[13]

Madison ultimately defined religion as a duty, determined by human beings. The obligations it entailed were to be interpreted by mankind and rested on individuals rather than on society, much less the state. Religion was "the duty which we owe to our Creator" and was something to be "discharged." Madison's view of its past was not positive. "Animosities and jealousies" had driven religion and societies apart. "Spiritual tyranny," built "on the ruins of the civil authority," emerged when its supporters mistakenly erected "ecclesiastical establishments" that manipulated the authority of the state to coerce both religious and secular opinion. Throughout, Madison assumed the plurality of religion and rejected Christianity's claim to sovereignty in society and with regard to the state.[14]

The contrast between Madison's vocabulary and that of his opponents in the debate further highlighted his daring reconceptualization. On the surface, proponents of multiple establishment also seemed to discuss religion generally and to emphasize Protestant Christianity as a generic phenomenon rather than as a truth possessed by specific traditions and groups. Thus an article in Richmond's *Virginia Gazette and Weekly Advertizer* advocating multiple establishment was titled, "On the Importance and Necessity of Religion to Civil Society." But the appearance was only superficial. Madison's opponents discussed "God" and a specifically Christian god, not an unidentified and undefined "creator." Christianity, not just "religion," propelled mankind to better governments and just societies. They believed that government and society depended upon religion to foster "mutual *trust* and *confidence* among men" because secular authorities could not accomplish these ends alone. In their view, public expressions of America's dependence on Christianity were therefore appropriate and useful. Such expressions recognized the true relationship between God and man and strengthened connections between God and individual men and women in society.[15]

The debate completely altered public opinion in Virginia. By all accounts, public sentiment turned strongly against multiple establishment during the election campaign. George Washington symbolized the magnitude of the shift. Never attached to religion in any deeply personal way but convinced both of its value in promoting order and of the danger in provoking discord, Washington at first supported the bill as much out of habit as out of conviction. But as the debate accelerated, he turned against the bill. If the debate stimulated discord, adoption of the multiple establishment act would "rankle, and perhaps convulse the state." When the 1785 elections returned an Assembly hostile to multiple establishment, Patrick Henry's bill died, and by a vote of 74 to 20 the legislators passed Thomas Jefferson's bill "for Establishing Religious Freedom."[16]

The 1786 Act for Establishing Religious Freedom completed Virginia's transformation of church-state relations in the post-revolutionary period. An alliance of evangelical Baptists, Methodists, and some Presbyterians, with support from the "Episcopalian rationalists," as Thomas Buckley has called them, secured the act's passage. The words "Almighty God" appeared in its opening sentence, and the Assembly eliminated several of Jefferson's most partisan rationalist phrases, including defenses of independent critical inquiry that were implicitly critical of Christianity and a more than noticeable slur on revealed religion. But Enlightenment conceptions dominated the words of the act nonetheless. It did not define religion, as Madison's "Remonstrance" did, but the Assembly explicitly rejected attempts to make Jesus the authority for their religious liberty and rooted it instead in a secular concept of "citizenry." In turn, they also rejected coercion in religion as both "sinful and tyrannical." Religious rights were described as "natural rights." By denying the magistrate's authority to "introduce his powers into the field of opinion," the act went far beyond mere prohibitions of aid to churches. It spoke instead of such incursions upon opinion as an "ill tendency" and "dangerous fallacy" which destroyed "all religious liberty," meaning not merely Christianity but religion broadly construed. And with the demise of the multiple establishment bill in mind, the Act for Establishing Religious Freedom noted that "the truth is great and will prevail if left to herself." Not religion generally, Christianity generally, or any particular denomination should demand assistance from the state.[17]

The Virginia debate and the Act for Establishing Religious Freedom directly affected the conceptualization and passage of the First Amendment to the Constitution. That the Constitution would be amended to prohibit some types of federal action in religious matters was a foregone conclusion after the ratification debates of 1787–88. The number of delegates to state conventions who had expressed concern about the potential danger the state posed to religion made this issue one that had to receive attention in early amendments. But the kind of protection needed remained a matter of doubt and even debate. It is significant that what was finally agreed on for the religious portion of the First Amendment, contained in its first sixteen words, revealed Enlightenment influence as fully as did the Virginia act of 1786.

Most important, the First Amendment used the term "religion" to frame discussion of government policy regarding things of the spirit and did not mention the term "church." In doing so, the First Amendment uprooted colonial practice. Before 1776 colonial assemblies legislated about "religion" in narrow ways that restricted legitimate religious opinion and practice to Christianity or, at best, to the Judeo-Christian tradition. Thus, though most still insisted that there was only one "true" religion and that it was Protestant Christianity, the First Amendment treated religion broadly. The

Congress rejected proposals whose defining adjectives and phrases would have narrowed the prohibitions on government activity to "church" matters. These included James Madison's first wording, which though it forbade establishment of "any national religion," also forbade only the abrogation of "civil rights . . . on account of religious belief or worship" and therefore left other rights, including "natural" ones, unaffected. Similarly, the Congress rejected wording that would have limited government inaction to establishing "religious doctrine," "articles of faith[,] or modes of worship"; to protecting only the "rights of conscience"; to prohibiting aid to "one Religious Sect or Society in preference to others"; and to "establishing any Religious Sect or Society" or "any particular denomination of religion in preference to another."

Congress also used the term "establishment" in a way that broadened rather than narrowed prohibitions against government activity in religion. This was evident in the amendment's most difficult phrase, "Congress shall make no laws respecting an establishment of religion." Some scholars and constitutional lawyers have argued that the term "establishment," and the indefinite article "an" that preceded it, narrowed the scope of forbidden congressional action to prohibitions against a national church or aid for a single religious group. The exact opposite was the case, however. Had the Congress used the definite article "the," so that the amendment read, "Congress shall make no laws respecting the establishment of religion," lawyers and scholars could fairly conclude that they indeed meant traditional colonial establishment of a single government-supported church or aid to only one or a few religious bodies. But the use of "an," together with the substitution of the word "religion" for the more traditional term "church," created broad, unprecedented restraints on federal activity in spiritual matters. Congressman Samuel Livermore from New Hampshire well expressed the intention of the amendment: "that Congress shall make no laws touching religion, or infringing the rights of conscience." In short, the amendment meant what it said and said what it meant. The federal government should not legislate on religious matters and should leave individuals alone in their pursuit of religious truth.[18]

The Virginia debate, the Virginia Act for Establishing Religious Freedom, and the First Amendment turned states away from the immediate postrevolutionary trend toward multiple establishment.

Without such influences, the state would likely have broadened support for numerous Protestant denominations even as they might also have lessened already minimal punitive measures against nonbelievers and the religiously indifferent. But between 1785 and 1800 these trends actually reversed themselves, with the Virginia debate and discussion of the First Amendment providing the principal extended discussions of the issues raised by multiple religious establishment. South Carolina's 1790 constitution abandoned the multiple establishment authorized by its 1778 constitution and guaranteed freedom of worship for Protestants, Catholics, and Jews but not for others. Multiple establishment bills failed in Georgia in 1782 and 1784. Although one passed in 1785, it was never enforced, and in 1789 a new constitution eliminated multiple establishment altogether. Multiple establishment bills also languished in Maryland, including a 1785 bill that failed by a margin of two to one; and in 1810 a constitutional amendment finally abolished the earlier authorization for a multiple church establishment. In New Hampshire multiple establishment collapsed as its local foundations rotted away. By 1815 half the state's towns had stopped collecting taxes to support Protestant congregations, and in 1819 the legislature repealed the statute that allowed the remaining towns to do so, thereby ending multiple establishment in the state in fact if not in theory.[19]

Only Connecticut and Massachusetts sustained multiple establishments after independence, though their byzantine complexity increasingly drained away the grandeur that state support for Christianity was designed to provide. In both states complicated certificate systems that relieved dissenting Presbyterians, Baptists, Quakers, and Episcopalians from parish church rates stimulated mistakes, misunderstandings, and arguments. Congregations vied for tax support or tax exemptions, then sued adherents who did not pay their promised dues. Fissures inside the established congregations, however, not outside agitation, caused the abandonment of multiple establishment. Congregationalist-Unitarian schisms sent established church litigants to court for over three decades, and government support for Protestantism degenerated into unseemly brawls for control of church buildings and tax receipts. Connecticut voters approved a new constitution in 1818 that finally abolished the multiple establishment altogether. Massachusetts voters did not amend their constitution to do so until 1833 and then only after a bitter contest that saw supporters of establishment decry the thorough collapse of morality and public order in an increasingly tendentious republic.[20]

As the state's authority in religion faded, denominational authority expanded. Religious leaders who might have been expected to advocate multiple establishment or vigorous government support for Christianity turned instead to the denominational institutions that they had inherited from the early eighteenth century and that had blossomed with special fullness after 1750. Their work completed the single most important institutional development of postrevolutionary Christianity: the shift of religious authority away from the state and toward the "voluntary" institutional bodies. Out of this shift came an extraordinary expansion of denominational institutions, new means to reach great numbers of individuals and groups, and a new confidence to shape society and its values.

Such events triggered their own distinctive tensions. The emphasis on denominational authority clashed with the egalitarian values of the American Revolution. Widespread evangelizing produced uneven, often disappointing, results, especially in contrast to Christianity's burgeoning institutional presence. By the 1850s some Christians bitterly demanded that the law recognize America's Christian and Protestant identity once again. They based their claims on a revised history of America's Christian past and its remarkable institutional presence in their own time, but not on its still-elusive popular support. These developments constituted, in their anxieties and in their achievements, a second major reshaping of America's institutional religious landscape in scarcely more than a century.

The rise of denominational institutions as major repositories of religious authority in antebellum America is best seen in their proliferation. Citizens who had disallowed government leadership in religion did not necessarily walk the pristine path of American individualism. They turned instead to institutions. Regional presbyteries, for example, whose meetings were attended by ministers and congregational elders, increased from 9 to 59 between 1776 and 1820, and the number of synods increased from 1 to 11. This denominational growth continued despite (or even perhaps because of) a doctrinal split into Old and New School groups in

1838. By 1855 the Old School Presbyterians had 30 synods and 148 presbyteries; the New School church had 24 synods and 108 presbyteries. Baptists experienced similarly explosive growth. In 1780 the country had only 6 Baptist associations. By 1820 it contained at least 100, and by 1860 the figure had risen to over 500. And the Methodists, who in 1783 possessed a single "conference" to manage matters for all the states (to which Methodist missionaries were in fact only just returning), claimed 6 bishops and 32 such conferences by 1843.[21]

The Protestant fascination for institutional proliferation places Catholic and Mormon development in a thoroughly different light, at least for historians. During the nativist crusades of the 1840s, Protestants charged that Catholics and Mormons held a collectivist ethic that sacrificed individual rights on the altar of authoritarian institutionalism. The record of Protestant institutional proliferation, however, suggests that the only significant difference among Protestant, Catholic, and Mormon institutional development stemmed from the fact that the Catholics and Mormons may have lagged behind their Protestant counterparts. In 1789 John Carroll of Maryland became the first American Catholic bishop and counted the whole of the country as his charge. By 1829, 9 bishops were eligible to attend the first Provincial Council in Baltimore, and by 1852, 31 bishops and archbishops attended the first Plenary Council, held in the same city. Diocesan expansion, of course, reflected this growth in the hierarchy. From a single see in 1789, American Catholicism expanded to 8 sees in 1820 and to 43 sees in 1860, all headed by bishops, archbishops, and a requisite bureaucracy parallel to that found in Protestant bodies.[22]

Mormon institutional proliferation began in the mid-1830s and accelerated in 1847, after Brigham Young led his Mormon followers to Utah following Joseph Smith's murder in Illinois. The early growth of institutional authority among the Mormons reflected the organizational sophistication common to many American religious groups. Smith and his successors created a wealth of offices and institutions, and their eclectic origins matched the Mormons' theological syncretism. By the time Brigham Young arrived in Salt Lake City, the Mormons were already familiar with titles such as prophet, president, bishop, First Presidency, stake, and ward. The authority conveyed by these offices and the power exercised through them both stimulated and reflected Mormonism's transition from cult to church. Institutional proliferation was not the sole factor that prevented Mormonism from descending into a maelstrom of personal bickering and schisms, but it was among the most important.[23]

The expansion of the American denominational superstructures stimulated phenomenal increases in the number of Christian congregations, gains that outstripped national population growth between 1780 and 1860. Baptists counted about 400 congregations in 1780, 2,700 in 1820, and 12,150 in 1860; Lutherans, 225 in 1780, 800 in 1820, and 2,100 in 1860; Presbyterians, nearly 500 in 1780, 1,700 in 1820, and 6,400 in 1860; Methodists, perhaps 50 in 1783, 2,700 in 1820, and nearly 20,000 in 1860. Roman Catholics counted about 50 congregations and missions in 1780, about 120 congregations in 1820, and 2,500 in 1860. Only Congregationalists and Episcopalians experienced relatively slow growth, Congregationalists counting about 750 congregations in 1780, 1,100 in 1820, and 2,200 in 1860 and Episcopalians about 400 in 1780, 600 in 1820, and 2,100 in 1860. In all, the total number of Christian congregations expanded from about 2,500 in 1780 to 11,000 in 1820 and 52,000 in 1860. By comparison, the United States population grew from about 4,000,000 in 1780 to 10,000,000 in 1820 and 31,000,000 in 1860.[24]

More congregations meant more landscape sacralization. Between 1780 and 1820 denominations probably constructed 10,000 new churches in America, and between 1820 and 1860 they probably added 40,000 more to the earlier total. In numbers alone, the church building became a ubiquitous feature of the early national and antebellum landscape. Quite unlike their seventeenth-century ancestors and even thoroughly outstripping the early eighteenth-century Anglicans, early national and antebellum denominational leaders fully understood the importance of Christianity's physical reminders. In accordance with this understanding, America's newly shaped land found itself with buildings fitted to those who inhabited it, even if their Christianity was more presumed than actually present. In the countryside, small and modest buildings reflected small and scattered populations. In the cities—what Richard Wade once called the "urban frontier"—buildings expressed greater cultural and social pretensions. Large Romanesque sanctuaries commanded awe, if not adherence, and aggressively occupied central physical spaces for which intense competition already existed. In both urban and rural settings, sanctified graveyards sharply limited the use of individual burial sites, a practice that had been common earlier and, in the southern colonies of the eighteenth century, was a legacy of seventeenth-century institutional lethargy.[25]

Cincinnati exemplified the explosion of urban church construction in antebellum America. The delicate print in Charles Cist's *Sketches and Statistics of Cincinnati in 1859* portrayed a cityscape filled with churches and church steeples (see Figure 17). And if readers worried that Cist exaggerated Christianity's institutional presence there in the way that city views sometimes exaggerated urban growth or urban planning, Cist carefully described each one of Cincinnati's 109 Christian congregations in his text: twenty-four Catholic, twenty-one Methodist, sixteen Episcopalian, nine New Side Presbyterian, eight Lutheran, seven Baptist, four Reformed Presbyterian, four Disciples of Christ, three Con-

17. View of Cincinnati, ca. 1859.

gregationalist, three United Brethren, three German Reformed, two Unitarian, two Universalist, one orthodox Quaker, one Hicksite Quaker, and one Swedenborgian, including four black Baptist and Methodist congregations. There were also eight Jewish synagogues. Clearly, Cincinnati's skyline proclaimed a Christian presence that was as diverse as it was visually striking.[26]

As they expanded the denominations embraced authority and power through their institutions as well as through their buildings. They did so via what might be called republican hierarchicalism. Denominations were republican not only in their love of virtue—actually in their love of Jesus, of course—but in their conviction that not quite all were equal in matters of governance. In most denominations, authority continued to flow down from the top, not rise up from the bottom. Those who attended denominational meetings were usually ministers and selected elders. Among Presbyterians, Congregationalists, and Methodists, ministers always outnumbered lay elders, just as they had in the colonial period. Only two denominations moved in different, though not necessarily democratic, directions. Baptists continued to hold complex notions of the ministerial role, and their meetings were attended by persons "in the ministry," broadly defined. After the Quaker reformation of the 1750s and 1760s and the purging experience of the American Revolution, the Society of Friends leavened their quarterly and yearly meetings, increased the role of women in formal church government, and further reduced the power of the so-called Public or ministering Friends. Most denominations, however, were simply not democratic by either contemporary or modern standards. Only certain individuals, usually prestigious, wealthy men despite the numerical predominance of women in the congregations, exercised the major responsibilities of church government. And though congregational leaders had important short-term financial and other powers, long-term authority resided with the denominations, where the clergy still predominated. Congregations might challenge that authority, but if they lost, they were forced to choose between denominational support and local freedom.[27]

The postrevolutionary denominations embraced authority but not authoritarianism. Theirs was a "mixed" government, in which good Christian laymen (not women) were defined by social status and religious experience and served ends validated by the Bible rather than by a fickle and mistrusted popular opinion. The Methodists, who were almost ostentatiously hierarchical, in 1789 created a council of bishops and presiding elders, though its recommendations could be vetoed by the bishop. Bishops in the Episcopal church had more spiritual than ecclesiastical authority and were forced to share the latter with parish clergy and some laymen; it was, as was observed then and later, a system of "mitre without scepter." Presbyterians continued to name elders to some standing presbytery and synod committees, a practice begun in the 1760s, but they did not expand this aspect of their church government in the antebellum period.[28]

In an ironic way, Catholics dramatically exemplified the trend toward republican hierarchicalism. In the aftermath of the Revolution, they eagerly accepted the republican ethos and rejected more democratic claims for church government. In their view, a republican church government provided for spiritual authority while protecting laypeople without degenerating into a crude mobocracy. To some, this had the practical implication of encouraging the use of lay "trustees" to manage local congregations and other Catholic institutions. The bishops themselves disagreed over these specific proposals: John England supported them; John Carroll opposed them. Still, even opponents agreed that ecclesiastical authoritarianism of an Old World variety was impossible in the American church, whatever its fate elsewhere.[29]

A comparison with American economic development reveals how the growth of denominational institutions after 1790 created national "spiritual economies" that preceded their material counterparts. By all accounts, national markets developed very slowly and erratically after 1776. Slavery guided economic expansion in the South but not in the North and the old Northwest. Some regions, especially the southern states, experienced more success in foreign trade in interchange between regions. Banking remained a source of intense local, regional, and national conflict through the 1830s. Wage and price disparities reinforced both regional and local economic differences and led to wasteful duplication and to bitter conflict among laborers and between them and their employers. Indeed, in economic life, the Civil War may not have shattered the national economic system so much as it fully exposed the long failure to achieve one.[30]

Many denominations, in contrast, had shaped their national

spiritual markets at least by 1820, and perhaps earlier. Their leaders believed from 1776 on that the internal market was indeed their major market. Worried about colonial spiritual lethargy since the seventeenth century, concerned about the rise of deism and skepticism among the political and social elite, propelled by a republican ideology to secure Christian foundations of American political virtue, and seeing in independence new opportunities to win adherents, religious leaders rushed to proselytize citizens in a growing nation. They never ignored foreign spiritual markets; evangelization among native Americans was increased from its surprisingly thin colonial practice, and the denominations developed proposals for African, Latin American, and even Asian missions with startling quickness after 1800. But their primary proselytizing efforts remained internal, not foreign, a sign of self-obsessiveness, perhaps, but for the denominations a superb mechanism for growth.[31]

Denominational institutions became the engine of national spiritual development. Much romanticizing aside, congregations sprang up infrequently from lay initiative, just as laicization or open congregational democracy rarely characterized a local church's government after its organization. Usually, new congregations resulted from delicate (and often indelicate) nurturing on the part of competing denominations, whose agents sought to shape the variegated spiritual inclinations of interested and half-interested laypeople. Itinerants sent out from presbyteries and synods, Baptist associations, Methodist conferences, and Episcopalian, Catholic, and Mormon sees—among others—gathered what mélange of former church members, gawkers, and settlers seeking companionship they could muster to listen to a sermon and receive elemental instruction in Christian doctrine ("orthodox" doctrine, of course). If all went well, which it frequently did not, those who came might promise to return to hear another itinerant sent from the same denomination. Later, if their numbers proved steady, they might request a resident minister from the denomination or, in a few cases, obtain the ordination of a local person after the individual had been tested to meet denominational standards. In the process, the group had become a Christian congregation.

As in the colonial period, denominational institutions gathered adherents and power by exercising authority. The authority they now exercised connected congregations via quickly expanding regions, and the resulting interdependent network of communication outstripped that of the primitive markets established by American business entrepreneurs. At heart, the denominations manipulated extensive systems of regional denominational meetings. The institutions in older, settled areas — in and around Philadelphia, for example — continued to follow patterns developed in the colonial period, though they frequently shrank to make room for new denominational meetings, better able to handle growth at the edges of these regions. In new areas, denominational leaders read maps with an intensity that challenged land speculators and prospective settlers. As they gauged a region's shape and development, their activity subtly imposed identities upon areas waiting for guidance.[32]

Regional denominational meetings were organized in as many different ways as geography and settlement patterns intersected and served the same function everywhere: they brought distant and potentially isolated congregations together. At yearly gatherings a congregation's minister and elder met other ministers and elders. They shared sorrows and joys, heard about difficulties and opportunities, and made important decisions about finances, doctrine, and evangelization. Minister and elder reported their own congregational development to the gathering and then reported on the denomination when they returned to their congregation. Such regional meetings were not necessarily provincial. Through the 1830s, at least, they reached out and up as vigorously as they reached out and down. They received letters from far distant meetings and, of course, responded with letters of their own. Their speakers frequently included itinerants who served other regions. They also received visitors from other regions and sent representatives to other regional meetings.

The Baptists in South Carolina's Bethel Association provide a particularly good example of the supple institutional creativity that shaped a regional and even national spiritual market out of what might otherwise have been isolated individual efforts. Bethel was a "back country" association of some fifteen churches, organized in 1789, containing congregations north and west of Columbia into the frontier portions of South and North Carolina. Perhaps wary of too much theological debate — not unlike New England's Freewill Baptists — it hedged on adopting the so-called

Philadelphia Confession drawn up by the Philadelphia Baptist Association in the 1740s. But at its formation, the Bethel Association did agree that "in general" it held to "the Calvinist sentiments." It also sought relations with other Baptists. It voted a day of thanksgiving "for the blessings of peace, harmony and concord . . . subsisting between us and the Charleston Association" and agreed to help form a committee of associations in the Carolinas.[33]

The Bethel Association shaped authority by exercising power. It settled numerous problems in its member congregations that emerged from disagreements about moral issues, finances, and even titles for ministers. "Reverend" seemed a fitting title for preachers, although "Brother" was thought to be more scriptural. It excommunicated recalcitrant clergymen and, in 1792, established its own rules for ordination. It also divided twice. Having grown to fifty congregations by 1800, it excused fourteen congregations to form the Broad River Association and nine congregations to form the Saluda Association, a process of division and subdivision that characterized Baptist denominational growth for the next century.[34]

Bethel Baptists participated in the national spiritual markets they were helping to create. They reached out to Baptists far away even as they reached down to their own member congregations. In 1794 the association received "circular" letters from the Charleston and Georgia associations, from Virginia's General Committee, and from a Baptist minister in Charleston, Oliver Hart. In turn, the Bethel Association authorized replies to them, received a messenger sent from the Georgia Association to attend the Bethel meeting, and sent two messengers each to the Charleston and Georgia meetings. By 1800 the Bethel Association routinely received letters from thirteen Baptist associations, including letters from Charleston, Philadelphia, Baltimore, Kentucky, Warren (in Rhode Island), and New Hampshire. It sent its own letter to four associations, received messengers from the Georgia and Hepzibah associations, and sent messengers to attend Charleston, Georgia, and Hepzibah association meetings.[35]

The denominations shaped the evangelizing labor that brought so many new Christian congregations into being between 1780 and 1860. Between 1790 and 1830 their major vehicle was the itinerant minister. Francis Asbury reputedly traveled three hundred thousand miles on behalf of the Methodists in his thirty years in America. But neither he nor the Baptist and Presbyterian itinerants wandered through wilderness and settlements undirected. Though the spirit may have moved them, their denominations led them. Methodist bishops, Presbyterian synods, Baptist associations, and Episcopalian conferences firmly managed the work of itinerants. They kept schedules, visited congregations in a certain order, inspected church discipline, determined who might or might not receive a "settled" minister, and answered to their superiors when they failed. Together, this planning and labor established lines of spiritual and denominational authority. Itinerants transformed wilderness into frontier and frontier into settlement by tying congregation to congregation, then melding these into regional and national denominational networks.[36]

Books, or at least the book trade, similarly expanded denominational authority. Christianity, Protestantism, Puritanism, and virtually every variety of sect, including evangelicalism, had long been associated with literacy and books, not only the Bible but popular pious tracts as well. But two factors made books even more important after 1780 than they had been before. First, literacy expanded significantly in eighteenth- and early nineteenth-century America. Even in New England, where literacy had already reached 60 percent for men and 40 percent for women by 1650, it climbed to 90 percent for men and 60 percent for women by the 1790s. Elsewhere the rise may have been steeper, though the result smaller. Literacy in the seventeenth-century Chesapeake Bay area most likely did not reach 30 percent for men and 15 percent for women, but by the early nineteenth century the figure was probably 70 percent for men and 50 percent for women. Second, American independence and denominational proliferation encouraged religious groups to use printed literature even more vigorously than before. Between 1780 and 1815 denominationally sponsored publications increased dramatically. That Congregationalists, Presbyterians, and Baptists failed to secure congressional sanction for a "pure" and exclusive edition of the Bible in the 1790s probably actually aided proselytizing, since the denominations quickly sponsored numerous competing editions and translations, all cheaply priced, for America's readers.[37]

The publication surge of the early national period exploded after 1820. Authority and communication networks laid down at ever more rapid rates and technological advances in printing increased the numbers of religious publications to astonishing levels. Fourteen religious newspapers in 1790 expanded to more than 600 by 1830, if anybody had time to count them. Religious books were pouring off the country's religious presses in even greater numbers. The American Bible and tract societies produced more than a million bibles and six million books and tracts a year, and the yearly total of religious publications probably amounted to more than ten billion pages by 1830. The religious publication industry took strength from interwoven regional identities: Portsmouth, Baltimore, Charleston, Pittsburgh, and Cincinnati were as important to it as were Boston, New York, and Philadelphia. Although the South lagged behind, especially after 1840, it never slipped back into illiteracy or into a religious culture that eschewed printed literature.[38]

A welter of cross-denominational societies furthered the inroads of institutional Christianity. Like earlier revivalism and religious renewal, these societies reflected the continuing vitality of transatlantic connections. The American Bible Society (founded in 1816) and the American Tract Society (1823) had their direct origins in London's Religious Tract Society (1799). By 1815 over sixty local and state Bible societies had been organized in the United States to provide a foundation upon which to form national organizations in the next decade. Indeed, Americans concerned about the moral fiber and social structure of the new republic learned great lessons from British efforts at reform. Societies promoting abolitionism, Sunday schools, penal reform, and temperance were all formed on British models and deepened the rich organizational life of early antebellum Christianity. If their membership was not always aware of the connections, as was sometimes clearly the case, the leadership at both local and national levels certainly was. For them the independence of the American societies meant the ability to pursue transatlantic connections that they had earlier had to reject.[39]

By 1850 America was overrun with reform societies, virtually all with strong denominational origins and connections. The American Colonization Society (1817) sought to end slavery, in part, by finding a home for slaves in Africa. The American Sunday School Union (1824) promoted the introduction of Sunday schools within congregations, especially in urban areas, and promoted a curriculum not unlike that of the late seventeenth- and early eighteenth-century Anglican Charity Schools. The American Temperance Society (1826) at first promoted temperate drinking but quickly came to demand abstinence. By 1831 it claimed more than 170,000 lay members and 2,000 local chapters, nearly all associated with Christian congregations. It was only one of several national temperance organizations that acted through Christian denominations to end drunkenness in America. The Washingtonian movement, begun in the 1840s, organized "lodges" of reformed drinkers who intended through their organization to find refuge "from the evils of intemperance, to afford mutual assistance in times of sickness, and to elevate our characters as men." Equally popular were the Sons of Temperance. Like the Washingtonian societies, they too were mutual aid groups with local lodges for reformed drinkers, but they also sold insurance. They claimed 6,000 lodges and 200,000 members in the 1840s.[40]

If temperance societies and Sunday schools had clearly popular implications, the formation of colleges capped the process of Christian institutional growth for upper-class segments of American society. Especially before 1840, advocates of college education treated their endeavors as elite enterprises, and the number of such institutions remained relatively small. In 1842 Francis Wayland, the Brown University educator, counted 101 colleges, 39 seminaries, 31 medical schools, and 10 law schools in the country, seemingly a large number but not overwhelmingly so in a nation of 20,000,000 people. Moreover, of the 182 colleges founded between 1776 and 1865, over half were begun after 1830. Virtually all the colleges were private and very small. In the 1810s American colleges were graduating scarcely 300 students a year, and as late as the 1850s that number had risen to only 900 per year. Yet however small, the colleges were Christian and were educating the Americans who would largely command antebellum institutional and political life. The colleges' abandonment of their role as a training ground for clergymen—hence the creation of seminaries—was predicated on a perception that they could be far more effective in shaping national values by training the lay social and political elite. The appeal here again was oligarchic rather than democratic, even in Jacksonian society. In a nation where social background and position counted very much indeed and where the public could be led astray by the breadth of spiritual expression increasingly evident everywhere, the Christian college provided a refuge of orthodoxy and, denominational leaders hoped, a citadel for the authority of Christian learning.[41]

Like American denominations, the early national and antebellum religious and reform societies were coercive institutions, but not conspiratorial or even necessarily conservative ones. They were cross-denominational, not nondenominational. Their membership consistently came from the mainstream Protestant groups, especially the Congregationalists, Presbyterians, and Baptists, who gathered together to promote Christianity and Christian social causes without specific denominational agendas. The societies' organization strongly paralleled that of the denominations to which most of their members were attached. They saturated the countryside with local societies who heard visiting speakers traveling prescribed routes, like denominational itinerants. They distributed books, tracts, and newspapers by the millions, and these only added to those already published by the denominations. If the religious and reform societies could not reshape America, they could at least drown it in a sea of paper and ink.[42]

The experience of two minorities, blacks and women, suggests how Americans who were ignored in the mainstream institutions could turn such institutional proliferation to their own uses. Black Americans shaped a new and increasingly distinctive Christian worship by creating powerful denominational institutions of their own. First in Philadelphia, through the organization of the African Methodist Episcopal Church under Richard Allen's leadership in 1816, black Christians used the discipline and muscle provided by institutional prowess to their own ends. As Gary Nash has explained, the creation of black denominations occurred only because black religious leaders challenged white authority in the city's Christian denominations. Allen succeeded in shaping an independent black Christianity in the city because he created a separate church rather than working within mixed congregations dominated by whites. Aided by formation of urban black churches in Baltimore and New York City, Allen soon had a denomination that expanded from 5 congregations in 1816 to more than 100 by 1850. By the 1850s black Baptists in the Midwest had organized their own Baptist associations — Ohio's Providence Baptist Association (1836) and Illinois's Wood River Baptist Association (1838) — to be followed by the organization of the American Baptist Missionary Convention in 1840, taking in northeastern black Baptists, and the Western Colored Baptist Convention in 1853.[43]

American women used the growth of denominational and cross-denominational institutions in two ways. On the one hand, they frequently found opportunities to exercise spiritual leadership in the interstices of male-dominated Protestant denominations. Nancy Towle, a Freewill Baptist itinerant, preached regularly from the mid-1810s until at least 1832 on circuits that first covered her native New England but subsequently included the entire eastern seaboard as far south as Charleston (where the first edition of her memoir was published). She preached before the U.S. Congress. She developed a network of female preaching companions with whom she shared at least as much about the subjugation of women in American religion and society as about the necessity of a Christian conversion. She also received significant aid from men, sometimes lay members of congregations in which she preached as an "exhorter," sometimes male ministers who were clear and direct in their support of her preaching. Other ministers and laymen opposed her work, however, and limits cropped up. David Marks, a Freewill Baptist minister, favorably mentioned the preaching of Towle as well as that of Sophia Humes, another woman preacher and sometime Towle companion. But neither appeared in Marks's account of denominational business meetings. Still, with other women preachers who often traveled independent circuits—Humes, Harriett Livermore, Salome Lincoln, Fanny Newell, and Clarissa Richmond—Towle provided a powerful model for female activity within the circumscriptions imposed on women by the antebellum Protestant denominations.[44]

On the other hand, women worked in their own institutions outside the denominations. The history of both religious and social reform in antebellum society is incomplete without the inclusion of women's organizations. Much of this activity, like the work of early female preachers, was generated by individual persistence. The lectures of Fanny Wright on a variety of reform topics and the antislavery activities of South Carolina's Grimké sisters had a profound impact on social reform generally in the United States, as well as on social reform among American women. The efforts of individuals soon resulted in distinctively women's organizations. From the Boston Female Antislavery Society to the American Sunday School Union, women mastered institutional politics with great skill in a society that still kept them from the most elemental forms of participation in secular politics. These institutions were not all exclusively women's institutions; often, they generated tension with other denominational bodies. But the tension, though often ostensibly over organizational matters, actually derived from the realization that the range of institutional work done by women activists was empowering, not only to Christianity and to the pursuit of social reform, but to women as well.[45]

The labor of the Christian institutions was not an end in itself. The work was attractive because it promised to bring Americans into the denominations and, hence, to make the American people Christian. Assessing the success of this effort is no easier in antebellum America than in colonial society. Although some church membership data is more voluminous, other data is nonexistent or unreliable, and because America expanded so dramatically it is more difficult to attach national significance to a local or even a regional study of the problems. The possibilities of adherence too grew more complex. As the population ballooned from 4,000,000 in 1780 to approximately 31,000,000 in 1860, the number and type of religious groups expanded as well. Immigration dictated part of the change. English settlers who constituted about 60 percent of all white residents in 1790 were less than 30 percent by 1860. Irish immigrants, nearly all at least nominally Catholic, accounted for more than 40 percent of all foreign-born settlers in the country. German immigrants, perhaps half Protestant, a third Catholic, and the remainder Jewish, accounted for another 20 percent. Non-Protestant immigrants alone were transforming a society where on the eve of the Revolution Protestantism had not successfully secured the allegiance of even English settlers.[46]

Indigenous religious development accounted for additional changes. From the War of 1812 to the Civil War, immigrant and native-born Americans faced increasing numbers of religious choices. Catholics and Jews appeared in a society that feared the former and had previously found the latter only a curiosity. An astonishing variety of religious-utopian-communitarian settlements, ranging from the Oneida community in New York to Fourierist experiments in Ohio and Indiana, fanned out across the expanding West. Religious renewal, revival, and schism brought forth a host of new groups — not only Mormons and spiritualists, but Mesmerists, Swedenborgians, Millerites, Adventists, "Christians," and dissident Baptist, Methodist, and Presbyterian groups — none of whom existed in the revolutionary era.[47]

This plenty could have produced a kind of spiritual paralysis. Hector St. John de Crèvecoeur suggested such an explanation for the low rate of church adherence in the 1780s, which he attributed to the already bewildering variety of sects and groups in America. But antebellum society seems to have been stimulated by religious diversity. Pluralism and institutional proliferation increased the number of worshipers. Upstate New York—the "burned-over district," charred by three decades of religious revival between 1820 and 1850—provides one important view of the result.

In the 1830s a Presbyterian minister in Oneida County, New York, took his own survey of church adherence among his largely rural and small-town neighbors. His conclusion was frightening, at least to him. Only about a quarter of those he surveyed sustained any significant connections with a Christian congregation, and the fraction would have been even lower had he not apparently ignored recently arrived European immigrants and those too poor or transient to be likely church adherents. Unbeknownst to the minister, however, his results in fact suggest a slow but significant rise in church adherence. A recent study of Cortland County, New York, between 1790 and 1860 demonstrates that membership in one of the four major Protestant denominations—Baptist, Congregational, Methodist, and Presbyterian—rose from about 10 percent in 1810 to about 20 percent in 1820 and that this figure remained quite stable through 1860 despite population growth. Including members of minor denominations probably indicates church adherence of between 25 and 30 percent, a significant improvement over the pattern in revolutionary society.[48]

The New York evidence fits national statistics regarding antebellum denominational affiliation. A study of church adherence based on the 1850 federal census and denominational membership statistics concludes that about 34 percent of the nation's population sustained a regular relationship with American churches. The pattern was not even across the country or within population groups. Especially in New England and in Ohio and Indiana, women still outnumbered men in Christian congregations, usually by a margin of two to one. Complaints of the period suggest that adherence in the increasingly populous cities lagged far behind that in rural areas, where, it should be emphasized, a majority of the adults still remained unaffiliated with the churches. And the antebellum figure was far from the 60 percent of adults who belonged to churches in America in the 1960s.[49]

Yet unlike Europe, Christian adherence in America was increasing rather than declining. If its patterns were uneven, they were also surprisingly broad, reaching into major segments of the antebellum population. Congregations attracted women and, through Sunday schools, proselytized children. They attracted urban immigrants, though they could not always hold them. They attracted American slaves, even if the slaves eventually created a Christianity of their own. And they attracted, and seemingly held against the lure of secularism, the nation's governing elite, supported by a middling, bourgeois population who continued to assume that church membership and holding public office went hand in hand—a remarkable achievement, considering the deep ambivalence or indifference of most Founding Fathers to the kind of Christian endeavor typical of antebellum society.[50]

As Christianization advanced in America, new and sometimes ugly demands for government guarantees of Christian hegemony emerged rather than receded. The infamous nativist campaigns of the antebellum period provided one important foundation for such efforts. Anti-Catholic, anti-Mormon, anti-Freemason nativism emerged from strong, unresolved tensions accompanying America's advancing religious complexity, Protestant institutional prowess, and persistent desires for simplification and individual freedom. Antebellum nativism also brought traditional European and early American mobocracy to antebellum society. Americans, of course, were no strangers to hatred and prejudice, especially in religion, and antebellum religious development offered them manifold opportunities to exercise their passion. They could attack and burn the Ursiline convent in Charlestown, Massachusetts, as they did in 1837, because they had for so long casually attacked other religious groups. As Paul Gilje has shown in his study of antebellum violence in New York City, evangelical Methodist meetings withstood assault on several occasions between 1780 and 1820. The fact that attention soon turned to Catholics, Mormons, and Freemasons in the 1830s and 1840s better demonstrated a shift in target than the development of a new cultural form in America.[51]

Demands for a return to legal coercion to guarantee "orthodox" Christian hegemony in America also increased as antebellum Christianization advanced. As in the nineteenth-century revolutions in Europe, these demands stemmed from the frustration that resulted when rising expectations—in this case, of Christian progress—remained only partially realized. Christian success might be lost when challenged by indigenous indifference and immigrant pluralism. Stephen Colwell's *The Position of Christianity in the United States* (1853) railed against the antebellum perversion of American religious liberty and demanded that government protect the "true Christianity" of its people from Catholics, Mormons, infidels, and atheists. In 1856, the otherwise optimistic and staid Robert Baird, historian and, like Colwell, an evangelical Presbyterian, voiced his concern that immigrants and natives alike misunderstood American religious freedom and were on the verge of reshaping the nation's traditional religious identity.[52]

In response, Baird, Colwell, and others evolved a myth of the American Christian past, one of the most powerful myths to inform the history of both American religion and American society. Their view contrasted sharply with the attitudes of denominational leaders during the revolutionary period. Revolutionary clergymen had worried that America was not at all a Christian society. They sought to make it so by sacralizing the Revolution in its aftermath, by creating powerful denominational institutions to harness the religious authority being abandoned by the state, and by proselytizing on an unprecedented scale.

Baird and Colwell, however, insisted that America had always been a Christian nation, from the settlement of Virginia and Massachusetts Bay to the writing of the Constitution. In this view the motives of exploration and emigration, colonial laws, revolutionary and army camp sermons, and calls for fast and thanksgiving days all demonstrated the nation's historic Christian practice. Laws passed to secure Christian allegiance in the populace now were taken to reflect it. A First Amendment written to prohibit government activity in religion now was interpreted as encouraging support for "orthodox" Christianity. Colwell thus argued that in adopting the First Amendment Americans "did not abdicate their Christian ascendancy nor proclaim that their institutions were purged of the Christian element. They avowed toleration, and not infidelity, as their great principle." Colwell believed that Americans also meant to support possible repression of non-Christian practice as well as support Christianity generally. "Any other religion inconsistent with Christianity may be prohibited, but the Christian religion is declared to be out of the reach of

Congressional interference. Legislation may promote the interests of religion by any measures not inconsistent with toleration."[53]

The myth of the American Christian past, couched as history, answered the anxieties that the unstable combination of institutional proliferation, partially successful proselytization, and the pursuit of power and authority by the denominations had introduced into antebellum religion and society. Perplexed by the gap between the denominations' astonishing national, regional, and local institutional growth and the still erratic levels of individual adherence to Christian congregations, the myth of the Christian past invoked "history" to shape the present. It pressed new historical "facts" on antebellum America as moral obligations. Americans would reap dire consequences if they trod paths different from those supposedly followed by their colonial predecessors, and the study of history now clearly revealed that those earlier paths had always been Christian ones.

If Colwell and Baird represented the darker side of Christian concern for power and authority in America, denominational activity probably constituted the churches' principal contribution to American antebellum democracy, though not for the reasons recent scholarship has suggested. Historians have criticized an earlier view of antebellum religious reformers as conservatives who stressed social control and opposed egalitarianism and democracy to stave off declining clerical influence and advancing democracy. They have noted the complex motives that moved ministers and denominations to sponsor social reform and have seen in their programs genuine interest in freeing men and women of the time from obvious harms ranging from alcoholism to slavery. They have stressed the ties to a highly positive and optimistic "premillennialism," which viewed such efforts as presaging Christ's second coming. In Nathan Hatch's recent analysis, *The Democratization of American Christianity,* the early national and antebellum evangelical Christian groups are viewed as genuine "republicans," if not democrats, who reflected substantial concern for individual liberty and freedom. Their drive for popularity and their promotion of antiauthoritarianism led to a persistent individualist ethos that underwrote the religious and social upheaval that has long distinguished modern American religion.[54]

Yet the antiauthoritarianism of many reformers and new religious groups proved as elliptical in the 1840s as it had been in the

1740s. Lorenzo Dow, the itinerant, all but ritualized his cant regarding evil in the Methodists' hierarchical church government. He denounced Methodist and papal government in nearly every public appearance, and he praised schisms, however wrenching, because they demonstrated that the search for religious truth was still going on. Yet Dow also knew the value and pleasure of authority. In the 1790s and early 1800s he sought and obtained Methodist approbation of his preaching, and even though he formally left the denomination he never eschewed the benefits of its organization. He traveled Methodist circuits throughout his lifetime, and Methodist listeners and local ministers found nothing objectionable in his free-grace theology and in his helpful, perhaps heartfelt, evocation of the original Methodist itinerants.[55]

Even Dow's rhetoric exhibited attention to "proper" authority. Dow regularly carried letters on his travels from political officials, especially Jeffersonian republicans like James Madison and a Georgia governor, to rescue him from potential difficulties. In 1804 Dow handed one such letter to a critic in Virginia who had publicly rebuked Dow as "a vile character" and refused to give him supplies. When the man had read no more than half the letter, Dow recounted that "he turned pale. He gave me what I wanted, and treated me as a king." In the 1800s as in the 1740s authority in truth's service was not only permissible but, twenty years after the American Revolution, so useful that one of its most "antiauthoritarian" purveyors could employ a monarchical metaphor to describe his considerable pleasure in its effects.[56]

Thus, the Christian contribution to a developing American democracy rested as fully on its pursuit of coercive authority and power as on its concern for individualism or its elusive antiauthoritarian rhetoric. This search for authority and power was not necessarily "conservative," as some critics have charged. Many denominational programs of religious and social change were markedly radical by their standards and ours. Nor were denominational leaders driven by a concern for a narrow "social control." They were concerned to shape American society and culture, not merely to manage the mundane day-to-day behavior of individuals. They were not egalitarians. They were more willing and eager to change the fundamental beliefs and behavior of whole peoples than to question their own assumptions and actions. They were frequently intolerant. They spread the desire for authority and power to unprecedented numbers of people through religious institutions whose sophistication and prowess matched and probably exceeded that of medieval Catholicism. Most of these denominational leaders were white, Anglo-Saxon, Protestant, and middle- and upper-class males, but others were women, American blacks, and newly arrived immigrants who then, and later, reached out and successfully grabbed what they were not offered but what they knew would empower them too. In pursuit of Christian power and authority through institutions of remarkable depth and discipline, these men and women shaped a society extraordinary in its religious energy, vigor, and will—a society indestructibly and inevitably American, bearing a rising Christian presence.

Conclusion

LINCOLN AND THE ALMOST CHOSEN PEOPLE

In *Democracy in America,* Alexis de Tocqueville provided an enduring description of religion in the antebellum era: "There is no country in the whole world in which the Christian religion retains a greater influence over the souls of men than in America." To Tocqueville, the cause was as simple as the effect: "The greatest part of British America was peopled by men who, after having shaken off the authority of the Pope, acknowledged no other religious supremacy: they brought with them into the New World a form of Christianity which I cannot better describe than by styling it a democratic and republican religion."[1]

Tocqueville comprehended antebellum religious antinomies with remarkable acumen. He recognized the inconsistencies of evangelical moralizing, the tension between individualism and institutionalism in religion, and the conflict between America's majoritarianism and its vibrant cultural pluralism. He appreciated the paradox of Catholics who committed themselves to republicanism in both politics and church government amid increasing anti-Catholic prejudice and violence. He saw the hypocrisy that lurked within the success and influence of Christianity in America.

How ironic, then, that Tocqueville's assessment of antebellum religion should have expressed such a narrow, ahistorical view of American religious development. Its origins might require historical explanation, but from Tocqueville's perspective no lengthy or elaborate account was in order. He understood American religion in Aristotelian terms. The spiritual sentiment present in the nation's infancy and youth—apparently largely Puritan, though

Tocqueville did not specify—had simply matured. America had emerged religious, Protestant, evangelical, and democratic from the spiritual seeds planted before 1630, and the seeds were most obviously those planted in New England. Faced with a complex and contradictory present that demanded constant attention, Americans need not be distracted by a more complex history of their own maturation, he thought.

But as we have seen, ambiguities characterized the development of religion in America from the very beginning. The European religious heritage did not provide a clear model on which to build a new society. Europe's laws enforced the Christian tradition not only because the conversion of the Roman Empire had demanded it but because lay indifference continued to require it. Without the law, churches half-filled on Easter would be nearly empty on other Sundays. Eclectic supernatural beliefs and practices permeated society. Some forms complemented Christianity and others opposed it; clergy and laity often disagreed on the extent of the contradictions. With the Protestant Reformation, the pluralism exhibited in medieval Catholicism exploded into more visible and hostile forms. The concept of "whose state, whose religion" masked European spiritual complexity. In "Puritan" England and on the Continent, that concept also hid both state power and state powerlessness. It served as important propaganda for the rise of the modern state, although historians have often mistakenly used it as a measure of spiritual orthodoxy among the early modern European laity.

American colonization and independence complicated already spotty European and English Christian practice. Christian institutional authority and even presence actually declined in seventeenth-century America; magic and the occult arts also crossed the Atlantic. The eighteenth-century colonies witnessed the renaissance of the state church tradition, the rise of denominational authority and power, the elaboration among Anglicans—and then among Dissenters—of startling doctrines of absolute obedience central to slavery and race relations in America, and an African spiritual holocaust that ultimately and ironically turned slave and free blacks to Christianity. The demise of traditional African religious systems was the most dramatic religious change in any period of American history before 1865, made all the more ironic by the continuing expansion of religious pluralism among European settlers.

It was the events of the critical period from 1680 to 1820 — not seventeenth-century New England Puritanism or the seemingly unique evangelical revivals beginning at Cane Ridge, Kentucky, in 1805 — that shaped America's most distinctive religious patterns. In the post-1680 Anglican renaissance, the renewal of Christian denominational authority, the effects of the African spiritual holocaust, the shifting of the old colonial church-state relationship, the further development of authority and power in the Christian denominations after the Revolution, and the development of highly volatile antebellum mixtures of popular supernatural views, the American religious tradition was born and reborn. Christianity's claim to the allegiance of the people rose in the process, while in Europe it weakened further. Although by 1865 American Christianity had yet to claim a majority of adults as church members and enormous segments of the population still remained not only outside the churches but skeptical of the faith for a variety of reasons, Christianization had passed the tests thrown up by seventeenth-century settlement, eighteenth-century skepticism, the American Revolution, and the tumultuous, almost chaotic, expansion of antebellum American society. These successes made the public and private roles of Christianity unique in what a century later was to become the West's most powerful society.

The patterns established by 1865 anticipated the future. In the late nineteenth and early twentieth centuries, religious America was not merely Calvinist or post-Puritan. Its history had continued to evolve in complex ways. Denominations and their adherents, seeking power and authority, turned to schism. Though the spiritualists faded, the Christian Scientists did not; both found ways to seek health through supernatural intervention in decades when modern medicine itself was being born. Blacks continued to pursue their own religious agenda within Christianity, exiling themselves after the Civil War from the old mixed congregations on the plantations, forming new congregations in the northern cities in the great migrations before and after World War II, and striking out with new liturgical developments that made the spiritual an indelible part of American Protestantism. The landscape was sacralized yet again, this time by Catholics and Jews as well, in the face of hostility and with a vigor that easily matched that of their Protestant predecessors. In short, as Americans moved into even more modern times, they did not move beyond now familiar processes of religious evolution.

This vigorous spiritual development and creativity found expression in the Civil War. In a society where organized Christianity had come to think of itself as both desiring and expressing authority and power, it is not surprising to note that its antebellum history can almost be read as a history of Civil War origins. In *Broken Churches, Broken Nation: The Churches and the Civil War,* C. C. Goen documents the ways in which religious divisions prefigured the secular divisions. The denominational schisms that occurred after 1830 never were caused by the slavery question alone. Theological, social, ethnic, and abolitionist sentiments all played important roles in hardening denominational institutions into increasingly provincial ones. But the Presbyterian split of 1837, the Methodist schisms of the 1840s and creation of the Methodist Episcopal Church, South, in 1845, and the formation of a separate Southern Convention for white Baptists in 1846 set the stage for greater, more profound divisions in society itself.[2]

The denominations furthered America's sectional tension. Quite unlike the experience in the American Revolution, denominational schisms preceded and prophesied the coming of the Civil War. Yet quite like the experience in the American Revolution, the denominations also served the needs of the state in both North and South. Some did this quietly; others acted more stridently. Some even launched major revival campaigns during the war, as had happened in New England in the 1770s and 1780s. In this context, Julia Ward Howe's "Battle Hymn of the Republic" described how the extraordinary rising institutional presence of Christianity in antebellum society could now be seen in the war camps themselves:

> I have seen him in the watch-fires of a hundred circling
> camps;
> They have builded him an altar in the evening dews and
> damps;
> I have read his righteous sentence by the dim and flaring
> lamps;
> His day is marching on.

I have read a fiery gospel, writ in burnished rows of steel,
"As ye deal with my contemners, so with you my grace shall deal";
Let the Hero, born of woman, crush the serpent with his heel,
Since God is marching on.

Howe's hymn was a proselytizing instrument, of course, whose assumption of Christian commitment in soldiers and the nation made it a powerful inducement to Christian adherence and practice. Few people better symbolized the continuing need for this proselytizing than Abraham Lincoln. Lincoln's religion has been the subject of considerable controversy. William H. Herndon, his former law partner, claimed that Lincoln attacked Christianity in his youth and "died an unbeliever." Others have appropriated him as a spiritualist, a Quaker, a Baptist, or a Presbyterian. Some have attached to him intense personal piety. Henry Ward Beecher's grandson, for example, claimed that after the Union loss at Bull Run Lincoln secretly visited Beecher in Brooklyn, where the two "wrestled together with the God of battles and the Watcher over the right until they had received the help which He had promised to those that seek His aid."[3]

Like many myths, the myths about Lincoln's religion point to important but often misplaced truths. Lincoln was indeed religious, perhaps profoundly so, and it is impossible to discuss him apart from religion. T. Harry Williams correctly describes Lincoln's thought as rooted in a complex religious sensibility. According to Williams, Lincoln was deeply guided by the conviction that "some supernatural force, God or a Guiding Providence largely directed the affairs of men," and that "there existed a Divine or higher law, of which men were aware and to which they should seek to approximate in their human law." Lincoln filled his speeches, letters, and writings with religious language. "The Almighty has His own purposes." "You have, under Providence, performed in this great struggle." "The will of God prevails." "This nation, under God." In short, without reference to the supernatural and providence, Lincoln would be diminished.[4]

But if Lincoln believed in the supernatural and in the reality of some transcendent power, he also exhibited the aloofness from churches and the indifference to major Christian tenets that still characterized so many of his fellow citizens, despite the expansion of the Christian institutional presence in antebellum society. At the most obvious level, Lincoln rejected the kind of formal commitments that American religious and denominational leaders like Stephen Colwell and Robert Baird demanded. Lincoln, like some other presidents, never joined a church. Lincoln's regard for churches does seem to have grown during his political career and presidency, and he was respectful of their presence in both the North and the South during the war, ordering military commanders to spare church buildings if possible during fighting. Yet despite ample opportunities to align himself with a denomination both long before and during his presidency, Lincoln never took that step.

More striking is the fact that Lincoln had little interest in Christ as either a religious or a historical figure. The contrast with Jefferson is especially notable. Jefferson spent considerable time after 1800 studying the teachings of Jesus, despite the fact that in the election of 1800 his opponents had tagged him as an atheist. Jefferson carefully assembled quotations from Christ on ethical and moral issues and finally produced his own "bible." But while Lincoln subsequently developed a formidable reputation as a religious man and was erroneously claimed as a member of several denominations, Christ interested him only marginally. Although Lincoln once referred to Christ as "the saviour of the world," the reference was singular and remained undeveloped. Few of Lincoln's writings and speeches revealed an interest in the doctrines and beliefs that separated Christianity from other major religious systems, and at no time did Lincoln evidence any sustained interest in such doctrines.

Lincoln's religious rhetoric was abstract, grand, fatalistic—almost Judaic in its emphasis on providence and, certainly, deliverance, but only loosely Christian at best and perhaps not substantially Christian at all. Whether in the Gettysburg Address or elsewhere, he talked of death and dying, of sacrifice, of heroism. His was a language of the transcendent supernatural, though not of transcendentalism. If he spoke about or alluded to salvation, it was a salvation of the nation and of the nation's soul, not individual salvation. When Peter Cartwright, the Methodist itinerant who was his opponent in the 1846 congressional race, accused Lincoln of "infidelity," Lincoln denied the charge but in a highly elliptical fashion. When he did speak of religion among individuals, he spoke not of Christ but only of a "Maker," as in a letter about his own dying father in 1851: "Tell him to remember to call upon, and confide in, our great, and good, and merciful Maker; who will not turn away from him in any extremity."[5]

Lincoln's religious sentiments also reflected the spiritual heterodoxy common to America since colonization. Lincoln's frequent and tormented dreams, to which he attributed divine significance, fit the spiritual world of his youth, where Methodists or other itinerants, such as Lorenzo Dow, regularly described dreams as they enunciated, justified, and explained the ways of God. Like them, Lincoln had numerous premonitions of death, his own as well as those of soldiers on the battlefield. Yet Lincoln also expressed a bitter fatalism that resonated both with traditional American lay skepticism and with some aspects of American occultism. He became distraught and embittered by the deaths of his children and refused to be consoled by traditional Christian piety. Mary Todd Lincoln brought spiritualists to the White House on at least eight occasions so she could speak to her dead children. Here too Lincoln was often aloof—he is believed to have attended only a few of the seances—though perhaps no more so than with denominational Christianity.[6]

Lincoln's religion, then, paralleled that of many of his contemporaries. He faced innumerable religious choices. He understood much of Christianity's appeal. He eschewed church membership and resisted practices and doctrines that distinguished contemporary Christianity. He better represented past American religious behavior, however, than future. After 1865 and especially after 1900, despite ceaseless warnings about secularization and decline, Americans increasingly turned to Christian congregations and church membership as a means of formulating and rationalizing their own religious convictions amid the vagaries of modern life. Those changes had originated in eighteenth-century developments that found renewed expression in antebellum society and that shaped the religious choices that Lincoln himself made. But Lincoln also represented the ambivalent spiritual inclinations among America's heterodox citizens, men and women whose religious practice had been reshaped by the events of the previous three hundred years but who, in Christian terms at least, still remained an "almost chosen people."

Notes

Introduction: Religion in the American Past

1. Melford E. Spiro, "Religion: Problems of Definition and Explanation," in *Anthropological Approaches to the Study of Religion,* ed. Michael Banton (London, 1966), pp. 85–126. For Spiro, the difficulty with the functional definition of religion is that one cannot determine what religion does until one knows what religion is. Such a criticism does not, of course, preclude a functional analysis of religion, its roles, and its effects.

2. Bronislaw Malinowski, *Magic, Science, and Religion,* ed. Robert Redfield (Garden City, 1954), p. 88; Patrick Collinson, "Das Opium des Volkes," *Journal of Religious History* 8 (1974–75), 105–111. For a somewhat different approach and a still important debate, see Hildred Geertz and Keith Thomas, "An Anthropology of Religion and Magic, I and II," *Journal of Interdisciplinary History* 6 (1975–76), 71–109.

3. Patricia U. Bonomi and Peter R. Eisenstadt, "Church Adherence in the Eighteenth-Century British American Colonies," *William and Mary Quarterly,* 3d ser., 39 (1982), 245–286; Edwin Scott Gaustad, *Historical Atlas of Religion in America,* rev. ed. (New York, 1976); Wade Clark Roof, "Concepts and Indicators of Religious Commitment: A Critical Review," in *The Religious Dimension: New Directions in Quantitative Research,* ed. Robert Wuthnow (New York, 1979), pp. 17–46; Roger Finke and Rodney Stark, "Turning Pews into People: Estimating Church Membership in Nineteenth-Century America," *Journal for the Scientific Study of Religion* 25 (1985), 180–192.

4. Richard T. Vann, *The Social Development of English Quakerism 1655–1755* (Cambridge, Mass., 1969), pp. 122–127, 155–156; Theodore D. Bozeman, *To Live Ancient Lives: The Primitivist Dimension in Puritanism* (Chapel Hill, 1989), pp. 360–362.

1. The European Religious Heritage

1. The Virginia Company charter quoted in Perry Miller, *Errand into the Wilderness* (Cambridge, Mass., 1956), p. 101; John Winthrop, "A Modell of Christian Charity," in *The Puritans: A Sourcebook of Their Writings,* ed. Perry Miller and Thomas H. Johnson (New York, 1938), pp. 195–199.

2. *Association Records of the Particular Baptists of England, Wales, and Ireland to 1660,* ed. B. R. White (London, 1971–73), pt. 1, p. 18.

3. The leading work on magic in early modern England is Keith Thomas, *Religion and the Decline of Magic* (New York, 1971). Other major studies include Robert Muchembled, *Popular Culture and Elite Culture in France, 1400–1750,* trans. Lydia Cochrane (Baton Rouge, 1985); Marc Bloch, *The Royal Touch: Sacred Mon-*

archy and Scrofula in England and France, trans. J. E. Anderson (London, 1973). Jeanne Favret-Saada, *Deadly Words: Witchcraft in the Bocage* (New York, 1980), describes the survival of magical beliefs into the twentieth century.

4. On varying uses of early modern European religious beliefs, see Alan Macfarlane, *Witchcraft in Tudor and Stuart England: A Regional and Comparative Study* (New York, 1970), pp. 115–134; Michael MacDonald, *Mystical Bedlam: Madness, Anxiety, and Healing in Seventeenth-Century England* (New York, 1981); *George Fox's "Book of Miracles",* ed. Henry J. Cadbury (Cambridge, 1948); Ronald C. Finucane, *Miracles and Pilgrims: Popular Beliefs in Medieval England* (Totowa, N.J., 1977).

5. Macfarlane, *Witchcraft in Tudor and Stuart England,* pp. 14–80; Robert Muchembled, *Les derniers bûchers: Un village de Flandre et ses sorcières sous Louis XIV* (Paris, 1981), pp. 147–186; Christina Larner, *Enemies of God: The Witch-hunt in Scotland* (Baltimore, 1981).

6. G. R. Elton, *England under the Tudors* (London, 1962), pp. 160–175, 398–429; Jean Orcibal, *Louis XIV et les protestants* (Paris, 1951); Larner, *Enemies of God,* pp. 69–79.

7. Mary Fulbrook, *Piety and Politics: Religion and the Rise of Absolutism in England, Wurttemberg, and Prussia* (New York, 1983), chap. 4, offers a comparative view of developing relationships between church and state.

8. Carl Bridenbaugh, *Vexed and Troubled Englishmen, 1590–1642: The Beginnings of the American People* (New York, 1967), pp. 247–250; David Little, *Religion, Order, and Law: A Study in Pre-Revolutionary England* (New York, 1969). On the potential for individual rebellion, see Carlo Ginzburg, *The Cheese and the Worms: The Cosmos of a Sixteenth-Century Miller,* trans. John and Anne Tedeschi (Baltimore, 1980).

9. J. Sears McGee, *The Godly Man in Stuart England: Anglicans, Puritans, and the Two Tables* (New Haven, 1976); Elton, *England under the Tudors,* pp. 148, 219, 307–308.

10. S. S. Acquaviva, *The Decline of the Sacred in Industrial Society,* trans. Patricia Lipscomb (Oxford, 1979), pp. 124–125; Roy Porter, *English Society in the Eighteenth Century* (London, 1982), pp. 76–77, 83, 386–387.

11. John R. Stilgoe, *Common Landscape of America, 1588 to 1845* (New Haven, 1982), pp. 18–19.

12. Elton, *England under the Tudors,* p. 148. Paradoxically, archaeological evidence indicates that Christianity's advance in early England benefited from the Christianization of pagan shrines, including those at Glastonbury. See C. A. Ralegh Radford, "Glastonbury Abbey," in *The Quest for Arthur's Britain,* ed. Geoffrey Ashe et al. (London, 1968), pp. 97–110.

13. Stilgoe, *Common Landscape,* pp. 219–231.

14. Henry Barrow quoted in Thomas, *Religion and the Decline of Magic,* pp. 58, 59; J. Phillips, *The Reformation of Images: Destruction of Art in England, 1535–1660* (Berkeley, 1973); anonymous Catholic quotation from Natalie Zemon Davis, "The Rites of Violence," in Davis, *Society and Culture in Early Modern France* (Stanford, 1975), p. 157.

15. R. W. Scribner, "Ritual and Popular Religion in Catholic Germany at the Time of the Reformation," *Journal of Ecclesiastical History* 35 (January 1984), 47–

77; Charles Phythian-Adams, *Desolation of a City: Coventry and the Urban Crisis of the Late Middle Ages* (Cambridge, 1979), pp. 175–179, 218–219.

16. On English iconoclasm, see Phillips, *The Reformation of Images;* on Continental varieties, see Robert Scribner, "Ritual and Reformation," in Scribner, *Popular Culture and Popular Movements in Reformation Germany* (London and Ronceverte, W.V., 1987), pp. 103–122; and Phyllis Mack Crew, *Calvinist Preaching and Iconoclasm in the Netherlands, 1544–1569* (Cambridge, 1978).

17. Keith Wrightson, *English Society, 1580–1680* (New Brunswick, N.J., 1982), pp. 187–191, 194–199; Patrick Collinson, *The Elizabethan Puritan Movement* (Berkeley, 1967), pp. 168–176, 191–196; Edward Leach quoted in Margaret Spufford, *Contrasting Communities: English Villagers in the Sixteenth and Seventeenth Centuries* (Cambridge, 1974), pp. 319–344; A. G. Dickens, *The English Reformation* (New York, 1964), pp. 191–192; A. G. Dickens, *Lollards and Protestants in the Diocese of York, 1509–1538* (London, 1959), pp. 171–172, 215–217; David M. Palliser, *The Reformation in York, 1534–1553* (London, 1971), pp. 18–21. On wills and literacy, see Spufford's Cambridgeshire study as well as her *Small Books and Pleasant Histories* (Athens, Ga., 1981).

18. Geoffrey Parker, *The Dutch Revolt* (Ithaca, 1977), pp. 202–203; J. van Roey, "De correlatie tussen het socialeberoepsmilieu en de godsdienskeuze te Antwerpen op het einde der XVIe eeuw," in *Sources de l'histoire religieuse en Belgique* (Louvain, 1968), pp. 239–258.

19. Keith Wrightson and David Levine, *Poverty and Piety in an English Village: Terling, 1525–1700* (New York, 1979), pp. 165–172.

20. John Bossy, "Blood and Baptism: Kinship, Community and Christianity in Western Europe from the Fourteenth to the Seventeenth Centuries," in *Sanctity and Secularity: The Church and the World,* ed. Derek Baker, Studies in Church History, 10 (Oxford, 1973), pp. 129–143; Wrightson, *English Society,* pp. 44–51; L. Bradley, "An Enquiry into Seasonality in Baptisms, Marriages, and Burials," *Local Population Studies,* no. 4 (Spring 1970), 21–40; no. 5 (Autumn 1970), 18–35; no. 6 (Spring 1971), 15–31.

21. William Christian, Jr., *Local Religion in Sixteenth-Century Spain* (Princeton, 1981); Emmanuel Le Roy Ladurie, *The Peasants of Languedoc,* trans. John Day (Urbana, 1974); Christopher Hill, "Puritans and 'The Dark Corners of the Land,'" *Transactions of the Royal Historical Society,* 5th ser., 13 (1965), 77–102.

22. Alexander Murray, "Piety and Impiety in Thirteenth-Century Italy," in *Popular Belief and Practice,* ed. G. J. Cuming and Derek Baker, Studies in Church History, 8 (Cambridge, 1972), pp. 92–94.

23. Parker, *The Dutch Revolt,* p. 203.

24. James M. Kittelson, "Successes and Failures in the German Reformation: The Report from Strasbourg," *Archiv für Reformationsgeschichte* 73 (1982), 153–175; Gerald Strauss, "Success and Failure in the German Reformation," *Past and Present,* no. 67 (May 1975), 30–63, quotation on p. 50.

25. G. Baccrabere, "La pratique religieuse dans le diocèse de Toulouse aux XVIe et XVIIe siècles," *Annales du Midi* 74 (1962), 287–314.

26. Humphrey Roberts and William Harrison quoted in Collinson, *Religion of the Protestants,* p. 205; *Archbishop Grindal's Visitation, 1574, Comperta et Detecta Book,* ed. W. J. Shiels, Borthwick Texts and Calendars: Records of the North-

ern Province, 4 (1977); Walter C. Renshaw, ed., "Ecclesiastical Returns for 81 Parishes in East Sussex Made in 1603," *Miscellaneous Records of the Sussex Record Society* 4 (1905), 1–17.

27. Lucien Febvre, *The Problem of Unbelief in the Sixteenth Century,* trans. Beatrice Goldfarb (Cambridge, Mass., 1984), pp. 131–146, 455–464. Lady Monson's dreams quoted in Thomas, *Religion and the Decline of Magic,* p. 168; on English atheism and skepticism, see ibid., pp. 166–173; Yorkshire quotations from Wrightson, *English Society,* p. 219.

28. Christopher Hill, "Plebeian Irreligion in Seventeenth-Century England," in *Studien über die Revolution,* ed. Manfred Kossok (Berlin, 1969), pp. 46–61.

29. Muchembled, *Popular Culture and Elite Culture in France,* pp. 43–107, 183–185; David D. Hall, *Worlds of Wonder, Days of Judgment: Popular Religious Belief in Early New England* (New York, 1989), chaps. 2, 5.

30. A. L. Rowse, *Simon Forman: Sex and Society in Shakespeare's Age* (London, 1974), pp. 14–36, 129–170, 200–222; Derek Parker, *Familiar to All: William Lilly and Astrology in the Seventeenth Century* (London, 1975), pp. 117–128; Thomas, *Religion and the Decline of Magic,* pp. 244–252, 300–322; Adam Eyre, "A Dyurnall, or Catalogue of all my Accions and Expences from the 1st of January, 1646–[47]," in *Yorkshire Diaries and Autobiographies in the Seventeenth and Eighteenth Centuries,* Surtees Society Publications, 65 (1875), pp. 62, 63; Wayne Shumaker, *The Occult Sciences in the Renaissance: A Study in Intellectual Patterns* (Berkeley, 1972), pp. 1–15, 108–159; William Lilly, *Christian Astrology Modestly Treated of in Three Books* (London, 1647), pp. 432–434, 442.

31. Macfarlane, *Witchcraft in Tudor and Stuart England,* pp. 115–134; *The Diary of Abraham de la Pryme, the Yorkshire Antiquary,* ed. Charles Jackson, Surtees Society Publications, 54 (1869), p. 56; Richard Gough, *The History of Myddle,* ed. David Hey (New York, 1981), p. 107.

32. Shumaker, *Occult Sciences in the Renaissance,* pp. 115, 128, 130; Thomas, *Religion and the Decline of Magic,* pp. 286–287, 295, 316–318; Rowse, *Simon Forman,* pp. 58–61, 83, 98, 205; Charles Webster, *From Paracelsus to Newton: Magic and the Making of Modern Science* (Cambridge, 1982), pp. 1–14, 48–74.

33. Finucane, *Miracles and Pilgrims,* pp. 59–99; Thomas, *Religion and the Decline of Magic,* pp. 26–50; *The Autobiography of Richard Baxter,* abridged by J. M. Lloyd Thomas, ed. N. H. Keeble (London, 1974), p. 78.

34. *George Fox's "Book of Miracles",* ed. Cadbury, pp. 2–3, 26–27, 42, 101; MacDonald, *Mystical Bedlam,* p. 229; E. Brooks Holifield, *Health and Medicine in the Methodist Tradition: Journey toward Wholeness* (New York, 1986), pp. 28–60.

35. Thomas, *Religion and the Decline of Magic,* pp. 180, 263–279, 371–385; John Butler, *Christologia; or, A Brief (but True) Account of the Certain Year, Month, Day and Minute of the Birth of Jesus Christ* (London, 1671); *Diaries and Letters of Philip Henry, M.A., of Broad Oak, Flintshire, A.D. 1631–1696,* ed. Matthew H. Lee (London, 1882), p. 194; *Association Records of the Particular Baptists,* ed. White, pt. 2, p. 65. For intriguing comments on Salmon's possible colonial American ventures, see Joseph I. Waring, *A History of Medicine in South Carolina, 1670–1825* (Charleston, S.C., 1964), p. 16; and Sebastian Smith, *The Religious Imposter; or, The Lifes of Alexander, a Sham-Prophet, Doctor, and Fortune-Teller* (Amsterdam [sic, for London], n.d.).

36. Ralph Merrifield, "The Use of Bellarmines as Witch-Bottles," *Guildhall Miscellany* 3 (1954), 1–15; Ralph Merrifield, "Witch Bottles and Magical Jugs," *Folklore* 66 (1955), 195–207; Thomas, *Religion and the Decline of Magic,* p. 544.

37. Joseph Blau, *The Christian Interpretation of the Cabala in the Renaissance* (New York, 1944); Frances Yates, *Giordano Bruno and the Hermetic Tradition* (Chicago, 1964); Yates, *The Rosicrucian Enlightenment* (London, 1974); Walter Pagel, *Paracelsus: An Introduction to Philosophical Medicine in the Era of the Renaissance* (New York, 1958); Betty Jo Teeter Dobbs, *The Foundations of Newton's Alchemy: or, "The Hunting of the Greene Lyon"* (New York, 1975).

38. MacDonald, *Mystical Bedlam,* pp. 13–71, 217–231.

39. Thomas Pickering, introduction to William Perkins, *The Damned Art of Witchcraft* (Cambridge, 1608), p. 3, quoted in Macfarlane, *Witchcraft in Tudor and Stuart England,* p. 89; William Perkins quoted in Wrightson, *English Society,* p. 205; John Gaule, *The Mag-Astro-Mancer; or, The Magicall-Astrological-Diviner Posed and Puzzled* (London, 1652), sig. A2; "Minutes of the Cambridge Classis," in *Minutes of the Bury Presbyterian Classis, 1647–1657,* Chetham Society, Remains Literary and Historical, new ser., 41 (1898), p. 198.

40. The classic contemporary account of English sectarianism is Thomas Edwards, *Gangraena* (London, 1646). Christopher Hill, *The World Turned Upside Down: Radical Ideas during the English Revolution* (London, 1972), offers the fullest modern treatment. See also Christopher Hill et al., *The World of the Muggletonians* (London, 1983); A. Hamilton, *The Family of Love* (London, 1981); Bernard S. Capp, *The Fifth Monarchy Men* (London, 1972); A. L. Morton, *The World of the Ranters* (London, 1970).

41. Patricia Caldwell, *The Puritan Conversion Narrative: The Beginnings of American Expression* (New York, 1983); Michael Walzer, *The Revolution of the Saints: A Study in the Origins of Radical Politics* (Cambridge, Mass., 1965), esp. pp. 219–224. For interior views of congregational discipline in seventeenth-century England, see *The Records of a Church of Christ in Bristol, 1640–1687,* ed. Roger Hayden, Bristol Record Society Publications, 27 (1974), esp. pp. 46–56; *Records of the Churches of Christ, Gathered at Fenstanton, Warboys, and Hexham, 1644–1720,* ed. Edward B. Underhill, Hanserd Knollys Society Publications, 9 (1854); replies to queries in *Association Records of the Particular Baptists,* ed. White; and *Minute Book of the Society of Friends in Bristol, 1667–1686,* ed. Russell Mortimer, Bristol Record Society Publications, 26 (1971).

42. Wrightson, *English Society,* pp. 214–220; "The Life of Master John Shaw," in *Yorkshire Diaries and Autobiographies,* p. 141; *The Autobiography of Richard Baxter,* ed. J. M. Lloyd Thomas (London, 1974), pp. 76–84.

43. E. A. Wrigley and R. S. Schofield, *The Population History of England, 1541–1871: A Reconstruction* (Cambridge, Mass., 1981), pp. 19, 24, 31, 153; R. S. Schofield and B. Midi Berry, "Age at Baptism," *Population Studies* 25 (1971), 455.

44. Wrigley and Schofield, *Population History of England,* p. 92; Roger Thomas, "The Breakup of Nonconformity," in Geoffrey F. Nuttall et al., *The Beginnings of Nonconformity* (London, 1964), pp. 33–60; William C. Braithwaite, *The Second Period of Quakerism,* 2d ed. (Cambridge, 1961), pp. 416–456; Arnold Lloyd, *Quaker Social History, 1669–1738* (London, 1950); C. G. Bolam et al., *English*

Presbyterians from Elizabethan Puritanism to Modern Unitarianism (London, 1968), pp. 73–92; R. Tudor Jones, *Congregationalism in England, 1662–1962* (London, 1962), pp. 46–71; Alexander Gordon, *Freedom after Ejection: A Review of Presbyterian and Congregational Nonconformity in England and Wales* (Manchester, 1917), pp. 1–150; Barry Levy, *Quakerism and the American Family: British Settlement in the Delaware Valley* (New York, 1988), pp. 58–85.

45. "Heads of Agreement," *Transactions of the Congregational Historical Society* 8 (1920–23), 38–48; Allan Brockett, *Nonconformity in Exeter, 1650–1875* (Manchester, 1962), pp. 74–95; Frank Buffard, *Kent and Sussex Baptist Associations* (Faversham, 1963), pp. 29–30; "Association Life to 1815," *Transactions of the Baptist Historical Society* 5 (1961), 24–28; H. Wheeler Robinson, "The Beginning of Association Life in Yorkshire and Lancashire," *Baptist Quarterly* 23 (1970), 208–211.

46. MacDonald, *Mystical Bedlam;* Dobbs, *Foundations of Newton's Alchemy;* Thomas, *Religion and the Decline of Magic,* pp. 51–77.

47. Thomas, *Religion and the Decline of Magic,* pp. 225, 579–583, 644.

48. Richard Saunders, *The Astrological Judgment and Practice of Physick* (London, 1677), unpaginated preface. On the vexing question of Newton's alchemy, see Dobbs, *Foundations of Newton's Alchemy;* and K. Figala, "Newton as Alchemist," *History of Science* 15 (1977), 102–137.

49. Macfarlane, *Witchcraft in Tudor and Stuart England,* pp. 200–211; Thomas, *Religion and the Decline of Magic,* pp. 641–663; E. William Monter, *Witchcraft in France and Switzerland: The Borderlands during the Reformation* (Ithaca, 1976), pp. 37–41; H. C. Erik Midelfort, *Witch-Hunting in Southwestern Germany, 1562–1584: The Social and Intellectual Foundations* (Stanford, 1972), pp. 6–7, 121–163; Hugh Trevor-Roper, *Religion, the Reformation, and Social Change* (London, 1967), pp. 90–192; Gustav Henningsen, *The Witches' Advocate: Basque Witchcraft and the Spanish Inquisition (1609–1614)* (Reno, 1980), pp. 227–307, 357–386; and Larner, *Enemies of God,* pp. 175–191.

50. Macfarlane, *Witchcraft in Tudor and Stuart England,* pp. 135–144; Jon Butler, "Witchcraft, Healing, and Historians' Crazes," *Journal of Social History* 18 (1984), 111–118.

51. Kay S. Wilkins, "Attitudes to Witchcraft and Demonic Possession in France during the Eighteenth Century," *Journal of European Studies* 3 (1973), 348–362; Clarke Garrett, "Witches and Cunning Folk in the Old Regime," in *Popular Culture in France,* ed. Jac Beauroy et al. (Sarasota, 1976), pp. 53–64; Wallace Notestein, *A History of Witchcraft in England from 1558 to 1718* (New York, 1911), pp. 313–344; Glyn P. Jones, "Folk Medicine in Eighteenth-Century Wales," *Folk Life* 7 (1970), 60–74; Monter, *Witchcraft in France and Switzerland,* pp. 185–190; Thomas, *Religion and the Decline of Magic,* pp. 663–668; Muchembled, *Popular Culture and Elite Culture,* pp. 235–278.

52. Natalie Zemon Davis, "Printing and the People," in Davis, *Society and Culture in Early Modern France,* p. 190; Jones, "Folk Medicine in Eighteenth-Century Wales"; Peter Burke, *Popular Culture in Early Modern Europe* (New York, 1978), pp. 270–286.

53. Wrightson and Levine, *Poverty and Piety in an English Village,* pp. 165, 169–170; *Extracts from the Diary of the Rev. Robert Meeke,* ed. H. J. Morehouse (Lon-

don, 1874), p. 44; vicar of Bladon quoted in *Bishop Fell and Nonconformity,* ed. Mary Clapinson, Oxfordshire Record Society Record Series, 52 (1977–78), p. xli.

54. Jean Delumeau, *Catholicism between Luther and Voltaire: A New View of the Counter-Reformation,* trans. Jeremy Moiser (Philadelphia, 1977), pp. 203–231; Jean Delumeau, "Au sujet de la dechristianization," *Revue d'histoire moderne et contemporaine* 22 (1975), 52–60; Olwen Hufton, "The French Church," in *Church and Society in Catholic Europe of the Eighteenth Century,* ed. William J. Callahan and David Higgs (Cambridge, 1979), pp. 13–33; Marc Venard, "Popular Religion in the Eighteenth Century," in ibid., ed. Callan and Higgs, pp. 138–154.

55. Norman Sykes, *Church and State in England in the Eighteenth Century* (Cambridge, 1934), pp. 115–121.

56. Catholic proselytization is described in the superb essays in *Church and Society in Catholic Europe in the Eighteenth Century,* ed. Callahan and Higgs.

57. J. H. Overton, *Life in the English Church, 1660–1714* (London, 1885), pp. 224–232, 296–306; G. V. Bennett, *White Kennett, 1660–1728, Bishop of Peterborough* (London, 1957), pp. 184–190; Norman Sykes, *From Sheldon to Secker: Aspects of English Church History, 1660–1728* (Cambridge, 1959), pp. 9–22.

58. Basil F. W. Clarke, *The Building of the Eighteenth-Century Church* (London, 1963), pp. 88–89, contains, as an example, details on the construction of new Anglican buildings in the West Riding of Yorkshire.

59. W. K. Lowther Clarke, *Eighteenth-Century Piety* (London, 1944), pp. 69–80; Edward Carpenter, *The Protestant Bishop, Being the Life of Henry Compton, 1632–1713, Bishop of London* (London, 1956), pp. 61–67, 208–232.

60. H. P. Thompson, *Thomas Bray* (London, 1954); W. K. Lowther Clarke, *A History of the S.P.C.K.* (London, 1959), pp. 19–58; Thomas Bray, "A Memorial Representing the Present State of Religion in the Continent of North America," in *Rev. Thomas Bray, His Life and Selected Works Relating to Maryland,* ed. Bernard C. Steiner, Maryland Historical Society Fund Publications, 27 (1901); H. P. Thompson, *Into All Lands: The History of the Society for the Propagation of the Gospel in Foreign Parts, 1701–1950* (London, 1951).

61. Hillel Schwartz, *The French Prophets: The History of a Millenarian Group in Eighteenth-Century England* (Berkeley, 1980); B. Robert Kreiser, *Miracles, Convulsions, and Ecclesiastical Politics in Early Eighteenth-Century France* (Princeton, 1978); Fulbrook, *Piety and Politics,* pp. 153–173; Bernard Semmell, *The Methodist Revolution* (New York, 1973).

62. David Higgs, "The Portuguese Church," in *Church and Society in Catholic Europe in the Eighteenth Century,* ed. Callahan and Higgs, p. 61; Raymond Callahan, "The Spanish Church," in ibid., p. 47.

63. This survey is taken from the visitation statistics compiled in *Archbishop Herring's Visitation Return, 1743,* ed. S. L. Ollard and P. C. Walker, Yorkshire Archaeological Society Record Series, 71–75 (1928–31).

2. The Crisis of Christian Practice in America

1. Perry Miller, "Religion and Society in the Early Literature of Virginia," in Miller, *Errand into the Wilderness* (Cambridge, Mass., 1956), p. 101; Robert F.

Berkhofer, Jr., *The White Man's Indian: Images of the American Indian from Columbus to the Present* (New York, 1978), pp. 3–32; William Penn to Thomas Janney, August 21, 1681, in *The Papers of William Penn,* ed. Richard S. Dunn and Mary Maples Dunn, 5 vols. (Philadelphia, 1981–87), II, 106.

2. George McClaren Brydon, *Virginia's Mother Church and the Political Conditions under Which It Grew,* 2 vols. (Richmond, 1947–52), I, 26–27.

3. Quoted in Brydon, *Virginia's Mother Church,* I, 24. Much of Virginia's early sermon literature is listed in Miller, "Religion and Society in the Early Literature of Virginia."

4. Whitaker quoted in Brydon, *Virginia's Mother Church,* I, 24.

5. Strachey quoted in Brydon, *Virginia's Mother Church,* I, 16.

6. *Lawes Divine, Morall and Martiall,* ed. David H. Flaherty (Charlottesville, Va., 1969); *Journals of the House of Burgesses of Virginia [1619–1776],* ed. H. R. McIlwaine and J. P. Kennedy, 15 vols. (Richmond, 1905–1915), I, 9–11.

7. James Horn, "Servant Emigration to the Chesapeake in the Seventeenth Century," in *The Chesapeake in the Seventeenth Century: Essays on Anglo-American Society and Politics,* ed. Thad W. Tate and David L. Ammerman (Chapel Hill, 1979), pp. 51–95; Edmund S. Morgan, *American Slavery, American Freedom: The Ordeal of Colonial Virginia* (New York, 1975), pp. 158–179.

8. *Minutes of the Council and General Court of Colonial Virginia, 1622–1632, 1670–1676,* ed. H. R. McIlwaine (Richmond, 1924), pp. 9, 18, 21, 22.

9. Ibid., pp. 105–107, 167.

10. Ibid., pp. 172, 175; Brydon, *Virginia's Mother Church,* I, 79–81.

11. *Minutes of the Council and General Court,* ed. McIlwaine, pp. 15, 17, 89, 107, 159, 167.

12. Ibid., pp. 96, 191.

13. Arthur Lyon Cross, *The Anglican Episcopate and the American Colonies* (Cambridge, Mass., 1902), pp. 13–24; see also J. H. Bennett, "English Bishops and Imperial Jurisdiction, 1660–1725," *Historical Magazine of the Protestant Episcopal Church* 32 (1963), 175–188.

14. *County Court Records of Accomack-Northampton, Virginia, 1632–1640,* ed. Susie M. Ames (Washington, D.C., 1954), pp. 40, 44; "Lower Norfolk County Records," *Virginia Magazine of History and Biography* 39 (1931), 15; 40 (1932), 36–37.

15. *County Court Records of Accomack-Northampton, 1632–1640,* ed. Ames, pp. xxxi, xlvii, 10, 24, 26, 45, 64, 92–93; Philip Alexander Bruce, *Institutional History of Virginia in the Seventeenth Century,* 2 vols. (New York, 1910), I, 211.

16. George C. Mason, "The Six Earliest Churches on the Eastern Shore of Virginia," *William and Mary Quarterly,* 2nd ser., 21 (1941), 199–207.

17. John R. Stilgoe, *Common Landscape of America, 1580 to 1845* (New Haven, 1982), pp. 18–19; *Minutes of the Council and General Court,* ed. McIlwaine, pp. 471, 472, 479, 481, 499, 505.

18. Kevin P. Kelly, "'In dispers'd Country Plantations': Settlement Patterns in Seventeenth-Century Surry County, Virginia," in *The Chesapeake in the Seventeenth Century,* ed. Tate and Ammerman, pp. 183–205; George C. Mason, "The Colonial Churches of Surry and Sussex Counties, Virginia," *William and Mary Quarterly,* 2d ser., 20 (1940), 285–305.

19. R[oger] G[reen], *Virginia's Cure; or, An Advisive Narrative concerning Virginia* (London, 1662), in *Tracts and Other Papers Relating Principally to the Origin, Settlement, and Progress of the Colonies of North America, from the Discovery of the Country to the Year 1776,* ed. Peter Force (Washington, D.C., 1844), III, no. 15, pp. 3–4.

20. James Walsh, "'Black Cotted Raskolls': Anti-Anglican Criticism in Colonial Virginia," *Virginia Magazine of History and Biography,* 88 (1980), 221–36; William Durand to John Davenport, July 15, 1642, in Jon Butler, ed., "Two 1642 Letters from Virginia Puritans," *Proceedings of the Massachusetts Historical Society* 84 (1972), 108; John Hammond, *Leah and Rachel; or, The Two Fruitful Sisters Virginia, and Maryland* (London, 1656), in Force, ed., *Tracts* III, no. 14, p. 9.

21. Margaret Stieg, *Laud's Laboratory: The Diocese of Bath and Wells in the Early Seventeenth Century* (Lewisburg, Pa., 1982), pp. 53–62.

22. Sacvan Bercovitch, *The Puritan Origins of the American Self* (New Haven, 1975), offers a particularly forceful explanation of the potential uses of biography and of the significance of Cotton Mather's often abused *Magnalia* in American history. It is intriguing that historians have failed to ask what significance the lack of a *Magnalia* meant for a developing concept of society in the Chesapeake.

23. Butler, ed., "Two 1642 Letters from Virginia Puritans"; Wesley Frank Craven, *The Southern Colonies in the Seventeenth Century* (Baton Rouge, 1949), pp. 228, 229; Bruce, *Institutional History of Virginia in the Seventeenth Century,* I, 252–261. Bruce described Durand as a minister, but none of the surviving records, including the Virginia legal records, offer that description.

24. Butler, ed., "Two 1642 Letters from Virginia Puritans."

25. Brydon, *Virginia's Mother Church,* I, 131–132; Samuel Eliot Morison, *Builders of the Bay Colony* (Boston, 1930), pp. 190–192.

26. *Lower Norfolk County Virginia Antiquary* 2 (1897), 12; Bruce, *Institutional History of Virginia,* I, 257; Babette M. Levy, "Early Puritanism in the Southern and Island Colonies," *Proceedings of the American Antiquarian Society* 70 (1960), 130; Craven, *Southern Colonies in the Seventeenth Century,* p. 228.

27. Anne F. Upshur and Ralph T. Whitelaw, eds., "Library of the Rev. Thomas Teackle," *William and Mary Quarterly,* 2d ser., 23 (1943), 298–308; Susie M. Ames, *Studies of the Virginia Eastern Shore in the Seventeenth Century* (Richmond, 1940), pp. 231–232. On books in the seventeenth-century southern colonies, see Richard Beale Davis, *Intellectual Life in the Colonial South* (Knoxville, 1978). The literature on books in New England is larger, of course, and among interesting recent works are David Cressy, "Books as Totems in Seventeenth-Century England and New England," *Journal of Library History* 21 (Winter 1986), 92–106; Norman Fiering, "The Transatlantic Republic of Letters," *William and Mary Quarterly,* 3d ser., 33 (1976), 642–660; and David D. Hall, *Worlds of Wonder, Days of Judgment: Popular Religious Belief in Early New England* (New York, 1989), pp. 21–70, 247–250.

28. On Anglican writings, compare Teackle's library with the ideal library developed by Thomas Bray, the Anglican reformer, in the 1690s and described in Edgar Legare Pennington, "The Beginnings of the Library in Charles Town, South Carolina," *Proceedings of the American Antiquarian Society* 44 (1934), 159–187; Charles T. Laugher, *Thomas Bray's Grand Design: Libraries of the Church of*

England in America, 1695–1785 (Chicago, 1973); and Lawrence C. Wroth, "Dr. Bray's 'Proposals for the Incouragement of Religion and Learning in the Foreign Plantations' — A Bibliographical Note," *Proceedings of the Massachusetts Historical Society* 65 (1932–36), 518–534. For descriptions of the works of many of the minor Puritan authors, some of whom took part in the parliamentary preaching in the 1640s, see John F. Wilson, *Pulpit in Parliament: Puritanism during the English Civil Wars, 1640–1648* (Princeton, 1969); on Caryl, see J. Sears McGee, *The Godly Man in Stuart England: Anglicans, Puritans, and the Two Tables* (New Haven, 1976), p. 28.

29. On popular Puritan piety, with which Teackle's library makes only occasional connections, see Charles Hambrick-Stowe, *The Practice of Piety: Puritan Devotional Disciplines in Seventeenth-Century New England* (Chapel Hill, 1982), and Jerald C. Brauer, "Types of Puritan Piety," *Church History* 56 (1987), 39–58.

30. Brydon, *Virginia's Mother Church,* I, 191–198. Bruce, *Institutional History of Virginia in the Seventeenth Century,* I, 222–252, 262–275; *The Life and Writings of Francis Makemie,* ed. Boyd S. Schlenther (Philadelphia, 1971), pp. 15–20; Bernard Bailyn, "Politics and Social Structure in Virginia," in *Seventeenth-Century America: Essays in Colonial History,* ed. James M. Smith (Chapel Hill, 1959), pp. 90–115; Morgan, *American Slavery, American Freedom,* pp. 250–270; Brydon, *Virginia's Mother Church,* I, 190.

31. Drawn from a survey of the records printed in *Charles Parish, York County, Virginia, History and Registers,* ed. Landon C. Bell (Richmond, 1932).

32. John Bossy, "Reluctant Colonists: The English Catholics Confront the Atlantic," in *Early Maryland in a Wider World,* ed. David B. Quinn (Detroit, 1982), pp. 149–166; John Tracy Ellis, *Catholics in Colonial America* (Baltimore, 1965), pp. 324–335.

33. Early Maryland population patterns are digested in Gloria L. Main, *Tobacco Colony: Life in Early Maryland, 1650–1720* (Princeton, 1982), pp. 9–16. On the social origins and mobility of seventeenth-century Maryland immigrants, see also Russell R. Menard, "Immigrants and Their Increase: The Process of Population Growth in Early Colonial Maryland," in *Law, Society, and Politics in Early Maryland,* ed. Aubrey C. Land et al. (Baltimore, 1977), pp. 88–110. Cecilius Calvert's injunctions to Catholics are quoted in Nelson W. Rightmyer, *Maryland's Established Church* (Baltimore, 1956), p. 6.

34. Rightmyer, *Maryland's Established Church,* pp. 153–221, contains the most complete list of Anglican clergymen known to have officiated in the colony until independence.

35. John D. Krugler, "'With promise of Liberty in Religion': The Catholic Lords Baltimore and Toleration in Seventeenth-Century Maryland, 1634–1693," *Maryland Historical Magazine* 79 (1984), 21–43; David S. Lovejoy, *The Glorious Revolution in America* (New York, 1972), pp. 85, 281–288; *The Glorious Revolution in America: Documents on the Colonial Crisis of 1689,* ed. Michael G. Hall et al. (Chapel Hill, 1964), pp. 165–166, 171–175, 179–186.

36. Jay Dolan, *The American Catholic Experience: A History from Colonial Times to the Present* (Garden City, N.Y., 1985), pp. 17–86. See also Ellis, *Catholics in Colonial America,* pp. 324–345. Ellis largely describes Jesuit work in the colony

that includes, between 1667 and 1674, 260 reputed conversions to Catholicism; but it is not clear whether these were conversions of active Protestants, lapsed Protestants, or lapsed Catholics. See ibid., p. 341.

37. Arnold Lloyd, *Quaker Social History, 1669–1738* (London, 1950); Richard Vann, *The Social Development of English Quakerism, 1655–1755* (Cambridge, Mass., 1969), pp. 96–101; Jon Butler, *Power, Authority, and the Origins of American Denominational Order: The English Churches in the Delaware Valley, 1680–1730,* American Philosophical Society Transactions, 68, pt. 2 (1978), pp. 17–18; Rufus Jones, *The Quakers in the American Colonies* (New York, 1911), pp. 278–282; Kenneth Carroll, *Quakerism on the Eastern Shore* (Baltimore, 1970), pp. 7–57; J. Reaney Kelly, *Quakers in the Founding of Anne Arundel County, Maryland* (Baltimore, 1963).

38. Christopher Hill, *The World Turned Upside Down: Radical Ideas during the English Revolution* (New York, 1972), pp. 186–207, describes the quite different appeal of Quaker doctrine to Commonwealth radicals. On Maryland, see Robert Clarkson to Elizabeth Harris, [9] mo/14/1657, printed in Carroll, *Quakerism on the Eastern Shore,* pp. 9–11; and Jones, *Quakers in the American Colonies,* pp. 265–294. Durand's Quaker membership is claimed in Jones, ibid., p. 267, and in "Two 1642 Letters from Virginia Puritans," ed. Butler, but is disproved in Carroll, *Quakerism on the Eastern Shore,* pp. 11, 14.

39. *Archives of Maryland,* 71 vols. to date (Baltimore, 1833–), V(1887), 130–131, 133.

40. Ellis, *Catholics in Colonial America,* p. 342; *Archives of Maryland,* LIV (1937), 129, 186–188, 267–268, 318, 600–609.

41. "Return of Romish Priests and Lay Brothers . . . ," May 24, 1698, in *Historical Collections Relating to the American Colonial Church,* ed. William S. Perry, 5 vols. (Hartford, Conn., 1875), IV, 20–23. Quaker buildings are described in Carroll, *Quakerism on the Eastern Shore,* pp. 29, 43–54; and Kelly, *Quakers in the Founding of Anne Arundel County.* Brief lists of Anglican church structures are found in Rightmyer, *Maryland's Established Church,* pp. 135–152. It is doubtful that two reputed early Anglican buildings ever existed—"Poplar Hill," supposedly constructed in 1642 in St. Mary's County, and a building on Kent Island, said to have been constructed about 1650. The *Hammond-Harwood House Atlas of Historical Maryland, 1608–1908,* ed. Edward C. Papenfuse and Joseph M. Coale III (Baltimore, 1982), does not settle problems about dating and locating seventeenth-century Maryland church buildings. Although it reproduces nearly all important early Maryland maps, early American cartographers did not use a consistent set of symbols to indicate church buildings and did not include all church buildings that existed when they made their maps.

42. *Archives of Maryland,* I(1883), 244–247; Thomas J. Curry, *The First Freedoms: Church and State in America to the Passage of the First Amendment* (New York, 1986), pp. 38–39.

43. *Archives of Maryland,* LIII (1936), 194. Main, *Tobacco Colony,* pp. 210–211, describes seventeenth-century Maryland funeral customs. Main's intriguing observations, however brief, offer a telling contrast to the assertion in David E. Stannard, *The Puritan Way of Death: A Study in Religion, Culture, and Social Change*

(New York, 1977), p. 129, that "in Virginia, for example, it took nearly a century for funerary ceremonies and monuments to acquire any substantial degree of cultural importance."

44. The literature on New England history and Puritanism is too vast to summarize here. Suffice it to say that even in the 1980s much of the argument about the substance and shape of the society still revolves around Perry Miller's scholarship, namely his *The New England Mind: The Seventeenth Century* (New York, 1939); *The New England Mind: From Colony to Province* (Cambridge, Mass., 1953); and *Errand into the Wilderness* (Cambridge, Mass., 1956). The most direct challenges to Miller have come from Darrett B. Rutman, *Winthrop's Boston: Portrait of a Puritan Town* (Chapel Hill, 1963); Darrett B. Rutman, *American Puritanism: Faith and Practice* (Philadelphia, 1970); John Demos, *A Little Commonwealth: Family Life in Plymouth Colony* (New York, 1970); Sumner Chilton Powell, *Puritan Village: The Formation of a New England Town* (Middletown, Conn., 1963); David D. Hall, *The Faithful Shepherd: A History of the New England Ministry in the Seventeenth Century* (Chapel Hill, 1972); and Philip Gura, *A Glimpse of Sion's Glory: Puritan Radicalism in Seventeenth-Century New England* (Middletown, Conn., 1984).

45. David Grayson Allen, *In English Ways: The Movements of Societies and the Transferral of English Local Law and Custom to Massachusetts Bay in the Seventeenth Century* (Chapel Hill, 1981), pp. 168, 178–179, 182, 198–199, 207; cf. Morgan, *American Slavery, American Freedom,* pp. 234, 405–410; Horn, "Servant Emigration to the Chesapeake." A dramatic instance of differences in Virginia and New England immigration patterns can be found in the two 1635 lists printed in *Remarkable Providences, 1600–1760,* ed. John Demos (New York, 1972), pp. 37–41.

46. John Allin, "Brief History of the Church of Christ . . . at Dedham in New England," in *Early Records of the Town of Dedham,* 6 vols. (Dedham, Mass., 1886–1936), II, 1–21; *Extracts from the Itineraries and Other Miscellanies of Ezra Stiles,* ed. Franklin B. Dexter (New Haven, 1916), p. 264; Powell, *Puritan Village,* pp. 107, 121. The most complete account of the early New England buildings, often including measurements, is found in Marian C. Donnelly, *The New England Meeting Houses of the Seventeenth Century* (Middletown, Conn., 1968).

47. Kenneth A. Lockridge, *A New England Town, the First Hundred Years: Dedham, Massachusetts, 1636–1736,* expanded ed. (New York, 1985), p. 31; Rutman, *Winthrop's Boston,* pp. 138–142.

48. Rutman, *Winthrop's Boston,* pp. 55, 109; *The Apologia of Robert Keayne: The Self-Portrait of a Puritan Merchant,* ed. Bernard Bailyn (New York, 1964); cf. *The Diary of Michael Wigglesworth, 1653–1657: The Conscience of a Puritan,* ed. Edmund S. Morgan (New York, 1965); John Dane, "A Declaration of Remarkable Providences in the Course of My Life," in *Remarkable Providences,* ed. Demos, pp. 80–88.

49. *Thomas Shepard's Confessions,* ed. George Selement and Bruce C. Woolley, Publications of the Colonial Society of Massachusetts, 58 (1981), pp. 99–101, 139–140; George Selement, "The Meeting of Elite and Popular Minds at Cambridge, New England, 1638–1645," *William and Mary Quarterly,* 3d ser., 41 (1984), 32–48; David D. Hall, "Toward a History of Popular Religion in Early New England," ibid., 49–55.

50. Quoted in Lockridge, *A New England Town,* pp. 4–5; Demos, ed., *Remarkable Providences,* pp. 53–56, 192–193.

51. Emery Battis, *Saints and Sectaries: Anne Hutchinson and the Antinomian Controversy in the Massachusetts Bay Colony* (Chapel Hill, 1962); Lyle Koehler, *The Search for Power: The "Weaker Sex" in Seventeenth-Century New England* (Urbana, 1980); Gura, *Glimpse of Sion's Glory;* Gura, "The Radical Ideology of Samuel Gorton: New Light on the Relation of English to American Puritanism," *William and Mary Quarterly,* 3d ser., 36 (1979), 78–100; Gura, "Samuel Gorton and Religious Radicalism in England, 1644–1648," ibid., 40 (1983), 121–124.

52. Battis, *Saints and Sectaries,* and Koehler, *The Search for Power,* remain the most exhaustive studies of the controversy, though *The Antinomian Controversy, 1636–1638: A Documentary History,* ed. David D. Hall (Middletown, Conn., 1968), offers the major sources and a still helpful introduction.

53. Hall, *Faithful Shepherd,* pp. 218–222; Rutman, *American Puritanism,* pp. 94–97; Robert F. Scholz, "Clerical Consociation in Massachusetts Bay: Reassessing the New England Way," *William and Mary Quarterly,* 3d ser., 29 (1972), 391–414.

54. Edmund S. Morgan, *Visible Saints: The History of a Puritan Idea* (Ithaca, 1963), pp. 64–112; Robert G. Pope, *The Half-Way Covenant: Church Membership in Puritan New England* (Princeton, 1969), pp. 13–42; Robert G. Pope, "New England versus the New England Mind: The Myth of Declension," *Journal of Social History* 3 (1969–70), 95–108.

55. Allen, *In English Ways,* pp. 89–95; Lockridge, *A New England Town,* pp. 79–90; Paul Boyer and Stephen Nissenbaum, *Salem Possessed: The Social Origins of Witchcraft* (Cambridge, Mass., 1974), pp. 37–59.

56. David Cressy, *Coming Over: Migration and Communication between England and New England in the Seventeenth Century* (New York, 1987), pp. 37–73; Henry A. Gemery, "Emigration from the British Isles to the New World, 1630–1700: Inferences from colonial populations," *Research in Economic Development* 5 (1980), 283–342; Douglas Jones, *Village and Seaport: Migration and Society in Eighteenth-Century Massachusetts* (Hanover, N.H., 1981); Douglas R. McManis, *Colonial New England: A Historical Geography* (New York, 1975), pp. 41–85.

57. Rutman, *Winthrop's Boston,* pp. 142–143.

58. Pope, *Half-Way Covenant;* Gerald F. Moran, "The Puritan Saint: Religious Experience, Church Membership, and Piety in Connecticut, 1636–1776" (Ph.D. dissertation, Rutgers University, 1973), p. 130; David M. Scobey, "Revising the Errand: New England's Ways and the Puritan Sense of the Past," *William and Mary Quarterly,* 3d ser., 41 (1984), 3–31.

59. Richard P. Gildrie, *Salem, Massachusetts, 1626–1682: A Covenant Community* (Charlottesville, Va., 1975), pp. 64, 163–164.

60. Bernard Bailyn, *The Peopling of British North America: An Introduction* (New York, 1986), esp. pp. 123–127; Jones, *Quakers in the American Colonies,* pp. 417–458; Frederick B. Tolles, *Meeting House and Counting House: The Quaker Merchants of Colonial Philadelphia, 1682–1763* (Chapel Hill, 1949), pp. 29–44; Elizabeth W. Fisher, "'Prophecies and Revelations': German Cabbalists in Early Pennsylvania," *Pennsylvania Magazine of History and Biography* 109 (1985), 299–333.

61. Gary B. Nash, *Quakers and Politics, Pennsylvania, 1681–1726* (Princeton,

1968), pp. 127–180; Jon Butler, "Into Pennsylvania's Spiritual Abyss: The Rise and Fall of the Later Keithians, 1693–1703," *Pennsylvania Magazine of History and Biography* 101 (1977), 151–170; Butler, *Power, Authority, and the Origins of American Denominational Order*, pp. 27–31, 43–47, 52–54, 64–67.

62. Richard W. Pointer, *Protestant Pluralism and the New York Experience: A Study of Eighteenth-Century Religious Diversity* (Bloomington, 1988), pp. 1–8.

63. "Governor Dongan's Report to the Committee of Trade on the Province of New York, dated 22d February, 1687," in *Documentary History of the State of New York*, ed. E. B. O'Callaghan, 4 vols. (Albany, 1849–51), I, 186.

64. S. Charles Bolton, *Southern Anglicanism: The Church of England in Colonial South Carolina* (Westport, Conn., 1982), offers a more positive treatment of religion and the Church of England in the colony.

65. Hugh T. Lefler and William S. Powell, *Colonial North Carolina: A History* (New York, 1973), pp. 192–195.

66. Reasonably dependable information about ecclesiastical architecture can be obtained from a number of disparate sources, among them John W. Reps, *The Making of Urban America: A History of City Planning in the United States* (Princeton, 1965); Isaac Newton Phelps Stokes, *The Iconography of Manhattan Island, 1498–1909*, 6 vols. (New York, 1915–28); Justin Winsor, ed., *The Memorial History of Boston*, 2 vols. (Boston, 1880–81); Walter Muir Whitehill, *Boston, A Topographical History* (Cambridge, Mass., 1959); and Harriett H. R. Ravenel, *Charleston: The Place and the People* (New York, 1906).

3. *Magic and the Occult*

1. *Minutes of the Council and General Court of Colonial Virginia, 1622–1632, 1670–1676*, ed. H. R. McIlwaine (Richmond, 1924), p. 112.

2. Ibid., p. 111, 112.

3. Ibid., p. 112, 114.

4. Ibid., pp. 114, 125–129. For the General Court's similar action in a 1624 transvestite episode, see p. 34.

5. R. G. Tomlinson, *Witchcraft Trials of Connecticut* (Hartford, Conn., 1978), pp. 13–18, 19–24; John P. Demos, *Entertaining Satan: Witchcraft and the Culture of Early New England* (New York, 1982), pp. 36–56; Paul Boyer and Stephen Nissenbaum, *Salem Possessed: The Social Origins of Witchcraft* (Cambridge, Mass., 1974).

6. John Demos, "Underlying Themes in the Witchcraft of Seventeenth-Century New England," *American Historical Review* 75 (1970), 1311–26; Carol F. Karlsen, *The Devil in the Shape of a Woman: Witchcraft in Colonial New England* (New York, 1987), pp. 77–116.

7. David D. Hall, *Worlds of Wonder, Days of Judgment: Popular Religious Belief in Early New England* (New York, 1989); Perry Miller, *The New England Mind: The Seventeenth Century* (New York, 1939), p. 228.

8. The distinction between wonders and miracles in contemporary literature is described in articles by D. P. Walker, "Valentine Greatrakes, the Irish Stroker and the Question of Miracles," in *Mélanges sur la littérature de la Renaissance à la mémoire de V.-L. Saulnier* (Geneva, 1984), 343–356; and D. P. Walker, "La cessazione dei miracoli," *Intersezioni* 3 (1983), 285–301.

9. Increase Mather, *An Essay for the Recording of Illustrious Providences . . .* (Boston, 1684), pp. 177, 253, 319. Increase Mather was equally sparse in his *Cases of Conscience concerning Evil Spirits Personating Men* (1693; London, 1862), p. 257; there his only use of the term miracle occurs when paraphrasing John Cotta's *The Triall of Witchcraft* (London, 1616), in which he quotes Cotta as arguing that the delivery of victims from witches' curses by having witches touch their victims constituted a "diabolical Miracle."

10. Chadwick Hansen, *Witchcraft at Salem* (New York, 1969), pp. 93–103. John Demos has warned historians against using the court record to determine whether any of the accused really practiced witchcraft and has suggested that the question can probably never be answered. Despite the problem of finding evidence that does not descend from the courts or Christian ministers, a sufficient range of evidence—legal, clerical, and literary—now seems to demonstrate that such practices did indeed occur, though it will never tell us whether the individuals accused at Salem engaged in witchcraft or in more benign occult activity. Demos, "Underlying Themes"; and Demos, "John Godfrey and His Neighbors: Witchcraft and the Social Web in Colonial Massachusetts," *William and Mary Quarterly,* 3d ser., 33 (1976), 242–265.

11. Tomlinson, *Witchcraft Trials of Connecticut,* p. 43; Richard Weisman, *Witchcraft, Magic, and Religion in Seventeenth-Century Massachusetts* (Amherst, Mass., 1984), pp. 53–72, 108–111.

12. Cotton Mather, "A Discourse on Witchcraft," in C. Mather, *Memorable Providences, Relating to Witchcrafts and Possessions* (Boston, 1689), pp. 19–21 (Mather's emphasis).

13. I. Mather, *Essay for the Recording of Illustrious Providences,* pp. 261, 266.

14. Cotton Mather, *The Angel of Bethesda,* ed. Gordon W. Jones (Barre, Mass., 1972), pp. 293–301.

15. Darrett B. Rutman, "The Evolution of the Religious Life of Early Virginia," *Lex et Scientia: The Journal of the American Academy of Law and Science* 14 (1978), 190–240; Richard Beale Davis, "The Devil in Virginia in the Seventeenth Century," in Davis, *Literature and Society in Early Virginia, 1608–1840* (Baton Rouge, 1973), pp. 14–41.

16. Minutes, Concord Monthly Meeting, 11–9 mo.–1695, 9–10 mo.–1695, 13–11 mo.–1695/6, 9–1 mo.–1696, and Minutes, Concord Quarterly Meeting, 3–12 mo.–1695; microfilm, Friends Historical Library, Swarthmore College, Swarthmore, Pa.; Amelia M. Gummere, *Witchcraft and Quakerism: A Study in Social History* (Philadelphia, 1908), pp. 46–47; Ezra Michener, *Retrospect of Early Quakerism: Being Extracts from the Records of Philadelphia Yearly Meeting and the Meetings Composing It* (Philadelphia, 1860), pp. 364–367.

17. *Records of the Courts of Chester County, Pennsylvania, 1681–1697* (Philadelphia, 1910), pp. 363–371. Although the term "negromancy" could have carried racial overtones in the colonial period, the point is difficult to establish. Seventeenth-century English writers used the term interchangeably with "necromancy" without apparent racial connotations, as in *A Plot Lately Discovered for the Taking of the Tower by Negromancie* (London, 1641).

18. *Records of the Court of Chester County, Pennsylvania, 1681–1697,* p. 393.

19. Ibid., pp. 398, 405, 406; *Records of the Courts of Chester County, Pennsylvania* (Danboro, Pa., 1972), II, 2, 3, 126, 160; and Herbert W. K. Fitzroy, "Richard

Crosbye Goes to Court, 1683–1697," *Pennsylvania Magazine of History and Biography* 62 (1938), 12–19. This occult activity surfaced amid a great deal of additional religious turmoil in Chester County in the same decade; see Jon Butler, "Into Pennsylvania's Spiritual Abyss: The Rise and Fall of the Later Keithians, 1693–1703," ibid., 101 (1972), 151–170.

20. Harold Jantz, "America's First Cosmopolitan," *Proceedings of the Massachusetts Historical Society* 84 (1972), 3–25; Robert C. Black III, *The Younger John Winthrop* (New York, 1966), pp. 87–88; and Ronald S. Wilkinson, "'Hermes Christianus': John Winthrop, Jr., and Chemical Medicine in Seventeenth-Century New England," in *Science, Medicine, and Society in the Renaissance: Essays to Honor Walter Pagel,* ed. Alan G. Debus (New York, 1972), pp. 222–241; Ronald S. Wilkinson, "The Alchemical Library of John Winthrop, Jr. (1606–1676) and His Descendants in Colonial America," *Ambix* 11 (1963), 33–51, and 13 (1965–66), 139–186; Ronald S. Wilkinson, "George Starkey, Physician and Alchemist," *Ambix* 11 (1963), 121–152.

21. *Charles Morton's Compendium Physicae,* [*1687*], Colonial Society of Massachusetts Publications, 33 (1940), pp. 28–30, 79, 161. In June 1692 Boston ministers warned that they could not "esteem Alterations made in the Sufferers, by a Look or Touch of the Accused to be an infallible Evidence of Guilt; but frequently liable to be abused by the Devil's Legerdemains." Cf. I. Mather, *Cases of Conscience,* pp. 262–266, 290.

22. Elizabeth W. Fisher, "'Prophecies and Revelations': German Cabbalists in Early Pennsylvania," *Pennsylvania Magazine of History and Biography* 109 (1985), 299–333, supersedes Julius F. Sachse, *The German Pietists of Provincial Pennsylvania, 1694–1708* (Philadelphia, 1895). See also Julius F. Sachse, ed., "The Diarium of Magister Johannes Kelpius," *Pennsylvania German Society Proceedings and Addresses* 25 (1914–15), separately paginated.

23. These book inventories are printed in *William and Mary Quarterly,* 1st ser., 2 (1893–94), 169–171; 3 (1894–95), 44–45, 133–134; 7 (1899–1900), 18–19, 230. William Penn and Francis Nicholson, sometime governor of several British colonies, subscribed to the English edition of *The Works of John Rudolph Glauber . . . ,* trans. Christopher Packe (London, 1689), which synthesized Christianity, Hermeticism, and alchemy.

24. Samuel Boulton, *Medicina Magica Tamen Physica: Magical, but Natural Physick* (London, 1665), pp. 117–119, 125. Teackle's ownership of both of the Croll volumes is suggested by its double appearance on the carefully drawn inventory, under its main title, *Bazilica Chymica,* and under its subtitle, *Royal and Practical Chemistry.*

25. Frances Yates, *Giordano Bruno and the Hermetic Tradition* (Chicago, 1964), pp. 416–423; Wayne Shumaker, *The Occult Sciences in the Renaissance: A Study in Intellectual Patterns* (Berkeley, 1972), pp. 160–251; Joscelyn Godwin, *Athanasius Kircher: A Renaissance Man and the Quest for Lost Knowledge* (London, 1979); Joseph Blau, *The Christian Interpretation of the Cabala in the Renaissance* (New York, 1944), pp. 41–64.

26. On early American almanacs see Herbert Leventhal, *In the Shadow of the Enlightenment: Occultism and Renaissance Science in Eighteenth-Century America* (New York, 1976), pp. 22–27, 32–36, 38–39, 47–56; George L. Kittridge, *The*

Old Farmer and His Almanac (Boston, 1904); and Marion B. Stowell, *Early American Almanacs: The Colonial Weekday Bible* (New York, 1977).

27. Nathaniel Ames, *An Astronomical Diary; or, An Almanack for . . . 1728* (Boston, 1728), unpaginated.

28. Daniel Leeds, *An Almanack for . . . 1697* (New York, 1697); Daniel Leeds, *An Almanack for . . . 1698* (New York, 1698); Jacob Taylor, *An Almanack for 1743* (Philadelphia, 1743), quoted in Leventhal, *In the Shadow of the Enlightenment,* p. 36; John Jerman, [*The American Almanack for . . . 1736*] (Philadelphia, 1736); Gilbert Cope, "Jacob Taylor, Almanac Maker," *Proceedings of the Chester County Historical Society* (1908), 10–28.

29. Jacob Taylor, *An Almanack for . . . 1705* (Philadelphia, 1705); *Ephemeris Sideralus; or, An Almanack for 1707* (Philadelphia, 1707).

30. D[aniel] L[eeds], *The Temple of Wisdom for the Little World* (Philadelphia, 1688); Daniel Leeds, *An Almanack and Ephereides for . . . 1693* (Philadelphia, 1693); Daniel Leeds, *An Almanack for . . . 1695* (Philadelphia, 1695); Daniel Leeds, *An Almanack . . . for 1697* (Philadelphia, 1697).

31. Edward W. James, "Grace Sherwood, The Virginia Witch," *William and Mary Quarterly,* 1st ser., 3 (1894–95), 96–101, 190–192, 243–244; 4 (1895–96), 18–22.

32. Nicholas Trott, "A Charge Delivered at the General Sessions . . . 1705/06," in L. Lynn Hogue, "An Edition of 'Eight Charges Delivered at so Many Several General Sessions . . . [1703–1707] by Nicholas Trott'" (Ph.D. dissertation, University of Tennessee, 1972), pp. 133–163. Michael Hindus kindly drew my attention to Hogue's work.

33. Francis Le Jau to Philip Stubs, April 15, 1707, in *The Carolina Chronicle of Dr. Francis Le Jau, 1706–1717,* ed. Frank J. Klingberg (Berkeley, 1956), p. 25.

34. Ebenezer Turrell, "Detection of Witchcraft," *Collections,* Massachusetts Historical Society, 2d ser., 10 (1823), 6–22; Demos, *Entertaining Satan,* pp. 389, 393.

35. Turrell, "Detection of Witchcraft," pp. 6–7, 11.

36. Ibid.

37. Autobiography of John Craig, manuscript collection, Historical Foundation of the Presbyterian and Reformed Churches, Montreat, N.C. Parts of the Craig manuscript have been printed in Howard M. Wilson, *The Tinkling Spring, Headwater of Freedom: A Story of the Church and Her People, 1732–1952* (Fisherville, Va., 1954), pp. 123–134.

38. Ibid.

39. Leventhal, *In the Shadow of the Enlightenment,* pp. 38–39, 262–264; William D. Stahlman, "Astrology in Colonial America: An Extended Inquiry," *William and Mary Quarterly,* 3d ser., 13 (1956), 551–563; Otho T. Beall, Jr., "*Aristotle's Master Piece,* in America: A Landmark in the Folklore of Medicine," ibid., 3d ser., 20 (1963), 207–222; *Aristotle's Master Piece* ([London?], 1755), pp. 96–119, 126–129.

40. Leventhal, *In the Shadow of the Enlightenment,* pp. 137–167; on Collinson, see Raymond P. Stearns, *Science in the British Colonies of America* (Urbana, 1970), pp. 515–516.

41. *The Journals of Henry Melchior Muhlenberg,* ed. and trans. Theodore G. Tappert and John W. Doberstein, 3 vols. (Philadelphia, 1942–58) I, 346–349.

42. Ibid., I, 576.

43. *The Diary of Ebenezer Parkman,* ed. Francis Wallett (Worcester, Mass., 1982), p. 218.

44. *The Literary Diary of Ezra Stiles,* ed. Franklin B. Dexter, 3 vols. (New York, 1910), I, 385–386; George C. Mason, "The African Slave Trade in Colonial Times," *American Historical Record* 1 (1872), 311–319; Kittridge, *Old Farmer and His Almanac,* pp. 39–41.

45. Alan Macfarlane, *Witchcraft in Tudor and Stuart England: A Regional and Comparative Study* (New York, 1970), pp. 200–210; Alan Macfarlane, *The Origins of English Individualism: The Family, Property and Social Transition* (Oxford, 1978), pp. 1–3, 59–60; Keith Thomas, *Religion and the Decline of Magic* (New York, 1971), pp. 570–583.

46. Jacob Taylor, *An Almanack and Ephemeris for . . . 1746* (Philadelphia, 1746). Leventhal, *In the Shadow of the Enlightenment,* pp. 47, 263, accepts Taylor's 1746 claim that he abandoned occultism as early as 1701, but a reading of Taylor's almanacs in the 1710s and 1720s suggests, at best, an ambivalent attitude toward these crafts.

47. Quoted in Samuel Briggs, *The Essays, Humor, and Poems of Nathaniel Ames, Father and Son, of Dedham, Massachusetts . . .* (Cleveland, 1891), p. 226.

48. *The New England Primer Enlarged* (Boston, 1737); Taylor, *Almanack and Ephemeris for . . . 1746.*

49. Michener, *Retrospect of Early Quakerism,* pp. 364–367.

50. *Records of the Presbyterian Church in the United States of America, . . . 1706–1788* (Philadelphia, 1904), p. 91; Whitefield J. Bell, Jr., "The Reverend Mr. Joseph Morgan, An American Correspondent of the Royal Society, 1732–1739," *Proceedings of the American Philosophical Society* 95 (1951), 254–261.

51. Alexander Hamilton, *Gentleman's Progress: The Itinerarium of Dr. Alexander Hamilton, 1744,* ed. Carl Bridenbaugh (Chapel Hill, 1948), pp. 35–36. Hamilton did not identify Morgan further or give his Christian name. My identification of Joseph Morgan is based on the strong parallels between Joseph Morgan's career, which is documented in Whitefield Bell's article and the introduction to Morgan's *Kingdom of Basaruah,* and Hamilton's description of the "old philosopher's" scientific, mathematical, and astrological interests and his eagerness to share his discoveries with prominent persons. One negative characteristic in the identification occurs in the landlord's comment that Morgan "had writ hom[e] to the States of Holland and some other great folks" about his discoveries. Although this suggests that the man was Dutch, the surname seems to deny it and the "home" referred to may have been the landlord's, not Morgan's, whose penchant for corresponding with "great folks" also closely parallels the Presbyterian minister's earlier career.

52. George W. Pilcher, *Samuel Davies: Apostle of Dissent in Colonial Virginia* (Knoxville, 1971), p. 93.

53. For a lay view of the time of George Whitefield's revivalist preaching, see Michael J. Crawford, ed., "The Spiritual Travels of Nathan Cole," *William and Mary Quarterly,* 3d ser., 33 (1976), 92–103.

54. Thomas, *Religion and the Decline of Magic,* pp. 17, 21, 86–88, 332–334, 341–345, 370.

55. George Webb, *The Office and Authority of a Justice of Peace* (Williamsburg, 1736), pp. 61, 361–362; Arthur P. Scott, "History of the Criminal Law in Virginia during the Colonial Period" (Ph.D. dissertation, University of Chicago, 1919), pp. 276–278; Anson Phelps Stokes, *Church and State in the United States,* 3 vols. (New York, 1950), I, 191–192; *Archives of Maryland,* 71 vols. to date (Baltimore, 1833–), XXXI (1936), 271–298; *Records of the Colony of Rhode Island and Providence Plantations,* ed. John R. Bartlett, 10 vols. (Providence, 1856–65), I, 166.

56. Stokes, *Church and State in the United States,* I, 168; Nicholas Trott, *The Laws of the British Plantations in America, Relating to the Church and to the Clergy, Religion and Learning* (London, 1725), pp. 74–76, 211–225, 231–232, 242–243, 255–256, 268–269, 288–290, 303, 324–326, 337, 345; Carl Zollmann, *American Church Law* (St. Paul, Minn., 1933), pp. 2–6.

57. Frederick C. Drake, "Witchcraft in the American Colonies, 1647–62," *American Quarterly* 20 (1968), 694–725; Macfarlane, *Witchcraft in Tudor and Stuart England,* pp. 23–63; Weisman, *Witchcraft, Magic, and Religion,* pp. 96–114.

58. Russell K. Osgood, "John Clark, Esq., Justice of the Peace, 1667–1728," in *Law in Colonial Massachusetts, 1630–1800,* Colonial Society of Massachusetts Publications, 62 (1984), p. 128; Nathaniel Bowen, *The New England Diary: or, Almanack for . . . 1727* (Boston, 1727).

59. A sample of magistrates' actions against anti-Christian behavior in Pennsylvania can be obtained by reading *Records of the Courts of Chester County, Pennsylvania, 1681–1697,* pp. 141, 244, 393; *Records of the Courts of Chester County, Pennsylvania,* [II], 22, 79, 145, 159; *Records of the Quarter Sessions and Common Pleas of Bucks County Pennsylvania, 1684–1700* (Meadville, Pa., 1943), pp. 20, 75, 76, 204, 346.

60. Jack Douglas, *American Social Order: Social Roles in a Pluralistic Society* (New York, 1971), p. 316. For a convenient explanation of labeling theory and demonstration of its use for historians, see Eric H. Monkkonen, *The Dangerous Class: Crime and Poverty in Columbus, Ohio, 1860–1880* (Cambridge, Mass., 1975). For an extensive critique of labeling theory, see Walter R. Grove, ed., *The Labelling of Deviance: Evaluating a Perspective* (Beverly Hills, Calif., 1975); and for a defense, see Ken Plummer's review of Grove in the *British Journal of Criminology* 17 (1977), 79–81.

61. *Proceedings of the Provincial Court of Maryland, 1658–1662,* in *Archives of Maryland,* XLI (1922), 203; Douglas Greenberg, *Crime and Law Enforcement in the Colony of New York, 1691–1776* (Ithaca, 1976), p. 112; *Documentary History of the State of New York,* ed. E.B. O'Callaghan, 4 vols. (Albany, 1849–51), III, 200.

62. On the aftermath of the Salem trials, see Boyer and Nissenbaum, *Salem Possessed,* pp. 217–221.

4. The Renewal of Christian Authority

1. Six books, each viewing America from a special perspective, describe some of the massive changes that overtook the eighteenth-century colonies: Bernard

Bailyn, *The Origins of American Politics* (New York, 1968); Gary B. Nash, *Urban Crucible: Social Change, Political Consciousness, and the Origins of the American Revolution* (Cambridge, Mass., 1979); Jack P. Greene, *The Quest for Power: The Lower Houses of Assembly in the Southern Royal Colonies, 1689–1776* (Chapel Hill, 1963); Henry F. May, *The Enlightenment in America* (New York, 1976); Michael Kammen, *People of Paradox: An Inquiry Concerning the Origins of American Civilization* (New York, 1972); and Peter Wood, *Black Majority: Negroes in Colonial South Carolina from 1670 to the Stono Rebellion* (New York, 1974).

2. On Blair, see Parke Rouse, *James Blair of Virginia* (Chapel Hill, 1971). Ned Landsman kindly reminded me of the importance of Blair's Scottish evangelistic interests and his probable evangelical sympathies.

3. Rouse, *James Blair of Virginia,* pp. 63–79, 137–151; Brydon, *Virginia's Mother Church and the Political Conditions under Which It Grew,* 2 vols. (Richmond, 1947–52), I, 225–240, 309–326.

4. Charles S. Sydnor, *Gentlemen Freeholders: Political Practices in Washington's Virginia* (Chapel Hill, 1952); Rhys Isaac, *The Transformation of Virginia, 1740–1790* (Chapel Hill, 1982), pp. 88–94, 131–135.

5. Del Upton, *Holy Things and Profane: Anglican Parish Churches in Colonial Virginia* (Cambridge, Mass., 1986), pp. 11–13, 63–65.

6. Upton, *Holy Things and Profane,* pp. 101–162.

7. Robert Beverley, *History and Present State of Virginia,* ed. David Freeman Hawke (Indianapolis, 1971), p. 134.

8. Presbyterian and Baptist historians tend to exaggerate the size and importance of early congregations in Virginia, such as the Accomack County congregation organized by Francis Makemie, the itinerant Presbyterian minister, in the 1690s. For a different treatment of Makemie and his place in Virginia society, see Timothy H. Breen, "Of Time and Nature: A Study of Persistent Values in Colonial Virginia," in Breen, *Puritans and Adventurers: Change and Persistence in Early America* (New York, 1980), pp. 164–196.

9. Nelson W. Rightmyer, *Maryland's Established Church* (Baltimore, 1956), pp. 14–54.

10. John W. Pratt, *Religion, Politics, and Diversity: The Church-State Theme in New York History* (Ithaca, 1967), pp. 40–42.

11. Pratt, *Religion, Politics, and Diversity,* pp. 44–52. Council payments to the Dutch, Anglican, and Huguenot ministers can be traced in *Calendar of* [*New York*] *Council Minutes, 1668–1783,* New York State Library Bulletin, 58 (1902), p. 131, passim; and *An Account of Her Majesty's Revenue in the Province of New York, 1701–09,* ed. Julius M. Block et al. (Ridgewood, N.J., 1966), p. 80, passim.

12. M. Eugene Sirmans, *Colonial South Carolina: A Political History, 1663–1763* (Chapel Hill, 1966), pp. 88–89. Sirmans overestimates technical difficulties in the 1706 church act.

13. Stephen Beauregard Weeks, *The Religious Development in the Province of North Carolina,* Johns Hopkins University Studies in Historical and Political Science, 10th ser., 5 (Baltimore, 1892), pp. 36–37, 46–47; Stephen Beauregard Weeks, *Church and State in North Carolina,* Johns Hopkins University Studies in Historical and Political Science, 11th ser., 6 (Baltimore, 1893), pp. 11–13; Hugh T. Lefler and William S. Powell, *Colonial North Carolina: A History* (New York, 1973), pp. 194–198.

14. H. P. Thompson, *Thomas Bray* (London, 1954); A General Plan of the Constitution of a Protestant Congregation or Society, Bray Papers, Sion College Manuscripts, pp. 62–63 (Library of Congress microfilm, University of California, Los Angeles).

15. Thomas Bray, "A Memorial Representing the Present State of Religion in the Continent of North America," in *Rev. Thomas Bray, His Life and Selected Works Relating to Maryland,* ed. Bernard C. Steiner, Maryland Historical Society Fund Publications, 27 (1901), pp. 167–168; John Calam, *Parsons and Pedagogues: The S.P.G. Adventure in American Education* (New York, 1971), pp. 62–102.

16. Henry W. Foote and John C. Perkins, *Annals of King's Chapel from the Puritan Age of New England to the Present Day,* 3 vols. (Boston, 1882–1940), I, 58–94; *The Papers of William Penn,* ed. Richard S. Dunn and Mary Maples Dunn, 5 vols. (Philadelphia, 1981–87), III, 443–449.

17. On the shifting settlement patterns of late seventeenth-century New England, see Kenneth A. Lockridge, *A New England Town, the First Hundred Years: Dedham, Massachusetts, 1636–1736,* expanded ed. (New York, 1985), pp. 91–164; Edward M. Cook, Jr., *The Fathers of the Towns: Leadership and Community Structure in Eighteenth-Century New England* (Baltimore, 1976), pp. 120–134; Paul Boyer and Stephen Nissenbaum, *Salem Possessed: The Social Origins of Witchcraft* (Cambridge, Mass., 1974), pp. 37–60; Philip Greven, Jr., *Four Generations: Population, Land, and Family in Colonial Andover, Massachusetts* (Ithaca, 1970), pp. 175–260. I have inferred my statements about late seventeenth-century New England immigrants from the town studies, although the subject has received no systematic, detailed, or even general study.

18. Michael Zuckerman, *Peaceable Kingdoms: New England Towns in the Eighteenth Century* (New York, 1970), pp. 36–37, 98–99, 113–114, 151–152; Cook, *Fathers of the Towns,* pp. 120–134.

19. Nicholas Trott, *The Laws of the British Plantations in America, Relating to the Church and the Clergy, Religion and Learning* (London, 1725). Trott's work seems to have gone unnoticed in the vast literature on early American religion, including the otherwise detailed treatment by Thomas J. Curry, *The First Freedoms: Church and State in America to the Passage of the First Amendment* (New York, 1986). Also see "Mr. Course's Proposal for printing Mr. Trotts Collection of American Laws relating to the Church Religion, &c.," Letters, ser. A, v. 14, p. 25, Papers of the Society for the Propagation of the Gospel in Foreign Parts, United Society for the Propagation of the Gospel Archives, London (microfilm, University of Minnesota, Minneapolis).

20. Quoted in Rightmyer, *Maryland's Established Church,* p. 25, from *Maryland Archives,* XX (1900), 106–111.

21. Pratt, *Religion, Politics, and Diversity,* pp. 43–57; Isaac Newton Phelps Stokes, *The Iconography of Manhattan Island, 1498–1909,* 6 vols. (New York, 1915–28), I, 159–203.

22. Weeks, *Religious Development in the Province of North Carolina,* pp. 36–37, 46–47.

23. Albert Simons and Samuel Lapham, Jr., eds., *The Early Architecture of Charleston* (Columbia, S.C., 1970); Samuel G. Stoney, *The Plantations of the Carolina Low Country,* ed. Albert Simons and Samuel Lapham, Jr. (Charleston, S.C., n.d.).

24. Peter Benes and Philip D. Zimmerman, *New England Meeting House and Church: 1630–1850* (Boston, [1979]), pp. 3–27; for a discussion of seventeenth-century craftsmanship, see Robert B. St. George, "Style and Structure in the Joinery of Dedham and Medfield, Massachusetts, 1635–1685," *Winterthur Portfolio* 13 (1979), 1–46.

25. Leonard Ellinwood, *The History of American Church Music* (New York, 1953), chap. 7.

26. Hamilton A. Hill, *History of the Old South Church (Third Church) Boston: 1669–1884* (New York, 1890), p. 228; Foote and Perkins, *Annals of King's Chapel,* I, 104–105; Andrew Le Mercier, *The Church History of Geneva* (Boston, 1732), pp. 215–216.

27. Gottlieb Mittelberger, *Journey to Pennsylvania,* ed. and trans. Oscar Handlin and John Clive (Cambridge, Mass., 1960), pp. 91–92; *The Diary of Ebenezer Parkman,* ed. Francis Wallett (Worcester, Mass., 1982), p. 126.

28. *Extracts from the Itineraries of Ezra Stiles and Other Miscellanies of Ezra Stiles,* ed. Franklin B. Dexter (New Haven, 1916), p. 230. In 1789, Stiles was informed of a Hebrew inscription on a rock in New Milford, Connecticut, which one local resident remembered seeing in the 1740s and which was inscribed with the date 1733. Stiles did not record the inscription in his diary, however. *The Literary Diary of Ezra Stiles,* ed. Franklin B. Dexter, 3 vols. (New Haven, 1910), III, 366.

29. The painting by Bishop Roberts, *A View of Charleston,* c. 1739, is owned by Colonial Williamsburg, Williamsburg, Virginia.

30. For a general account of rising American craftsmanship after 1680 see Wendy A. Cooper, *In Praise of American Decorative Art, 1650–1820* (New York, 1980); John A. Dix, *History of the Parish of Trinity Church in the City of New York,* 6 vols. (New York, 1898–1950), I, 154, 222; Graham Hood, *American Silver: A History of Style, 1650–1900* (New York, 1971); Foote, *Annals of King's Chapel,* I, 211, 214, 421, II, 102, 170; M. K. D. Babcock, "The Organs and Organ Builders of Christ Church, Boston, 1736–1945," *Historical Magazine of the Protestant Episcopal Church* 14 (1945), 241–263; Ellinwood, *History of American Church Music,* chap. 4.

31. William Berrian, *An Historical Sketch of Trinity Church, New York* (New York, 1847), pp. 321–365; Foote, *Annals of King's Chapel,* I, 89, 116–117, II, 118.

32. Robert F. Scholz, "Clerical Consociation in Massachusetts Bay: Reassessing the New England Way and Its Origins," *William and Mary Quarterly,* 3d ser., 29 (1972), 391–414; David D. Hall, *The Faithful Shepherd: A History of the New England Ministry in the Seventeenth Century* (Chapel Hill, 1972), pp. 108–115, 218–222.

33. J. William T. Youngs, *God's Messengers: Religious Leadership in Colonial New England, 1700–1750* (Baltimore, 1976). Alexander Blaikie, *A History of Presbyterianism in New England* (Boston, 1881), tends to exaggerate "presbyterian" influence in eighteenth-century New England, although the matter probably will remain a mystery; most minutes of the New England presbyteries before 1750 are lost.

34. These changes among the Quakers are the principal subject of William C. Braithwaite, *The Second Period of Quakerism,* 2d ed. (Cambridge, 1961); Richard

T. Vann, *The Social Development of English Quakerism, 1655–1755* (Cambridge, Mass., 1969), pp. 122–143; Arnold Lloyd, *Quaker Social History, 1660–1738* (London, 1950), pp. 56, 112.

35. Minutes, Philadelphia Quarterly and Monthly Meeting, January 9, 1692; March 6, 1683; June 5, 1683; Minutes, Philadelphia Yearly Meeting, September 4, 1683; microfilm, Friends Historical Library, Swarthmore.

36. George Fox to Christopher Taylor et al., May 20, 1685, Etting Papers, vol. 27, Historical Society of Pennsylvania, printed in the *Pennsylvania Magazine of History and Biography* 29 (1903), 105–106; Fox to the Friends in the Ministry in Pennsylvania and New Jersey, July 30, 1685, in *Selections from the Epistles of George Fox,* ed. Samuel Tuke (Cambridge, Mass., 1879) pp. 297–298.

37. [George Keith], "Gospel Order and Discipline," *Journal of the Friends Historical Society* 10 (1913), 70–76; Jon Butler, "'Gospel Order Improved': The Keithian Schism and the Exercise of Quaker Ministerial Authority in Pennsylvania," *William and Mary Quarterly,* 3d ser., 31 (1974), 431–452; Jon Butler, "Into Pennsylvania's Spiritual Abyss: The Rise and Fall of the Later Keithians, 1693–1703," *Pennsylvania Magazine of History and Biography* 101 (1977), 151–170.

38. Minutes, Middletown Monthly Meeting, January 4, 1700; Minutes, Bucks Quarterly Meeting of Ministers and Elders, February 22, 1709/10; January 24, 1714/15; February 23, 1714/15; Minutes, Concord Quarterly Meeting, August 2, 1714; Minutes, Philadelphia Yearly Meeting, September 18–22, 1714; microfilm, Friends Historical Library, Swarthmore. Ezra Michener, *Retrospect of Early Quakerism: Being Extracts from the Records of Philadelphia Yearly Meeting and the Meetings Composing It* (Philadelphia, 1860), pp. 156–158, 169–171, 178.

39. Minutes, Philadelphia Monthly Meeting, October 28, 1694, microfilm, Friends Historical Library, Swarthmore; Epistle, Women's Meeting at Burlington to Friends, September 21, 1698, Miscellaneous Epistles, Friends Historical Library, Swarthmore.

40. Alfred C. Underwood, *A History of the English Baptists* (London, 1947), pp. 130–132; W. T. Whitley, *The Baptists of London, 1617–1928* (London, n.d.), pp. 47–48.

41. Minutes, Pennepek Baptist Church, pp. 42, 44, American Baptist Historical Society, Rochester, N.Y.; Norman H. Maring, *Baptists in New Jersey: A Study in Transition* (Valley Forge, Pa., 1964), p. 32; *Records of the Welsh Tract Baptist Meeting, Pencader Hundred, New Castle County, Delaware, 1701 to 1828,* Historical Society of Delaware Papers, 42 (Wilmington, Del., 1904), pp. 8–10.

42. Minutes, Pennepek Baptist Church, p. 43.

43. Minutes, Pennepek Baptist Church, pp. 47, 56–58; *Minutes of the Philadelphia Baptist Association, from A.D. 1707, to A.D. 1807; Being the First One Hundred Years of Its Existence,* ed. A. D. Gillette (Philadelphia, 1851), p. 26, 30; David Benedict, *General History of the Baptist Denomination in America* (New York, 1855), pp. 562–563; Nathaniel Jenkins to the Congregation at Piscataway, December 30, 1730, in *The Diary of John Comer,* ed. C. Edwin Burrows, Rhode Island Historical Society Collections, 8 (1893), 117–118. Details of Baker's offenses, omitted from the printed letter, can be found in a copy in the manuscript of John Comer's diary at the Rhode Island Historical Society, Providence, R.I.

44. *Minutes of the Philadelphia Baptist Association,* ed. Gillette, pp. 50–54.

45. Ibid., pp. 85, 157.

46. Ned Landsman, *Scotland and Its First American Colony, 1683–1765* (Princeton, 1985), pp. 48–72; Marilyn J. Westerkamp, *Triumph of the Laity: Scots-Irish Piety and the Great Awakening, 1625–1760* (New York, 1988), pp. 3–43; Walter R. Foster, *Bishop and Presbytery: The Church of Scotland, 1661–1688* (London, 1958), pp. 1–11, 89–95; A. Ian Dunlop, *William Carstares and the Kirk by Law Established* (Edinburgh, 1967), pp. 62–99.

47. Francis Makemie to Benjamin Colman, March 28, 1707, in *The Life and Writings of Francis Makemie,* ed. Boyd S. Schlenther (Philadelphia, 1971), pp. 252–253.

48. *Records of the Presbyterian Church in the United States of America, 1706–1788* (Philadelphia, 1904), pp. 17, 42, 341, 461. Attendance lists are usually found at the beginning of the minutes for each presbytery session. Also see "The Records of the Presbytery of New Castle upon Delaware," *Journal of Presbyterian History* 14 (1931), 299–300.

49. *Records of the Presbyterian Church, 1706–1788,* pp. 2, 10, 11–12, 13, 15, 18–19, 22–24, 27–29, 36, 42; Horton Davies, *The Worship of the English Puritans* (London, 1948), pp. 228–231; Walter R. Foster, *Bishop and Presbytery: The Church of Scotland, 1661–1688* (London, 1958), pp. 93–96; Richard Webster, *A History of the Presbyterian Church in America* (Philadelphia, 1857), pp. 333, 339.

50. *Records of the Presbyterian Church, 1706–1788,* pp. 45, 150, 400–401.

51. Leonard R. Riforgiato, *Missionary of Moderation: Henry Melchior Muhlenberg and the Lutheran Church in English America* (Lewisburg, Pa., 1980), pp. 158–182, quotation on p. 165.

52. Jon Butler, *Power, Authority, and the Origins of American Denominational Order: The English Churches in the Delaware Valley, 1680–1730,* American Philosophical Society Transactions, 68, pt. 2 (Philadelphia, 1978), pp. 75–78. The Presbyterian schism of the 1740s is discussed here in Chapter 6.

53. Jack D. Marietta, *The Reformation of American Quakerism, 1748–1783* (Philadelphia, 1984), pp. 73–128. For different views of eighteenth-century Quaker development, see Hermann Wellenreuther, *Glaube und Politik in Pennsylvania, 1681–1776* (Cologne, 1972); and Jean R. Soderlund, *Quakers and Slavery: A Divided Spirit* (Princeton, 1985).

54. Frederick V. Mills, Sr., "Anglican Expansion in Colonial America," *Historical Magazine of the Protestant Episcopal Church* 39 (1970), 315–324; John F. Woolverton, *Colonial Anglicanism in North America* (Detroit, 1984), pp. 27–30.

5. Slavery and the African Spiritual Holocaust

1. The literature on slavery is immense. Without prejudicing other excellent studies, recent indispensable works include Winthrop D. Jordan, *White over Black: American Attitudes toward the Negro, 1550–1812* (Chapel Hill, 1968); Richard S. Dunn, *Sugar and Slaves: The Rise of the Planter Class in the English West Indies, 1624–1713* (Chapel Hill, 1972); Philip Curtin, *The Atlantic Slave Trade* (Madison, 1969); Edmund S. Morgan, *American Slavery, American Freedom: The Ordeal of Colonial Virginia* (New York, 1975); and Peter H. Wood, *Black Majority: Negroes in Colonial South Carolina from 1670 to the Stono Rebellion* (New York, 1974).

2. Robert V. Wells, *The Population of the British Colonies in America before 1776: A Survey of Census Data* (Princeton, 1975), pp. 149–151, 161–162.

3. T. H. Breen and Stephen Innes, *"Myne Owne Ground": Race and Freedom on Virginia's Eastern Shore, 1640–1676* (New York, 1980), pp. 72–109; Jordan, *White over Black,* p. 82.

4. Wells, *Population of the British Colonies,* p. 265; Wood, *Black Majority,* pp. 142–166; Gary B. Nash, *Forging Freedom: The Formation of Philadelphia's Black Community 1720–1840* (Cambridge, Mass., 1988), pp. 8–16.

5. Moses I. Finley, *Ancient Slavery and Modern Ideology* (New York, 1980); Dunn, *Sugar and Slaves,* esp. pp. 224–229; Gary Puckrein, *Little England: Plantation Society and Anglo-Barbadian Politics, 1627–1700* (New York, 1984).

6. Dunn, *Sugar and Slaves,* pp. 224–229, 314–317.

7. Morgan, *American Slavery, American Freedom,* p. 301.

8. Thomas Smith as quoted in Jordan, *White over Black,* p. 50.

9. For a sampling of English objections to slave baptism, see *The Carolina Chronicle of Dr. Francis Le Jau, 1706–1717,* ed. Frank J. Klingberg (Berkeley, 1956), pp. 50, 52, 54, 55, 60, 76, 81, 86, 97, 102, 116, 121, 124, 129; Jordan, *White over Black,* p. 183.

10. Virginia statute of 1699 quoted in Jordan, *White over Black,* p. 184, also see pp. 180–187.

11. Jordan, *White over Black,* pp. 180–186; Le Jau to SPG, September 18, 1711, in *Carolina Chronicle of Dr. Francis Le Jau,* ed. Klingberg, p. 102.

12. Orlando Patterson, *Slavery and Social Death: A Comparative Study* (Cambridge, Mass., 1982), esp. chap. 7.

13. Kenneth Scott, "The Slave Insurrection in New York in 1712," *New-York Historical Society Quarterly* 45 (1961), 43–74; Ferenc M. Szasz, "The New York Slave Revolt of 1741: A Re-Examination," *New York History* 48 (1967), 215–230; Daniel Horsmanden, *The New-York Conspiracy,* ed. Thomas J. Davis (1744; Boston, 1971); Wood, *Black Majority,* pp. 311, 317. Choices made in economic life are described in Philip D. Morgan, "Work and Culture: The Task System and the World of Lowcountry Blacks, 1700 to 1880," *William and Mary Quarterly,* 3d ser., 39 (1982), 563–599.

14. William Fleetwood, *The Relative Duties of Parents and Children, Husbands and Wives, Masters and Servants* (London, 1705).

15. Ibid., pp. 339, 342–346. The words "no body" were not a misprint for "nobody"; they referred to Parliament and courts that refused to excuse blasphemous and illegal behavior by servants on the grounds that their superiors had ordered it.

16. Ibid., p. 346.

17. Ibid., pp. 346–347.

18. William Fleetwood, *A Sermon Preached before the Society for the Propagation of the Gospel in Foreign Parts, at the Parish Church of St. Mary-le-Bow, on Friday the 16th of February, 1710/11* (London, 1711), p. 13. Fleetwood's sermon is reprinted in Frank J. Klingberg, *Anglican Humanitarianism in Colonial New York* (Philadelphia, 1940), pp. 195–212.

19. Fleetwood, *A Sermon Preached before the* [*S.P.G.*], *1710/11,* p. 13.

20. Ibid., p. 18.

21. Ibid., pp. 16–17. See also Jordan, *White over Black,* pp. 191–192.

22. A. Leon Higginbotham, Jr., *In the Matter of Color: Race and the American Legal Process, the Colonial Period* (New York, 1978), pp. ix, 193–198, passim; Jordan, *White over Black,* p. 108.

23. Berkeley's sermon is reprinted in *Twelve Anniversary Sermons Preached before the Society for the Propagation of the Gospel in Foreign Parts* (London, 1845), pp. 52–69; Secker's sermon is reprinted in Klingberg, *Anglican Humanitarianism,* pp. 213–233.

24. Information on book orders placed by Anglican ministers in America is discussed at several points in *Religious Philanthropy and Colonial Slavery: The American Correspondence of the Associates of Dr. Bray, 1717–1777,* ed. John C. Van Horn (Urbana, 1985); Thomas Wilson, *Knowledge and Practice of Christianity Made Easy to the Meanest Capacities* (London, 1741), pp. xvi–xvii.

25. Le Jau to SPG, October 20, 1709, in *Carolina Chronicle of Dr. Francis Le Jau,* ed. Klingberg, p. 60.

26. Le Jau to SPG, February 20, 1712, in *Carolina Chronicle of Dr. Francis Le Jau,* ed. Klingberg, p. 108.

27. Fleetwood, *A Sermon Preached before the* [*S.P.G.*], *1710/11,* pp. 18, 19.

28. Thomas Bacon, *Four Sermons Preached at the Parish Church of St. Peter, in Talbot County, . . .* (London, 1753), p. 13.

29. Bacon, *Four Sermons,* pp. 30, 31, 34.

30. J. P. Kenyon, *Revolution Principles: The Politics of Party 1689–1720* (Cambridge, 1977), pp. 64–65, 88–89; G. V. Bennett, *The Tory Crisis in Church and State, 1688–1730: The Career of Francis Atterbury, Bishop of Rochester* (Oxford, 1975), pp. 103–116; Geoffrey Holmes, *The Trial of Doctor Sacheverell* (London, 1973), pp. 31–34, 138–142, passim.

31. Eugene Genovese, *Roll, Jordan, Roll: The World the Slaves Made* (New York, 1974), p. 5; Alan Gallay, "The Origins of Slaveholders' Paternalism: George Whitefield, the Bryan Family, and the Great Awakening in the South," *Journal of Southern History* 53 (August 1987), 369–394. The evidence below, particularly that taken from Thomas Bacon's *Four Sermons,* explains why the claim for earlier Anglican origins takes precedence. This does not mean, however, that evangelicals might not have extended the Anglican view of paternal authority on the plantation in significant ways.

32. Francis Le Jau and Charles Martyn quoted in Frank J. Klingberg, *An Appraisal of the Negro in Colonial South Carolina: A Study in Americanization* (Washington, D.C., 1941), p. 5.

33. Bacon, *Four Sermons,* pp. 83–84.

34. The evidence outlined in Klingberg's *Appraisal of the Negro in Colonial South Carolina* reveals both the range and limits of clerical objection to planter behavior.

35. Finley, *Ancient Slavery,* p. 121; William G. McLoughlin and Winthrop D. Jordan, eds., "Baptists Face the Barbarities of Slavery in 1710," *Journal of Southern History* 29 (1963), 495–501.

36. Wood, *Black Majority,* pp. 285–326; Gerald W. Mullin, *Flight and Rebellion: Slave Resistance in Eighteenth-Century Virginia* (New York, 1972), pp. 33–62.

37. Le Jau to SPG, February 23, 1713, in *Carolina Chronicle of Dr. Francis Le Jau,* ed. Klingberg, p. 130.

38. Samuel Quincy, *Twenty Sermons* (Boston, 1750), pp. 38–54, 235–254, 255–264; William Brogden, *Freedom and Love* (Annapolis, 1750), pp. 12, 13.

39. Josiah Smith, *The Duty of Parents to Instruct Their Children* (Boston, 1730), pp. 17–18; John Gordon, *A Thanksgiving Sermon on the Defeat of the Rebels* (Annapolis, 1746), pp. 1, 18, 20, 27; S[ophia] H[ume], *An Exhortation to the Inhabitants of the Province of South Carolina, to Bring Their Deeds to the Light of Christ, in Their Own Consciences* (Philadelphia, 1747), pp. 53, 126.

40. South Carolina *Gazette,* March 28, 1743; Thomas Bacon to SPG, August 4, 1750, in *Historical Collections Relating to the American Colonial Church,* ed. William S. Perry, 5 vols. (Hartford, Conn., 1875), IV, 324–325; Charles Woodmason, *The Carolina Backcountry on the Eve of the Revolution: The Journal and Other Writings of Charles Woodmason, Anglican Itinerant,* ed. Richard J. Hooker (Chapel Hill, 1953), p. 13.

41. Lang quoted in Mechal Sobel, *Trabelin' On: The Slave Journey to an Afro-Baptist Faith* (Westport, Conn., 1979), p. 61.

42. On what Edmund Morgan describes as "affinities between slavery and republicanism" in late eighteenth-century Virginia, see his *American Slavery, American Freedom,* pp. 363–387.

43. Fredrike T. Schmidt and Barbara R. Wilhelm, "Early Pro-Slavery Petitions in Virginia," *William and Mary Quarterly,* 3d ser., 30 (January 1973), 133–146.

44. John Thomson, *An Explication of the Shorter Catechism Composed by the Assembly of Divines, Commonly Called, the Westminster Assembly* (Williamsburg, 1749), p. 161; Stephen J. Stein, "George Whitefield on Slavery: Some New Evidence," *Church History* 42 (1973), 243–256. In general, historians have exaggerated abolitionist sentiment among colonial revivalists, as will be discussed in Chapter 6. For more positive evaluations of eighteenth-century revivalism and antislavery thought, see, among others, Jordan, *White over Black,* pp. 212–214, and Patricia U. Bonomi, *Under the Cope of Heaven: Religion, Society, and Politics in Colonial America* (New York, 1986), pp. 124–126.

45. James David Essig, "'A Very Wintry Season': Virginia Baptists and Slavery, 1785–1797," *Virginia Magazine of History and Biography* 88 (1980), 170–185; Donald G. Mathews, *Slavery and Methodism: A Chapter in American Morality, 1780–1845* (Princeton, 1965), chap. 1.

46. Sobel, *Trabelin' On,* pp. 3–21, 39–48; John W. Blassingame, *The Slave Community: Plantation Life in the Antebellum South* (New York, 1972), pp. 32–40.

47. Genovese, *Roll, Jordan, Roll,* pp. 209–232; Gilbert Osofsky, *Harlem: The Making of a Ghetto: Negro New York, 1890–1930* (New York, 1966), pp. 143–144.

48. Gerald W. Mullin, *Flight and Rebellion: Slave Resistance in Eighteenth-Century Virginia* (New York, 1972), pp. ix–xi. This static view of black religion under slavery permeates such classic works as Genovese's *Roll, Jordan, Roll* and Lawrence W. Levine, *Black Culture and Black Consciousness: Afro-American Folk Thought from Slavery to Freedom* (New York, 1977), although Genovese and Levine each acknowledge that there must have been some change between the colonial and national periods. Some of this change is outlined in Albert J. Raboteau, *Slave Religion: The "Invisible Institution" in the Antebellum South* (New York, 1978).

49. Sobel, *Travelin' On,* p. 25; Blassingame, *Slave Community,* pp. 32–33; Melville Herskovits, *The Myth of the Negro Past* (Boston, 1941); Genovese, *Roll, Jordan, Roll,* p. 210.

50. Lorenzo J. Greene, *The Negro in Colonial New England, 1620–1776* (New York, 1942); Raboteau, *Slave Religion,* pp. 108–110.

51. As an example of a book that superbly summarizes the recent literature on African cultural resilience in America, see Mechal Sobel, *The World They Made Together: Black and White Values in Eighteenth-Century Virginia* (Princeton, 1987).

52. Allan Kulikoff, *Tobacco and Slaves: The Development of Southern Cultures in the Chesapeake, 1680–1800* (Chapel Hill, 1986); Ira Berlin, "Time, Space, and the Evolution of Afro-American Society on British Mainland North America," *American Historical Review* 85 (1980), 47–78; Marcus W. Jernegan, "Slavery and Conversion in the American Colonies," *American Historical Review* 21 (1916), 504–527; Luther P. Jackson, "Religious Development of the Negro in Virginia from 1760 to 1860," *Journal of Negro History* 16 (1931), 168–239.

53. Scott, "The Slave Insurrection in New York in 1712"; Jordan, *White over Black,* pp. 20–24, 180–187; Sobel, *The World They Made Together,* pp. 79–99, 171–203.

54. On William Byrd, see *The Secret Diary of William Byrd of Westover, 1709–1712,* ed. Marion Tinling (Richmond, 1941); *Another Secret Diary of William Byrd of Westover, 1739–1741, with Letters and Literary Exercises, 1696–1726* (Richmond, 1942); and Kenneth Lockridge, *The Diary, and Life, of William Byrd II of Virginia, 1694–1744* (Chapel Hill, 1987). On Landon Carter, see *The Diary of Colonel Landon Carter of Sabine Hall, 1752–1778,* ed. Jack P. Greene (Charlottesville, Va., 1965).

55. Robert Beverley, *History and Present State of Virginia,* ed. David Freeman Hawke (Indianapolis, 1971), pp. 102–111; Thomas Jefferson, *Notes on the State of Virginia* (1781; New York, 1964), pp. 150–155.

56. John Sharpe to SPG, June 23, 1712, in "The Negro Plot of 1712," *New York Genealogical and Biographical Record* 21 (1890), 162–163; Horsmanden, *New-York Conspiracy,* pp. 369–370, 421–431; Wood, *Black Majority,* pp. 308–317; Mullin, *Flight and Rebellion,* pp. 159–160. On slave revolts generally, see Eugene Genovese, *From Rebellion to Revolution: Afro-American Slave Revolts in the Making of the Modern World* (Baton Rouge, 1980).

57. This is not to say that the historical study of religion in western Africa, especially during the slave-trading centuries from 1500 to 1850, need be as closed a subject as it remains. Nearly all the work on which historians of slavery base their judgments about slave religion is rooted in studies of African religion that typically build their analysis on nineteenth- and twentieth-century evidence. Such studies, including the superb works by John Mbiti, *Introduction to African Religion* (London, 1975), Geoffrey Parrinder, *African Traditional Religion* (London, 1954), and Dominique Zahan, *The Religion, Spirituality, and Thought of Traditional Africa* (Chicago, 1970), as well as the relevant introductory segments of Sobel's *Trabelin' On* and *The World They Made Together,* need to be supplemented by attempts to trace persistent and shifting themes and practices in specific western African religious traditions from the fifteenth to the nineteenth centuries.

58. Charles Ball, *Fifty Years in Chains; or, The Life of an American Slave* (New York, 1858), pp. 9, 15. Allan Kulikoff kindly brought Ball's narrative to my attention.

59. William D. Piersen, "White Cannibals, Black Martyrs: Fear, Depression, and Religious Faith as Causes of Suicide among New Slaves," *Journal of Negro History* 62 (1977), 147–159.

60. Le Jau to SPG, October 20, 1709, and June 13, 1710, in *Carolina Chronicle of Dr. Francis Le Jau*, ed. Klingberg, pp. 61, 77.

61. The problem of cultural devastation was first and most thoroughly explored in Stanley M. Elkin, *Slavery: A Problem in American Institutional and Intellectual Life* (New York, 1963). Accepting Elkin's description of this cultural devastation should not, however, obligate historians to accept his more controversial interpretation of the existence and origins of the Sambo personality type among black slaves.

62. On the background of these systems, see Sobel, *Trabelin' On,* pp. 3–21, and Raboteau, *Slave Religion,* pp. 3–92.

63. "T[homas] Walduck's Letters from Barbados, 1710–11," *Barbados Museum and Historical Society* 15 (1947–48), 148–149; Sobel, *Trabelin' On,* p. 43; Philip D. Morgan, "Black Society in the Lowcountry, 1760–1810," in *Slavery and Freedom in the Age of the American Revolution,* ed. Ira Berlin and Ronald Hoffman (Charlottesville, Va., 1983), p. 138.

64. Jerome S. Handler and Frederick W. Lange, *Plantation Slavery in Barbados: An Archaeological and Historical Investigation* (Cambridge, Mass., 1978), pp. 171–215; the Ligon quotation is found on p. 182.

65. Sobel, *Trabelin' On,* pp. 44, 197–200; Sobel, *The World They Made Together,* pp. 214–225; both discuss early nineteenth-century burial practices. For a report on an archaeological excavation of an antebellum plantation, see John S. Otto, *Canon's Point Plantation, 1794–1860: Living Conditions and Status Patterns in the Old South* (New York, 1984).

66. Many of the secular developments are summarized in Kulikoff, *Tobacco and Slaves,* and in Berlin, "Time, Space, and the Evolution of Afro-American Society."

67. On Anglican proselytization, often ignored or slighted by historians, see Klingberg, *Appraisal of the Negro in Colonial South Carolina;* Edgar Legare Pennington, *Thomas Bray's Associates and Their Work among the Negroes* (Worcester, Mass., 1939); Van Horne, ed., *Religious Philanthropy and Colonial Slavery.*

68. Sobel, *The World They Made Together,* pp. 178–203; John B. Boles, ed., *Masters and Slaves Together: Race and Religion in the American South, 1740–1870* (Lexington, Ky., 1988).

69. Isaac, *Transformation of Virginia,* pp. 171–172; Sobel, *Trabelin' On,* pp. 99–135; Sobel, *The World They Made Together,* pp. 178–203.

70. Isaac, *Transformation of Virginia,* pp. 161–177.

71. For an introduction to African-American religious syntheses in several New World slave societies, see George E. Simpson, *Black Religions in the New World* (New York, 1978); and Roger Bastide, *African Civilisations in the New World,* trans. Peter Green (New York, 1971).

6. The Plural Origins of American Revivalism

1. For a review of the problem of the "Great Awakening" as treated by modern historians and a general description of the important secondary works to 1982, see Jon Butler, "Enthusiasm Described and Decried: The Great Awakening as Interpretative Fiction," *Journal of American History* 69 (1982–83), 305–325. The best general studies of the revivals are J. M. Bumsted and John E. Van de Wetering, *What Must I Do To Be Saved? The Great Awakening in Colonial America* (Hinsdale, Ill., 1976), and relevant sections of David Lovejoy, *Religious Enthusiasm in the New World: Heresy to Revolution* (Cambridge, Mass., 1985); Christine Hyerman, *Commerce and Culture: The Maritime Communities of Colonial Massachusetts, 1690–1750* (New York, 1984); and Harry S. Stout, *The New England Soul: Preaching and Religious Culture in Colonial New England* (New York, 1986).

2. Gilbert Burnet, *A Discourse of the Pastoral Care* (London, 1692), p. xii.

3. On the *Book of Common Prayer,* see Horton Davies, *The Worship of the English Puritans* (London, 1948), chaps. 6, 9.

4. *The Carolina Chronicle of Dr. Francis Le Jau, 1706–1717,* ed. Frank J. Klingberg (Berkeley, 1956); Charles Woodmason, *The Carolina Backcountry on the Eve of the Revolution: The Journal and Other Writings of Charles Woodmason, Anglican Itinerant,* ed. Richard J. Hooker (Chapel Hill, 1953).

5. On the poor and on parish responsibilities for them, see Stephen E. Wiberley, Jr., "Four Cities: Public Poor Relief in Urban America, 1700–1775" (Ph.D. dissertation, Yale University, 1975), which discusses Anglican relief in Charleston; on parish life in Virginia, see Charles Sydnor, *Gentlemen Freeholders: Political Practices in Washington's Virginia* (Chapel Hill, 1952), pp. 58–65, 88–94.

6. Thomas Barton quoted in Henry F. May, *The Enlightenment in America,* (New York, 1976), p. 67. Eighteenth-century Anglican piety is in need of more systematic study, but see May's discussion, ibid., pp. 66–69, as well as W. K. Lowther Clarke, *Eighteenth-Century Piety* (London, 1944).

7. On Anglican educational activity, see John Calam, *Parsons and Pedagogues: The S.P.G. Adventure in American Education* (New York, 1971).

8. Frank J. Klingberg, ed., "Commissary Johnston's Notitia Parochialis," *South Carolina Historical and Genealogical Magazine* 48 (1947), 26–34.

9. Evolving public ceremonialism in the colonies is in need of study, although some of its effects can be discerned through histories of early American art. For a discussion of this business among colonial Huguenot silversmiths, see my own book, *The Huguenots in America: A Refugee People in New World Society* (Cambridge, Mass., 1983), pp. 131–132, 178–180.

10. Rhys Isaac, *The Transformation of Virginia, 1740–1790* (Chapel Hill, 1982), offers a high church view of Virginia Anglicanism; on Cornbury, see Lewis Morris to SPG, May 30, 1709, SPG manuscripts, letters, ser. C, Box 1, no. 2, United Society for the Propagation of the Gospel Archives, London (microfilm, University of Minnesota, Minneapolis).

11. Klingberg, ed., "Commissary Johnston's Notitia Parochialis."

12. Ibid.

13. Richard D. Shiels, "The Feminization of American Congregationalism,

1730–1835," *American Quarterly* 33 (1981), 46–62; Paul R. Lucas, *Valley of Discord: Church and Society along the Connecticut River, 1636–1725* (Hanover, N.H., 1976), pp. 141–142, 244–245; Laurel Thatcher Ulrich, *Good Wives: Image and Reality in the Lives of Women in Northern New England, 1650–1750* (New York, 1982); Edward M. Cook, Jr., *The Fathers of the Towns: Leadership and Community Structure in Eighteenth-Century New England* (Baltimore, 1976), pp. 119–142.

14. Michael Zuckerman, *Peaceable Kingdoms: New England Towns in the Eighteenth Century* (New York, 1970), pp. 112–113; Jonathan M. Chu, *Neighbors, Friends, or Madmen: The Puritan Adjustment to Quakerism in Seventeenth-Century Massachusetts Bay* (Westport, Conn., 1985); Christine Leigh Hyerman, "Specters of Subversion, Societies of Friends: Dissent and the Devil in Provincial Essex County, Massachusetts," in *Saints and Revolutionaries: Essays on Early American History*, ed. David D. Hall et al. (New York, 1984), pp. 38–74.

15. The century's best-known dispute, of course, pitted Jonathan Edwards against his Northampton congregation, a dispute Edwards lost. See Patricia J. Tracy, *Jonathan Edwards, Pastor: Religion and Society in Eighteenth-Century Northampton* (New York, 1980), pp. 171–194. See also Robert E. Brown, *Middle-Class Democracy and the Revolution in Massachusetts, 1691–1780* (Ithaca, 1955), pp. 103–105.

16. Some notion of the humdrum of a minister's activity can be gained through *The Diary of Ebenezer Parkman,* ed. Francis G. Wallett (Worcester, Mass., 1982), as well as relevant portions of Tracy, *Jonathan Edwards, Pastor;* Stout, *New England Soul;* and J. William T. Youngs, *God's Messengers: Religious Leadership in Colonial New England, 1700–1750* (Baltimore, 1976).

17. Stout, *New England Soul,* offers the most thorough examination of the topic. See especially chap. 8.

18. Ibid., pp. 79–80, 82–83, 121–122, 167–174.

19. Ibid., p. 155; Richard P. Gildrie, "The Ceremonial Puritan Days of Humiliation and Thanksgiving," *New England Historical and Genealogical Register* 136 (1982), 3–16, describes such days for the seventeenth century. Also see William D. Love, *The Fast and Thanksgiving Days of New England* (Boston, 1895).

20. *Edward Taylor's "Church Records" and Related Sermons,* ed. Thomas M. Davis and Virginia L. Davis (Boston, 1981), pp. 174–242. The congregation did hear several ecclesiastical disputes brought to it from neighboring congregations. Tracy, *Jonathan Edwards, Pastor,* pp. 171–183.

21. On Yorkshire discipline, see Chapter 1 above, and *Archbishop Herring's Visitation Return, 1743,* ed. S. L. Ollard and P. C. Walker, Yorkshire Archaeological Society Record Series, 71–75 (1928–31).

22. Richard Bushman, *From Puritan to Yankee: Character and the Social Order in Connecticut, 1690–1765* (Cambridge, Mass., 1967), pp. 164–168; Bruce E. Steiner, "New England Anglicanism, A Genteel Faith?" *William and Mary Quarterly,* 3d ser., 27 (1970), 122–135; Bruce E. Steiner, "Anglican Officeholding in Pre-Revolutionary Connecticut: The Parameters of New England Community," ibid., 31 (1974), 369–406.

23. Ned Landsman, *Scotland and Its First American Colony, 1683–1765* (Princeton, 1985); Bernard Bailyn, *The Peopling of British North America: An Introduction* (New York, 1986); Elizabeth W. Fisher, "'Prophecies and Revelations': Ger-

man Cabbalists in Early Pennsylvania," *Pennsylvania Magazine of History and Biography* 109 (1985), 299–333; Ernest Lashlee, "Johannes Kelpius and His Woman in the Wilderness: A Chapter in the History of Colonial Pennsylvania Religious Thought," in *Glaube, Geist, Geschichte: Festschrift für Ernst Benz,* ed. Gerhard Muller and Winfried Zeller (Leiden, 1967), pp. 327–338; Stephanie G. Wolf, *Urban Village: Population, Community, and Family Structure in Germantown, Pennsylvania, 1683–1800* (Princeton, 1976).

24. Dietmar Rothermund, *The Layman's Progress: Religious and Political Experience in Colonial Pennsylvania, 1740–1770* (Philadelphia, 1961), pp. 1–16; Marianne Wokeck, "The Flow and Composition of German Immigration to Philadelphia, 1727–1775," *Pennsylvania Magazine of History and Biography* 105 (1981), 249–278; Sally Schwartz, *"A Mixed Multitude": The Struggle for Toleration in Pennsylvania* (New York, 1987); and A. G. Roeber, "In German Ways? Problems and Potentials of Eighteenth-Century German Social and Emigration History," *William and Mary Quarterly,* 3d ser. (1987), 750–774.

25. Lovejoy, *Religious Enthusiasm in the New World,* pp. 156–158, 162–168; Rufus M. Jones, *The Quakers in the American Colonies* (New York, 1966), pp. 265–353; Isaac, *The Transformation of Virginia,* pp. 161–205.

26. Jon Butler, "Into Pennsylvania's Spiritual Abyss: The Rise and Fall of the Later Keithians, 1694–1703," *Pennsylvania Magazine of History and Biography* 101 (1977), 151–170; Butler, *The Huguenots in America,* pp. 88, 111–13; Leo Schelbert, "From Reformed Preacher in the Palatinate to Pietist Monk in Pennsylvania: The Spiritual Path of Johann Peter Muller, 1709–1796," in *Germany and America: Essays on Problems of International Relations and Immigration,* ed. Hans L. Trefousse (New York, 1980), pp. 139–150; *Die Korrespondenz Heinrich Melchior Muhlenbergs aus der Anfangszeit des deutschen Luthertums in Nordamerika,* ed. Kurt Aland (Berlin, 1986); Frederick B. Tolles, *Quakers and the Atlantic Culture* (New York, 1960); Jack D. Marietta, *The Reformation of American Quakerism, 1748–1783* (Philadelphia, 1984), pp. 73–128.

27. John A. Dix, *History of the Parish of Trinity Church in the City of New York,* 6 vols. (New York, 1889–1950), I, 304.

28. Perry Miller, *The New England Mind: From Colony to Province* (Cambridge, Mass., 1953), pp. 105–118. Miller's irony in entitling the chapter "Revivalism" is suggested in his title for the next chapter, "Intolerance." See also C. C. Goen, *Revivalism and Separatism in New England, 1740–1800: Strict Congregationalists and Separate Baptists in the Great Awakening* (New Haven, 1962), p. 6; Lucas, *Valley of Discord,* pp. 199–202; Edwin Gaustad, *Great Awakening in New England* (New York, 1957), pp. 16–20; Sydney Ahlstrom, *A Religious History of the American People* (New Haven, 1972), pp. 314–329.

29. Alexander Garden, *Take Heed How Ye Hear* (Charleston, S.C., 1741); [Charles Chauncy], *The Wonderful Narrative; or, A Faithful Account of the French Prophets, Their Agitations, Ecstasies* [sic] *and Inspirations* (Boston, 1742); Hillel Schwartz, *The French Prophets: The History of a Millenarian Group in Eighteenth-Century England* (Berkeley, 1980); Jonathan Edwards, *Some Thoughts concerning the Present Revival* (1742), in *The Great Awakening,* ed. C. C. Goren (New Haven, 1972), pp. 313, 330, 341; Lovejoy, *Religious Enthusiasm in the New World,* pp. 178–194; Bumsted and Van de Wetering, *What Must I Do to Be Saved?* pp. 40–53;

James Tanis, *Dutch Calvinistic Pietism in the Middle Colonies: A Study of the Life of Theodorus Jacobus Frelinghuysen* (The Hague, 1968).

30. Gaustad, *Great Awakening in New England,* p. 111; John B. Frantz, "The Awakening of Religion among the German Settlers in the Middle Colonies," *William and Mary Quarterly,* 3d ser., 33 (April 1976), 266–288; Charles H. Maxson, *The Great Awakening in the Middle Colonies* (Chicago, 1920), pp. 1–10, 28, 32; Wesley M. Gewehr, *The Great Awakening in Virginia, 1740–1790* (Durham, 1930), p. 254.

31. Bushman, *From Puritan to Yankee,* pp. 135–143, 183–220; Landsman, *Scotland and Its First American Colony,* pp. 227–255; Isaac, *Transformation of Virginia,* pp. 161–205.

32. *George Whitefield's Journals,* [ed. Iain Murray] (London, 1960), p. 476; Susan O'Brien, "A Transatlantic Community of Saints: The Great Awakening and the First Evangelical Network, 1735–1755," *American Historical Review* 91 (1986), 811–832.

33. Leonard J. Trinterud, *The Forming of an American Tradition: A Re-Examination of Colonial Presbyterianism* (Philadelphia, 1949), pp. 100–121, describes the formation of the New York Synod, though it ties the development too closely to Whitefield.

34. Backus quoted in Alan Heimert, *Religion and the American Mind from the Great Awakening to the Revolution* (Cambridge, Mass., 1966), p. 206; on Whitefield, see Stout, *New England Soul,* pp. 192–194.

35. Edwards, *Some Thoughts concerning the Present Revival,* pp. 279–383, 401–405, 483–489; Gilbert Tennent, *The Danger of an Unconverted Ministry,* in *The Great Awakening,* ed. Alan Heimert and Perry Miller (Indianapolis, 1967), pp. 90, 97; Rothermund, *Layman's Progress,* p. 160; Maxson, *Great Awakening in the Middle Colonies,* p. 146.

36. Samuel Blair, *A Short and Faithful Narrative* [1744], in *The Great Awakening: Documents on the Revival of Religion, 1740–1745,* ed. Richard L. Bushman (Chapel Hill, 1969), pp. 71–77.

37. Harry S. Stout and Peter Onuf, "James Davenport and the Great Awakening in New London," *Journal of American History* 70 (1983–84), 556–578.

38. *Max Weber on Charisma and Institution Building: Selected Papers,* ed. S. N. Eisenstadt (Chicago, 1968), esp. pp. 18–27, 48. Weber sometimes confused issues by using the adjective "charismatic" as often as the noun "charisma." Also see Bryan R. Wilson, *The Noble Savages: The Primitive Origins of Charisma and Its Contemporary Survival* (Berkeley, 1975), pp. 2–3, 5, 110–111.

39. Christina Larner, *Enemies of God: The Witch-hunt in Scotland* (Baltimore, 1981), pp. 157–174; Ned Landsman, "Revivalism and Nativism in the Middle Colonies: The Great Awakening and the Scots Community in East New Jersey," *American Quarterly* 34 (1982), 149–164.

40. Landsman, "Revivalism and Nativism in the Middle Colonies," pp. 155–156. I have not counted the mutually unsatisfactory one-year stay of Gilbert Tennent at New Castle, Delaware, where he began his ministry in 1726. Charles Tennent did not serve a predominantly Scottish congregation but did spend his entire career at White Clay Creek, Delaware. See De Benneville K. Ludwig, "Memorabilia of the Tennents," *Journal of Presbyterian History* 1 (1902), 344–354.

41. William Tennent [Sr.], manuscript sermons, Presbyterian Historical Society, Philadelphia. One sermon has been published: Thomas C. Pears, Jr., ed., "William Tennent's Sacramental Sermon," *Journal of Presbyterian History* 19 (1940), 76–84. On Gilbert Tennent's millennialist views, see the brief comments in James West Davidson, *The Logic of Millennial Thought: Eighteenth-Century New England* (New Haven, 1977), p. 149n. Gilbert Tennent is notably absent from the discussion in Christopher M. Beam, "Millennialism and American Nationalism, 1740–1800," *Journal of Presbyterian History* 54 (1976), 182–199. In Heimert's *Religion and the American Mind,* Gilbert Tennent figures prominently as an evangelical but not as a millennialist.

42. George Selement, "The Meeting of Elite and Popular Minds at Cambridge, New England, 1638–1645," *William and Mary Quarterly,* 3d ser., 41 (1984), 32–48; on the Log College, see Trinterud, *The Forming of an American Tradition,* pp. 63–64, 74, 82, 169–195.

43. Gilbert Tennent, "Prefatory Discourse," in John Tennent, *The Nature of Regeneration Opened* (Boston, 1735), pp. i–ix.

44. Thomas Henderson to Elias Boudinot, n.d. [1805], no. 11M7, ms. manuscript group I, New Jersey Historical Society, Trenton, N.J.; Archibald Alexander, *Biographical Sketches of the Founder and Principal Alumni of the Log College* (Philadelphia, 1851), pp. 127–134; Carl Bridenbaugh, "'The Famous Infamous Vagrant' Tom Bell," in Bridenbaugh, *Early Americans* (New York, 1981), pp. 121–149.

45. Elias Boudinot, *Life of the Rev. William Tennent, late Pastor of the Presbyterian Church at Freehold, N.J.* (Trenton, N.J., 1833), pp. 20–24; Boudinot's sketch, based on letters he received from members of Tennent's Freehold congregation, first appeared anonymously in the *Evangelical Intelligencer* 2 (1806), 97–103, 145–166, 201–207, then as *Memoirs of the Life of William Tennent, . . . An Account of His Being Three Days in a Trance and Apparently Living* (Trenton, N.J., 1810); Alexander, *Biographical Sketches,* pp. 150–152. Alexander offered a naturalistic explanation for the loss of Tennent's toes to deflate supernatural implications he found embarrassing. On missing body parts, see Douglas B. Price, "Miraculous Restoration of Lost Body Parts: Relationship to the Phantom Limb Phenomenon and to Limb-Burial Superstitions and Practices," in *American Folk Medicine: A Symposium,* ed. Wayland D. Hand (Berkeley, 1976), pp. 49–72.

46. John Tennent, *The Nature of Regeneration Opened,* pp. ii, iii; Jonathan Edwards, *Religious Affections,* ed. John E. Smith (New Haven, 1959), p. 21; Thomas Prince, *The Christian History Containing Accounts of the Revival and Propagation of Religion in Great-Britain and America for the Year 1744, 5* (Boston, 1745), pp. 292–293.

47. *The Querists, Part III* (Philadelphia, 1741), p. 91; "The Wonderful Wandering Spirit," in *The Great Awakening,* ed. Heimert and Miller, pp. 147–151; also see *The Querists; or, An Extract of Sundry Passages Taken Out of Mr. Whitefield's Printed Sermons, Journals and Letters* (Philadelphia 1740), p. 44.

48. George Whitefield, *A Short Account of God's Dealings with the Reverend Mr. George Whitefield* (London, 1740), pp. 8, 48–49; Daniel Rogers, diary, 1740–53, October 31, 1740, manuscript collection, New-York Historical Society, New York, N.Y. Compare Rogers's description with that in *Whitefield's Journals,* [ed. Murray], p. 484.

49. Whitefield quoted in Clarke Garrett, *Spirit Possession and Popular Religion from the Camisards to the Shakers* (Baltimore, 1987), p. 83.

50. Stuart C. Henry, *George Whitefield: Wayfaring Witness* (Nashville, 1957), pp. 95–114.

51. *The Literary Diary of Ezra Stiles*, ed. Franklin B. Dexter, 3 vols. (New York, 1910), I, 80.

52. "The Spiritual Travels of Nathan Cole," in *The Great Awakening: Event and Exegesis*, ed. Darrett B. Rutman (New York, 1970), p. 44.

53. See also the 1741 Whitefield portrait now in the National Portrait Gallery, London, and reproduced, among other places, in James Henretta and Gregory Nobles, *Evolution and Revolution: American Society, 1600–1820* (Lexington, Mass., 1987), p. 106, and the eighteenth-century portrait owned by the Ipswich Historical Society and pictured in Katherine Whiteside, "Early American Pleasure, The Whipple House . . . ," *House and Garden*, July 1987, pp. 110–119.

54. Heimert, *Religion and the American Mind*, p. 48; Joel Headley, *The Chaplains and Clergy of the Revolution* (New York, 1864), pp. 92–93; Leroy M. Lee, *The Life and Times of the Reverend Jesse Lee* (Louisville, Ky., 1948), p. 246; [Abel Stevens], *Sketches and Incidents; or, A Budget from the Saddle-Bags of a Superannuated Itinerant* ed. George Peck (Cincinnati, 1848), p. 120; *Memoirs of the Life of David Marks, Minister of the Gospel*, ed. Marilla Marks (Dover, N.H., 1846), p. 335.

55. William Becket to George Whitefield, June 9, 1740, William Becket's Notices and Letters, manuscript collections, Historical Society of Pennsylvania, Philadelphia.

56. Howard C. Kee, *Miracle in the Early Christian World: A Study in Sociohistorical Method* (New Haven, 1983); Ramsay MacDonald, *Christianizing the Roman Empire, 100 A.D. — 400 A.D.* (New Haven, 1984); *George Fox's "Book of Miracles,"* ed. Henry J. Cadbury (Cambridge, 1948); Richard Bushman, *Joseph Smith and the Beginnings of Mormonism* (Urbana, 1984); David Harrell, Jr., *All Things Are Possible: The Healing and Charismatic Revivals in Modern America* (Bloomington, 1975).

57. Historians generally homogenize evangelical revivalist style. For a general introduction to evangelicalism, see Leonard I. Sweet, "The Evangelical Tradition in America[: Introduction]," in *The Evangelical Tradition in America*, ed. Sweet (Macon, Ga., 1984), pp. 1–86; on revivalism generally, see Whitney R. Cross, *The Burned-Over District: The Social and Intellectual History of Enthusiastic Religion in Western New York, 1800–1850* (New York, 1950); Timothy L. Smith, *Revivalism and Social Reform: American Protestantism on the Eve of the Civil War* (Nashville, 1957); and William G. McLoughlin, *Revivals, Awakenings, and Reform: An Essay on Religion and Social Change in America, 1607–1977* (Chicago, 1978).

58. Two studies claim relatively high rates at mid-century: Patricia U. Bonomi and Peter R. Eisenstadt, "Church Adherence in the Eighteenth-Century British American Colonies," *William and Mary Quarterly*, 3d ser., 39 (1982), 245–246; and Richard W. Pointer, *Protestant Pluralism and the New York Experience: A Study of Eighteenth-Century Religious Diversity* (Bloomington, 1987), pp. 29–31, 151. On New England church adherence patterns, see Gerald F. Moran, "The Puritan Saint: Religious Experience, Church Membership, and Piety in Connecticut, 1636–1776" (Ph.D. dissertation, Rutgers University, 1973); and Richard P. Gildrie, *Salem, Massachusetts, 1626–1682: A Covenant Community* (Char-

lottesville, Va., 1975), pp. 64, 163–164. Difficulties with the various estimates center on the count of congregations, the "averages" used to indicate congregation size, and the differences that result from the fact that some historians count adults while others count adults and children. These technical problems are beyond the scope of the general study here, though I hope to address them in a subsequent publication.

59. The statistics from Radnor, Apoquimminy, and Newcastle have been collected from the "Notitia Parochialis" scattered through the voluminous reports of SPG ministers, contained in SPG manuscripts, ser. A, B, and C, United SPG Archives, London (microfilm, University of Minnesota, Minneapolis).

60. Hector St. John de Crèvecoeur, *Letters from an American Farmer and Sketches of Eighteenth-Century America,* ed. Albert E. Stone (New York, 1981), p. 76.

7. A Revolutionary Millennium?

1. Joseph Tracy, *The Great Awakening: A History of the Revival of Religion in the Time of Edwards and Whitefield* (Boston, 1841); Joel T. Headley, *The Chaplains and Clergy of the Revolution* (New York, 1864), p. 14; Frank Moore, ed., *The Patriot Preachers of the American Revolution* (New York, 1862); John W. Thornton, *The Pulpit of the American Revolution* (Boston, 1860). Still valuable comments on the historiography of religion and the Revolution are contained in Alan Heimert, *Religion and the American Mind from the Great Awakening to the Revolution* (Cambridge, Mass., 1966), pp. 1–24.

2. Carl Bridenbaugh, *Mitre and Sceptre: Transatlantic Faiths, Ideas, Personalities, and Politics, 1689–1775* (New York, 1962); Heimert, *Religion and the American Mind;* Harry S. Stout, *The New England Soul: Preaching and Religious Culture in Colonial New England* (New York, 1986); Harry S. Stout, "Religion, Communication, and the Ideological Origins of the American Revolution," *William and Mary Quarterly,* 3d ser., 34 (October 1977), 519–541; Rhys Isaac, *The Transformation of Virginia, 1740–1790* (Chapel Hill, 1982); Rhys Isaac, "Evangelical Revolt: The Nature of the Baptists' Challenge to the Traditional Order in Virginia, 1765–1775," *William and Mary Quarterly,* 3d ser., 31 (July 1974), 345–368; Patricia U. Bonomi, *Under the Cope of Heaven: Religion, Society, and Politics in Colonial America* (New York, 1986).

3. *Historical Collections Relating to the American Colonial Church,* ed. William S. Perry, 5 vols. (Hartford, Conn., 1871), III, 290; Bridenbaugh, *Mitre and Sceptre,* pp. 23–53, 260–287; Arthur Lyon Cross, *The Anglican Episcopate and the American Colonies* (Cambridge, Mass., 1902).

4. Bridenbaugh, *Mitre and Sceptre,* pp. 207–229.

5. Jonathan Mayhew, *A Discourse concerning Unlimited Submission and Non-Resistance to the Higher Powers* (Boston, 1750), quoted in Thornton, *Pulpit of the American Revolution,* pp. 73–74; William Livingston, *The Independent Reflector,* ed. Milton Klein (Cambridge, Mass., 1963), pp. 367–375.

6. Bridenbaugh, *Mitre and Sceptre,* pp. 333–334.

7. David Skaggs, "Thomas Cradock and the Chesapeake Golden Age," *William and Mary Quarterly,* 3d ser., 30 (1973), 93–116; John Gordon, *Sermon on the*

Late Rebellion (Williamsburg, 1746); *Records of the Tuesday Club of Annapolis, 1745–56,* ed. Elaine G. Breslaw (Urbana, 1988).

8. Thomas Cradock quoted in Skaggs, "Thomas Cradock and the Chesapeake Golden Age," p. 101.

9. *The Life of the Reverend Devereux Jarratt, Rector of Bath Parish, Dinwiddie County, Virginia, Written by Himself* (Baltimore, 1806), p. 30; S[ophia] H[ume], *An Exhortation to the Inhabitants of the Province of South Carolina, to Bring Their Deeds to the Light of Christ, in Their Own Consciences* (Philadelphia, 1747).

10. Christopher M. Jedrey, *The World of John Cleaveland: Family and Community in Eighteenth-Century New England* (New York, 1979), pp. 108–109; Skaggs, "Thomas Cradock and the Chesapeake Golden Age," pp. 100–101.

11. Jedrey, *World of John Cleaveland,* pp. 126–127; Samuel Langdon, *Government Corrupted by Vice, and Recovered by Righteousness* (Boston, 1775), in *Religion and the Coming of the American Revolution,* ed. Peter Carroll (Waltham, Mass., 1970), pp. 128–142.

12. Samuel Webster quoted in Stout, *New England Soul,* p. 285; see also ibid., chap. 14; Bonomi, *Under the Cope of Heaven,* pp. 209–210.

13. Stout, *New England Soul,* chap. 14; David L. Holmes, "The Episcopal Church and the American Revolution," *Historical Magazine of the Protestant Episcopal Church* 47 (1978), 267–283.

14. *Minutes and Letters of the Coetus of the German Reformed Congregations in Pennsylvania, 1747–1792* (Philadelphia, 1903), pp. 350, 352.

15. Mark Noll, *Christians in the American Revolution* (Washington, D.C., 1977), pp. 65–68; Nathan O. Hatch, *The Sacred Cause of Liberty: Republican Thought and the Millennium in Revolutionary New England* (New Haven, 1977), pp. 22, 61; *Records of the Presbyterian Church in the United States of America . . . , 1706–1788* (Philadelphia, 1904), pp. 466–469.

16. Four Presbyterian ministers endorsed the view of the Anglican minister, George Mickeljohn, whose sermon, *On the Important Duty of Subjection to the Civil Powers* (Newbern, N.C., 1768), is reprinted in *Some Eighteenth Century Tracts concerning North Carolina,* ed. William K. Boyd (Raleigh, N.C., 1927), pp. 393–412.

17. The 1775 Philadelphia Synod letter is in *Records of the Presbyterian Church, 1706–1788,* pp. 166–169. Readers should know that this interpretation of prerevolutionary Presbyterian sentiment differs considerably from Noll, *Christians in the American Revolution,* pp. 51–52, 60, 65–68, 76, and, to a lesser extent, from Leonard J. Trinterud, *The Forming of an American Tradition: A Re-examination of Colonial Presbyterianism* (Philadelphia, 1949), pp. 242–257.

18. Wallace Brown, *The King's Friends: The Composition and Motives of the American Loyalist Claimants* (Providence, 1965), pp. 267–268, passim; Wallace Brown, *The Good Americans: The Loyalists in the American Revolution* (New York, 1969), pp. 56–58, 243–244, 253–254; Trinterud, *Forming of an American Tradition,* pp. 244–245; Leonard R. Riforgiato, *Missionary of Moderation: Henry Melchior Muhlenberg and the Lutheran Church in English America* (Lewisburg, Pa., 1980), pp. 201–212.

19. Samuel Seabury quoted in Bernard Bailyn, *Ideological Origins of the American Revolution* (Cambridge, Mass., 1967), p. 312; John F. Woolverton, *Colonial Anglicanism in North America* (Detroit, 1984), pp. 227–233.

20. "Journal of William Tennent," in *Documentary History of the American Revolution: Consisting of Letters and Papers relating to the Contest for Liberty, Chiefly in South Carolina, from Originals in the Possession of the Editor, and Other Sources,* ed. R. W. Gibbes, 3 vols. (New York, 1853–55), II, 225–238; Charles Woodmason, *The Carolina Backcountry on the Eve of the Revolution: The Journal and Other Writings of Charles Woodmason, Anglican Itinerant,* ed. Richard J. Hooker (Chapel Hill, 1953), pp. 188–189.

21. "Journal of William Tennent," pp. 231, 232.

22. Woolverton, *Colonial Anglicanism,* pp. 228–233.

23. Baptist membership statistics can be found with the report of each yearly association meeting in *Minutes of the Philadelphia Baptist Association, from A.D. 1707, to A.D. 1807; Being the First One Hundred Years of Its Existence,* ed. A. D. Gillette (Philadelphia, 1851).

24. Leah Townsend, *South Carolina Baptists, 1670–1805* (Florence, S.C., 1935), p. 115; Trinterud, *Forming of an American Tradition,* p. 255.

25. On Methodism, see Doris E. Andrews, "Popular Religion and the Revolution in the Middle Atlantic Ports: The Rise of the Methodists, 1770–1800" (Ph.D. dissertation, University of Pennsylvania, 1986); Noll, *Christians in the American Revolution,* pp. 103–122.

26. *The Diary of Isaac Backus,* ed. William McLoughlin (Providence, 1979), p. 973; Jack D. Marietta, *The Reformation of American Quakerism, 1748–1783* (Philadelphia, 1984), pp. 240–248.

27. Trinterud, *Forming of an American Tradition,* pp. 254–255.

28. *Records of the Presbyterian Church, 1706–1788,* pp. 478, 481, 483, 488; *Minutes and Letters of the Coetus,* pp. 362, 365, 372; Oliver Hart, *Dancing Exploded* (Charleston, S.C., 1778).

29. George Washington quoted in George H. Williams, "The Chaplaincy in the Armed Forces of the United States of America in Historical and Ecclesiastical Perspective," in *Military Chaplains: From Religious Military to a Military Religion,* ed. Harvey Cox (n.p., n.d.), pp. 11–58, quotation at p. 18.

30. Charles H. Metzger, "Chaplains in the American Revolution," *Catholic Historical Review* 21 (1945–46), 31–79; Ned Landsman, *Scotland and Its First American Colony, 1683–1765* (Princeton, 1985), pp. 48–96, 227–255.

31. *Journal of the Rev. Ammi Robbins, a Chaplain in the American Army, in the Northern Campaign of 1776* (New Haven, 1850), pp. 4, 5, 10, 30.

32. *Diaries and Letters of William Emerson 1743–1776, Minister of the Church in Concord* [*and*] *Chaplain in the Revolutionary Army,* ed. Amelia F. Emerson (n.p., 1972), pp. 59, 61–70, 77.

33. *Journal of Ammi Robbins,* p. 27; Amos Farnsworth quoted in Walter F. Wallace, "'Oh, Liberty! Oh Virtue! Oh, My Country!' An Exploration of the Minds of New England Soldiers during the American Revolution" (M.A. thesis, Northern Illinois University, 1974), p. 88. See also a sermon by one Dr. Tenney, "Whiskey Triumphant over Turner," Valley Forge, Pa., May 1778; and Benjamin Trumbull, sermon on Nehemiah 4:14, North Haven, Conn., May 23, 1775, and New York, August 4, 1776; manuscript collection, New-York Historical Society, New York.

34. *Journal of Ammi Robbins,* p. 41.

35. Ibid., p. 37; Wallace, "'Oh Liberty!,'" pp. 65–66.

36. Lieutenant Isaac Bangs quoted in Wallace, "'Oh Liberty!,'" p. 65; *Journal of Ammi Robbins,* p. 20.

37. *Journal of Ammi Robbins,* pp. 7, 16, 33, 34; Wallace, "'Oh Liberty!,'" pp. 65–66.

38. *Records of the Presbyterian Church, 1706–1788,* p. 488; *Minutes of the Philadelphia Baptist Association,* ed. Gillette, p. 169.

39. Gordon Wood, *The Creation of the American Republic, 1776–1787* (Chapel Hill, 1969), pp. 114–118, 344–389; J. R. Pole, *Foundations of American Independence, 1763–1815* (Indianapolis, 1972), pp. 80–87.

40. John Winthrop, "A Modell of Christian Charity," in *The Puritans: A Sourcebook of Their Writings,* ed. Perry Miller and Thomas H. Johnson (New York, 1938), p. 195; Massachusetts Constitution of 1780 quoted in Wood, *Creation of the American Republic,* p. 427; Riforgiato, *Missionary of Moderation,* pp. 210–228; William G. McLoughlin, *Isaac Backus and the American Pietistic Tradition* (Boston, 1967), pp. 193–208.

41. Kenneth Silverman, *A Cultural History of the American Revolution: Painting, Music, Literature, and the Theater in the Colonies and the United States from the Treaty of Paris to the Inauguration of George Washington, 1763–1789* (New York, 1976), esp. pp. 443–536; Joseph J. Ellis, *After the Revolution: Profiles of Early American Culture* (New York, 1979).

42. Mark A. Noll et al., *The Search for Christian America* (Westchester, Ill., 1983), pp. 74–76; *The Writings of Christopher Gadsden,* ed. Richard Walsh (Columbia, S.C., 1966), pp. 213, 286, 294; Paul F. Boller, Jr., *George Washington and Religion* (Dallas, 1963), still offers the most systematic treatment of religious beliefs among any of the Founding Fathers.

43. Adams and the Massachusetts *Centinel* quoted in Silverman, *Cultural History of the American Revolution,* p. 491; Thomas Paine, *Common Sense,* ed. Isaak Kramnick (New York, 1976), pp. 89, 100, 104.

44. The best bibliography of published New England chaplains' sermons is found in Wallace, "'Oh Liberty!'" Chaplains' sermons listed in *American Bibliography: A Chronological Dictionary of All Books, Pamphlets, and Periodical Publications Printed in the United States of America, 1639–1800,* ed. Charles Evans, 14 vols. (New York, 1903–1959), sometimes, but not always, can be identified by title.

45. Abraham Keteltas quoted in Hatch, *Sacred Cause of Liberty,* p. 61; Elhanan Winchester quoted in Ruth Bloch, *Visionary Republic: Millennial Themes in American Thought, 1756–1800* (New York, 1985), p. 59.

46. Ebenezer Baldwin and Elhanan Winchester quoted in Bloch, *Visionary Republic,* pp. 59, 79–80; Abraham Keteltas quoted in Hatch, *Sacred Cause of Liberty,* p. 61. See also James West Davidson, *The Logic of Millennial Thought: Eighteenth-Century New England* (New Haven, 1977), pp. 248–250.

47. Bloch, *Visionary Republic,* pp. 105–110.

48. I have been helped particularly on this topic by a senior thesis by Julie Edmunds, "Apocalyptic Thinking in Eighteenth-Century America," Department of History, Yale University, May 1987. For a superb brief analysis see the

introductory essay in Jonathan Edwards, *Apocalyptic Writings: "Notes on the Apocalypse" and An Humble Attempt,* ed. Stephen J. Stein (New Haven, 1977), pp. 1–15; see also Bloch, *Visionary Republic,* and Davidson, *Logic of Millennial Thought.*

49. Anonymous columnist in the *New-England Chronicle* quoted in Bloch, *Visionary Republic,* p. 80; Wood, *Creation of the American Republic,* pp. 344–389. Gordon Wood's retrospective essay, "Ideology and the Origins of a Liberal America," *William and Mary Quarterly,* 3d ser., 44 (1987), 628–640, places more stress on the importance of religion and evangelicalism than his original treatment.

50. Richard Beale Davis, *Intellectual Life in the Colonial South, 1585–1763* (Knoxville, 1978), pp. 1344–1400; Richard Beale Davis, ed., *The Colonial Virginia Satirist: Mid-Eighteenth-Century Commentaries on Politics, Religion, and Society* (Philadelphia, 1967); William Meade, *Old Churches, Ministers, and Families of Virginia,* 2 vols. (Philadelphia, 1906–1910), I, 174–175.

51. On the origins of deism, see Robert E. Sullivan, *John Toland and the Deist Controversy: A Study in Adaptations* (Cambridge, Mass., 1982); on deism in prerevolutionary America see Henry F. May, *The Enlightenment in America* (New York, 1976), pp. 20–23, 116–132.

52. Jedidiah Morse quoted in G. Adolf Koch, *Republican Religion: The American Revolution and the Cult of Reason* (New York, 1933), p. 252.

53. Koch, *Republican Religion,* pp. 253–284; Vernon Stauffer, *New England and the Bavarian Illuminati* (New York, 1918).

54. Fawn Brodie, *Thomas Jefferson: An Intimate History* (New York, 1974), pp. 431–432.

55. Conrad Wright, *The Beginnings of Unitarianism in America* (Boston, 1955), remains the standard account of the movement. For Unitarianism's connection to the Enlightenment, see May, *The Enlightenment in America,* pp. 351–357.

56. On the Unitarians in Philadelphia and Boston, see the excellent studies by Elizabeth M. Geffen, *Philadelphia Unitarianism, 1796–1861* (Philadelphia, 1961); Daniel Walker Howe, *The Unitarian Conscience* (Cambridge, Mass., 1970). On southern Unitarianism, see Clarence Gohdes, "Some Notes on the Unitarian Church in the Antebellum South," in *American Studies in Honor of William Kenneth Boyd,* ed. David K. Johnson (Durham, 1940), pp. 327–366.

57. Richard Pointer, *Protestant Pluralism and the New York Experience: A Study of Eighteenth-Century Religious Diversity* (Bloomington, 1987), pp. 103–120, 141–144; Stephen A. Marini, *Radical Sects of Revolutionary New England* (Cambridge, Mass., 1982), pp. 40–59; Clarke Garrett, *Spirit Possession and Popular Religion from the Camisards to the Shakers* (Baltimore, 1987), pp. 160–194.

58. Devereux Jarratt quoted in David L. Holmes, "Devereux Jarratt: A Letter and Reevaluation," *Historical Magazine of the Protestant Episcopal Church* 47 (1978), 37–49; Marini, *Radical Sects of Revolutionary New England,* pp. 64–67, 139–144; Elias Smith, *The Life, Conversion, Preaching, Travels, and Sufferings of Elias Smith* (Portsmouth, N.H., 1816), pp. 125, 134.

59. Amos Taylor quoted in Marini, *Radical Sects of Revolutionary New England,* p. 78. On the Shakers, see the excellent accounts by Marini, ibid., pp. 75–80, 148–153; and Garrett, *Spirit Possession and Popular Religion,* pp. 169–214.

60. Benjamin Randel quoted in Marini, *Radical Sects of Revolutionary New England,* p. 66; Freeborn Garrettson, *American Methodist Pioneer: The Life and Jour-

nals of the Rev. Freeborn Garrettson, 1752–1827, ed. Robert D. Simpson (Rutland, Vt., 1984), pp. 53, 98, 101, 102, 107–108, 138, 142, 154; Elias Smith, *Life,* pp. 173, 216–217.

61. Marini, *Radical Sects in Revolutionary New England,* pp. 172–176; John Ripon, *Baptist Annual Register* (London, 1790–93); Frank Baker, *From Wesley to Asbury: Studies in Early American Methodism* (Durham, 1976).

8. Toward the Antebellum Spiritual Hothouse

1. Charles Brockden Brown, *Wieland; or, The Transformation,* ed. Fred L. Pattee (New York, 1926), p. 262.

2. Ibid. pp. 8–9, 12, 13. Brown's source for Camisard history was most likely François Mission, ed., *A Cry from the Desart* [sic]; *or, Testimonials of Miraculous Things Lately Come to Pass in the Cevennes* (London, 1707), a widely circulated translation of *Le Théâtre sacré des Cévennes* (London, 1706). See also Clarke Garrett, *Spirit Possession and Popular Religion from the Camisards to the Shakers* (Baltimore, 1987); Hillel Schwartz, *The French Prophets: The History of a Millenarian Group in Eighteenth-Century England* (Berkeley, 1980); David Lovejoy, *Religious Enthusiasm in the New World: Heresy to Revolution* (Cambridge, Mass., 1985), pp. 168–177, 188; and Elizabeth Fisher, "'Prophecies and Revelations': German Cabbalists in Early Pennsylvania," *Pennsylvania Magazine of History and Biography* 109 (July 1985), 299–333.

3. Quoted in Edmund S. Morgan, "The Witch and We, the People," *American Heritage* (August-September 1983), 6–11. Steven Rosswurm originally drew my attention to this incident in "Arms, Culture, and Class: The Philadelphia Militia and 'Lower Orders' in the American Revolution, 1765–1783" (Ph. D. dissertation, Northern Illinois University, 1979), pp. 46, 48.

4. *The Literary Diary of Ezra Stiles,* ed. Franklin B. Dexter, 3 vols. (New York, 1910), III, 62, 351; Brown, *Wieland,* p. 204.

5. Richard Dorson, *American Folklore* (Chicago, 1977), pp. 35–38; Herbert Leventhal, *In the Shadow of the Enlightenment: Occultism and Renaissance Science in Eighteenth-Century America* (New York, 1976), pp. 77–78; *The Autobiography of Brantley York* (Durham, 1910), pp. 7–8. For the history of supernatural fiction in later decades, see Howard Kerr et al., eds., *The Haunted Dusk: American Supernatural Fiction, 1820–1920* (Athens, Ga., 1983); and Howard Kerr, *Mediums, and Spirit-Rappers, and Roaring Radicals: Spiritualism in American Literature, 1850–1900* (Urbana, 1972).

6. Leventhal, *In the Shadow of the Enlightenment,* pp. 112–118; Evon Z. Vogt and Ray Hyman, *Water Witching U.S.A.* (Chicago, 1959), pp. 12–22.

7. D. Michael Quinn, *Early Mormonism and the Magic World View* (Salt Lake City, 1987), p. 16; Frederick H. Quitman, *A Treatise on Magic: or, On the Intercourse between Spirits and Men; with Annotations* (Albany, 1810), p. 73; Robert Scott, *Letters to the Rev. Frederick H. Quitman, Occasioned by His Late Treatise on Magic* (Poughkeepsie, 1810).

8. *Autobiography of Brantley York,* pp. 8–9.

9. Marion B. Stowell, *Early American Almanacs: The Colonial Weekday Bible* (New York, 1977), and Samuel Briggs, *The Essays, Humor, and Poems of Nathaniel*

Ames, Father and Son, of Dedham, Massachusetts . . . (Cleveland, 1891); Quinn, *Early Mormonism and the Magic World View*, pp. 19–22.

10. Alan Taylor, "The Early Republic's Supernatural Economy: Treasure Seeking in the American Northeast, 1780–1830," *American Quarterly* 38 (Spring 1986), 6–33.

11. Ibid.

12. Joshua Gordon, "Witchcraft Book," South Caroliniana Library, University of South Carolina, Columbia, S.C. A Joshua Gordon filed for revolutionary war compensation from the North Carolina government, and another person by that name appeared as a resident of York County, South Carolina, in the 1790 federal census; information from the Joshua Gordon file, South Caroliniana Library, University of South Carolina, courtesy Allen Stokes. The charms in the Gordon manuscript are difficult to decipher. Anita Rutman, a superb paleographer, suggests an alternate reading of the second charm: "Your Saviour Sweeting Blood with wry[?]" and comments that "'wry' can, according to the *OED*, be defined as 'a twisting or tortuous movement,' which would make some sense and a fairly rhythmic little incantation." Rutman to the author, August 6, 1978.

13. Ibid. The cures in the Gordon manuscript closely follow the style of seventeenth-century English cures described in Keith Thomas, *Religion and the Decline of Magic* (New York, 1971), pp. 177–192.

14. Dorson, *American Folklore*, pp. 17–18; Joseph Doddridge quoted in Tom Peete Cross, "Witchcraft in North Carolina," *Studies in Philology* 16 (1919), 224.

15. Information on the Philadelphia Social History Project was kindly supplied by Elisabeth Lightbourn. On the Project's methodology, see Theodore Hershberg and Robert Dockhorn, "Occupational Classification," *Historical Methods* 9 (March-June 1976), 59–77. The Project's sampling techniques—complete data for black residents and first-generation German and Irish immigrants but a sample of only one out of every six native-born whites—make its recovery of any obscure or suspect occupations among Philadelphia whites all the more remarkable.

16. Leventhal, *In the Shadow of the Enlightenment*, pp. 129–131.

17. See S. Foster Damon, "De Brahm, Alchemist," *Ambix* 24 (1977), 77–88; Leventhal, *In the Shadow of the Enlightenment*, pp. 129–131.

18. Marguerite B. Block, *The New Church in the New World: A Study of Swedenborgianism in America* (New York, 1932), pp. 73–111; Robert Fuller, *Mesmerism and the American Cure of Souls* (Philadelphia, 1982); Robert Fuller, *Americans and the Unconscious* (New York, 1986). Robert Ellenberger, *The Discovery of the Unconscious* (New York, 1970), describes Mesmerism's place in the history of modern psychology.

19. Shomer S. Zwelling, "Robert Carter's Journey: From Colonial Patriarch to New Nation Mystic," *American Quarterly* 38 (Fall 1986), 613–636. The profile of Baltimore's New Jerusalem congregation is found in Terry D. Bilhartz, *Urban Religion and the Second Great Awakening: Church and Society in Early National Baltimore* (Rutherford, N.J., 1986), pp. 24, 158–166.

20. Robert Darnton, *Mesmerism and the End of the Enlightenment in France* (Cambridge, Mass., 1968); Robert S. Ellwood, Jr., *Alternative Altars: Unconventional and Eastern Spirituality in America* (Chicago, 1979), pp. 91–92; R. Laurence Moore, *In Search of White Crows: Spiritualism, Parapsychology, and American Culture*

(New York, 1977), pp. 9, 15; Sydney Ahlstrom, *A Religious History of the American People* (New Haven, 1972), p. 1019.

21. Paul Goodman, *Towards a Christian Republic: Antimasonry and the Great Tradition in New England, 1826–1836* (New York, 1988). For a contemporary view of Masonic heresies, see John Fellows, *An Exposition of the Mysteries; or, Religious Dogmas and Customs of the Ancient Egyptians, Pythagoreans, and Druids. Also, An Inquiry into the Origins, History, and Purport of Freemasonry* (New York, 1835).

22. E. Brooks Holifield, *Health and Medicine in the Methodist Tradition: Journey toward Wholeness* (New York, 1986), pp. 28–38; *The Journal of Joseph Pilmore, Methodist Itinerant for the Years August 1, 1769 to January 2, 1774,* ed. Frederick E. Maser and Howard T. Maag (Philadelphia, 1969), pp. 66, 68, 75; James P. Horton, *A Narrative of the Early Life, Remarkable Conversion, and Spiritual Labors of James P. Horton, Who Has Been a Member of the Methodist Episcopal Church upward of Forty Years* (n.p., 1839), p. 184.

23. Henry Smith, *Recollections and Reflections of an Old Itinerant,* ed. George Peck (New York, 1848), pp. 213, 214–217; Lorenzo Dow, *History of the Cosmopolite; or, The Writings of Rev. Lorenzo Dow, containing His Experiences and Travels, in Europe and America, up to near His Fiftieth Year,* rev. ed. (Cincinnati, 1860), p. 210; *The Life and Times of George Peck, D.D., Written by Himself* (New York, 1874), p. 22; Freeborn Garrettson, *American Methodist Pioneer: The Life and Journals of the Rev. Freeborn Garrettson, 1752–1827,* ed. Robert D. Simpson (Rutland, Vt., 1984), p. 101.

24. William H. Williams, *The Garden of American Methodism: The Delmarva Peninsula, 1769–1820* (Wilmington, Del., 1984), p. 129; Benjamin Abbott, *The Experiences and Gospel Labours of the Rev. Benjamin Abbott,* ed. John Ffirth (1805; New York, 1832), pp. 78, 91; Garrettson, *American Methodist Pioneer,* p. 148.

25. *Life and Times of George Peck,* pp. 27, 28.

26. Morton T. Kelsey, *God, Dreams, and Revelation: A Christian Interpretation of Dreams* (Minneapolis, 1968).

27. Garrettson, *American Methodist Pioneer,* p. 108.

28. Ibid., pp. 107–108; *Life and Times of George Peck,* pp. 25, 97–98.

29. Abbott, *Experiences and Gospel Labours,* pp. 24, 32, 130–132.

30. Garrettson, *American Methodist Pioneer,* pp. 53, 98, 101, 102; *Life and Times of George Peck,* p. 51; Abbott, *Experiences and Gospel Labours,* pp. 5, 18, 24.

31. Abbott, *Experiences and Gospel Labours,* p. 123; Frank Baker, *Methodism and the Love-Feast* (London, 1957), p. 10.

32. Abbott, *Experiences and Gospel Labours,* pp. 215, 216, 220, 222, 227, 229, 235, 237; the quotation taken from p. 237 has been modernized.

33. Christine L. Hyerman, "The Origins of an Evangelical Consensus in the Old South: From the American Revolution to the Great Revival," in *Religion in a Revolutionary Age,* ed. Ronald L. Hoffman (Charlottesville, Va., forthcoming).

34. Among the laments, see [Abel Stevens], *Sketches and Incidents; or, A Budget from the Saddle-Bags of a Superannuated Itinerant,* ed. George Peck (Cincinnati, 1848).

35. Horton, *A Narrative,* p. 75; Dow, *History of the Cosmopolite,* pp. 18, 117, 119, 129, 131, 203, 208, 331–332; Charles C. Sellers, *Lorenzo Dow: The Bearer of the Word* (New York, 1928), pp. 223, 224.

36. Dean C. Jessee, "New Documents and Mormon Beginnings," *Brigham*

Young University Studies 24 (1984 [1986]), 397–428; David Hewett, "The Mark Hoffman Story," *Maine Antique Digest* (June 1986), C1–C8. John Brooke kindly furnished these materials. See also Klaus J. Hansen, *Mormonism and the American Experience* (Chicago, 1981); Richard L. Bushman, *Joseph Smith and the Beginnings of Mormonism* (Urbana, 1984); Jan Shipps, *Mormonism: The Story of a New Religious Tradition* (Urbana, 1985); and Quinn, *Mormonism and the Magic World View.*

37. Gordon Wood, "Evangelical America and Early Mormonism," *New York History* 61 (1980), 359–386; Joseph Smith, *History of the Church of Jesus Christ of Latter-day Saints,* ed. B. H. Roberts, 7 vols. (Salt Lake City, 1932–51), I, 3.

38. For the importance of the *Book of Mormon*'s political context, see Nathan O. Hatch, *The Democratization of American Christianity* (New Haven, 1989).

39. Martin Harris quoted in Quinn, *Mormonism and the Magic World View,* p. 114; *The Personal Writings of Joseph Smith,* ed. Dean C. Jessee (Salt Lake City, 1984), pp. 202–204.

40. Lucy Mack Smith, *Biographical Sketches of Joseph Smith the Prophet and His Progenitors for Many Generations* (Liverpool, 1853), pp. 91–92; Bushman, *Joseph Smith and the Beginnings of Mormonism,* p. 74; Quinn, *Mormonism and the Magic World View,* pp. 54–58.

41. Quinn, *Mormonism and the Magic World View,* pp. 53–77, 128–133, 173–174.

42. *Personal Writings of Joseph Smith,* p. 90.

43. Nancy Towle, *Vicissitudes Illustrated in the Experience of Nancy Towle in Europe and America,* 2d ed. (Portsmouth, N.H., 1833), p. 152; B. H. Roberts, *A Comprehensive History of the Church of Jesus Christ of Latter-day Saints,* 6 vols. (Salt Lake City, 1930), I, 202, 265, II, 19–22.

44. *Autobiography of Rev. Tobias Spicer* (New York, 1852), p. 111; Breck England, *The Life and Thought of Orson Pratt* (Salt Lake City, 1985), pp. 30–33.

45. *Personal Writings of Joseph Smith,* pp. 63, 93, 94, 101–103, 104, 129–130, 163, 294–296, 662.

46. Shipps, *Mormonism,* 67–85.

47. Quinn, *Mormonism and the Magic World View,* pp. 192–224.

48. On the transformation of late nineteenth- and early twentieth-century Mormonism, a topic that generates as much discord as does the discussion of early Mormon magic, see Hansen, *Mormonism and the American Experience;* and Shipps, *Mormonism.*

49. On the black church in America, see Albert Raboteau, *Slave Religion: The "Invisible Institution" in the Antebellum South* (New York, 1978). Robert Baird's well-known work, *Religion in America* (New York, 1856), provided no statistical information or even substantial descriptions of religion among black Americans, slave or free, in its 696 pages.

50. Raboteau, *Slave Religion;* Gary B. Nash, *Forging Freedom: The Formation of Philadelphia's Black Community, 1720–1840* (Cambridge, Mass., 1988), pp. 109–114.

51. Will B. Gravely, "African Methodisms and the Rise of Black Nationalism," in *Rethinking Methodist History: A Bicentennial Historical Consultation,* ed. Russell E. Richey and Kenneth E. Rowe (Nashville, 1985), pp. 111–124; Nash, *Forging Freedom,* p. 231. Mechal Sobel stresses the importance of African elements in Afro-American Baptist congregational life before 1800 in *Trabelin' On:*

The Slave Journey to an Afro-Baptist Faith (Westport, Conn., 1979) and *The World They Made Together: Black and White Values in Eighteenth-Century Faith* (Princeton, 1987), though she agrees that African elements also increased rather than decreased after 1820.

52. John W. Blassingame, *The Slave Community: Plantation Life in the Antebellum South* (New York, 1972), pp. 61–63; Nash, *Forging Freedom,* p. 128.

53. Nash, *Forging Freedom,* pp. 212–233; Carol V. R. George, *Segregated Sabbaths: Richard Allen and the Rise of Independent Black Churches, 1760–1840* (New York, 1973); Gravely, "African Methodisms." Readers should be aware that the interpretation offered here portrays a process thoroughly different from that stressed in the work of W. E. B. Dubois and, most recently, in Sterling Stuckey, *Slave Culture: Nationalist Theory and the Foundations of Black America* (New York, 1987), pp. 34–38, 88–91, 256–258.

54. Blassingame, *Slave Community,* pp. 64–76; Stuckey, *Slave Culture,* p. 91.

55. On spiritualism, the most dependable published treatment is found in Moore, *In Search of White Crows.*

56. *Spiritual Telegraph* 1 (1853), 19–20, 74–75, 91–95, 196–197, 206–207, 307–308, 367–372; 2 (1853), 23, 48–51, 60–64, 97–98, 106–107, 128–138, 180–181, 232–241, 376–381, 403–405, 426–428, 447–448, 466–467, 484–487, 490–492, 514. The international aspects of spiritualism have not received further extensive study since the publication of Frank Podmore's excellent work, *Modern Spiritualism: A History and a Criticism,* 2 vols. (London, 1902).

57. *Spiritual Telegraph* 2 (1853), 160–164, 346–347, 410–411; Moore, *In Search of White Crows,* pp. 40–64.

58. *Shekinah* 1 (1852), 105–119; 2 (1853), 49–59, 193–208; Janet Oppenheim, *The Other World: Spiritualism and Psychical Research in England, 1850–1914* (New York, 1985).

59. R. Laurence Moore, "The Occult Connection? Mormonism, Christian Science, Spiritualism," in *The Occult in America: New Historical Perspectives,* ed. Howard Kerr and Charles L. Crow (Urbana, 1983), pp. 135–161.

60. Ann Braude, "Women in American Spiritualism" (Ph.D. dissertation, Yale University, 1987).

61. For the Chase letters, see *Spiritual Telegraph* 1 (1853), 249–251, 382–385, 423; 2 (1853), 57–58, 139–141.

62. The class orientation of the spiritualist movement is evident from the observations in Kerr, *Mediums, and Spirit-Rappers, and Roaring Radicals,* and Moore, *In Search of White Crows.* On Higginson, see Tilden G. Edelstein, *Strange Enthusiasm: A Life of Thomas Wentworth Higginson* (New Haven, 1968); and Thomas Wentworth Higginson, *Army Life in a Black Regiment,* ed. Howard Mumford Jones (East Lansing, 1960).

9. Christian Power in the American Republic

1. This view has received its finest recent exposition in Nathan O. Hatch, *The Democratization of American Christianity* (New Haven, 1989). Earlier studies pursuing similar themes include Alice Felt Tyler, *Freedom's Ferment: Phases of American Social History from the Colonial Period to the Outbreak of the Civil War* (Minne-

apolis, 1944); Martin Marty, *Pilgrims in Their Own Land: 500 Years of Religion in America* (New York, 1984); and even Perry Miller, *The Life of the Mind in America from the Revolution to the Civil War* (New York, 1965).

2. Leonard W. Levy, *The Establishment Clause: Religion and the First Amendment* (New York, 1986), argues strongly for the so-called separationist position but also offers extremely fair summaries of the other arguments and includes a bibliography of the most important legal history studies. Also see John F. Wilson and Donald Drakeman, eds., *Church and State in American History,* 2d ed. (Boston, 1987); and Thomas J. Curry, *The First Freedoms: Church and State in America to the Passage of the First Amendment* (New York, 1986).

3. Curry, *The First Freedoms,* pp. 161–162.

4. Levy, *The Establishment Clause,* pp. 25–62; Curry, *The First Freedoms,* pp. 134–192.

5. Levy, *Establishment Clause,* pp. 26–46.

6. Levy, *Establishment Clause,* pp. 4–24, 40; William G. McLoughlin, *New England Dissent, 1630–1833: The Baptists and the Separation of Church and State,* 2 vols. (Cambridge, Mass., 1971), I, 217; Chester J. Antieau et al., *Freedom from Federal Establishment: Formation and Early History of the First Amendment Religion Clauses* (Milwaukee, 1964), p. 23.

7. William Tennent quoted in William G. McLoughlin, "The Role of Religion in the Revolution: Liberty of Conscience and Cultural Cohesion in the New Nation," in *Essays on the American Revolution,* ed. Stephen G. Kurtz and James H. Hutson (Chapel Hill, 1973), p. 217; cf. Levy, *Establishment Clause,* p. 8; Antieau et al., *Freedom from Federal Establishment,* pp. 45–46, 54.

8. Curry, *The First Freedoms,* pp. 134–192.

9. Isaac Backus's thanksgiving and fast day preaching of the 1770s is recorded in *The Diary of Isaac Backus,* ed. William G. McLoughlin (Providence, 1979), pp. 928, 959, 982, 1009, 1015, 1021, 1071, and his preaching for the 1800s is recorded on pp. 1482, 1486, 1493, 1504. Backus's call for congressional protection for the Bible is recorded on pp. 1295–96. See also McLoughlin, "The Role of Religion in the Revolution," p. 211; and McLoughlin, *Isaac Backus and the American Pietistic Tradition* (Boston, 1967), p. 150.

10. Among the most important recent books on later eighteenth-century Virginia are Rhys Isaac, *The Transformation of Virginia, 1740–1790* (Chapel Hill, 1982), and Richard Beeman, *The Evolution of the Southern Backcountry: A Case Study of Lunenburg County, Virginia, 1746–1832* (Philadelphia, 1984), though both tend to confirm the picture of the aristocracy offered in Charles S. Sydnor, *Gentlemen Freeholders: Political Practices in Washington's Virginia* (Chapel Hill, 1952).

11. Curry, *First Freedoms,* pp. 134–148; Levy, *The Establishment Clause,* pp. 51–60; Thomas J. Buckley, S. J., *Church and State in Revolutionary Virginia, 1776–1787* (Charlottesville, 1977), pp. 38–70.

12. Virginia petitions quoted in Levy, *The Establishment Clause,* pp. 56, 57. See also Buckley, *Church and State in Revolutionary Virginia,* pp. 113–152.

13. James Madison, "Memorial and Remonstrance," in *The Papers of James Madison,* 14 vols. to date (Chicago and Charlottesville, Va., 1962–), VIII, 295–306; Buckley, *Church and State in Revolutionary Virginia,* pp. 131–136.

14. *Papers of James Madison,* VIII, 295–306. Madison was indebted to Locke, of course, as Thomas Buckley notes, and quoted him several times in the "Memorial and Remonstrance."

15. Buckley, *Church and State in Revolutionary Virginia,* pp. 141–142. If we allow for considerable separation in time and place, these views were not terribly different from those expressed in John Winthrop's famous *Arbella* sermon of 1632.

16. Ibid., pp. 157–159.

17. Buckley, *Church and State in Revolutionary Virginia,* pp. 190–191, reprints the Act for Religious Freedom and identifies Jefferson's original phrasing and the Burgesses' deletions.

18. "House and Senate Debates (1789)," in *Church and State in American History,* ed. Wilson and Drakeman, pp. 75–78. Although my reading of the First Amendment agrees in substance with that offered by Levy, *The Establishment Clause,* I have come to it through sometimes different means and have given greater emphasis to the amendment's precise wording and choice of terms.

19. Levy, *The Establishment Clause,* pp. 38–41, 47–50. New Hampshire did not amend its constitution to prohibit support for any religious group until 1877, and this occurred, in part, because the state's Supreme Court intrepreted the state constitution's support for religious equality to require tax exemption for Catholic as well as for Protestant schools. See Chester J. Antieau, *Religion under The State Constitutions* (Brooklyn, 1965), pp. 127–128.

20. Levy, *The Establishment Clause,* pp. 34–38; John D. Cushing, "Notes on Disestablishment in Massachusetts, 1780–1833," *William and Mary Quarterly,* 3d ser., 26 (April 1969), 169–190. The most detailed and nuanced treatment of New England disestablishment is found in McLoughlin, *New England Dissent.*

21. *Minutes of the General Assembly of the Presbyterian Church in the United States of America from Its Organization, A.D. 1789 to A.D. 1820 Inclusive* (Philadelphia, [1847]), p. 743; *Minutes of the Philadelphia Baptist Association, from A.D. 1707, to A.D. 1807; Being the First One Hundred Years of Its Existence,* ed. A. D. Gillette (Philadelphia, 1851), pp. 169–172; Edwin Scott Gaustad, *Historical Atlas of Religion in America,* rev. ed. (New York, 1976); Robert Baird, *Religion in America,* rev. ed. (New York, 1856), pp. 462, 487, 496.

22. Jay P. Dolan, *The American Catholic Experience: A History from Colonial Times to the Present* (Garden City, N.Y., 1985), pp. 104–105. Information on the growth of the American Catholic hierarchy and ecclesiastical structure has been extracted from Joseph B. Code, *Dictionary of the American Hierarchy, 1789–1964* (New York, 1964). Charles Lamb, of the University of Notre Dame Archives, kindly supplied this information.

23. Jan Shipps, *Mormonism: The Story of a New Religious Tradition* (Urbana, 1985), pp. 83, 131–137; Leonard Arrington and David Bitton, *The Mormon Experience: A History of the Latter-Day Saints* (New York, 1979), p. 351.

24. These figures are taken from Gaustad, *Historical Atlas of Religion in America.*

25. John R. Stilgoe, *Common Landscape of America 1580 to 1845* (New Haven, 1982), pp. 218–241.

26. Charles Cist, *Sketches and Statistics of Cincinnati in 1859* (Cincinnati, 1859), pp. 192–198.

27. Despite historians' rhetoric about American Protestant laicization and, hence, democratization, systematic studies of "membership" patterns in denominational bodies are all but unwritten. For a start on the topic, see Jack D. Marietta, *The Reformation of American Quakerism 1748–1783* (Philadelphia, 1984), pp. 129–186; and Jean R. Soderlund, *Quakers and Slavery: A Divided Spirit* (Princeton, 1985). Presbyterian attendance patterns can be traced in *Minutes of the General Assembly of the Presbyterian Church, 1789 to 1820,* which incorporated attendance lists into the minutes of each year's session.

28. William H. Williams, *The Garden of American Methodism: The Delmarva Peninsula, 1769–1820* (Wilmington, Del., 1984), pp. 172–174; Frederick V. Mills, *Bishops by Ballot: An Eighteenth-Century Ecclesiastical Revolution* (New York, 1978), pp. 302–307.

29. Patrick W. Carey, *People, Priests, and Prelates: Ecclesiastical Democracy and the Tensions of Trusteeism* (Notre Dame, Ind., 1987), pp. 158–171, 193–206; Patrick W. Carey, *An Immigrant Bishop: John England's Adaptation of Irish Catholicism to American Republicanism* (New York, 1982), pp. 96–97; Patrick W. Carey, "Republicanism in American Catholicism, 1785–1860," *Journal of the Early Republic* 3 (1983), 413–437.

30. Susan Previant Lee and Peter Passell, *A New Economic View of American History* (New York, 1979), pp. 130–222; Stuart Bruchey, *The Roots of American Economic Growth, 1607–1861: An Essay in Social Causation* (New York, 1965), pp. 74–123.

31. On the debate over the place of national and foreign markets in American economic development, readers are best advised to start with Alexander Hamilton's famous "Report on Manufactures," and continue to one of the superb new economic histories, such as Lee and Passell, *A New Economic View of American History.* On the ambiguities of missions to American Indians and foreign lands both before and after the Revolution, see the opening chapters in William R. Hutchison, *Errand to the World: American Protestant Thought and Foreign Missions* (Chicago, 1987).

32. On communication networks in the early republic, see Allan R. Pred, *Urban Growth and the Circulation of Information: The United States System of Cities, 1790–1840* (Cambridge, Mass., 1973), pp. 12–19.

33. Leah Townsend, *South Carolina Baptists, 1670–1805* (Florence, S.C., 1935), pp. 261–270.

34. Ibid.

35. Ibid.

36. On itinerant ministries, see John Boles, *The Great Revival 1787–1805* (Lexington, Ky., 1972); and L. C. Rudolph, *Francis Asbury* (Nashville, 1966).

37. William J. Gilmore, "Elementary Literacy on the Eve of the Industrial Revolution: Trends in Rural New England, 1760–1830," *Proceedings,* American Antiquarian Society, 92 (1982), 87–171; David D. Hall, *Worlds of Wonder, Days of Judgment: Popular Religious Belief in Early New England* (New York, 1989), chap. 1; Wesley Norton, *Religious Newspapers in the Old Northwest to 1861* (Athens, Ohio, 1977).

38. David P. Nord, "The Evangelical Origins of Mass Media in America,

1815–1835," *Journalism Monographs* 88 (1984), 1–30; *The Millerites and Early Adventists: An Index to the Microfilm Collection of Rare Books and Manuscripts,* ed. Jean Hoornstra (Ann Arbor, 1978); Walter Sutton, *The Western Book Trade: Cincinnati as a Nineteenth-Century Publishing and Book-Trade Center* (Columbus, Ohio, 1961).

39. Frank Thistlewaite, *The Anglo-American Connection in the Early Nineteenth Century* (Philadelphia, 1959), remains an outstanding example of this theme.

40. James B. Stewart, *Holy Warriors: The Abolitionists and American Slavery* (New York, 1976); Joseph R. Gusfield, *Symbolic Crusade: Status Politics and the American Temperance Movement* (Edwardsville, Ill., 1963); W. R. Rorabaugh, *The Alcoholic Republic: An American Tradition* (New York, 1979); Anne M. Boylan, *The Sunday School: The Formation of an American Institution, 1790–1880* (New Haven, 1988).

41. Donald G. Tewksbury, *The Founding of American Colleges and Universities before the Civil War: With Particular Reference to the Religious Influences upon the College Movement* (New York, 1932); Francis Wayland, *Thoughts on the Present College System* (Boston, 1842), p. 8; Burton J. Bledstein, *The Culture of Professionalism: The Middle Class and the Development of Higher Education in America* (New York, 1976), pp. 240–242.

42. On the voluntary societies, see Clyde Griffin, *Their Brothers' Keepers: Moral Stewardship in the United States, 1800–1865* (New Brunswick, N.J., 1960), pp. 23–43, 61–80.

43. Gary B. Nash, *Forging Freedom: The Formation of Philadelphia's Black Community, 1720–1840* (Cambridge, Mass., 1988), pp. 227–233; David M. Reimers, *White Protestantism and the Negro* (New York, 1965), pp. 3–24.

44. Nancy Towle, *Vicissitudes Illustrated, in the Experience of Nancy Towle, in Europe and America,* 2d ed. (Portsmouth, N.H., 1833); *The Life of Elder Abel Thornton* (Providence, 1828), pp. 113–115; Elizabeth Hoxie, "Harriett Livermore: 'Vixen and Devotee,'" *New England Quarterly* (1945), 39–50; *Memoirs of Fanny Newell* (Springfield, Mass., 1832).

45. Nancy F. Cott, *The Bonds of Womanhood: "Women's Sphere" in New England, 1780–1835* (New Haven, 1977), pp. 132–135, 151–154, 178–182; Mary P. Ryan, *Cradle of the Middle Class: The Family in Oneida County, New York, 1790–1865* (New York, 1981), pp. 116–144; Boylan, *The Sunday School;* Nancy A. Hewitt, *Women's Activism and Social Change: Rochester, New York, 1822–1872* (Ithaca, 1984).

46. Gaustad, *Historical Atlas of American Religion,* remains the best single source of statistical information on antebellum religious groups.

47. Ibid., part two.

48. Ryan, *Cradle of the Middle Class,* pp. 75–77, 257; Curtis D. Johnson, "Islands of Holiness: Rural Religion in Cortland County, New York, 1790–1860" (Ph. D. dissertation, University of Minnesota, 1985), p. 167.

49. Roger Finke and Rodney Stark, "Turning Pews into People: Estimating Church Membership in Nineteenth-Century America," *Journal for the Scientific Study of Religion* 25 (1985), 180–192; Roger Finke and Rodney Stark, "American Religion in 1776: A Statistical Portrait," *Sociological Analysis* 49 (1988), 39–51; Edwin Scott Gaustad, ed., *The Rise of Adventism: Religion and Society in Mid-Nineteenth-Century America* (New York, 1974), p. xiii; Carroll Smith-Rosenberg,

Religion and the Rise of the American City: The New York City Mission Movement, 1812–1870 (Ithaca, 1971); Marion I. Bell, *Crusade in the City: Revivalism in Nineteenth-Century Philadelphia* (Lewisburg, Pa., 1977); Hewitt, *Women's Activism and Social Change;* Paul E. Johnson, *A Shopkeeper's Millennium: Society and Revivals in Rochester, New York, 1815–1837* (New York, 1978).

50. Stark and Finke, "Turning Pews into People," p. 187; on politics and church membership, see Lee Benson, *The Concept of Jacksonian Democracy: New York as a Test Case* (New York, 1961), esp. pp. 198–213.

51. Paul A. Gilje, *The Road to Mobocracy: Popular Disorder in New York City, 1763–1834* (Chapel Hill, 1987), pp. 206–220; David Brion Davis, "Some Themes of Countersubversion: An Analysis of Anti-Masonic, Anti-Catholic, and Anti-Mormon Literature," *Mississippi Valley Historical Review* 47 (1960), 205–224.

52. Baird, *Religion in America;* Stephen Colwell, *The Position of Christianity in the United States, in Its Relations with Our Political Institutions, and especially with Reference to Religious Instruction in the Public Schools* (New York, 1853).

53. Colwell, *Position of Christianity in the United States,* pp. 20, 23. See also Benjamin Franklin Morris, *Christian Life and Character of the Civil Institutions of the United States, Developed in the Official and Historical Annals of the Republic* (Philadelphia and Cincinnati, 1864).

54. Clifford S. Griffin, *Their Brothers' Keepers: Moral Stewardship in the United States, 1800–1865* (New Brunswick, N.J., 1960); John R. Bodo, *The Protestant Clergy and Public Issues, 1812–1848* (Princeton, 1954); Lois Banner, "Religious Benevolence as Social Control: A Critique of an Interpretation," *Journal of American History* 40 (June 1973), 23–41; Hatch, *Democratization of American Christianity.*

55. Lorenzo Dow, *The History of the Cosmopolite; or, The Writings of Rev. Lorenzo Dow, Containing His Experiences and Travels, in Europe and America, up to near His Fiftieth Year,* rev. ed. (Cincinnati, 1860), pp. 27–31, 42–43, 51, 177, 199–200, 215, 219, 277–279. On Methodist attitudes toward Dow, see Smith, *Recollections and Reflections of an Old Itinerant,* p. 51; *Autobiography of Rev. Tobias Spicer,* pp. 227–231.

56. Dow, *History of the Cosmopolite,* quotation on p. 185; see also p. 251.

Conclusion: Lincoln and the Almost Chosen People

1. Alexis de Tocqueville, *Democracy in America,* trans. Henry Reeve, ed. Phillips Bradley (New York, 1945), I, 311.

2. C. C. Goen, *Broken Churches Broken Nation: The Churches and the Civil War* (Macon, Ga., 1986); Sydney Ahlstrom, *A Religious History of the American People* (New Haven, 1972), pp. 657–669.

3. Henry Ward Beecher's grandson quoted in William J. Wolf, *The Almost Chosen People: A Study of the Religion of Abraham Lincoln* (New York, 1959), p. 27, see also pp. 17–32; D. Elton Trueblood, *Abraham Lincoln: Theologian of American Anguish* (New York, 1973), pp. 3–26.

4. *Abraham Lincoln: Selected Speeches, Messages, and Letters,* ed. T. Harry Williams (New York, 1957), p. vi.

5. Wolf, *The Almost Chosen People,* pp. 40–42, 69–78; Lincoln quoted in Stephen B. Oates, *With Malice toward None: The Life of Abraham Lincoln* (New York, 1977), p. 103.

6. Jean H. Baker, *Mary Todd Lincoln, A Biography* (New York, 1987), pp. 217–222.

Index